# *Italian Master Drawings*

## 1350–1800

FROM THE JANOS SCHOLZ COLLECTION

SELECTED AND DESCRIBED BY

JANOS SCHOLZ

DOVER PUBLICATIONS, INC., NEW YORK

Published in Canada by General Publishing Company, Ltd., 30 Lesmill Road, Don Mills, Toronto, Ontario.
Published in the United Kingdom by Constable and Company, Ltd., 10 Orange Street, London WC 2.

*Italian Master Drawings, 1350–1800, from the Janos Scholz Collection* is a new work, first published by Dover Publications, Inc., in 1976.

The publisher is grateful to Dr. Charles Ryskamp, Director of The Pierpont Morgan Library, New York, and to the Trustees of the Library, for permission to reproduce these drawings, which now belong to the Library.

*International Standard Book Number: 0-486-23257-3*
*Library of Congress Catalog Card Number: 75-19835*

Manufactured in the United States of America
Dover Publications Inc.
180 Varick Street, New York, N.Y. 10014

# INTRODUCTION

*From the age of six, I had a mania for drawing the forms of things. By the time I was fifty, I had published an infinity of designs, but all I have produced before the age of seventy is not worth taking into account. At seventy-five I have learned a little about the real structure of nature—of animals, plants and trees, birds, fishes and insects. In consequence, when I am eighty, I shall have made still more progress. At ninety I shall penetrate the mystery of things; at a hundred I shall certainly have reached a marvelous stage, and when I am a hundred and ten, everything I do—be it but a line or dot—will be alive. I beg those who live as long as I, to see if I do not keep my word.*

*Written at the age of seventy-five by me—once Hokusai—today Gwakio-rojin, "the old man, mad about drawing." (1760–1849)*

The words of this great Japanese artist evoke a strange parallel in my mind. It is a humble parallel, since the most significant component of Hokusai's life—the creative part—is entirely missing from my own. But an appreciation of form, symmetry, balance and harmony in the visible universe has always been important to me, especially since the time when, approaching middle age, I too became "mad about drawing." I should like to tell something about the form my "madness" has taken, the collecting of master drawings, which has occupied my existence for several decades.

The illustrations in this volume are from my collection of about 1500 drawings by Italian masters of the past, most of them preparatory sketches for paintings. These pictures should serve above all for visual enjoyment. The primary function of all art is to give pleasure and to embellish our often grayish existence. But for those readers who care to probe beneath the easily obtainable first impression there is ample occasion for mental exercise. In fact, the collection was formed with this dual purpose in mind: to educate as well as to offer aesthetic pleasure.

Much has been said and written about the peculiar "immediate" character of sketches and drawings, and this immediacy will always constitute much of their charm and attraction. But it should be remembered that in most cases the sketch is the first step on a long road of artistic production that may lead to a painting, a sculpture or a work of architecture. This explains not only the importance of drawings in art-historical research—usually centered on analysis rather than on aesthetics—but also the significance of this delicate form of art as a prime educational tool of great effectiveness on all levels of artistic concern.

It was with this basic idea in mind that my collection was brought together over a span of forty years. I have been trained in various disciplines, all of them requiring meticulous preparatory work and high performance standards. Therefore, when I embarked on this venture of gathering study material in the graphic arts, I determined that the collection should show artistic excellence and continuous progress in as many directions as possible. The task of assembling such material seemed almost insurmountable, for vast vistas of knowledge appeared in the distance which had to be approached, examined and absorbed. Of necessity my quest ultimately became an obsession.

Despite the slowness of my progress, the unremitting search soon turned into an almost pleasurable daily routine. Part of this routine involved a practical and useful self-education, obtained by constantly reading, observing, comparing and remembering. Another important factor in this training was personal contact with many scholars, curators, fellow collectors and dealers. Such contacts are often just as important in the development of an effective scholar-collector as are the necessary innate gifts.

The student of master drawings needs a peculiar sensitivity because of the comparative scarcity of concrete evidence to guide him in his explorations. It is true that there are solid bases for research; knowledge of associated paintings, archive work and the recognition of graphological characteristics all help the scholar to achieve the solution of a given problem. Still, the role of constructive speculation in this field is enormous, and we should remember Hokusai's wise recommendation of caution. It takes a good part of a lifetime to master any profession thoroughly. Having spent more than half of mine analyzing the peculiarities, character, style and environment of numerous artists, I will not be accused of exaggerating when I say that the study of drawings by the masters is one of the most exacting and exciting of pursuits.

My basic rules for collecting were manifold. Primary consideration was always given to excellence of execution, artistic impact, historical significance and, above all, to the joy these delicate and precious works could give to those who are sensitive to this most intimate form of art. The satisfaction of handling drawings is great, for it continues to grow as our understanding deepens.

During my years of search and research it became obvious that we in this hemisphere lacked the original material for comparison that is to be found in such abundance in the print cabinets of the Old World. The old European collections have given scholars a wealth of good, bad and indifferent examples on which they can sharpen their eyes, develop their judgment, practice careful sifting, and bring into focus artistic values often hidden in portfolios for centuries. For this reason a primary aim in forming my collection was to obtain as many different examples as possible by the same master. Here the considerations I had to keep in mind were those that are of paramount importance in art-historical research: for instance, the chronology within the graphic oeuvre of one specific master, or the role that the act of drawing played in the creative process during the fulfillment of a complicated artistic commission. This latter point alone could lead the inquiring mind in various directions, from the purely artistic working habits of a painter, through all sorts of interesting side issues, to the understanding of his way of life, mind and intellect.

The necessity of reading correctly the meaning of an artist's task makes the study of master drawings one of the most challenging areas in all artistic research. The very vastness of the scope, the infinite variety of purpose behind these so often only reconnoitering lines, the correct interpretation of a carefully hidden psychological content, all this offers rich satisfaction to the researcher, akin to that which a scientist feels when making a significant discovery in his own field.

Automatically, the critical analysis of technique led to an almost graphological probing, which was also suggested to me many years ago by James Rorimer. This helped me gain a better understanding of artistic personalities and, as a corollary, supplied an efficient method of detecting forgeries in the drawing field. Continued work in this direction led to an accumulation of practical knowledge and a keener critical appraisal which later on proved to be extremely useful in art-historical teaching. When special seminar courses in the connoisseurship of drawings were added to the curriculum in various universities and soon proved very popular, my early experiments provided a completely new element, that of a keen eye-training based on the study of original works of art, an approach entirely different from the existing one of using mainly slides and photographs.

It was at this point that the importance of a study collection as an educational tool became generally recognized. During many years of conducting drawing-connoisseurship seminars I noticed that the concentrated observation needed for judging an original drawing proved to be beneficial to students and scholars from *all* art disciplines. Far East specialists and classical archaeologists received a powerful boost to their perceptive faculties, while Northern Renaissance men or those interested in Italian Baroque sculpture also benefited from the new approach. This is easy to understand, because in the long run a work of art, its form and dramatic content, projective capacity and execution, can and should be judged in only one way: by approaching the object with an all-encompassing clinical observation, evaluating its merits or shortcomings candidly. Only after this process has been completed should a realistic decision be made as to whether the work under scrutiny is representative of a greater or lesser master's better or poorer achievement.

The above reflections could be considered basic tenets to be followed when looking for material to be included in an effective study collection. Still, the task is complicated and one has to be prepared for eventual adjustments and sudden reactions, because surprises offered by artistic vagaries are encountered frequently when going through an artist's output. The critic is prone to speculate, and often forced to generalize to some extent, when commenting on, let us say, significant changes in a hand, occurring sometimes without obvious reasons. Experience proves that there was some reason for most changes. These reasons can be of superficial character, like speed, overabundance of visual impressions or a buoyant mood, or else the results of deep spiritual experience. Changes like these show up more clearly in master drawings than in any other art form.

I started out as a collector with a strong innate sense for preserving material of all kinds and ages. After a great deal of meandering about in many fields, the graphic arts became my main point of interest, but it was only after a few years of systematically collecting old master prints that I concentrated on the domain of old master drawings. In all my collecting efforts I followed a basic direction, acquiring, describing and classifying. During the print-collecting period, I bought a considerable number of graphics, especially the works of the Netherlandish landscapists, including the complete oeuvre of Everdingen, Waterlo and the van de Veldes, and a fine group of Breughels. Piece by piece, a complete set of prints by Claude and Ostade were also obtained from the then bottomless resources of the British market. The great printmakers such as Rembrandt, Ruysdael and Lucas van Leyden were also represented by fine impressions, but even by then (1936) the rare prints were hard to get and beyond my means.

During these early years an occasional drawing would join the print collection. It was inevitable that while scouring hundreds of portfolios at a time when the material from dispersed old collections was abundant and not yet thoroughly picked over by keen amateurs, an eager and inquisitive collector could discover fine things. At first my purchasing was hesitant, since caution and lack of knowledge held me back a good deal, but before long a certain split-second reaction to subject, quality and condition became an additional aid, along with my memory, which by then was fairly effective.

Thus my pleasure in making discoveries and purchasing at a good price increased all the time, especially when I started to look beyond first considerations, like originality and authenticity, and began to search for deeper artistic values, such as dramatic impact and narrative content. The happy equilibrium between historical importance, scholarly classification and the sheer artistic quality of a work is, and should always remain, the primary criterion for the inclusion of any item in a study collection. Without these factors an object is ineffective except, perhaps, as a negative quantity, a bad example, since explaining a low point of artistic production can also be useful in analytical teaching.

As more and more drawings were added to my print collection, I gradually realized that the interest produced by an original piece of graphic art—a drawing—is enormously greater than that aroused by a print. Because of the intervention of a mechanical process in printmaking, there is an insurmountable barrier between the artist and the product. I suppose this is why so many of the great print connoisseurs of the past ultimately turned to the study of original master drawings. Fortunately, this shift of emphasis came rather early in my case, at a time when my curiosity and desire to learn were at a high pitch, and the material to be found and studied was much easier to come by than nowadays.

Since I was a very busy concert musician, I had the welcome opportunity to travel extensively and to meet interesting people and see collections otherwise difficult of access. Moreover, the visual training of a musician helps to develop memory, and the capacity to retain details, peculiarities and pertinent facts is an invaluable item in the arsenal of a scholar-collector. During these long years of work I have met individuals with the most prodigious memories which they could bring into play at a moment's notice. The versatility of memory, ranging from the most complex humanistic mysteries to the minutest bits of professional knowledge, is what I have admired so much in the scholars I have had the privilege to know.

The list of friends and acquaintances among the art historians who, by their advice, admonitions, teaching and practical hints, have helped me ever so generously, is enormous. It includes the elite of all those who, through their gifts and hard work, have brought the study of master drawings to its impressive present-day level. Of course, without the necessarily limited efforts of nineteenth-century scholars of drawing, we would be far behind today. But most of our knowledge has been gained in the last fifty years, with their concentrated emphasis on stylistic analysis, clinical probing in many directions, technical research and serious archive work. It was during this time span that my collection was being assembled. The availability of new literature, and the avalanche of specialized or general exhibitions with scholarly catalogues at hand to enlighten the visitor and challenge the curious, were a great help and encouragement to me.

The earliest phases of my collecting life brought me into contact with two great scholars whose example has remained with me all these years. As my collecting activities began in London, from the very start (1935) I had the good fortune to meet A. E. Popham of the British Museum, who, with his legendary helpfulness and kindness, introduced me patiently to the mysteries of collecting master drawings. No matter how minor the object was that I showed him at the beginning, his interest was aroused and his advice—pertinent and accurate—was gladly given. When I began to come to him with more important items, like the large architectural drawing by Piranesi (Plate 144), which I unearthed in a small shop around the corner from the British Museum for a few shillings, he seemed to find pleasure in my efforts and encouraged me to discontinue the collecting of prints and concentrate on drawings only. My contact with Popham remained uninterrupted until his death.

During the same year in which I bought the Piranesi (1937) I made one of the most important art-historical encounters of my life. On my way back home to Hungary, I showed the Piranesi to a young, aristocratic-looking man at the Albertina in Vienna. It was Otto Benesch, the great Rembrandt scholar, whose friendship I valued and whose memory I cherish. Not only our mutual interest in drawings, but an even more powerful tie—our love of music—bound us together in a lifelong fellowship. From Benesch I acquired many things, above all an almost religious respect for beauty in all its forms. He also impressed on me the fact that beauty is to be found all around us if we take the trouble to search it out, try to understand its essence and then absorb it. To listen to him analyze a work of art was an experience I shall always remember, for he had a multifaceted approach that partook of the sensitivity of a performing musical artist as well as the classical humanist's penetration in depth. Benesch's humanity and sense of humor were exhilarating. He always approached a knotty problem of subject analysis by looking for the simplest solution and not by straining his brain in deep and obscure mental exercise, as often done by art analysts of certain schools. His great strength was that he could outdo any of the hard-core symbol experts and iconographers, because his classical education was of such formidable solidity that almost nothing fazed him. There was always a little reserve of ideas or obscure information which brought him close to the desired solution.

Shortly afterward two other Austrian scholars came into my life, Hans and Erica Tietze, who, with their Viennese brightness and charm, strange peculiarities and vast knowledge, gave me their affectionate attention and friendship. I have been attracted since my childhood to the art of the Venetian painters, so it was fascinating for me to know these two scholars during the years in which they were building up their catalogue of drawings by the Venetian masters of the Renaissance. My admiration for their work grew by observing their systematic efforts and their incredibly many-sided knowledge, used with split-second efficiency. To these were added an almost encyclopedic grasp of the older source literature not only in their main subject area but also in all the collateral aspects. Although the type of material covered in their book has increased immensely since it first appeared, the basic work is, and will remain epoch-making in our field.

During the Second World War Frits Lugt came to Oberlin, Ohio, where he spent some time. This visit left an indelible imprint on all persons in our country interested in the study and collecting of master drawings. This keen scholar and sensitive collector soon became interested in my work and offered me help, advice and, above all, practical hints on collecting which have remained as guidelines for me during all these years of search. The incredible kindness and encouragement Frits Lugt showed me are among the most precious memories I have. Wisdom, knowledge and speed were some of the characteristics of this great personality and probably also the real secret of his fabulous achievement as a scholar-collector. A main rule—that of beauty and quality in a work of art—he passionately professed to all his friends. It was so important to him that a work of art should be handsome and well executed that the attribution to one or another artist did not even enter his mind when observing an object for the first time. This point of view, so utterly adverse to that of Academia, became almost an obsession with Lugt. How often he said to me: "Do not worry about this or that attribution or connection in the art-historical field. First look carefully and see whether the work of art is good or bad. If you judge it to be of fine quality, try to acquire it for a reasonable sum. Later on you can classify it at your leisure." This sound advice helped me a great deal. However, my professional training left in me a mania for system and order which on occasion forced me to lower my standards, usually for historical considerations. For this same reason I desired to build a study collection of drawings rather than a smaller selective collection with only handsome pieces to delight the eye alone.

While looking around for material, it struck me that although the holdings in old master drawings in the United States were considerable, their general characteristics were those of a star collection rather than a conglomeration of mixed high and low quality, like those in the European print cabinets and collections. As noted earlier, we lacked the older stock that resulted from the European *Wunderkammer* (cabinet of rarities) type of collecting, the kind of graphic material preserved in the larger European libraries, and lastly the important old private holdings of individuals who had had the desire and knowledge to assemble their own cabinet of graphic arts. In the United States there were hardly any persons like the latter. Yet, some such material was imported even in the eighteenth century, and we must be grateful to those pioneers who left treasures in Bowdoin College, Baltimore and Mobile, or later on in Sacramento, Brookline, the Biltmore Estates in North Carolina, and Philadelphia. These treasures are now known and carefully guarded. But until recent years some smaller private collections of imported drawings all over the continent either eluded detection or were completely neglected by their successive owners. During my concert tours I tracked these down, and on more than one occasion I was able to salvage remnants of material brought over here many years earlier. This scouting work was fascinating, for it brought me into contact with many interesting personalities. I have observed with admiration the innate desire of the American people to surround themselves with fine things, which they may not have understood in the modern critical sense, but to whose beauty they responded naturally.

When the giant American collectors started amassing their loot, drawings played only a minor role, although material was readily available at the time. The example of J. Pierpont Morgan was a unique phenomenon, unfortunately not followed either by our great museums in their early days or by other private collectors. This is one of the main reasons that our important drawing collections are often lacking in depth despite their occasional dazzling brilliancy. Moreover, the governing fads or taste of the time were a major factor in the rather lopsided way institutions and collectors bought; hence the predominant position held in American collections by drawings of the Tiepolos, Francesco Guardi, the eighteenth-century French masters, Ingres and Goya, to point out just a few instances.

After the First World War the situation changed to a great extent. Men like Robert Lehman, Frank Mather, Dan F. Platt, Philip Hofer (trained at Harvard by Paul Sachs) and Winslow Ames started highly successful collecting careers, while others, like Dr. Max A. Goldstein in St. Louis or Gurley in Chicago, bought rather in width than in depth. All this aroused interest among art-minded people and, as a result, the hitherto easily obtainable material on the local market started to vanish. Another boost in the appreciation of master drawings came from the European refugees who brought to America not only their prize possessions but also an active competitive sense. In the wake of the refugee collectors came an influx of highly trained, sensitive-eyed dealers, many of them carrying coveted art-historical degrees from old European universities, and they too stirred up a good deal of activity.

To live through these years was another important part of my education. The varied and highly desirable new material on the market once more stimulated my search into American holdings, which were becoming not only passionately interesting but also quite lucrative in every sense. It was obvious that we no longer had to get drawings in the London or Paris market for viciously marked-up prices, while fine items were available at home for modest amounts.

If we observe only the situation around 1935, the year when I started to collect drawings more actively, the age-old saying that it is impossible to find a fine thing seems farcical. It was easy to get a good Giambattista Tiepolo drawing on 57th Street for much less than a hundred dollars, while a Giandomenico Pulcinello sheet changed hands on Third Avenue for thirty-five dollars. The early material was even more neglected because it was not well enough known to stir sufficient interest. And so it happened that in one of the still active art-book stores, a small genuine Dürer drawing turned up among other things and was offered for sale at the price of a good dinner. The Paolo Veronese fur-cape study reproduced in this book (Plate 63) was for many decades in an old American collection, and when the books from that source were sold, the drawing came along with others and was marked at less than a dollar. All we needed then was a good eye, some knowledge, speedy reactions and a small amount of money. The same was true when prints and drawings appeared in the out-of-the-way auction galleries. The material surfacing from older American sources was quite astonishing. Long-lost works by known artists mentioned in the literature were sometimes sold in obscure places. To cite only one example, I bought a Rubens and an Ostade drawing, both published over fifty years ago, at a furniture sale here in New York. A few years later I gave them both to the Metropolitan Museum, where they now form part of the fine cabinet of master drawings.

As I indicated above, my purchases of drawings started late in 1935 in London. In the dealer Spencer's small house on New Oxford Street, not far from the British Museum, I spent hours going over hundreds of portfolios. The results were slight in the beginning, but later on an occasional masterpiece slipped into the parcel I took home. One of my first purchases at Spencer's was the Pietro da Cortona drawing for the Palazzo Mattei ceiling in Rome (Plate 91), which has since become famous as one of the earliest *modello* drawings by the artist. During the year 1938 a great many drawings from the Platt Collection in Princeton, N.J., came on the market in New York. This was an opportunity for starting my Tiepolo group with fine examples from the Algarotti-Cheney material which Platt had bought from Parsons in London.

A few years later, a fascinating album became available here in New York, containing many sheets by Bolognese artists and other masters from the early sixteenth century to the late seventeenth. Many drawings by all the Carraccis, a glorious group by Cavedone and pristine chalk drawings by Lanfranco, besides the many Reni and Domenichino examples, acted as a seed for establishing a representative Bolognese group in my study collection. As occasions arose, this section was augmented by early examples and also by those of the able eighteenth-century painters working in Bologna. This part of the collection now contains close to 300 drawings.

During a visit to Hungary in 1939 I heard about a collection in Eisenstadt, Austria, the delightful residence of the Eszterházy family. It contained the material collected by a Viennese stage designer, Michael Mayr, who died about 1870 and left everything to his granddaughter. This purchase started my interest in stage design, resulting in the publication of several books on the subject and in numerous exhibitions all over the United States. Again much curiosity was aroused and, on account of this, America now possesses many important drawings for the stage. As my concern with painters' drawings became more pronounced, I ceded about a thousand items related to the theater to our great stage designer, the late Donald Oenslager, who built it up into probably the best collection of stage material in the world.

During the Second World War much activity took place in the art market. Drawings came to the fore quite often, and still at reasonably modest prices. In 1942 I purchased a large part of the Brandegee drawings. The bulk of this Massachusetts collection was by then already in the Cooper Union Museum in New York, thanks to the astuteness of Dr. Rudolf Berliner, one of the really great scholars in the decorative field, who recognized the prime importance of this material for the art school of that venerable institution and persuaded the trustees to buy. Today the Cooper Union holdings, part of our National Collections, comprise one of the most important agglomerations of graphic arts connected with decoration anywhere. My group from the Brandegee collection, originally brought together by Giovanni Piancastelli in Italy, contained many fine things, like the Lanfranco study in this volume (Plate 80) and the rare Cavallino sketch (Plate 101).

On a concert tour in 1945 I visited St. Louis, where I met the widow of one of our earliest American collectors of drawings, Dr. Max A. Goldstein. This man systematically acquired prints and drawings from about 1910 on, and amassed a numerically enormous collection. Part of it was sold at auctions, but the bulk remained in the house, and I persuaded the owner to let me have it. The mere work of sorting it out took about a year, for there were thousands of prints, broadsides and ephemera of all kinds, but principally master drawings. Among this material I found very fine things by some of the great masters, like Rembrandt, three drawings by Rubens, several van Dycks, and among the Italians the "St. Catherine" by Montagna (Plate 14) and the landscape by Titian (Plate 32), to mention just a few.

By that time I was quite convinced that my efforts should be concentrated solely on drawings by Italian painters, because I believed that the Italian school more than any other showed a line of continuous organic development, most strongly pronounced in its drawings. There is a fascination in this unbroken line from the very beginnings to the end of the eighteenth century, for it keeps a distinct graphological character alive, even throughout all the major changes in style or artistic movements. In my opinion this character disappears with Neoclassicism, when a strong foreign influence obliterates this distinctive "Italian" quality in drawing. It remains dormant for quite a few decades, to be reborn with renewed vigor and brilliancy only toward the end of the nineteenth century in the work of the great draughtsmen who lead into our time. For these reasons I decided quite arbitrarily to limit my collection to works earlier than the advent of Neoclassicism.

During a trip to Europe I saw at a dealer's in Paris an album of architectural drawings of the Renaissance which had turned up at auction in the Hôtel Drouot. I bought the album at once, although the dealer said that the Louvre was also actively interested. This precious lot included French funeral monument projects of the sixteenth century and the architectural material connected with many of Michelangelo's works and other Italian buildings. It is now conserved in the Metropolitan Museum, to which I presented it many years ago.

In 1949 I ran across a group of drawings in Switzerland which originally belonged to a famous old Italian collection. This *Wunderkammer*-like collection was begun in the sixteenth century and kept in the Moscardo family until the Napoleonic years, when part of it passed into the Museo in Verona, while some of the paintings and drawings remained in the possession of collateral relatives. Much of the private holdings were sold in the 1920s, but after the Second World War Swiss dealers acquired a fine group of miscellaneous material from the owners. The group which I was fortunate enough to find became the core of my Venetian and North Italian holdings in Renaissance and even earlier material. Quite a few fine sheets from this noble collection are reproduced in this book, such as the Zoppo "Man carrying faggots and vegetables" (Plate 7) and the Pisanello scrollwork (Plate 8A). The group was particularly strong in drawings by Brescian, Paduan, Veronese and Vicentine painters and is today the main source anywhere for the study of these painters' graphic works.

About 1952 a dealer approached me with the possibility of examining a large group of drawings that belonged originally to the Royal House of Savoy (rulers of Italy) and had been brought over to Switzerland after the family went into exile. There were about a thousand items in this collection, mostly by Italian painters and decorators from the early fifteenth century to about 1800, at which time the drawings were mounted in albums. Among these I found a fine lot of scenic inventions by the Bibienas, the works of fresco painters from the mid-sixteenth century to the great decorators of the Piedmontese Rococo, coach designs and quite a few projects for jewelry and goldsmiths' work, sculptors' sketches and plans by architects. All these are now in the Print Department of the Metropolitan Museum. I kept for my own collection only painters' drawings of quality and historical significance. In the Savoy collection I found among other works the early Umbrian "St. John the Baptist" (Plate 2) and the enchanting "Head of a boy" by Francesco Guardi (Plate 146).

In the summer of 1955 I visited the gallery of Reichlen, a well-known dealer in Lausanne, who expressed some interest in a painting by a Swiss artist which I had in my possession. He showed me some drawings that he had kept apart in his shop ever since acquiring them from a source in the country. The old portfolios contained hundreds of sheets originally belonging to the print and drawing cabinet of Louis Armand de Mestral de Saint-Saphorin, a Swiss nobleman who served the King of Denmark as ambassador in many European posts. When he died in Vienna in 1805, he left behind an impressive collection of works of art, including his print and drawing collection. Part of these graphic works were sold in Vienna in 1806, but some material remained in Switzerland and was left by his will to a brother, whose descendants still have some items in their possession. I was able to trace the extent of this collection through the manuscript catalogue in the family archives. As far as can be estimated, de Mestral must have had about 30,000 prints and close to 5000 drawings. His main interest was in the works of Giambattista Tiepolo, which he probably acquired while on diplomatic service in Madrid. The second Italian painter amply represented in his collection was the Bolognese Rococo painter Donato Creti; according to the lists, he must have had about 150 Creti drawings. It was a well-rounded collection of all schools and periods, with examples dating as far back as the mid-fifteenth century. Since my main interest by this time was in the Italian masters, I selected several hundred Italian works in exchange for my Swiss painting. De Mestral must also have owned an album that once belonged to a well-known seventeenth-century collector, Gaspar Guzmán y Haro, a Spanish viceroy of Naples. Among the de Mestral drawings I discovered the finely drawn title page of one of the Guzmán albums, probably by Calandrucci. I presented this to Frits Lugt on his eightieth birthday as a small token of friendship and gratitude. Among the de Mestral drawings in this book are examples by Parmigianino, Primaticcio, dell'Abbate, Giordano, Strozzi and Giambattista Tiepolo.

Occasional single purchases here and abroad added some more important examples. The Raphael tondo (Plate 27) was actually brought to my door, while the fourteenth-century Tuscan drawing (Plate 1) turned up in California and found its way to New York. The interest in my collecting shown by dealers here and abroad was particularly gratifying to me, because it proved that they were often more concerned with my efforts in behalf of education than with their own profits. Thus I was able to add to the collection such rarities as the Correggio sheet (Plate 33A) or the little Leonardo head (Plate 18B) practically as gifts from friendly dealers. I hope that these people will appreciate the fact that their treasures now form an important part of a whole that will give pleasure to a wide public for years to come.

From the very start, my zeal in collecting was accompanied by the desire to share whatever I had with others. My connections with the now legendary publisher Herbert Bittner and with my friend, the noble scholar A. Hyatt Mayor, led not only to several books about my collection, but also to exhibitions. I have frequently lent material to museums and universities to encourage the appreciation and deeper understanding of the drawing medium. From my earliest exhibitions in 1940 to the present day, drawings from the study collection have been shown either singly or in numbers, here and abroad, in more than 150 exhibitions. Fortunately, because of my private status, bureaucratic red tape and restrictions were cut down to a minimum. The risks were great and still remain serious. Still, the fact that these works of art should be seen and enjoyed overcame all other considerations, and it is my hope that this policy of sharing will be continued.

In selecting the illustrations for the present book my principal aim, after the natural consideration of aesthetics, was to show the scope, depth and general character of the collection. From the large and varied material at hand, I tried to choose drawings that would please not only the occasional reader but also the specialist. I wanted the pictures to demonstrate what a working study collection of master drawings means to me.

The future of the study collection and of the perhaps equally significant research library gave me a great deal of thought. I never wavered in my belief that the collection and library, as I have brought them together, should remain united in order to continue to serve the original purpose of teaching others something about the intimate and powerful beauty that emanates from these sheets. My educational work in the last fifteen years proved to me that I was on the right path, especially when I saw the positive results in young scholars who came to me in the very beginning and who today occupy coveted leading positions in the art-historical and museum world. This gives me a satisfaction which I can hardly describe.

I have now lived nearly half a century in New York and have become deeply attached to this city, although my travels throughout the United States made my sincere admiration grow in many directions. My collection, which can now be considered almost as a standard reference institution for students, could have been usefully installed in many quarters. The main argument for leaving it in New York was the manifold opportunities this city offers to all those interested in art-historical education. Its great museums and collections, its libraries of incredible scope and wealth, its universities and other institutions of learning make New York the center of art-historical studies and research. If this statement sounds exaggerated, I hasten to say that I am the last person to underestimate the grand efforts made by our other centers of learning all over the United States.

After choosing New York as the repository for my collection, I finally settled on that distinguished home of culture and learning, The Pierpont Morgan Library. The eminent collection of drawings there is, in its catholicity, the finest in the country. The quality of its holdings, and also the way in which they have been husbanded in the last decades, are exemplary. Additions to the already quite considerable treasures have been wisely and courageously handled by the staff and the very helpful trustees. When I approached the Director, Dr. Charles Ryskamp, I found an understanding for the far from negligible problems of transfer that was visionary, bold and scholarly. That everything should stay together, drawings and extensive research library, forming a corpus of study material to complement the already existing holdings, was appreciated and assured.

Thus, the possibility of a major center in the United States for studying the history of Italian draughtsmanship became a reality when the Library accepted my offering. Let us hope that this move will encourage other collectors to make their treasures available to the Library in the future for the enjoyment of all those interested in drawings, which are, after all, the authentic key to the hands and achievements of the great masters.

NEW YORK, MAY 1975

# LIST OF ILLUSTRATIONS

Dimensions are in millimeters, height before width.

1. *Tuscan master. Second quarter of the 14th century.*
FIGURES AND DECORATIVE ELEMENTS. Pen, various shades of brown ink, on vellum. 305 x 760 mm.
Drawn on the verso of a deed dated 1321, these sketches are from life and also copied from paintings, sculptures or book illuminations. They probably represent material recorded by an artist for future use, a frequent practice in medieval pattern books.

2. *Umbrian painter. Third quarter of the 14th century.*
ST. JOHN THE BAPTIST AND ANOTHER FIGURE. Pen, brown ink, on white paper. 253 x 125 mm.
This early example belongs to a group of drawings, now scattered in various collections, which Bernhard Degenhart attributed to an Umbrian hand. Other scholars are inclined to consider it as a working drawing by a Sienese artist.

3. *Lorenzo Monaco. Florentine, about 1370–1425.*
THE MAN OF SORROWS. Pen and brush, brown ink and watercolors, on fine silk or linen, cut out around the edges and laid down on paper. 97 x 82 mm.
One of the few drawings that can be attributed to this master with a certain amount of justification. It is closely related to Lorenzo's painting of the same subject in the Bergamo Gallery. Being drawn on cloth, it could have been intended for a needlework panel.

4. *Gentile Bellini. Venetian, 1429–1507.*
A CAMEL. Pen, brown ink, on white paper. 160 x 214 mm.
Probably drawn during the artist's sojourn in Constantinople, where he went on a diplomatic mission. This is an interesting early representation of an animal placed in a vast landscape setting, done realistically from life.

5. *Antonio Pisanello, attributed to. Venetian, before 1395–1455.*
TWO YOKED WATER BUFFALOS. Pen and brush, brown ink over preliminary work with metalpoint, on white paper turned yellow. 113 x 193 mm.
A very vivid drawing apparently from life. The subject is known to exist in two other versions from the circle of the Venetian painter.

6. *Stefano da Verona. Veronese, about 1375–1438.*
GROUP OF FIVE FIGURES. Pen, brown ink, on white paper. 196 x 147 mm.
Similar in execution to other autograph examples by the master in Paris and Vienna, this drawing shows the strong influence of Pisanello's art on Stefano. Intended for use in a composition like the Adoration of the Magi, the work can be dated about 1435.

7. *Marco Zoppo. Venetian, 1433–1478.*
MAN CARRYING FAGGOTS AND VEGETABLES. Pen, brown ink over black chalk, on white paper toned slightly pink. 198 x 165 mm.
The drawing dates from the maturity of this able painter. Marco Zoppo used this type of figure in his decorations of various buildings all over the Venetian territories. The present drawing has a companion sheet in the National Gallery of Scotland, Edinburgh.

8A. *Antonio Pisanello.*
DESIGN FOR SCROLLWORK. Pen, dark brown ink over preparatory work with metalpoint, on white paper. 120 x 90 mm.
One of two existing pages from a small notebook by the painter containing sketches for decorative elements to be used in paintings, sculpture or metalwork.

8B. *Antonio Pisanello, circle of.*
BARKING DOG. Pen, brown ink over preliminary work with metalpoint, on white paper. 63 x 99 mm.
This small animal was surely drawn by one of the Veronese studio assistants of Pisanello about 1440–1450.

9. *Francesco di Giorgio. Sienese, 1439–1502.*
DESIGN FOR A PADDLE BOAT AND ANOTHER VESSEL. Pen, light brown ink over preparatory red chalk work, on white paper. 242 x 214 mm.
Page from a dismembered notebook of this eminent painter, architect and engineer-inventor, containing various pieces of military machinery, vessels and pontoon bridges. A large number of these designs is preserved in later copies in the British Museum, Siena and elsewhere.

10. *Lorenzo di Credi. Florentine, 1456–1537.*
HEAD OF A YOUTH. Metalpoint, on pink prepared paper. 128 x 115 mm.

To be dated about 1490–1500, this delicate head can be compared stylistically to examples in Florence, Boston and elsewhere.

*11. Piero di Cosimo. Florentine, 1462–1521.*
ST. FRANCIS RECEIVING THE STIGMATA. Pen, grayish-brown ink over preliminary work with metalpoint, heightened with white, on light blue prepared paper. 110 x 148 mm.

When in the collection of the painter Jonathan Richardson, Sr., the drawing was attributed to Leonardo da Vinci. It is, however, the work of Piero, done around 1500. On the verso is a pen-and-ink sketch for a seated Madonna with the Christ Child, identical in execution to an example by the master in the Uffizi, Florence (343E).

*12. Antonio Vivarini. Venetian, about 1415–1484.*
ST. CATHERINE STANDING IN A NICHE. Pen, brown ink with blue washes, on white paper. 270 x 104 mm.

The elegant, elongated figure of the saint recalls strongly Mantegna's art, an influence which penetrated Venetian territories during the great Paduan's life. The Vivarini family, who worked in Murano, became especially attached to this new style.

*13. Bartolomeo Vivarini. Venetian, 1432–about 1491.*
ST. JOHN THE EVANGELIST AND ST. JOHN THE BAPTIST. Pen, light brown ink, on white paper. 136 x 75 mm.

On the verso of this little drawing is a project for an altarpiece representing the Assumption of the Virgin, done in the same loose and somewhat angular pen-and-ink manner typical of the art of this minor, but popular, religious painter.

*14. Bartolomeo Montagna. Vicenza, about 1450–1523.*
ST. CATHERINE. Pen and brush, brown ink, heightened with gray washes, over preparatory work with metalpoint, on brownish paper. 146 x 140 mm.

The popular saint is represented here seated on the wheel of her martyrdom, which is a quite rare version. Montagna's style not only is dependent on Venetian prototypes but also shows a strong Northern influence, so clearly evident in this work.

*15. Andrea Mantegna, studio of. Paduan, about 1500.*
DESIGN FOR AN ELABORATE PILASTER. Pen, brown ink over preliminary work with metalpoint, on white paper. 283 x 206 mm.

Page from a sketchbook by an immediate collaborator of Mantegna with a masterfully conceived Renaissance design for a work probably to be executed ultimately in marble. There are architectural details on the verso.

*16. Vittore Carpaccio. Venetian, about 1445–1526.*
THE PRESENTATION OF THE VIRGIN AT THE TEMPLE. Pen, brown ink, on white paper. 119 x 117 mm.

The composition, destined for a predella painting, belongs to a set of five drawings by the Venetian, scattered in various collections. They all represent biblical subjects and date from the maturity of the painter, about 1500–1510.

*17. Bernardo Parentino. Venetian, about 1437–1531.*
ROMAN TRIUMPHAL PROCESSION. Pen, brown ink, on white paper turned yellow. 324 x 416 mm.

This overcrowded, elaborate work is clearly influenced by Mantegna's *Triumphs*. Parentino, an Istrian by birth, decorated churches and buildings in the Venetian provinces, where he became a principal artistic personality after Andrea Mantegna's death.

*18A. Giuseppe Arcimboldi. Lombard, about 1530–1593.*
MAN WEARING A FANCY PLUMED HAT. Pen, brown ink, on white paper. 118 x 95 mm.

Arcimboldi is best known for his grotesque human figures made up of fruits or flowers. Suggesting a theatrical costume, this sketch is one of many examples by this inventive, strange and amusing painter to be found in collections here and abroad.

*18B. Leonardo da Vinci. Florentine, 1452–1519.*
PROFILE HALF-LENGTH VIEW OF A PEASANT. Black chalk, on white paper. 68 x 45 mm.

Published only recently as a work of the 1490s by the great Florentine, this subject was known from various drawings, originals at Windsor and early school versions in Milan and the Spencer Collection, New York Public Library. The present drawing once belonged to Baron Vivant-Denon, Napoleon's Director of Fine Arts.

*19A. Giovanni Agostino da Lodi. Lombard, working around 1500.*
OLD BEARDED MAN IN PROFILE. Red chalk, on white paper. 58 x 64 mm.

The exquisite technical achievement of this little-known artist, influenced by Leonardo da Vinci's activity in Milan, places him among the most significant Lombard followers of the great Florentine.

*19B. Giovanni Agostino da Lodi.*
HEAD OF A YOUTH. Red chalk, on white paper. 55 x 60 mm.

Companion piece to the previous drawing.

*20. Bernardino Luini. Lombard, 1480/85–1532.*
HEAD OF A WOMAN AND VARIOUS SKETCHES. Metalpoint, on gray prepared paper. 103 x 138 mm.

Luini came under Leonardo's spell when the Florentine worked in Milan. In the present drawing this leaning is so evident that the eminent Leonardo scholar William Suida was inclined to give this example to a close contemporary of Leonardo rather than Luini.

*21. Ambrogio Bergognone. Lombard, 1481–1518.*
ST. AUGUSTINE MATRICULATING AT THE UNIVERSITY OF CARTHAGE. Pen and brush, brown ink, heightened with white, on eggplant-colored prepared paper. 191 x 241 mm.

The subject of this picture was only recently identified by Creighton Gilbert as an event from the life of St. Augustine, and it was Gilbert who assigned the work to Bergognone. Formerly the sheet was given to Luini, but recent research established it and its companion as designs for a predella painting by Ambrogio.

*22. Gianfrancesco Bembo. Cremonese, working 1514–1526.*
BUST OF A MAN WEARING A BIRETTA. Red and black chalk, some light brown pastel and touches of gray wash, on white paper. 204 x 181 mm.

This imposing portrait sketch, done from life, should be related to a painting in the Budapest Gallery, which, although not of the same sitter, offers striking similarities in style, costume and, above all, volume and surface treatment.

*23. Francesco Bonsignori. Veronese, about 1455–1519.*
HEAD OF A MAN IN PROFILE. Red and white chalk, on brownish paper. 207 x 150 mm.

This impressive profile portrait, probably from a living model, was given traditionally to Bonsignori while in the collection of Sir Thomas Lawrence. Lately the name of another possible author, that of the Bolognese-Ferrarese Amico Aspertini, has been tentatively suggested.

*24. Vincenzo Catena. Venetian, about 1470–1531.*
DRAPERY STUDY. Black chalk, brown wash, heightened with white, on olive-green colored paper. 180 x 186 mm.

This is the only existing drawing by the significant artist which can be connected with his painted oeuvre. It is the study for the garment of the angel in the *Annunciation* by Catena, 1515, as pointed out by Creighton Gilbert.

*25. Defendente Ferrari. Piedmontese, about 1470–1535.*
SHEPHERD, LEANING ON HIS STAFF. Pen and brush, brown and black inks, purple-red washes, heightened with white, on orange-tinted paper. 172 x 97 mm.

Originally thought to be Ferrarese, this quite luminous, dramatic sheet should be placed in Piedmont, and is especially close to the known oeuvre of Defendente Ferrari.

*26. Baccio Della Porta, called Fra Bartolomeo. Florentine, 1472–1517.*
STANDING APOSTLE OR SAINT, HOLDING A BOOK. Black and white chalk, on light brown paper. 270 x 110 mm.

A free and painterly study, probably from a live model, with emphatic attention paid by the artist to the folds and volume of the garment.

*27. Raffaelo Santi, called Raphael. Urbino-Rome, 1483–1520.*
MALE FIGURE SYMBOLIZING AN EARTHQUAKE. Metalpoint, heightened with white, on gray prepared paper. Diameter: 114 mm.

Study for the figure personifying the earthquake in the Vatican tapestry *The Liberation of St. Paul*, for which Raphael made the cartoon in 1515.

*28. Giannicola di Paolo Manni, called Lo Smica. Umbrian, about 1460–1544.*
ST. ANTHONY ABBOT. Black and white chalk, on gray paper, perforated along the contours for transfer onto a panel. 375 x 262 mm.

This cartoon was considered by earlier owners to be the work of Perugino. However, it should be ascribed to Manni about 1500, when he was working closely with his master Perugino on the decorations of the Cambio in Perugia.

*29. Ferrarese master. About 1500.*
DESIGN FOR AN ELABORATE TITLE PAGE. Pen, brown ink, on white paper. 254 x 186 mm.

This design could have been intended for a manuscript or a woodcut. The composition leans strongly on Ferrarese art, as can be seen especially in the pilaster decorations and the solution of the heraldic top border. The scene with the cardinal seated in his library conversing with scholars may point to Florentine prototypes.

*30. Lorenzo Lotto. Venetian, about 1480–1536.*
HEAD OF A BEARDED MAN. Black and white chalk, on grayish-blue paper. 185 x 134 mm.

This expressive head, strongly influenced by Titian's art, should be considered as a work of the last phase of Lotto's life.

*31. Giovanni Girolamo Savoldo. Brescian, 1480–1548.*
MAN'S HEAD AND HAND. Black and white chalk, on blue-gray paper. 245 x 170 mm.

Probably intended as a sketch for the head of Christ, this work from the painter's maturity seems to be a study from a live model. It relates well to the handful of splendid heads by Savoldo recorded in various collections.

*32. Tiziano Vecellio, called Titian. Venetian, 1487–1576.*
ST. THEODORE IN A LANDSCAPE. Pen, brown ink, on white paper. 195 x 293 mm.

The event represented is from the life of the popular Venetian saint. He puts a guardian dragon to sleep so that a mother can bring her ailing child to be bathed in the miraculous well. The landscape is a view of the master's birthplace, with the Marmarola mountain range in the distance.

*33A. Antonio Allegri, called Correggio. Parma, 1489–1534.*
STUDY OF A MALE FIGURE, A PUTTO AND A DECORATIVE FRIEZE. Red chalk, pen and brown ink, on white paper. 103 x 82 mm.
Sketch for one of the apostles in the cupola of S. Giovanni Evangelista, Parma, carried out about 1520. The companion to this lively drawing is in the British Museum. Among other owners, it belonged to two English painters, Sir Peter Lely and Sir Joshua Reynolds.

*33B. Francesco Mazzuola, called Parmigianino. Parma, 1503–1540.*
STANDING FEMALE FIGURE, FACING RIGHT. Pen, brown ink over black chalk, on white paper. 102 x 69 mm.
Connected with Parmigianino's major project, the vault of S. Maria della Steccata, Parma. The painter began the ceiling decorations in 1531 and worked on them until the end of his life.

*34. Francesco Mazzuola, called Parmigianino.*
STUDIES OF PUTTI AND A SEATED BOY. Red chalk, on white paper. 191 x 159 mm.
Considered by A. E. Popham to be an early work by the master, done about 1524, this sheet is strikingly similar to the exquisite putto studies by Parmigianino in the Louvre, Paris.

*35. Francesco Mazzuola, called Parmigianino.*
WOMEN CARRYING BASKETS AND AMPHORAE. Pen and brush, brown ink, heightened with white, over black chalk preparation, on light brown tinted paper. 233 x 204 mm.
This recently discovered work, in the master's best pen-and-wash technique, can be dated about 1530 and compared with the celebrated preparatory sketches for the decorations of the Steccata, most of which are conserved in London, Paris and Florence.

*36. Camillo Boccaccino. Cremonese, 1501–1546.*
THE PROPHET ISAIAH AND KING DAVID. Pen and brush, brown ink, heightened with white, on light brown paper. 290 x 252 mm.
Preparatory drawing for the decoration of the organ shutters in S. Vincenzo, Piacenza, dated 1530, as established by John Gere.

*37. Polidoro Caldara, called Polidoro da Caravaggio. Roman, about 1500–1543.*
CHRIST ON THE MOUNT OF OLIVES. Pen and brush, brown ink over black chalk, heightened with white, on gray-green paper; squared for transfer. 387 x 263 mm.
A dramatic composition by this gifted follower of Raphael, from the latter part of his career. The almost theatrical, highly successful treatment of depth, space and lighting is a significant characteristic of Polidoro.

*38. Francesco Primaticcio. Bolognese, 1504–1570.*
CIRCE CHANGING THE COMPANIONS OF ULYSSES INTO SWINE. Black chalk, on white paper. 142 x 190 mm.
Primaticcio designed and executed various scenes from the *Odyssey* in the palace of Fontainebleau during his long stay in France. This example is one of the handful of preparatory sketches remaining in collections here and abroad.

*39. Nicolò dell'Abbate. Modena, about 1512–1571.*
PEOPLE WALKING IN A LANDSCAPE; IN THE DISTANCE, IDEALISTIC VIEW OF ROME. Pen and brush, brown ink, heightened with lead-white (oxidized), on light brown tinted paper. 224 x 188 mm.
This recently discovered sheet is the right-hand portion of the original composition, which is known from two old copies, in the British Museum and in Göteborg. Another drawing by Abbate, in the Albertina, Vienna, representing an episode from the life of Coriolanus, seems to be part of the same large project.

*40. Giulio Romano. Roman, 1493–1546.*
ST. JEROME AND ST. AUGUSTINE. Pen and brush, brown ink, heightened with white, on pink-tinted paper; squared for transfer. 273 x 201 mm.
Imposing detail study for the right-hand portion of a large project, representing the four Fathers of the Church attending a sacred event. To be dated about 1520–1524.

*41. Domenico Beccafumi. Sienese, 1484/86–1551.*
SEATED MALE FIGURE. Pen and brush, brown ink over black chalk, on white paper. 181 x 210 mm.
Strongly under the spell of Michelangelo, this figure, intended probably for a river god in some large work, represents the best sides of Beccafumi's multifaceted painterly and technical gifts.

*42. Jacopo Ripanda. Ferrarese, working about 1490–1530.*
TWO GROTESQUE HEADS. Brush, various shades of blue ink, heightened with white, on blue prepared paper. 153 x 206 mm.
It has been suggested that these exaggerated heads may be intended as decorations for faience apothecary jars or plates. Although the close affinity to works by Ripanda is obvious, the alternative of Giacomo Francia's possible authorship has been lately mentioned.

*43. Gaudenzio Ferrari. Piedmontese, 1480–1546.*
THE CONVERSION OF PAUL. Brush, various shades of brown ink, heightened with white, over black chalk, on blue-gray paper. 273 x 363 mm.
This drawing, the design for part of the decoration of a Gothic church, should be dated from the maturity of the able and immensely popular painter-decorator.

*44. Jacopo da Pontormo. Florentine, 1494–1557.*
HALF-LENGTH FIGURE OF A YOUTH. Red chalk, on white paper. 157 x 127 mm.
Study for the Virgin in Pontormo's painting *The Deposition of Christ* in S. Felicità, Florence. The work dates from about 1525. There is another autograph sketch for the same figure in the Uffizi, Florence.

*45. Francesco Salviati. Florentine, 1510–1563.*
A MONSTER. Red chalk, on white paper. 108 x 184 mm.
Awe-inspiring sketch of an imaginary, half marine, half land-based dragon-like creature, a type which was often depicted by Renaissance artists—painters and sculptors alike.

*46. Taddeo Zuccaro. Tuscan, 1529–1566.*
GROUP OF WARRIORS. Pen and brush, brown ink, on white paper; squared for transfer. 222 x 161 mm.
Detail study for the left section of Taddeo's large painting *Charles before Orbetello*, in the Palazzo Farnese, Rome, which today houses the French embassy.

*47. Federigo Barocci. Urbino, 1526–1612.*
ST. FRANCIS RECEIVING THE STIGMATA. Pen and brush, brown and black ink, heightened with pinkish white, on blue prepared paper. 366 x 278 mm.
Compositional study for the painting in the Galleria Nazionale, Urbino, presently on loan to the Museo Civico, Fossombrone. An earlier sketch for this imposing project is in the British Museum.

*48. Bernardino Barbatelli, called Poccetti. Florentine, 1548–1612.*
THE SEVEN SAINTLY FOUNDERS SUPERVISING THE BUILDING OF THE MONASTERY OF MONTE SENARIO IN 1234. Black chalk, on white paper. 204 x 283 mm.
Preparatory design for the lunette painted by Poccetti in the cloister of the Santissima Annunziata, Florence.

*49. Moretto da Brescia. Brescian, about 1498–1554.*
ST. AUGUSTINE AND ST. CATHERINE. Pen and brush, brown ink, on white paper. 216 x 253 mm.
The two seated saints vividly recall similar figures in the church of S. Giovanni Evangelista, Brescia, executed by Moretto about 1521. The broader treatment of the pen and wash work, the ample volume of the figures and folds and the speed of execution indicate a more mature dating for this drawing.

*50. Girolamo Romanino. Brescian, about 1485–1561.*
STANDING SOLDIERS. Red chalk, on white paper. 290 x 201 mm.
Elegant study for a lansquenet, probably from life. Romanino used this type of Germanic soldier in his frescoes in the Cremona Cathedral and in the Colleoni Castle, Malpaga. The drawing can be dated between 1519 and 1527.

*51. Giulio Campi. Cremonese, about 1502–1572.*
ST. ROCH, SEATED IN A LANDSCAPE. Pen, brown ink, on brownish paper. 365 x 274 mm.
The moving legend of St. Roch, who healed the sick and subsequently suffered a martyr's death, is placed here in surroundings which combine Northern elements with the great Venetian landscape tradition of Giorgione and Titian.

*52. Bernardino Campi. Cremonese, about 1522–1590/95.*
MONK STANDING, WITH A KNEELING MAN. Black chalk, on pink-tinted paper; squared for transfer. 245 x 103 mm.
Figure studies, apparently from life, for the left-hand portion of a large composition. The saintly monk presents the kneeling donor to the main actor in the altarpiece.

*53. Antonio Campi. Cremonese, died 1591.*
STANDING MALE FIGURE. Black and white chalk, on gray-blue paper; squared for transfer. 243 x 249 mm.
Companion to the sheet in the Ashmolean Museum, Oxford, representing a very similar standing figure of a prophet. The Oxford example is given to Bernardino Campi. The two drawings, however, differ much in execution and volume from the secure works by Bernardino, whose style was greatly influenced by Giulio Romano.

*54. Bartolomeo Passarotti. Bolognese, 1529–1592.*
GROTESQUE HEAD. Pen, brown ink, on white paper. 244 x 175 mm.
Passarotti, a compulsive imitator of Michelangelo's pen technique, left many strange heads like the present one to posterity. These strikingly ugly representations constitute an important initial step toward Bolognese caricature art, brought to perfection later by the Carraccis and Guercino.

*55. Bartolomeo Schedone. Modena, 1578–1615.*
HANDS AND HEADS. Black and white chalk, on gray paper. 407 x 276 mm.
Delightful studies from life by this eminent early Baroque master, full of velvety surface rendering and youthful charm.

*56. Jacopo da Ponte, called Jacopo Bassano. Bassano, 1517/18–1592.*
HEAD OF A BEARDED OLD MAN. Colored chalks, on gray paper. 274 x 188 mm.
To be dated about 1563–1564, this is one of the many studies by the great Venetian done in pastels. The dashing virtuosity of his drawings places Jacopo Bassano among the most painterly artists of the Italian Renaissance.

57. *Leandro da Ponte, called Leandro Bassano. Bassano, 1557–1622.*

HALF-LENGTH FIGURE OF A CAVALIER. Black and white chalk, with some black oil chalk, on blue-gray paper. 190 x 141 mm.

The attribution of this stately portrait, with its obvious leanings on Titian and Paolo Veronese, is not altogether solved. There is a certain loose baroque swing in the posture of the knight which is alien to the rather stolid sitters seen in Leandro's large portrait oeuvre.

58. *Giovanni Antonio da Pordenone. Venetian, 1484–1539.*

HALF-LENGTH FIGURE OF A MAN WEARING A PLUMED HAT. Red chalk, on white paper. 195 x 138 mm.

This belongs to a group of works centering around the creation of Pordenone's masterpiece, the *Crucifixion* fresco in the Cremona Cathedral, painted 1520–1521. Pordenone's dashing linework, the velvety surface rendering and the superb grasp of light effects are quite unique among his contemporaries.

59. *Giovanni Antonio da Pordenone.*

THE ADORATION OF THE MAGI. Pen and wash, brown ink, heightened with white, on blue-gray paper. 246 x 333 mm.

Attributed by an earlier collector to Pomponio Amalteo, the principal follower of Pordenone, this drawing has been recently identified by Charles Cohen as an original by the older master. It is connected with his work in the church of S. Maria di Campagna, Piacenza. Another version of this subject is at Windsor Castle.

60. *Jacopo Tintoretto. Venice, 1518–1594.*

STANDING MAN. Black chalk and brown oil paint, on blue paper. 344 x 170 mm.

This figure was probably drawn from a wax model or a mannequin, which Tintoretto often used in his studio. The oil-paint outline was a method of transferring and reversing the sense of the composition whenever necessary during the preparation of a work.

61. *Jacopo Tintoretto.*

CROUCHING MAN. Black and some white chalk, on gray paper; squared for transfer. 172 x 156 mm.

This seems to be a study for a figure in the *Vision of Ezekiel,* Scuola San Rocco, Venice. Tintoretto began his major project in the Scuola in 1564, continuing for more than twenty years.

62. *Paolo Veronese. Verona-Venice, 1528–1588.*

HEAD OF A MAN. Black and white chalk, on gray-blue paper. 265 x 198 mm.

Realistic and splendidly observed study from a living model. With the simplest of graphic means, the artist solves problems of shape, volume, shimmering surface and brilliant light effects with great ease.

63. *Paolo Veronese.*

STUDY OF A FUR CAPE. Black and white chalk, on gray-green paper. 319 x 210 mm.

Among the chalk studies by Paolo, this imposing sheet finds no rival. The brillant linework, velvety and quite forceful at the same time, can be compared only with the master's celebrated wash drawing of a suit of armor in Berlin.

64. *Andrea Meldolla, called Schiavone. Venetian, 1522–1563.*

APOLLO AND MARSYAS. Pen and brush, brown and gray ink over black chalk, heightened with white, on blue-gray paper. 273 x 265 mm.

Marsyas was a satyr who challenged the god Apollo to a music contest. The subject is also known from a very similar version by Parmigianino in The Pierpont Morgan Library. Indeed, besides the great Venetians, the art of Parmigianino was one of the vital sources of Schiavone's development.

65. *Federigo Zuccaro. Tuscan, 1540/41–1609.*

EMPEROR FREDERIC BARBAROSSA BEFORE POPE ALEXANDER III. Pen and brush, brown ink over black chalk, on white paper. 266 x 214 mm.

When banned from Rome in 1581, Federigo Zuccaro spent some time in Venice, where he was commissioned to paint this historical event for the Ducal Palace. It replaced an earlier version by Jacopo Tintoretto which perished during the 1577 fire. The painter planned several versions for the project, of which this seems to be the earliest.

66. *Francesco Vanni. Siena, 1563–1610.*

SCENES FROM THE LIFE OF ST. CATHERINE OF SIENA. Black and some white chalk, on blue-gray paper. 277 x 213 mm.

Spirited compositional and detail studies by this sensitive artist, who followed in the footsteps of Federigo Barocci in Siena.

67. *Antonio d'Enrico, called Tanzio da Varallo. Lombard, 1574/81–1635.*

KNEELING MONK. Red and white chalk, on red-tinted paper. 236 x 160 mm.

Drapery study for St. Francis in an altarpiece, painted for the Oratorio of San Carlo at Sabbia, Valsesia, between 1628 and 1633. This figure, with its rather static character, recalls the utterly theatrical stations of the Passion done by Tanzio on the Sacro Monte in Varallo.

68. *Lattanzio Gambara. Brescian, 1530–1573/74.*

JOSHUA, STANDING. Black charcoal and white chalk, on gray-green paper. 425 x 273 mm.

This imposing picture is the preparatory study for the gigantic figure appearing on the left wall flanking the main entrance inside the Duomo in Parma. Gambara did considerable work in this church between 1567 and 1571.

69. *Giuseppe Cesari, called Cavaliere d'Arpino. Roman, 1568–1640.*
HALF-LENGTH FIGURE OF A MAN HOLDING A BANNER. Black chalk, on white paper. 218 x 144 mm.

Following the tradition of his great Roman predecessors, Cavaliere d'Arpino enjoyed an enviable position as a draughtsman well into the seventeenth century. Clarity, economical use of all facets of drawing technique and an unerring sense of proportion characterize his works.

70. *Paolo Farinato. Veronese, 1524–1606.*
SIEGE OF A TOWN. Pen, brown ink, on white paper. 188 x 318 mm.

This picture may represent the siege of Verona, a project which Farinato contemplated but, to our knowledge, did not execute. The subject, however, was painted by Contarini for the Ducal Palace in Venice at a somewhat later date. The drawing should be dated about 1560, when Farinato was strongly influenced by Titian.

71. *Lodewyck Toeput, called Pozzoserrato. Antwerp-Treviso, about 1550–1603/05.*
LANDSCAPE WITH A STAG HUNT. Pen and brush, blue ink over black chalk, on white paper. 284 x 400 mm.

The happy marriage of Flemish training with Venetian space and light here creates a most effective image, full of action and joyful exuberance, recalling the lovely murals by this able decorator in the Villa Maser, near Treviso.

72. *Jacopo Negretti, called Palma Giovane. Venice, 1544–1628.*
CHRIST AND HIS DISCIPLES. Pen and brush, dark brown ink over black chalk, heightened with white, on brownish paper. 403 x 207 mm.

In this work the prolific draughtsman is still under the tutelage of his master, Jacopo Tintoretto; hence, the sheet should be dated in the late 1560s.

73. *Giuseppe Porta, called Salviati. Venetian, about 1520–1575.*
BELLEROPHON KILLING THE CHIMERA. Pen and brush, brown ink over black chalk, heightened with white, on gray paper; squared for transfer. 276 x 232 mm.

According to the historian Ridolfi, Porta decorated the facade of Nicolò Bernardo's house in the Campo San Polo, Venice, for which this design may be the preparatory stage. The work is a happy fusion of Roman art and that of Tintoretto and Veronese.

74. *Pietro Faccini. Bolognese, 1562–1602.*
HEAD OF S. FILIPPO NERI. Red chalk, on yellow-tinted paper. 220 x 207 mm.

It is the merit of Chandler Kirwin to have been the first to recognize the subject of this dramatic portrait as the venerated and amiable saint. Among the known images of S. Filippo Neri, this may be the one example to have been drawn from life and not from the death masks conserved in Rome and Naples.

75. *Lodovico Cardi, called Il Cigoli. Florentine, 1559–1613.*
MONK IN PRAYER BEFORE THE CROSS. Pen and brush, brown ink over red chalk, on white paper. 143 x 108 mm.

According to the autograph inscription, this is a preparatory sketch for a portrait of Padre Tommaso, General of the Monastery in Città di Castello. Cigoli, who is better appreciated in his spectacular colored brush drawings and architectural prospects, uses his brilliant wash technique effectively in this work.

76. *Luca Cambiaso. Genoese, 1527–1585.*
MARRIAGE OF THE VIRGIN. Pen and brush, brown ink, on white paper. 138 x 307 mm.

Preparatory drawing for the painting in the Lercari Chapel, Duomo di S. Lorenzo, Genoa, carried out about 1567. There is another sketch for this fresco in the British Museum. The drawings of this forward-looking draughtsman were much admired and in great demand in his time; hence, Cambiaso often made versions of his own compositions.

77. *Bernardo Buontalenti. Florentine, 1536–1608.*
SKETCHES FOR THEATRICAL COSTUMES. Pen and brush, brown ink, on white paper turned yellow. 194 x 297 mm.

The eminent architect and designer was chief engineer for many Florentine theatrical productions during the latter part of the sixteenth century. Buontalenti planned his effective costumes to the minutest detail, just as he did with architectural projects, as can be seen on the verso of this sheet, which is covered with sketches for portals, window casings and chimney pieces.

78. *Giovanni Battista Paggi. Genoese, 1554–1627.*
AN ARCHER. Black and white chalk, on light brown paper. 406 x 220 mm.

Paggi worked toward the end of the sixteenth century in Florence. This accounts for the strong influence artists like Empoli and Passignano had on this painter, who nevertheless proved during his entire career to be the most gifted and faithful Genoese follower of Luca Cambiaso.

79. *Fabrizio Boschi. Florentine, 1570–1642.*
AN ARCHER. Red and black chalk, on white paper. 299 x 205 mm.

This vigorous study from a live model was long given to Matteo Roselli, a Florentine contemporary of Boschi. It has been recently identified by Dr.

Christel Thiem as a preparatory sketch for a known altarpiece by the latter artist, who in an effective way continues the sixteenth-century Florentine drawing tradition into the next century.

*80. Giovanni Lanfranco. Parma-Rome, 1582–1647.*
STUDIES FOR THE HEAD OF A YOUTH. Black and white chalk, on buff-colored paper. 268 x 221 mm.

A close follower of the best Carracci tradition, Lanfranco was at his peak when drawing in this medium, often from living models. This study is for the St. John in one of the pendentive frescoes in Gesù Nuovo, Naples, done about 1636.

*81. Annibale Carracci. Bolognese, 1560–1609.*
NUDE MAN STRIKING WITH A CLUB. Black and white chalk, on gray-green paper. 422 x 272 mm.

Probably drawn from a live model, this is a study for one of the figures in the Palazzo Farnese frescoes, Rome, painted during the years 1597–1604.

*82. Annibale Carracci.*
LANDSCAPE WITH FIGURES. Pen, dark brown ink, on white paper. 250 x 194 mm.

Landscape composition in two sections, the upper a rather explicit academic sorting out of details, while the lower is a vigorous nature study in the best vein of this accomplished artist.

*83. Domenico Zampieri, called Domenichino. Bolognese, 1581–1641.*
LANDSCAPE WITH A FORTIFIED TOWN IN A LAKE. Pen and brown ink, on white paper. 428 x 326 mm.

Pleasing and neat picture of a town, probably an imaginary composition which underlines well Domenichino's classical training and somewhat dry pen-and-ink technique.

*84. Giacomo Cavedone. Bolognese, 1577–1660.*
THE VIRGIN UNDER THE CROSS. Black and white chalk, on blue-gray paper. 242 x 364 mm.

Cavedone was probably the most imaginative painter and draughtsman among the earlier Bolognese Baroque masters. He observed and transformed his strong heritage from the Venetians effectively, as can be seen in this moving composition.

*85. Guido Reni. Bolognese, 1575–1642.*
HAND AND ARM STUDIES. Black, red and white chalk, on buff-colored paper. 160 x 298 mm.

A brilliant sheet of studies from a live model in the effective *à trois crayons* technique that became so popular in France in the eighteenth century.

*86. Giovanni Francesco Barbieri, called Guercino. Bolognese, 1591–1666.*
DEATH OF S. FILIPPO NERI. Pen and brush, brown ink, on white paper. 248 x 290 mm.

This is the detail study for the lower portion of the altarpiece in S. Maria in Galliera, Bologna, painted 1646/47. The consummate art of Guercino as a draughtsman was rarely surpassed by other artists of his time. Dramatic use of shading, light, surface treatment, strong or delicate variations of contours, all play together in a harmonious and lively action to produce some of the most significant graphic masterpieces left to posterity.

*87. Giovanni Francesco Barbieri, called Guercino.*
LANDSCAPE WITH VOLCANO. Brush, brown ink, on blue-gray paper. 258 x 372 mm.

A rapid and forceful rendering of an astounding natural phenomenon, drawn with utmost speed, economy and virtuosity.

*88. Ottavio Leoni. Paduan, 1578–1630.*
PORTRAIT OF MONSIGNOR PORTA. Black and white chalk, on gray paper. 218 x 157 mm.

Done by the able and busy portraitist in 1619, this represents one of the many official-looking renderings of personalities in and around Rome. The considerable talent of Leoni as a printmaker is easily discernible in this almost miniature-like image.

*89. Giovanni Lorenzo Bernini. Roman, 1598–1680.*
CARICATURE OF A CAVALIER. Pen and brown ink, on white paper. 207 x 144 mm.

Bernini is much too little known as a caricaturist. His overpowering talents as sculptor, painter and architect outshine his subtle, fun-poking side. Unfortunately, only a fistful of these witty sheets remain for posterity. The present example, done rapidly and with utmost economy, exhibits an elegance, a sense of humor and a gift for clinical observation of emotional content and amusing detail rarely encountered in other artists.

*90. Pietro Berettini, called Pietro da Cortona. Roman, 1596–1669.*
HALF-LENGTH FIGURE OF A WOMAN. Black and white chalk, on brown paper pieced together. 660 x 643 mm.

Large full-scale cartoon drawing for a fresco by the eminent Roman decorator, which was used for transfer onto the plaster surface. This can be observed from the indentations along the contours of this floating female figure. The work can be dated about 1635.

*91. Pietro Berettini, called Pietro da Cortona.*
THE QUEEN OF SHEBA BEFORE SOLOMON. Pen and brush, brown ink, heightened with white and washed with blue and gray watercolors, on brown paper. 220 x 360 mm.

Elaborate model drawing for the fresco in the Palazzo Mattei, Rome. This was one of Cortona's first major commissions and its great success started the painter off on his phenomenal career.

*92. Pietro Testa. Roman, 1611–1650.*
THE DREAM OF JOSEPH. Pen and brush, brown ink, on white paper. 271 x 215 mm.
Testa, one of the significant printmakers of the Roman Baroque, shows in this intimate picture his innate talent for concise composition, warm coloring and refined sentiment. In addition, the strong influence of Poussin and Claude, his French colleagues in Rome, is also discernible.

*93. Baldassare Franceschini, called Il Volterrano. Florentine, 1611–1689.*
TRIUMPH OF THE ROVERE. Red chalk and washes, on white paper turned yellow. 338 x 217 mm.
Design for the central portion of the ceiling in the Sala del Volterrano, Palazzo Pitti, Florence. It was commissioned to celebrate the fame of Vittoria della Rovere, wife of Ferdinand II de' Medici, Grand Duke of Tuscany.

*94. Orazio Gentileschi. Florentine, 1562–1657.*
HEAD OF A YOUTH. Black and white chalk, on buff-colored paper. 373 x 272 mm.
The head of this young man served as a model for that of St. Cecilia, the patron saint of music, in an altarpiece by Gentileschi now in the Brera, Milan.

*95. Jacopo Chimenti, called Jacopo da Empoli. Florentine, 1551–1640.*
HEAD OF A YOUTH. Black and white chalk, on gray paper. 360 x 246 mm.
A good work by this able artist, who drew a great deal in the manner of the noted sixteenth-century Florentines, especially that of Pontormo. His large output, preserved mainly in the Uffizi, Florence, is rather monotonous and repetitive, however.

*96. Stefano della Bella. Florentine, 1610–1664.*
CONVENTION IN A CHURCH. Pen and brush, brown ink, gray washes over preliminary lead-pencil tracing, on white paper. 268 x 403 mm.
This Convention of the Knights of St. Stephen, taking place in Pisa, demonstrates magisterially della Bella's talent as a master printmaker and inventive scenic designer.

*97. Alfonso Parigi. Florentine, died 1656.*
PROJECT FOR FUNERARY DECORATIONS. Pen and brush, brown ink, on white paper. 253 x 281 mm.
Designed for the obsequies of Ferdinand II, Emperor of Austria, held in S. Lorenzo, Florence, 1637. Stefano della Bella prepared the exterior decorations, while the younger Parigi made this drawing for the interior of the church.

*98. Giovanni Manozzi, called Giovanni da San Giovanni. Florentine, 1592–1636.*
ST. PAUL LED INTO DAMASCUS. Pen and brush, brown ink, on white paper. 177 x 397 mm.
Preparatory design for the lunette in the Inghirami Chapel of the Duomo in Volterra. San Giovanni completed the extensive frescoes on the life of St. Paul in 1622.

*99. Pierfrancesco Mola. Coldrerio-Rome, 1612–1660.*
MAN DICTATING HIS WILL. Pen and brush, dark brown ink over black chalk, on white paper. 254 x 390 mm.
Scene from the life of a certain bearded man who is known from a series of drawings by Mola and Guercino. All these pictures are of domestic scenes, slightly caricaturistic and often realistically explicit, bordering on the obscene. The subject must have been a popular personage in his time, living probably somewhere near Bologna.

*100. Giovanni Battista Salvi, called Sassoferrato. Roman, 1609–1685.*
PORTRAIT OF A CLERIC. Black, red and white chalk, on blue paper. 191 x 265 mm.
Extremely sensitive rendering of a subject that shows the mastery of this once very popular religious painter. Sassoferrato continued with much skill the tradition of such portraitists as the Carraccis and Leoni.

*101. Bernardo Cavallino. Neapolitan, 1616–1654.*
STUDY OF A WOMAN WALKING. Black and white chalk, on gray-green paper. 379 x 272 mm.
Sketch for a painting of the Vergine Immacolata in a private collection, Palermo. This is one of the very few remaining autograph drawings by this most delicate painter, who during his lifetime was already praised by writers as one of the "truly great."

*102. Mattia Preti. Rome-Naples, 1613–1699.*
ST. SEBASTIAN. Black chalk, on white paper. 338 x 240 mm.
This figure, which gives the impression of hanging in space, could well be a sketch prepared by the painter for a sculptor. Preti painted this subject several times and there are similar examples by him in various collections, all of which should be dated about 1650.

*103. Luca Giordano. Neapolitan, 1632–1705.*
STANDING CHERUB HOLDING A CLUB. Black chalk, on white paper. 262 x 202 mm.
The much-traveled artist, while working in Spain, completed his masterpiece in the Escorial, the Grand Staircase decorations, about 1694. This delicate sketch was used there in the lunettes of the stairwell, flanking the windows.

*104. Salvator Rosa. Naples-Rome, 1615–1673.*
JAEL AND SISERA. Pen and brush, brown ink, on white paper. 152 x 140 mm.
A late work by the virtuoso draughtsman, full of dramatic impact and dazzling performance. Rosa, a

many-faceted genius, was one of the outstanding Baroque graphic artists.

*105. Paolo de Matteis. Neapolitan, 1662–1729.*
THE HOLY FAMILY AND ST. JOHN. Pen and brush, dark brown ink, on white paper. 250 x 184 mm.

This gifted follower of Salvator Rosa and also of the Roman Baroque achieved quite a reputation as a draughtsman. His strong Neapolitan chiaroscuro, as well as a sense for compact compositional schemes recalling the painters of the mid-seventeenth century in Rome, justify the high opinion his contemporaries had for de Matteis' art.

*106. Daniele Crespi. Lombard, 1590/95–1630.*
ST. BRUNO AND COUNT ROGER OF CALABRIA. Pen and brush, brown ink, heightened with white, on gray-green paper. 249 x 267 mm.

Project for the painting in the Carthusian monastery of Garegnano, completed in 1629. Crespi composed a cycle of paintings from the life of this popular saint of Lombardy, including this scene, in which the saint wakes Count Roger from his sleep to warn him of danger.

*107. Bernardo Strozzi. Genoese, 1581–1644.*
CHERUBS DANCING AROUND THE CHRIST CHILD, WHO HOLDS THE CROSS. Pen, brown ink, on white paper. 238 x 360 mm.

Early in his life, Strozzi adhered strongly to Genoese tradition, especially that of Cambiaso and his immediate followers. There is also a powerful Central-Italian influence discernible here, harking back to earlier compositional schemes of the mid-sixteenth century.

*108. Giovanni Benedetto Castiglione. Genoese, 1616–1670.*
TRAVELERS RESTING UNDER A TREE. Pen and brush, dark brown ink, on white paper turned yellow. 273 x 403 mm.

Castiglione was one of the most inventive graphic personalities of the Italian Baroque. In this very late work, which seems to be from life, he reaches far into the future, into the world of Goya and Daumier. His passionate admiration for Rembrandt shines through in every drawing he made.

*109. Giovanni Andrea de' Ferrari. Genoese, 1598–1669.*
JACOB PROMISING LABAN SEVEN YEARS OF SERVICE. Black and red chalk, with some gray washes, on white paper. 133 x 260 mm.

The delicate gray washes in this chalk drawing create a velvety, subtle effect which is quite personal and characteristic of this Genoese Baroque painter. With his superlative drawing skill, Andrea de' Ferrari influenced many of the younger Genoese artists.

*110. Pierfrancesco Mazzucchelli, called Il Morazzone. Lombard, 1571/73–1626.*
SEATED MALE FIGURE. Brush, brown ink over black chalk, on gray-green paper. 258 x 297 mm.

The impressive study, probably for an apostle, should be compared with similar figures in the Lombard master's frescoes. Morazzone was an extremely prolific decorator, who received his training partly in Rome. He there came into contact with Caravaggio's art and from then on adopted a dramatic differentiation of light and shade, which is particularly significant in his late work, like this drawing.

*111. Giovanni Battista Benaschi. Turin-Naples, 1636–1688.*
TRUMPETERS. Black and white chalk, on slightly faded blue paper. 380 x 539 mm.

According to contemporary sources, this painter was Lanfranco's pupil. If so, he must have been a very young boy at the time. Benaschi undoubtedly absorbed much of Lanfranco's manner and then carried these traditions into a new, liquid and forceful late-Baroque language, which earned him much praise.

*112. Alessandro Maganza. Vicenza, 1556–about 1640.*
STUDIES FOR A ST. SEBASTIAN. Pen and brush, brown ink over black chalk, on white paper. 277 x 190 mm.

There are few draughtsmen among the North Italians of the outgoing Renaissance who demonstrate such virtuosity and emotional content as can be found in the drawings of Alessandro Maganza. The abandon with which his pen and brush move over the surface recalls the achievement of earlier Venetians. This gifted minor painter became one of the revitalizing factors which brought about the revival of Venetian drawing art during the last decades of the seventeenth century.

*113. Francesco Maffei. Venetian, 1606–1660.*
THE VISITATION. Pen and brush, dark brown ink, red and brown washes, on white paper. 185 x 145 mm.

Maffei is one of the few major figures of the Venetian seventeenth century who left their mark by producing utterly splendid works. Outstanding in his oeuvre are the large historical canvases in and around Vicenza. He painted several versions of the Visitation. This late drawing could be a study for his painting in Arzignano, done about 1645.

*114. Domenico Tintoretto. Venice, 1560–1635.*
CHRIST ON THE MOUNT OF OLIVES. Brush, brown ink over black chalk, on blue-gray paper. 218 x 308 mm.

This theatrically conceived picture by the son of the great Tintoretto is a key document for our understanding of the transition from the Venetian Renaissance to the oncoming Baroque. Despite the somewhat hesitant placing of figures, there is evidence of careful study of the past, a slight undercurrent of Parmigianino's art and an eager search for a new dramatic light and expression.

*115. Domenico Maria Canuti. Bolognese, 1620–1684.*
STUDY OF A DEAD OR SLEEPING MAN. Red and white chalk over black chalk, on brown paper. 306 x 506 mm.

The strong impact of the Carraccis must have followed Canuti throughout his very active career as a decorator. In this powerful picture, with its astounding surface treatment and anatomical exactness, the artist reached his summit as a draughtsman.

*116. Federico Bencovich. Venetian, about 1677–1753.*
HERCULES FREEING PROMETHEUS. Pen and brush, brown ink, on red-tinted paper. 303 x 251 mm.

The popular subject of the liberation of Prometheus is treated here by this much-traveled artist in a way that links the classic Baroque to a much more alive idiom, which will lead ultimately to the great Venetian eighteenth century.

*117. Carlo Maratta. Roman, 1625–1713.*
HALF-LENGTH FIGURE OF A FAUN. Red chalk, on brown paper. 250 x 244 mm.

Detail study for a figure in the Palazzo Altieri, Rome. Pope Clement X Altieri commissioned Maratta to decorate several rooms in his palace. The painter, then the most admired decorator in Rome, painted the principal ceiling and provided sketches like the present one to his assistants, who then completed the other frescoes.

*118. Andrea Sacchi. Roman, 1599–1661.*
EPISODE FROM THE LIFE OF A SAINT. Pen, brown ink over red chalk, on white paper. 250 x 185 mm.

This dramatic event, the saint's rescue of a monk from drowning in a river, recalls another drawing by the painter at Windsor Castle. They are almost identical in medium, technique and even composition. Like the Windsor example, the present sheet should be dated about 1625.

*119. Pierleone Ghezzi. Roman, 1674–1755.*
VIOLONCELLIST PLAYING HIS INSTRUMENT. Pen, brown ink over black chalk, on white paper. 251 x 195 mm.

The abbé manipulating the bow and cello in the true early-eighteenth-century manner is, according to an inscription on the verso of the drawing, the house-musician of a Monsieur de Bacqueville, a French nobleman who probably resided in Rome in the 1720s.

*120. Giuseppe Passeri. Roman, 1654–1714.*
ST. PETER FREED FROM PRISON. Pen and brush, dark brown ink, reddish-brown washes, heightened with white, on red-tinted paper. 280 x 230 mm.

This painter-historian left a large oeuvre of highly finished, brilliant drawings, like the present sheet. While his attractive pictures are a joy to look at, his biographies of painters remain a source of great importance for Roman art-historical research.

*121. Alessandro Magnasco. Genoese, about 1667–1749.*
SEATED MONK IN A LANDSCAPE. Brush, grayish-brown ink, heightened with white, on light brown paper. 259 x 210 mm.

Design for an altarpiece honoring the Blessed Agostino Novelli, a noted Augustinian monk. The drawing is not connected with a known painting by the master; however, it should be dated rather late in Magnasco's career, during his stay in Milan (thus before 1735).

*122. Domenico Piola. Genoese, 1627–1703.*
ALLEGORY OF THE SOLSTICE. Pen and brush, brown ink over black chalk, on white paper. 300 x 428 mm.

This popular and very active decorator was a brilliant draughtsman. His large graphic oeuvre, preserved mostly in Genoa but also in American collections, is varied and fascinating on account of the skill with which Piola jotted down rapidly his attractive inventions.

*123. Paolo Girolamo Piola. Genoese, 1666–1724.*
THE TOILET OF BATHSHEBA. Pen and brush, brown ink over black crayon, heightened with white, on blue-gray paper. 290 x 424 mm.

Paolo Girolamo, son of Domenico, learned from his father how to make good use of his innate talents. He became just as popular as his father, perhaps surpassing Domenico with his more graceful and transparent compositions.

*124. Gaspare Vanvitelli. Utrecht-Rome, 1647–1736.*
THE ROMAN CAMPAGNA. Pen and brush, brown ink and gray washes, on white paper. 267 x 413 mm.

This wide-open view, one of the most successful pictures in Vanvitelli's oeuvre, seems to have been done from nature. The present drawing and its companion in the Munich Print Cabinet, which represents a hill town near Rome, form a link between the heroic landscape style of Claude and the oncoming Settecento of Canaletto and his contemporaries.

*125. Domenico del Mondo. Neapolitan, 1717–1806.*
HORATIUS COCLES DEFENDING THE BRIDGE. Pen and brush, dark brown ink, gray and brown washes, heightened with white, on white paper. 210 x 307 mm.

In Roman legendary history, Cocles saved the city by defending a Tiber bridge against invading Etruscans. Domenico del Mondo, the popular painter and teacher, found a way of assembling elements from an earlier Neapolitan graphic vocabulary. With his rapid, young drawing style, he was leading into Neoclassicism and even further, into the Romantic era.

*126. Gian Gioseffo dal Sole. Bolognese, 1654–1719.*
THE BIRD CATCHERS. Pen and brush, brown ink over red chalk, on white paper. 204 x 270 mm.

Dal Sole, much esteemed by his contemporaries, was a successful decorator and teacher. His art bears witness to the Bolognese heritage, that of Guido Reni in particular. His drawn oeuvre, which is not large, presents him as a gentle, effective and convincing storyteller, while his landscape inventions mark him as one of the more significant *vedutisti* of his time.

*127. Donato Creti. Bolognese, 1671–1749.*
SATYR. Black chalk, on white paper. 251 x 206 mm.

Although born in Cremona, Creti became one of the most significant and admired artists of Bologna. He traveled a great deal and wherever he went left traces of his noble, delicious art, which became the summit of the Bolognese Rococo.

*128. Gaetano Gandolfi. Bolognese, 1734–1802.*
THE DEAD CHRIST. Black oiled charcoal, red and white chalk, on buff-colored paper. 441 x 315 mm.

Sketch for the figure of Christ taken from the Cross. The complicated and subtle blending of various media into a homogeneous expressive unit is a telling proof of this remarkable artist's great gifts. Gaetano Gandolfi, the draughtsman, constitutes a brilliant culmination of Bolognese graphic art throughout the centuries.

*129. Gaetano Gandolfi.*
THE MARRIAGE FEAST AT CANA. Pen and brush, dark brown ink and gray washes, on white paper. 245 x 206 mm.

Preparatory sketch for the splendid canvas in the Pinacoteca, Bologna. There is another version of this subject in the Albertina, Vienna. On the verso of the present sheet the artist sketched out the almost embryonic concept of this imposing composition.

*130. Sebastiano Ricci. Venetian, 1659–1734.*
ROMAN BATTLE. Pen and brush, brown and gray ink over lead pencil, on white paper. 220 x 300 mm.

The subject might be the battle of the Sabines and the Romans. Sebastiano is one of the most significant graphic artists of the Venetian territories. With his Bolognese training and Venetian enthusiasm, he created singlehanded a style of drawing which became a source of inspiration for the entire Venetian Settecento.

*131. Marco Ricci. Venetian, 1676–1729.*
BRIGANDS ATTACKING TRAVELERS. Pen and brush, brown ink over black chalk, on white paper. 372 x 538 mm.

A master of landscape art, Marco drew this favorite subject of his several times. There are two other versions at Windsor Castle and a tempera painting on leather in Buckingham Palace.

*132. Giovanni Battista Piazzetta. Venice, 1682–1754.*
HEAD OF A LEVANTINE. Black and white chalk, on gray paper. 375 x 301 mm.

This expressive head is obviously drawn from life. There is another version of the same sitter in the Venice Academy collection. The grand heads by Piazzetta, done in his inimitable, velvety, dramatic manner are among the most precious remnants of Venetian art.

*133. Giovanni Antonio Pellegrini. Venetian, 1675–1741.*
HOLY BISHOP IN GLORY. Pen and brush, brown ink over red chalk, on white paper. 264 x 207 mm.

Another gifted precursor of the Tiepolos was Pellegrini. His drawings are of a painterly quality, full of light, summary and almost explosive in execution, bristling with life and sparkle.

*134. Giovanni Battista Tiepolo. Venice-Madrid, 1696–1770.*
MAN LED INTO PRISON. Pen and brush, brown and gray ink over lead pencil, on white paper. 410 x 282 mm.

The composition and technique of the sheet, which indicate an early date, about 1730, would suggest a connection with the great historical paintings Tiepolo executed about that time. However, it seems that the design was never used in a painting. On the other side of this drawing are the preliminary sketches for the Fava altarpiece, completed by the artist about 1732.

*135. Giovanni Battista Tiepolo.*
MADONNA AND CHILD ADORED BY SAINTS. Pen and brush, golden-brown ink over black chalk, on white paper. 356 x 257 mm.

As the autograph note by Tiepolo indicates, this impressive altarpiece study was either done in or commissioned by a person in Varese, a Lombard town. The painter, after an earlier trip, returned again to Milan about 1740 and it can be assumed that this sheet was drawn during the two years he spent there.

*136. Giovanni Battista Tiepolo.*
HERCULES STANDING. Black chalk, on white paper. 600 x 445 mm.

Returning from his second journey to Lombardy, Giambattista renewed his relationship with Piazzetta and interested himself in the older master's teaching activities. At that time he drew a number of large-scale academic studies, like this Hercules. He even furnished material for a book on drawing which Piazzetta published in Venice.

*137. Giovanni Battista Tiepolo.*
HEAD OF A MAN WEARING A TURBAN. Red and white chalk, on blue paper. 314 x 209 mm.

Giambattista, a grand virtuoso with chalk, left a number of astounding studies like this head. They range from the early years to the end of his long career. Terisio Pignatti proposes for this example a date after 1753.

*138. Giovanni Domenico Tiepolo. Venetian, 1727–1804.*
THE HOLY TRINITY IN GLORY. Pen and brush, brown ink with light brown washes over red chalk, on grayish-buff paper. 257 x 304 mm.

A free adaptation of a composition of his father (Giambattista) which Giandomenico used in the church of Casale sul Sile, done in 1781. This is a significant example of the younger Tiepolo's mature style, and a rare instance of a preparatory drawing that can be securely connected with one of his painted works.

*139. Giovanni Domenico Tiepolo.*
ORIENTAL RIDER AND ANOTHER FIGURE. Pen and brush, brown ink over black crayon, on white paper. 182 x 252 mm.

Giandomenico made many versions and variations of this type of subject. A few he used in his paintings, but one could speculate that he may have had prints in mind when assembling this rich repertory of amusing pictures.

*140. Gaspare Diziani. Bologna-Venice, 1689–1767.*
ADAM AND EVE EXPELLED FROM PARADISE. Pen and brush, brown ink over black chalk, watercolors, on white paper. 279 x 187 mm.

The brilliant little picture served as a *modello* for an easel painting or a larger canvas to be put into a paneled wall. Diziani was an able master who absorbed well the art of his peers and produced a considerable, fine graphic oeuvre.

*141. Giovanni Antonio Guardi. Venetian, 1699–1760.*
THE MARTYRDOM OF SAINT CLEMENT. Pen and brush, brown ink and gray washes, on white paper. 422 x 265 mm.

It was Otto Benesch who recognized this sheet as the work of Giovanni Antonio Guardi, when he was assembling material for his book on Venetian drawings in American collections in 1947. The drawing is a free and luminous copy of a lost painting by another Venetian, Giovanni Battista Pittoni.

*142. Antonio Canal, called Canaletto. Venetian, 1697–1768.*
IMAGINARY VENETIAN VIEW. Pen and wash, brown ink, brown and gray washes over black chalk, on white paper. 286 x 203 mm.

In this view Canaletto used various architectural elements to create a pleasing picture, a *capriccio*, as it was called at the time. Supreme as a master of view painting, the great Venetian enriched posterity greatly through his oeuvre.

*143. Antonio Canal, called Canaletto.*
THE PRESBYTERY OF S. MARCO. Pen and brown ink over black chalk, on white paper. 292 x 191 mm.

Preliminary drawing for a painting now in the Victoria and Albert Museum, London. It shows the south pulpit. Probably sketched quickly on the spot, it represents a kind of drawing by the artist that served him as a guide for further work in the studio.

*144. Giovanni Battista Piranesi. Venetian, 1720–1778.*
ARCHITECTURAL FANTASY. Pen and brush, dark brown ink, on white paper. 329 x 491 mm.

The great draughtsman and printmaker was undoubtedly one of the most powerful scene designers of the eighteenth century. There are hardly any sketches known by him that can be directly connected with the stage, but still one wonders whether this grandiose invention could not have been meant as a backdrop for a theatrical performance.

*145. Francesco Guardi. Venetian, 1712–1793.*
THREE SAILING BOATS AND A GONDOLA. Pen and brush, brown ink over lead pencil, on white paper. 204 x 250 mm.

Rapid sketches of various vessels by the eminent Venetian, in his liquid and painterly technique. Obviously done on the Canal, the drawing was later used in one of his paintings, now in London.

*146. Francesco Guardi.*
HEAD OF A BOY. Black and red chalk, on buff-colored paper. 179 x 125 mm.

During his youth Francesco Guardi painted quite a few portraits. Among his many drawings there are only a comparatively small number of heads or figures. This young boy, surely done from a live model, is a rarity in his oeuvre not only as a subject but also for its delicate chalk technique and as a testimony of the painter's keen powers of observation.

*147. Francesco Guardi.*
VIEW WITH AN OBELISK AND FIGURES. Pen and brush, brown ink, gray and brown washes, on white paper. 232 x 145 mm.

Among Francesco's many landscape drawings, this view takes a special place. The picture, representing an idealized view of the outskirts of Padua, is in its noble simplicity and airy composition a sublimation of the Venetian's way of observing and recreating. He used this little sketch in one of his painted *capricci*, translating the lucid drawing technique into a shimmering little jewel of a painting.

*148. Giacomo Guardi. Venetian, 1764–1835.*
ENTRANCE TO THE ARSENAL IN VENICE. Pen and brush, brown ink, gray washes over black crayon, on white paper. 279 x 420 mm.

Giacomo, Francesco Guardi's son, often participated in his father's work, especially toward the end of the master's life. This drawing, recalling the father's painting now in Vienna, may have been an early effort by the son to learn and understand his master's art. Giacomo became a very popular artist in his own right, painting small colored views of Venice and selling them to the ever-present tourists.

*149. Francesco Zuccarelli. Tuscan, 1702–1788.*

LANDSCAPE WITH A LAKE AND A HORSEMAN. Pen and brush, brown ink, gray washes, heightened with white, over black chalk, on white paper. 295 x 462 mm.

Although Tuscan and trained in Rome, Zuccarelli became Venetian through circumstance. Settling in Venice in 1735, he started a studio, where he produced idyllic landscapes like the present drawing. His pen and wash technique, as effective and individual as it is, owes a great debt to Claude and the other classical view painters of the seventeenth century.

*150. Fedele Fischetti. Neapolitan, 1734–1789.*

THE AGE OF GOLD. Pen and brush, black and gray ink, gray washes over black crayon, on white paper. 346 x 460 mm.

An elaborate project for the ceiling in the Queen's apartments in the royal palace of Caserta, near Naples. Fischetti was an able decorator and effective designer, who also used his gifts for planning and designing tapestries for his royal patrons.

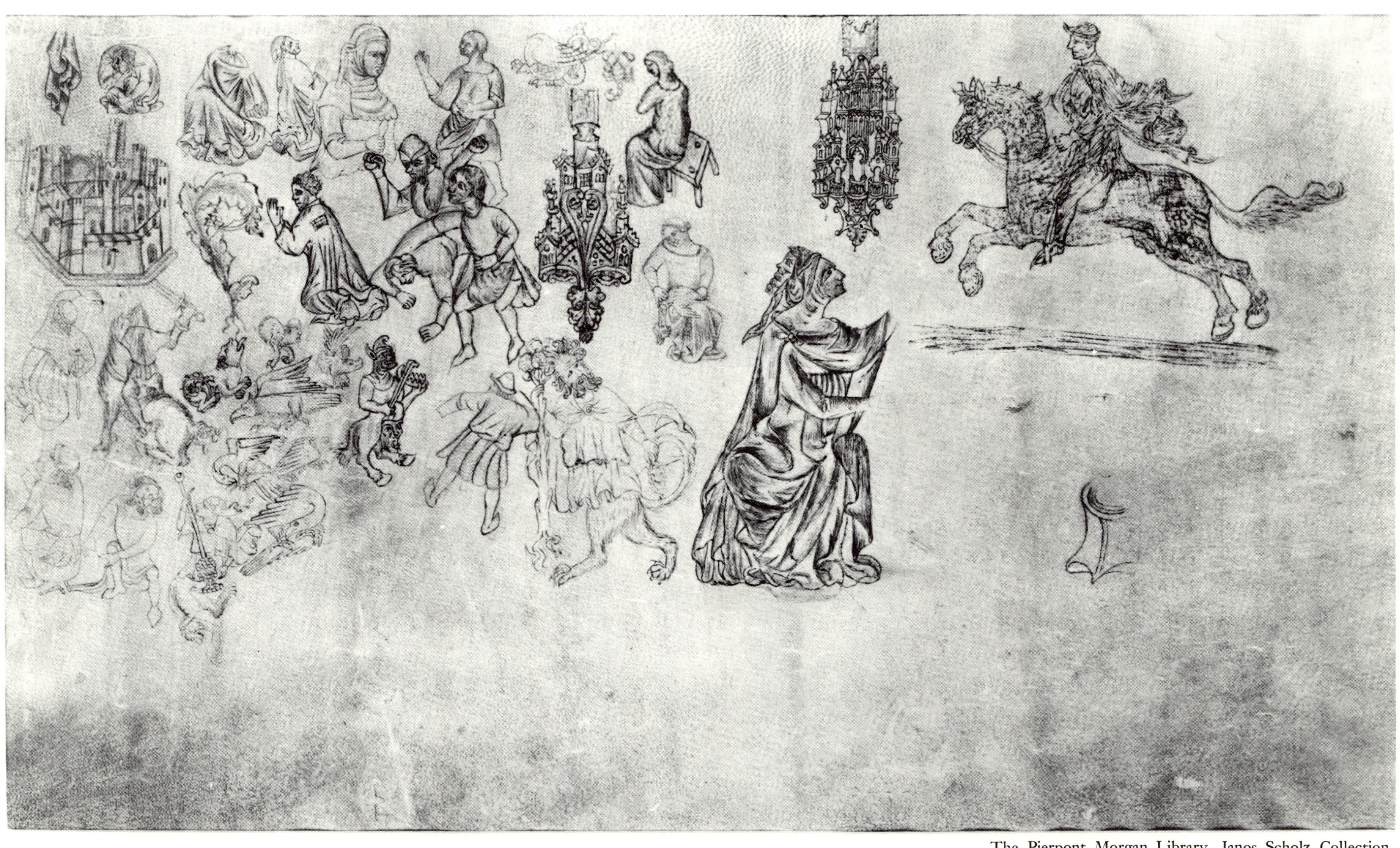

The Pierpont Morgan Library, Janos Scholz Collection

1. *Tuscan master (second quarter of the 14th century).* FIGURES AND DECORATIVE ELEMENTS.

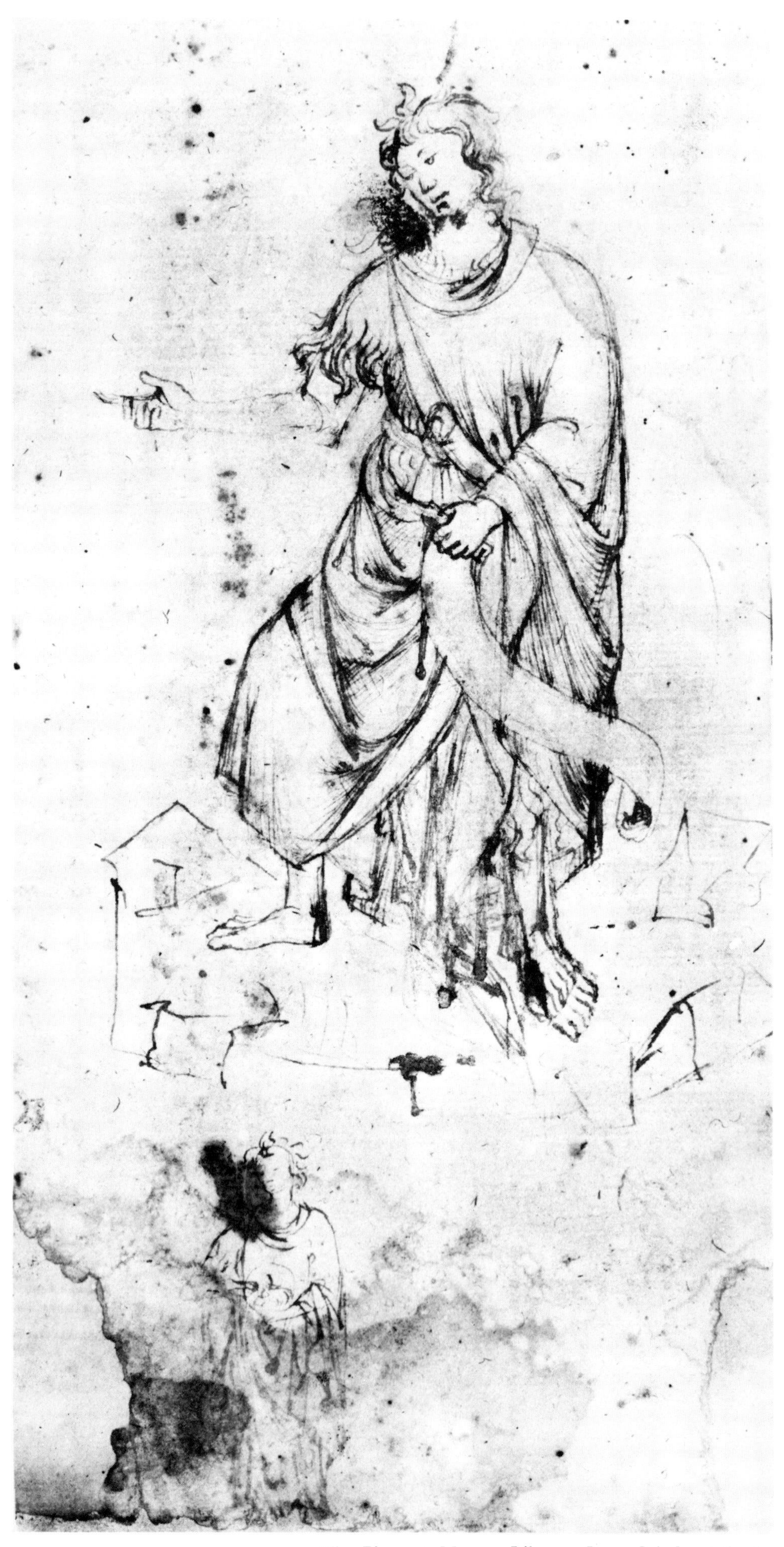

The Pierpont Morgan Library, Janos Scholz Collection

2. *Umbrian painter (third quarter of the 14th century).*
ST. JOHN THE BAPTIST AND ANOTHER FIGURE.

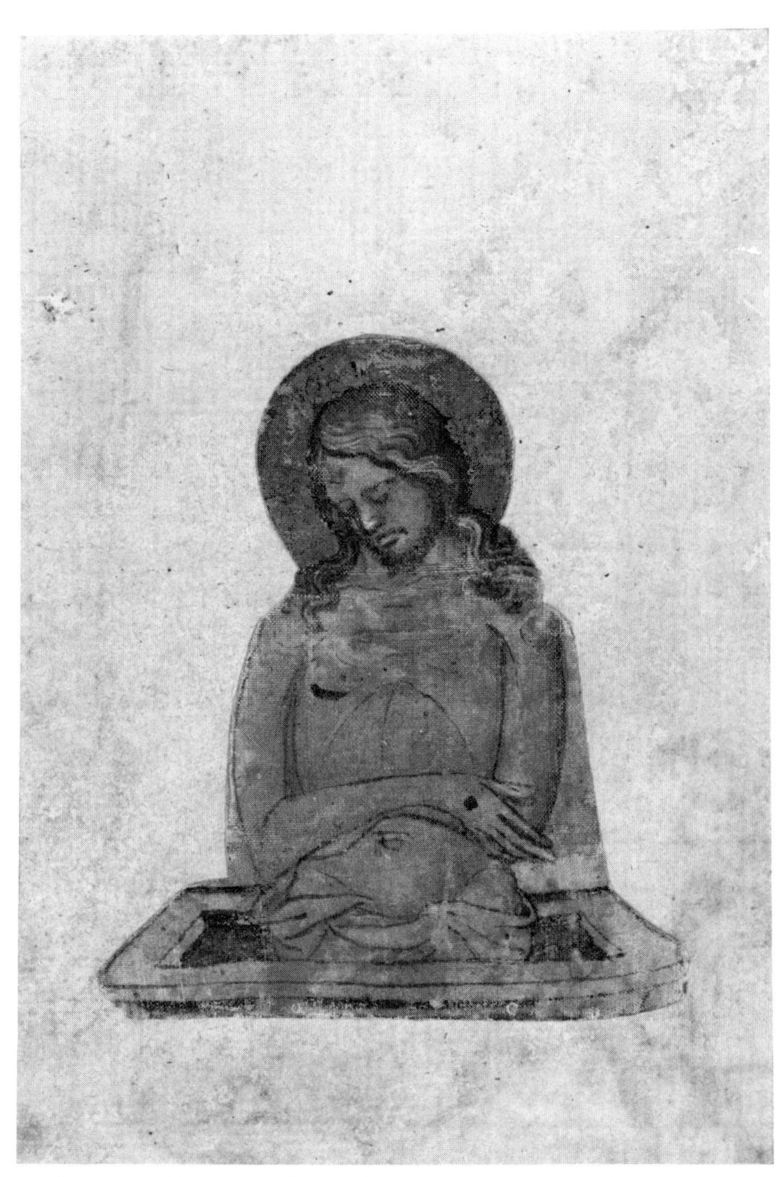

*3. Lorenzo Monaco (Florentine, about 1370–1425).*
THE MAN OF SORROWS,

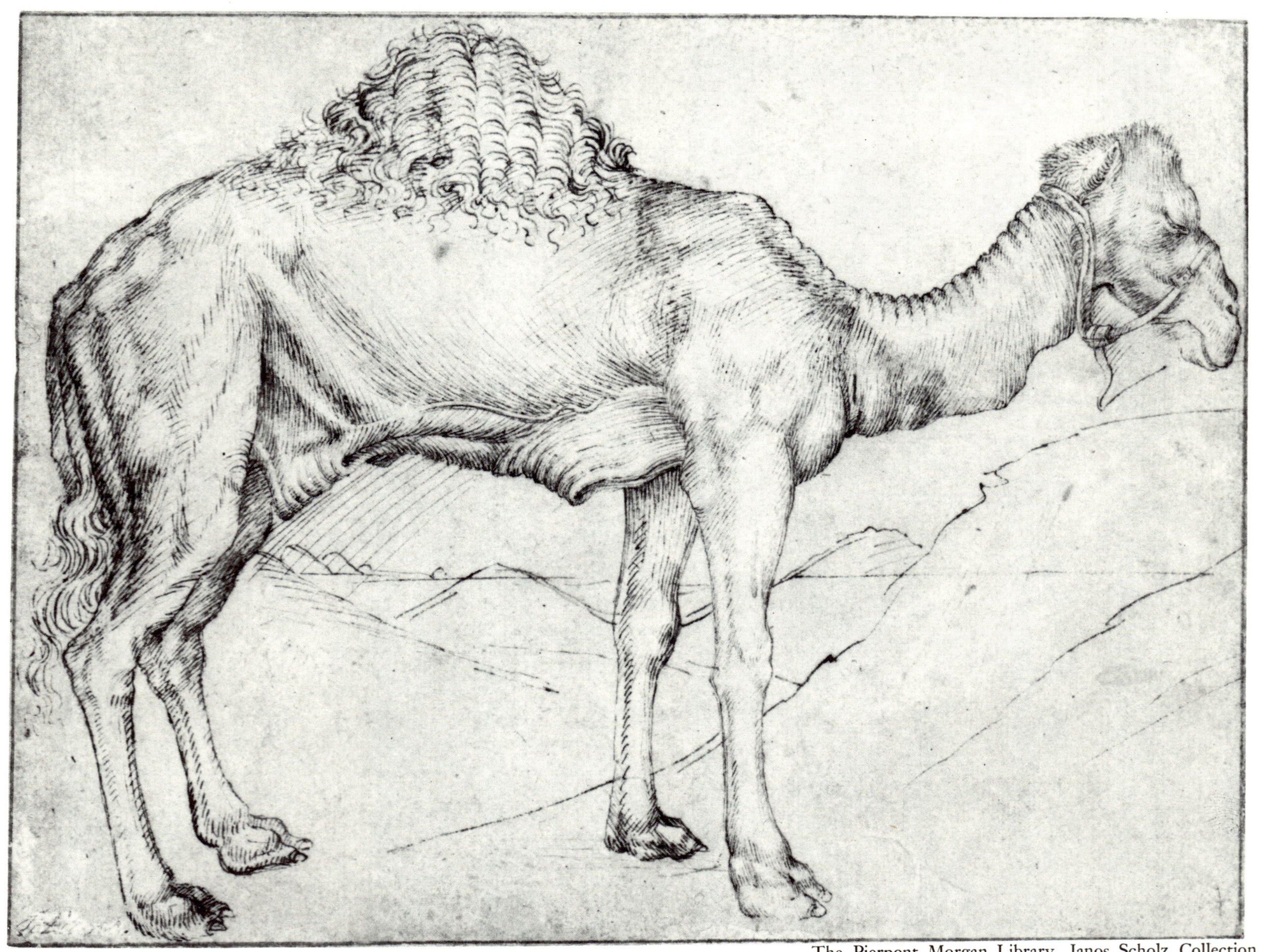

The Pierpont Morgan Library, Janos Scholz Collection

4. *Gentile Bellini (Venetian, 1429–1507).* A CAMEL.

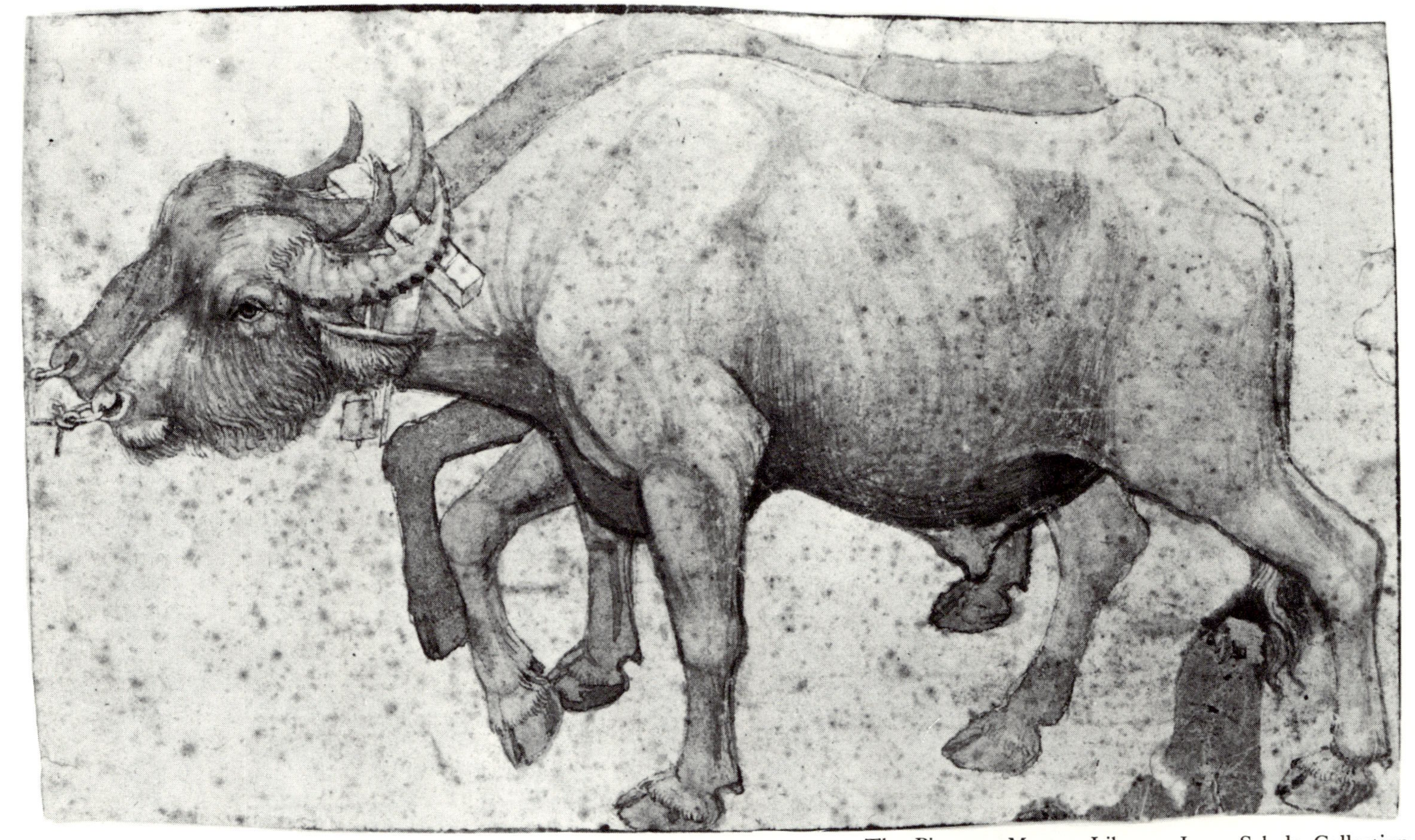

The Pierpont Morgan Library, Janos Scholz Collection

5. *Attributed to Antonio Pisanello (Venetian, before 1395–1455).*
TWO YOKED WATER BUFFALOS.

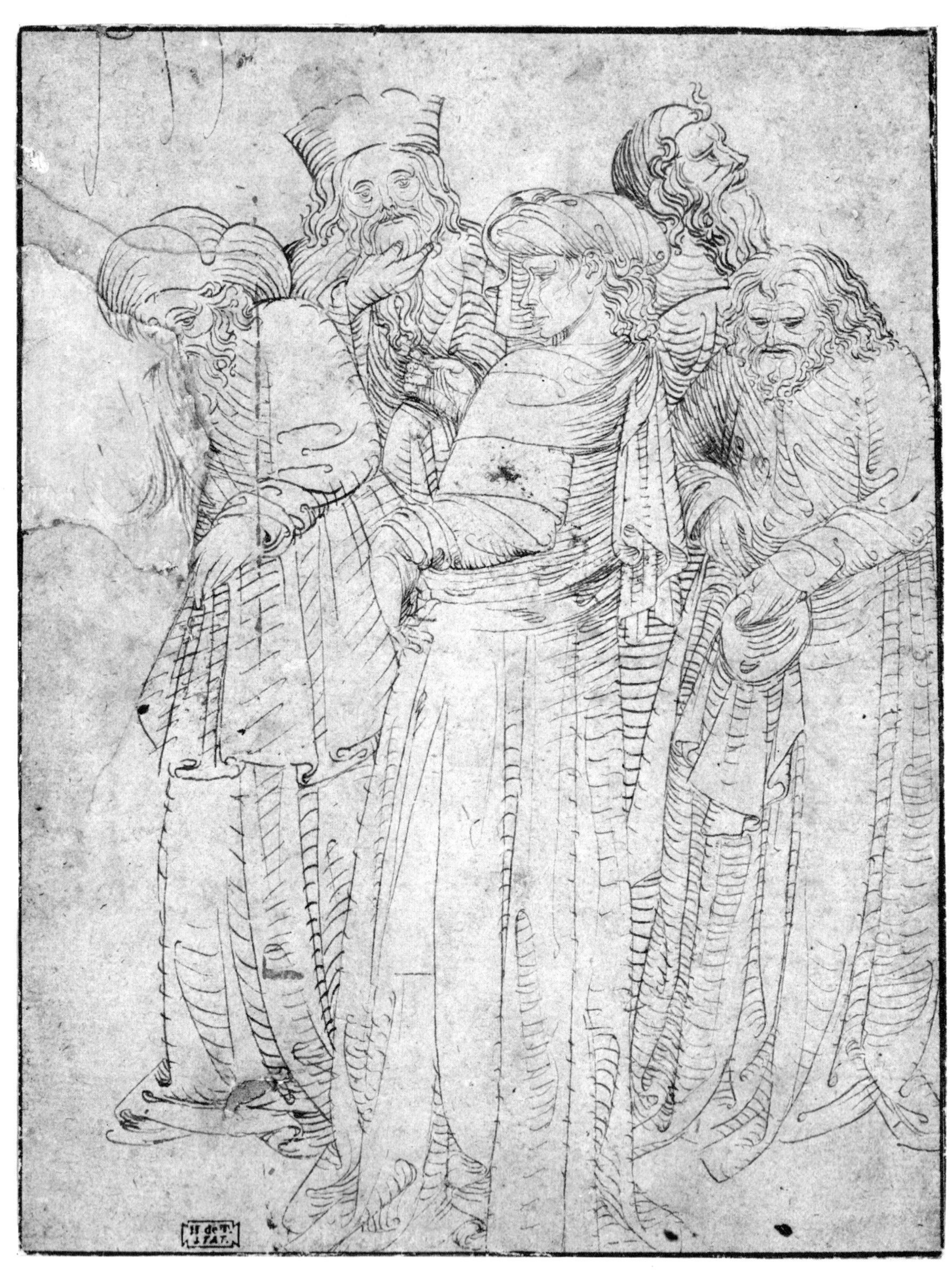

6. *Stefano da Verona (Veronese, about 1375–1438).* GROUP OF FIVE FIGURES.

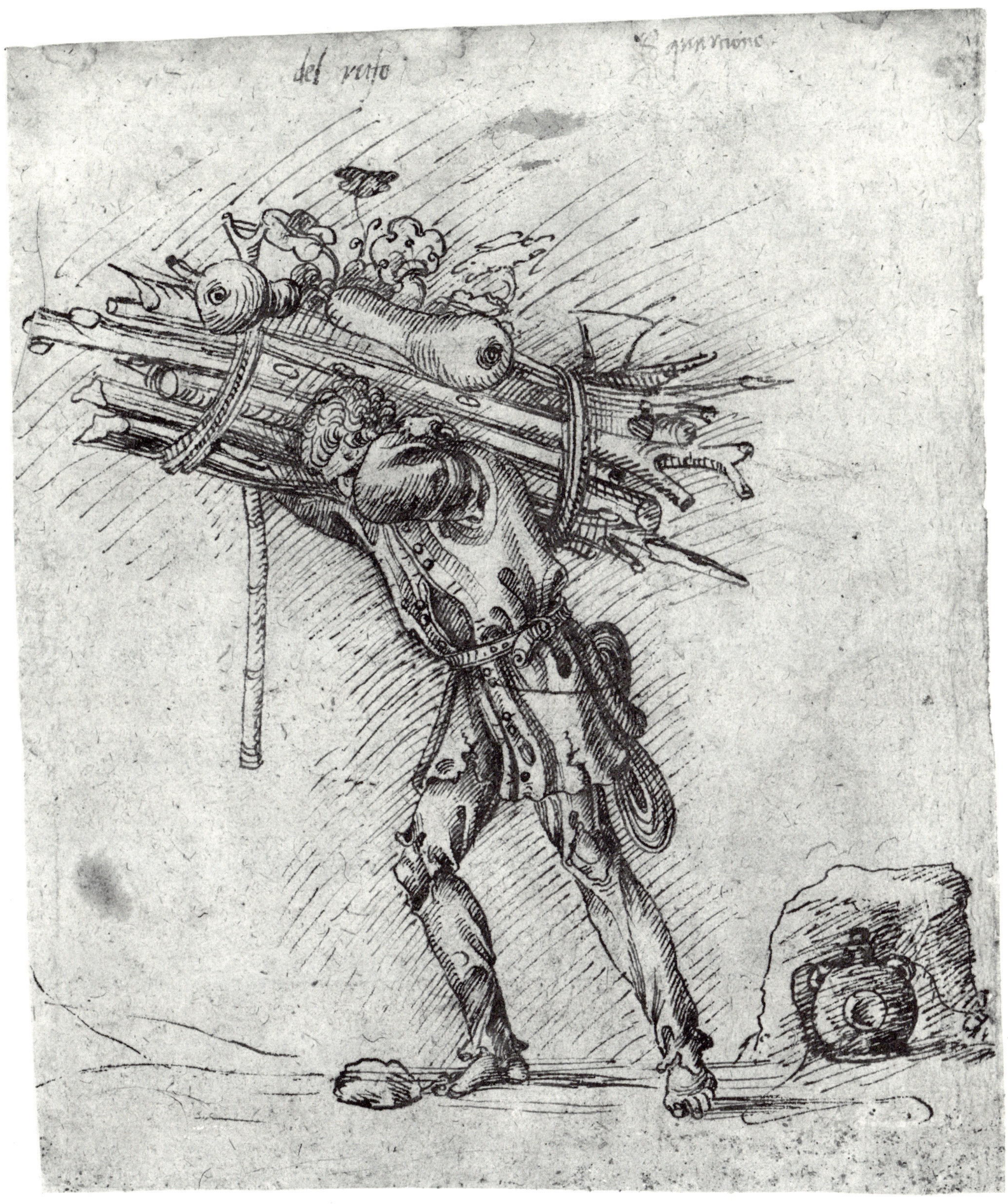

7. *Marco Zoppo (Venetian, 1433–1478).* MAN CARRYING FAGGOTS AND VEGETABLES.

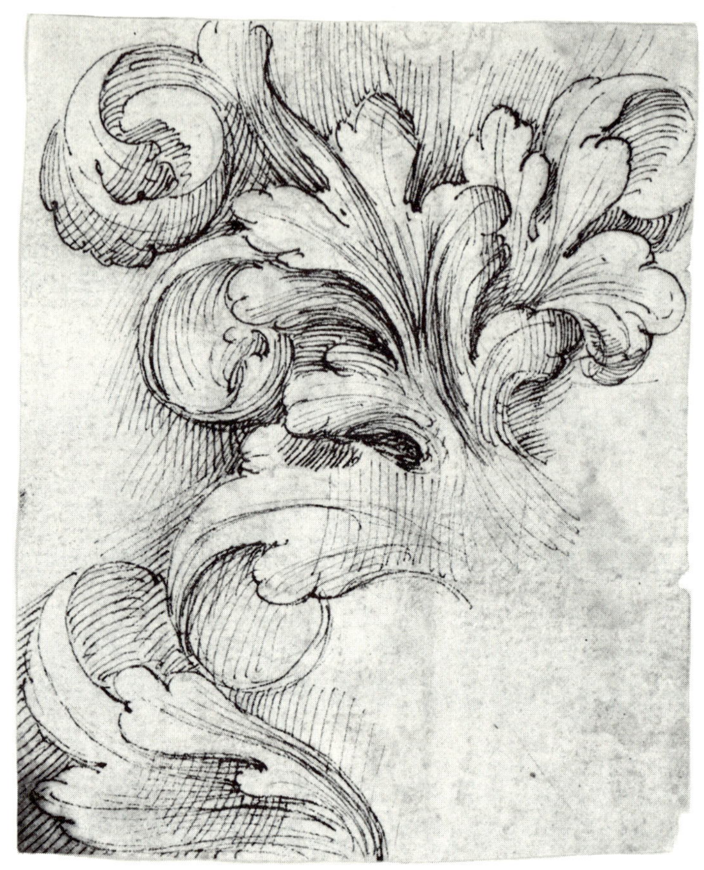

*8A. Antonio Pisanello.* DESIGN FOR SCROLLWORK.

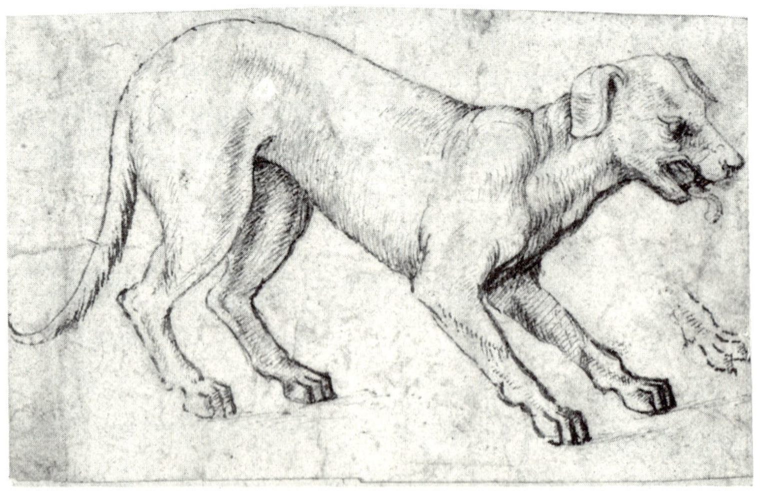

*8B. Circle of Antonio Pisanello.* BARKING DOG.

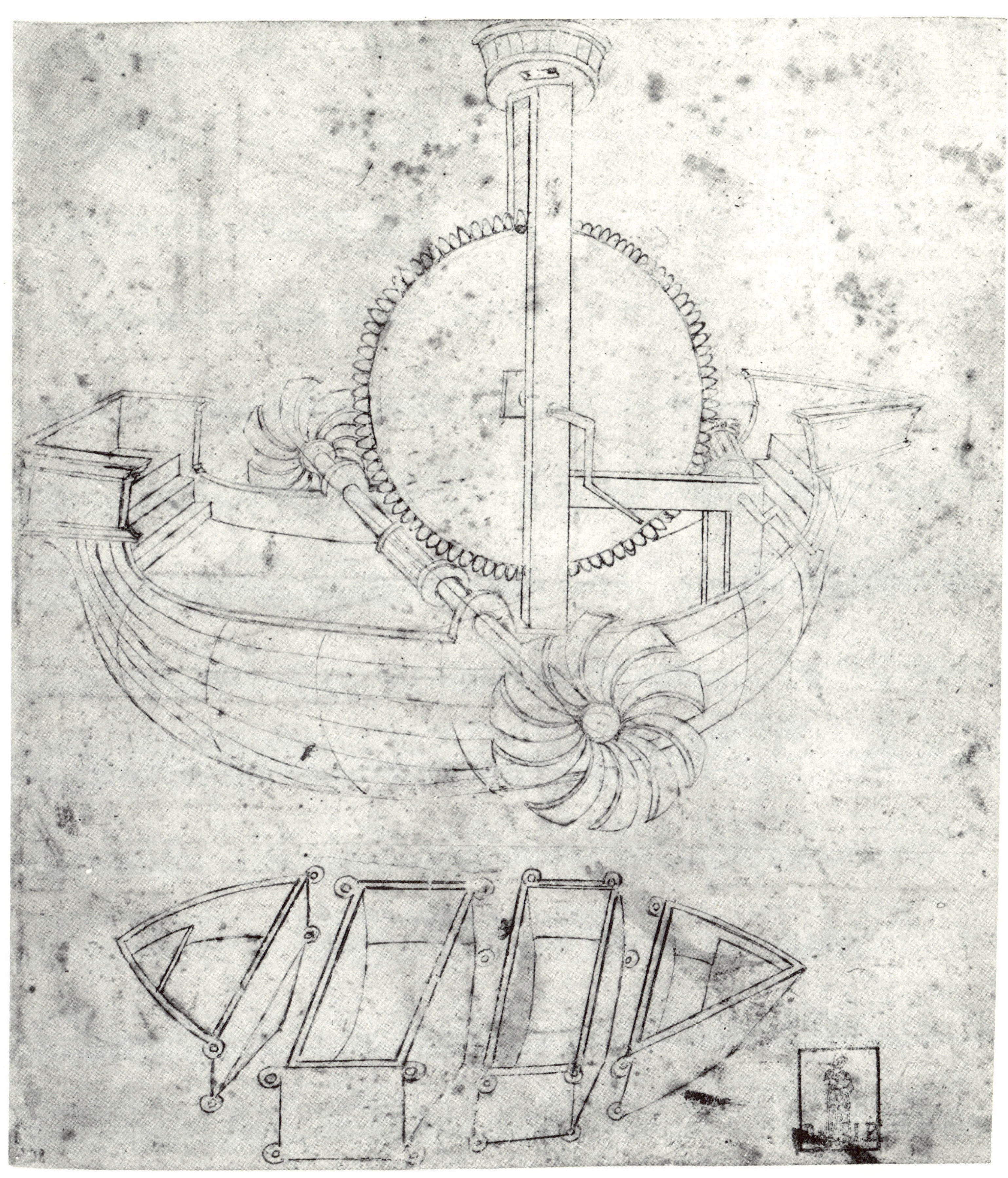

9. *Francesco di Giorgio (Sienese, 1439–1502).* DESIGN FOR A PADDLE BOAT AND ANOTHER VESSEL.

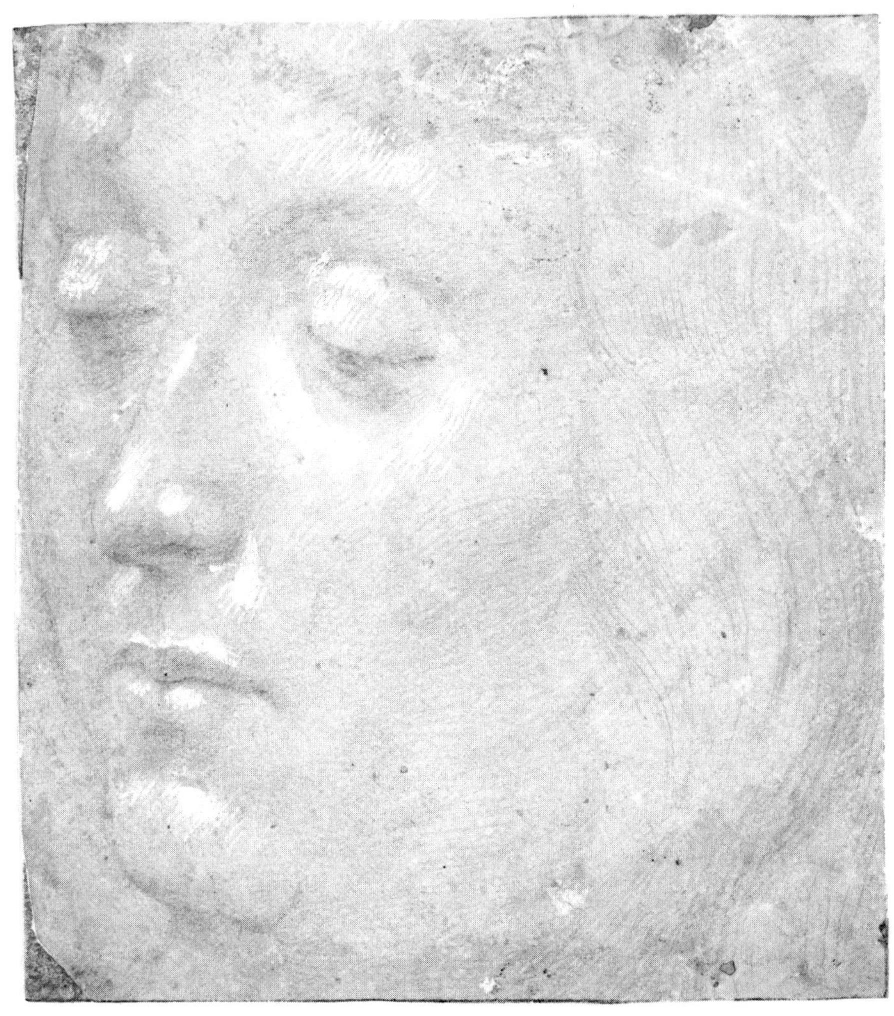

10. *Lorenzo di Credi (Florentine, 1456–1537).* HEAD OF A YOUTH.

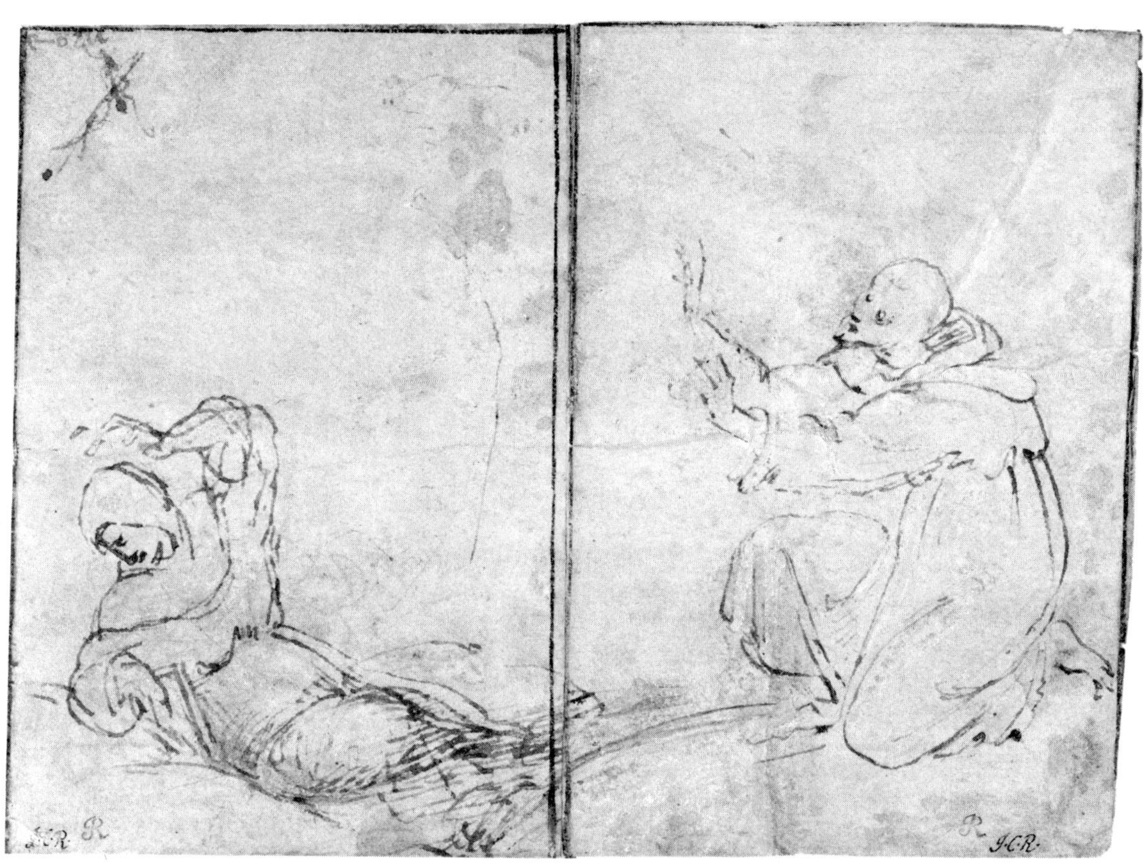

*11. Piero di Cosimo (Florentine, 1462–1521).* ST. FRANCIS RECEIVING THE STIGMATA.

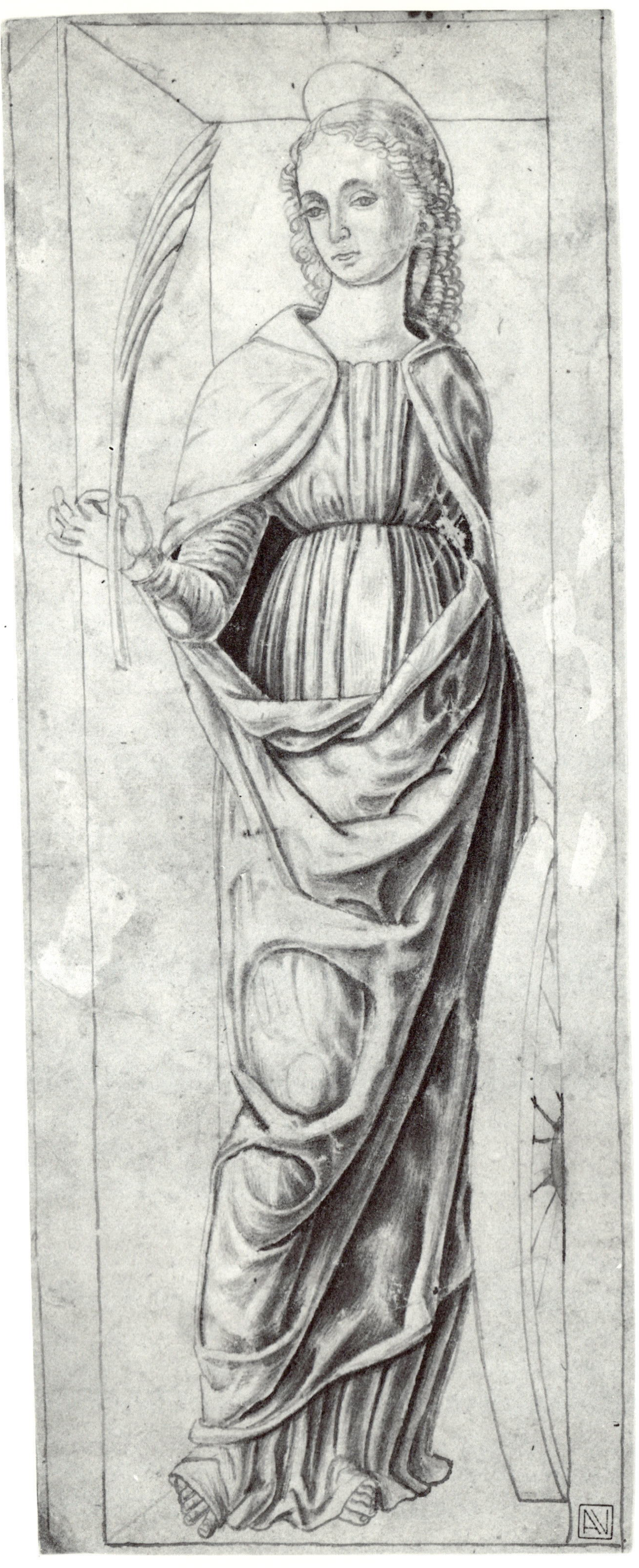

12. *Antonio Vivarini (Venetian, about 1415–1484).*
ST. CATHERINE STANDING IN A NICHE.

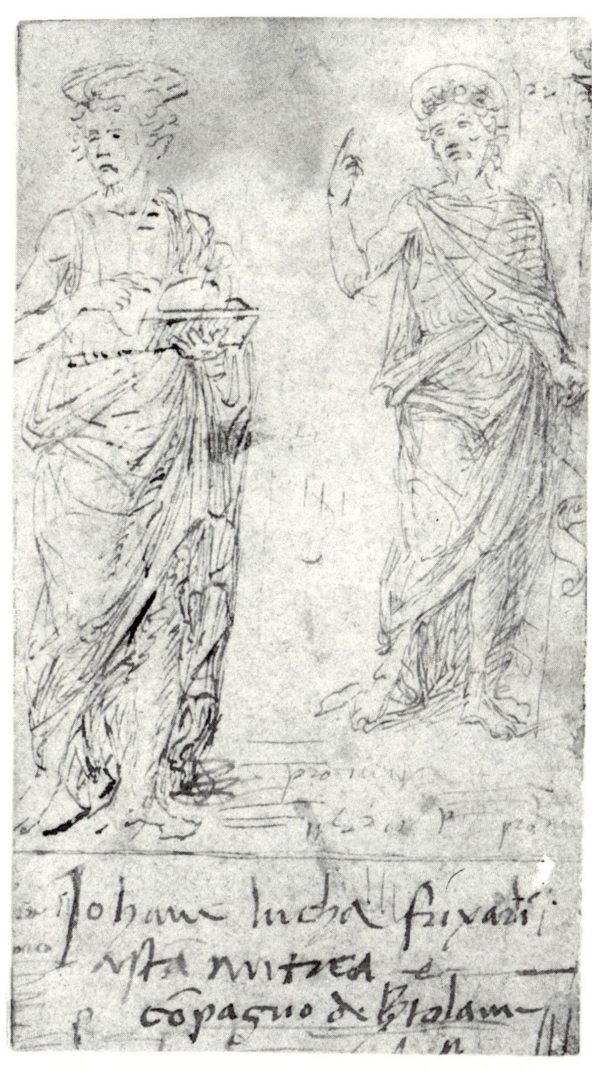

*13. Bartolomeo Vivarini (Venetian, 1432–about 1491).* ST. JOHN THE EVANGELIST AND ST. JOHN THE BAPTIST.

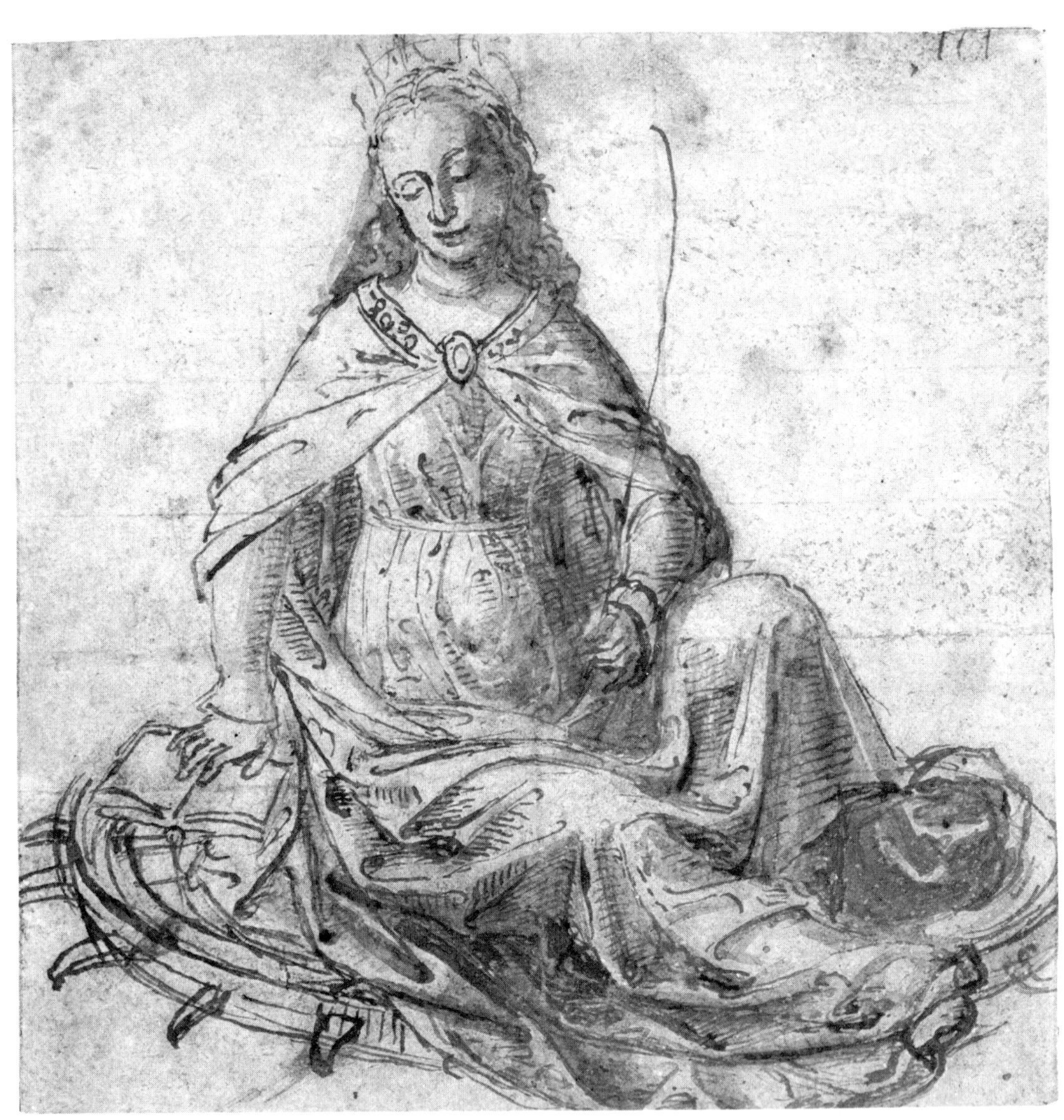

*14. Bartolomeo Montagna (Vicenza, about 1450–1523).* ST. CATHERINE.

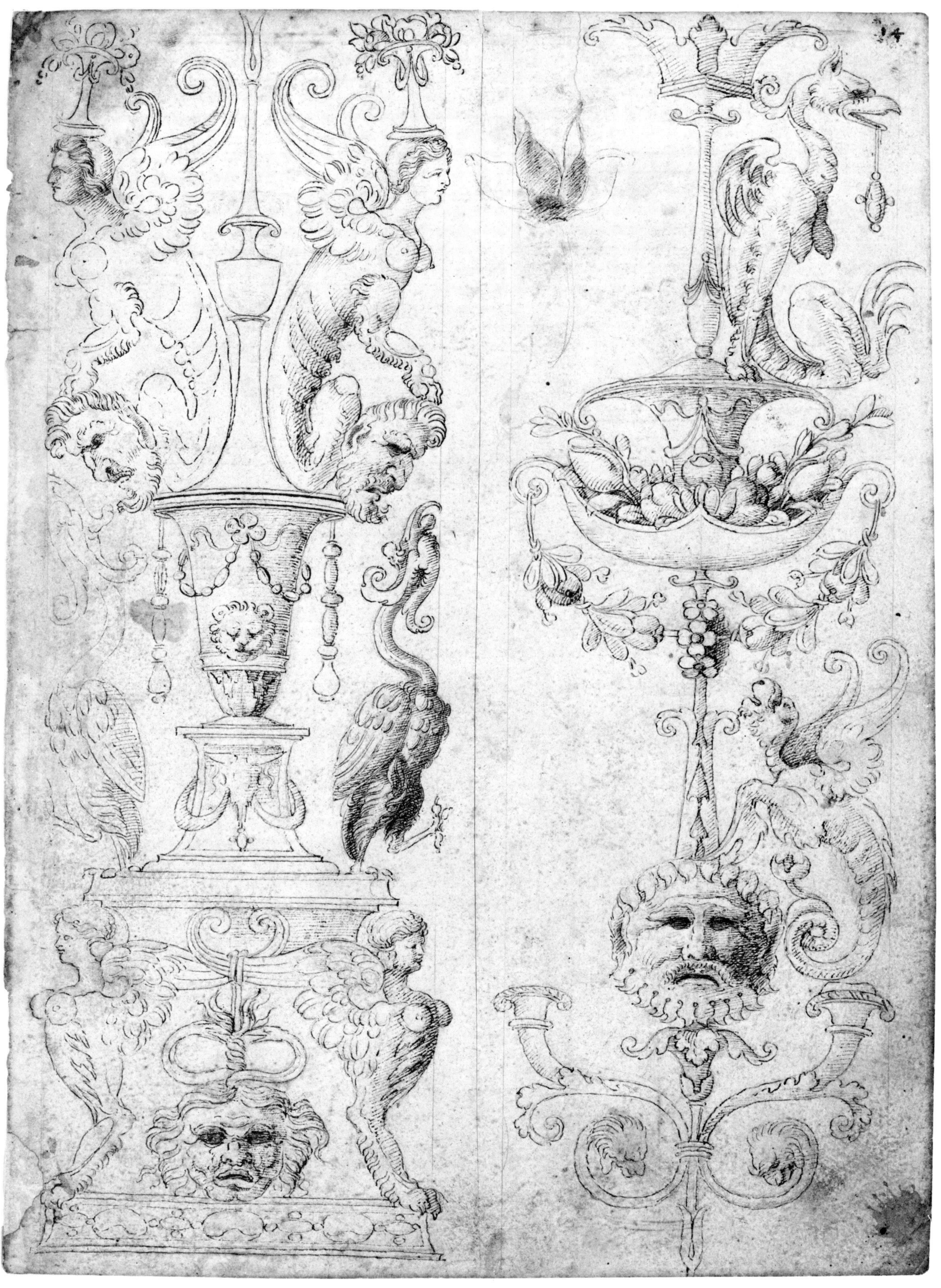

*15. Studio of Andrea Mantegna (Paduan, about 1500).* DESIGN FOR AN ELABORATE PILASTER.

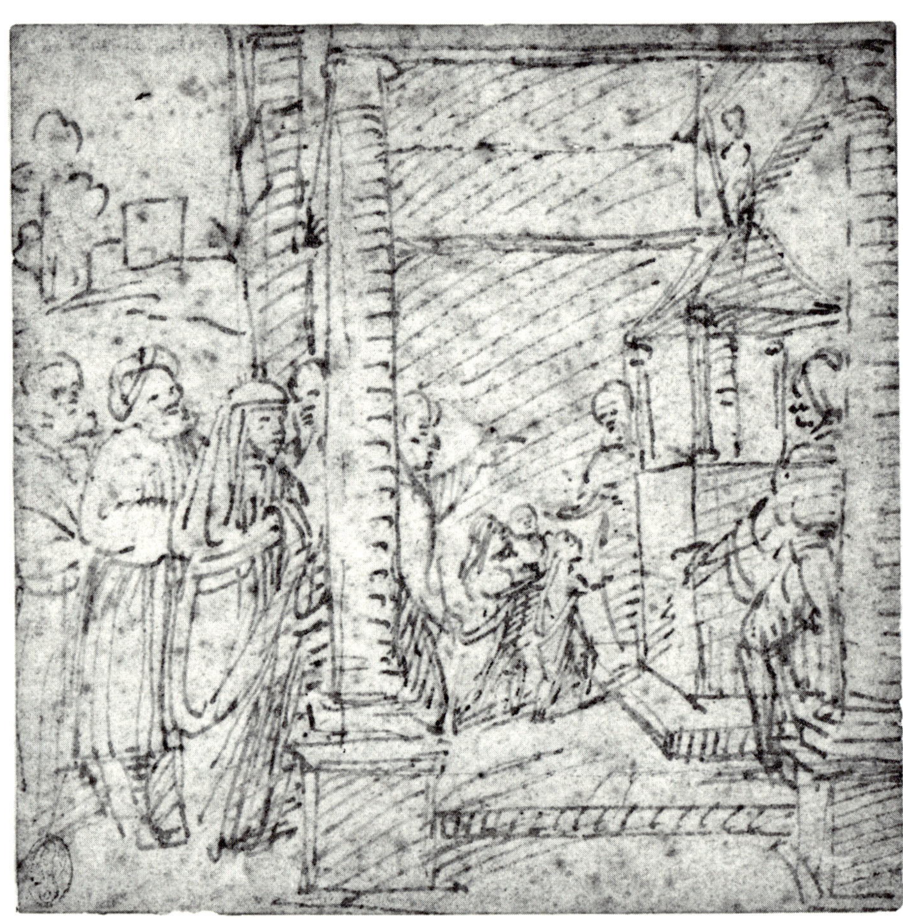

*16. Vittore Carpaccio (Venetian, about 1445–1526).* THE PRESENTATION OF THE VIRGIN AT THE TEMPLE.

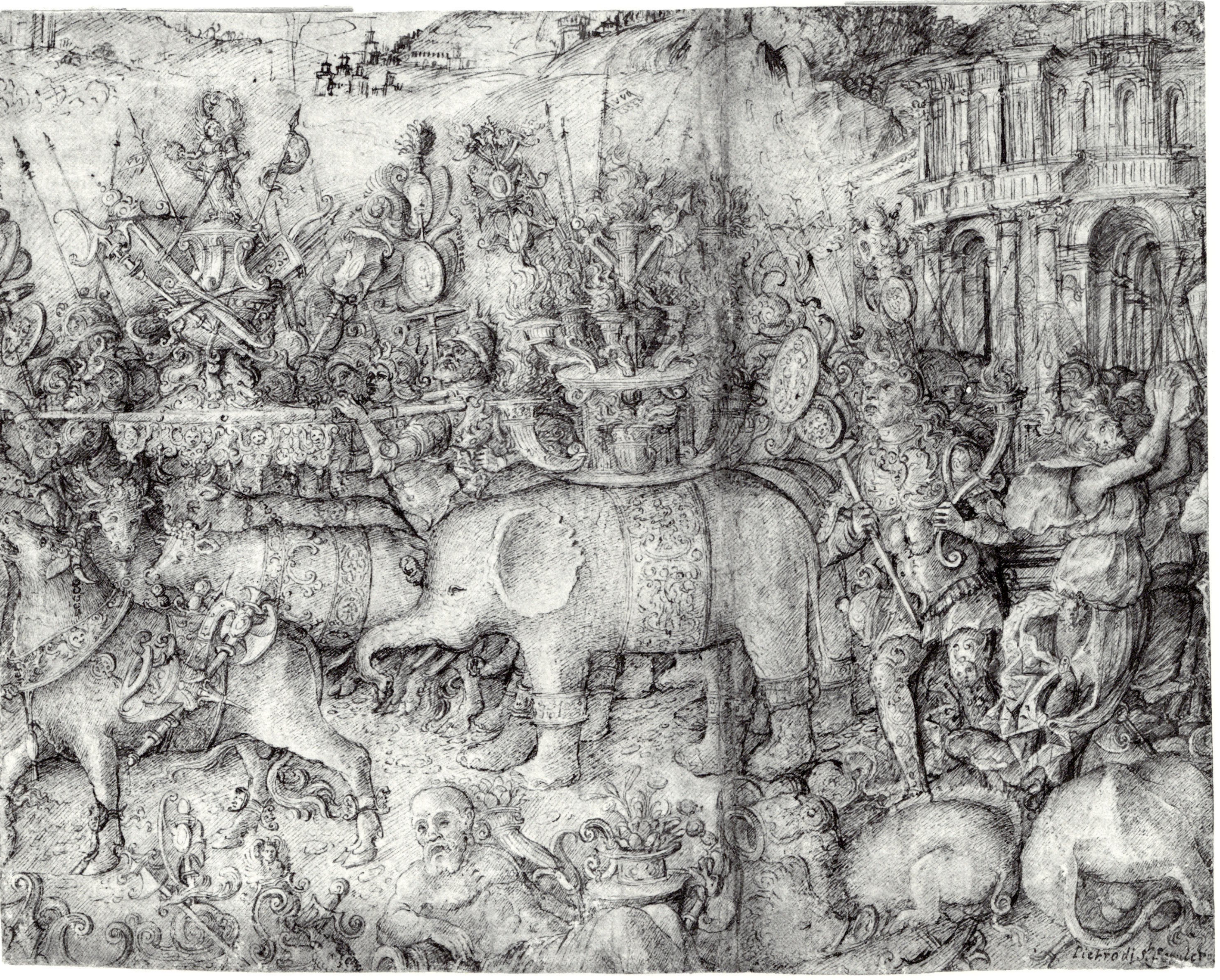

17. *Bernardo Parentino (Venetian, about 1437–1531).* ROMAN TRIUMPHAL PROCESSION.

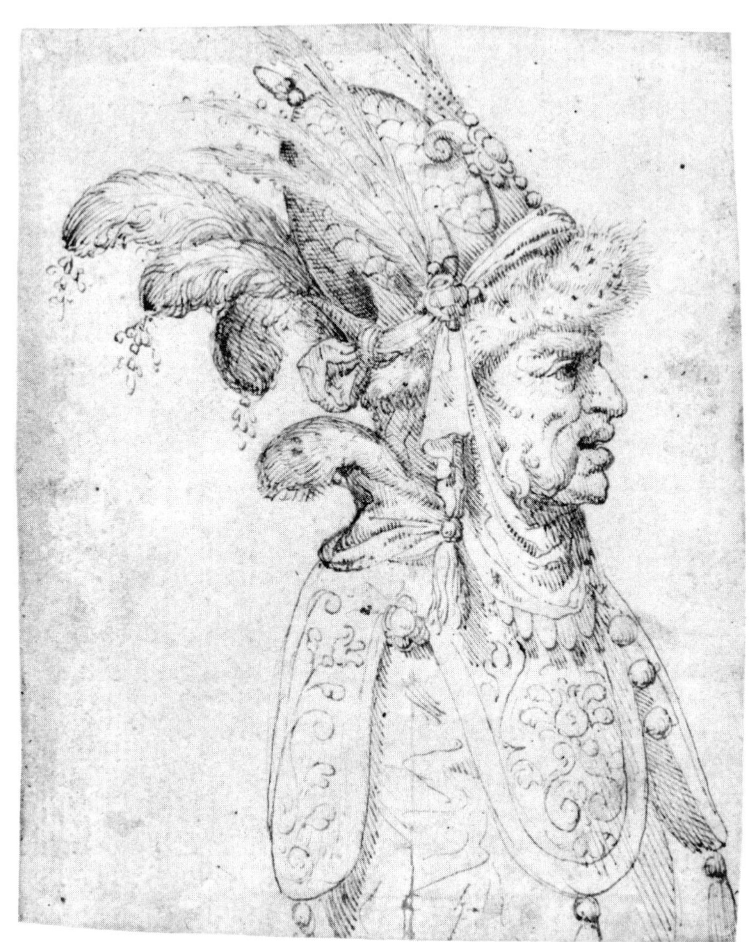

*18A. Giuseppe Arcimboldi (Lombard, about 1530–1593).*
MAN WEARING A FANCY PLUMED HAT.

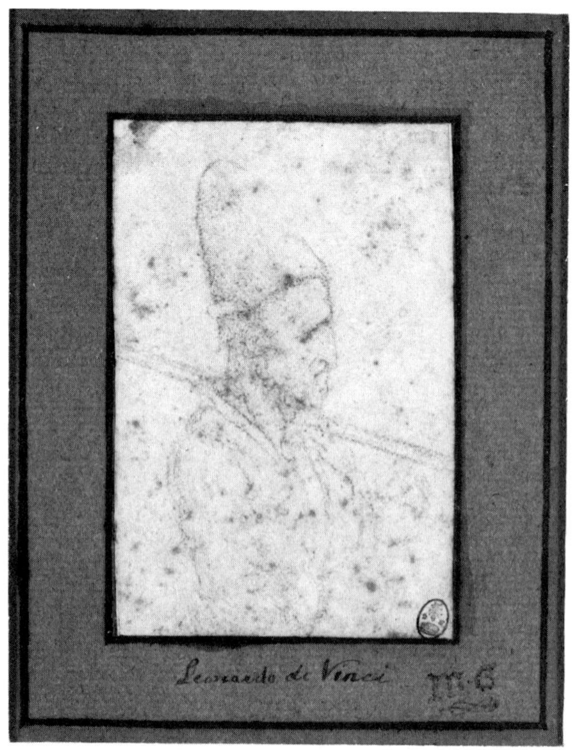


*18B. Leonardo da Vinci*
*(Florentine, 1452–1519).*
PROFILE HALF-LENGTH VIEW OF A PEASANT.

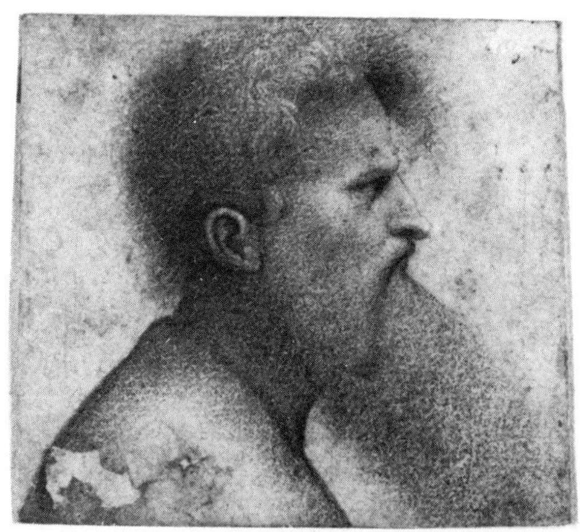

The Pierpont Morgan Library,
Janos Scholz Collection

*19A. Giovanni Agostino da Lodi (Lombard, working around 1500).*
OLD BEARDED MAN IN PROFILE.

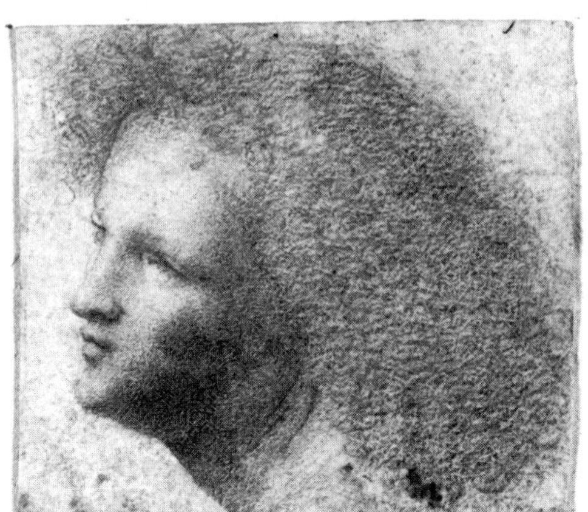

The Pierpont Morgan Library,
Janos Scholz Collection

*19B. Giovanni Agostino da Lodi.*
HEAD OF A YOUTH.

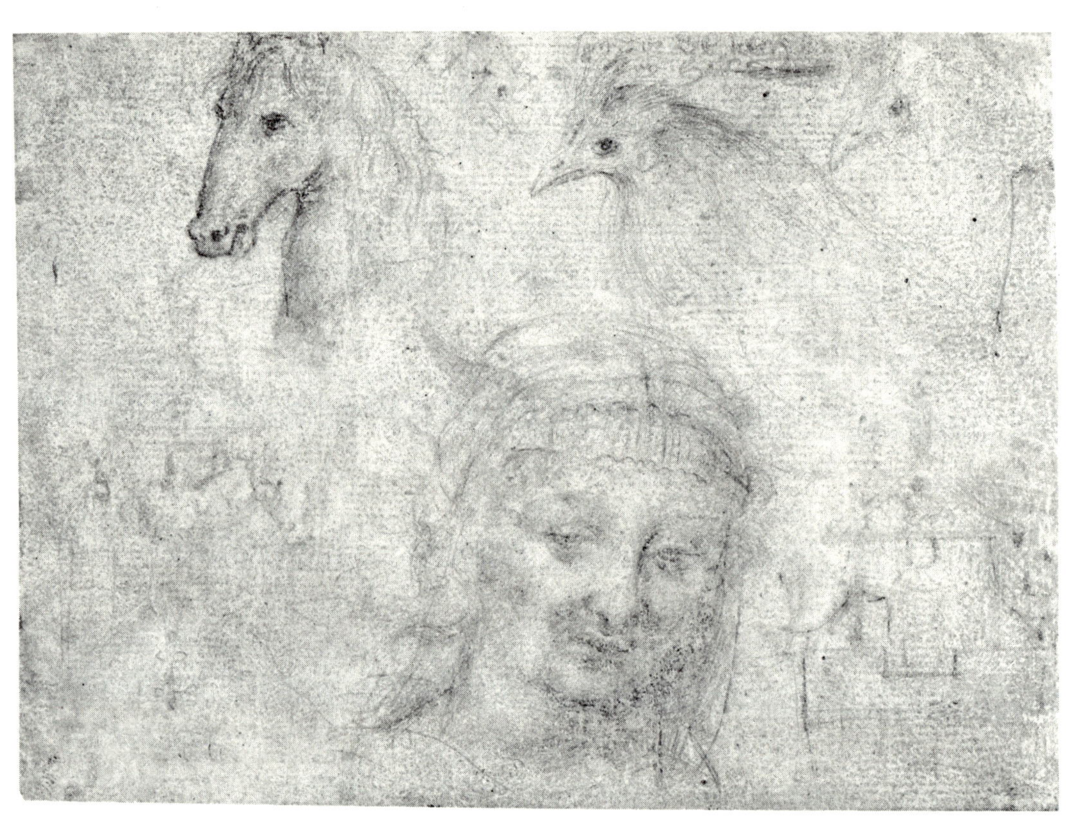

20. *Bernardino Luini (Lombard, 1480/85–1532).*
HEAD OF A WOMAN AND VARIOUS SKETCHES.

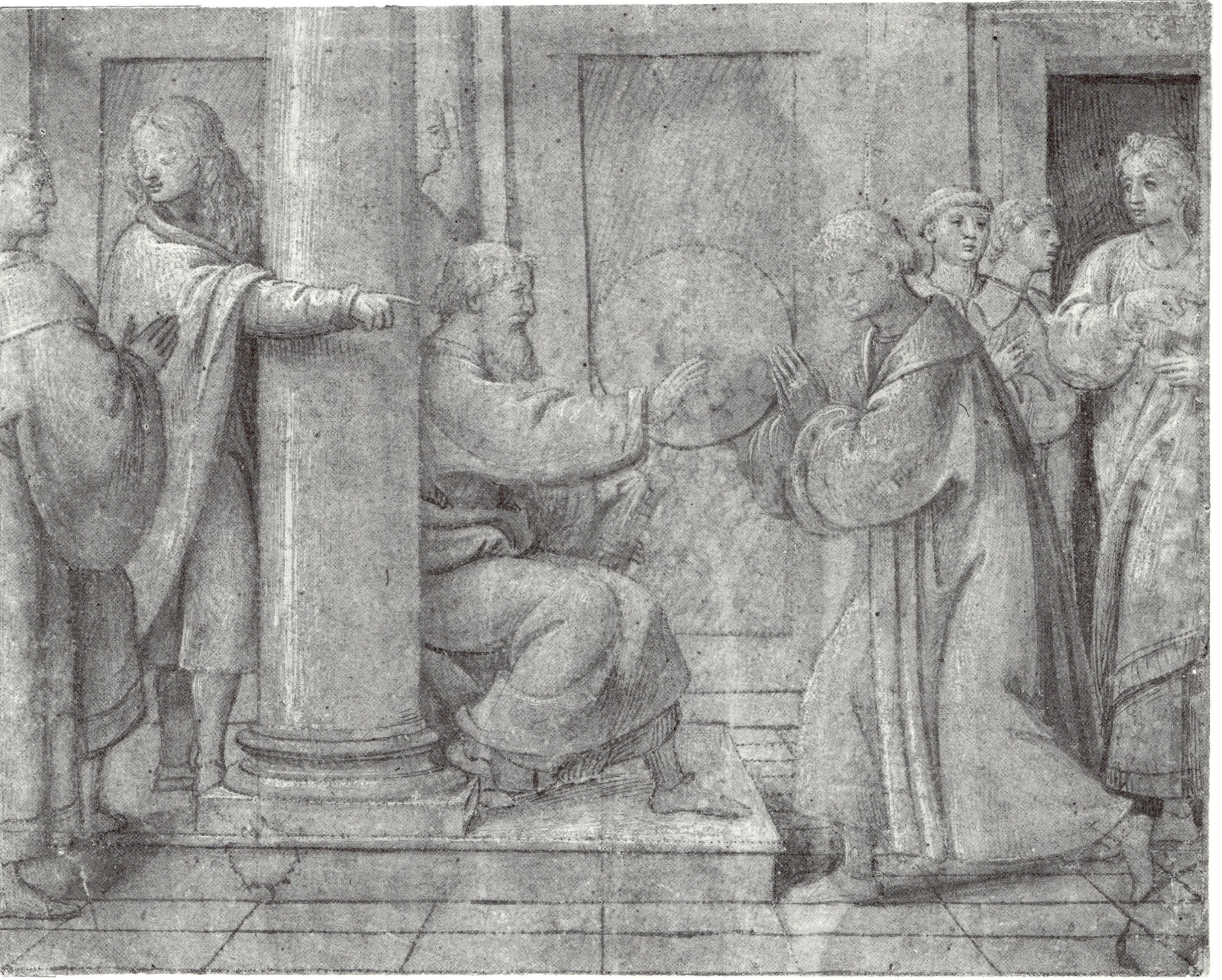

21. *Ambrogio Bergognone (Lombard, 1481–1518).* ST. AUGUSTINE MATRICULATING AT THE UNIVERSITY OF CARTHAGE.

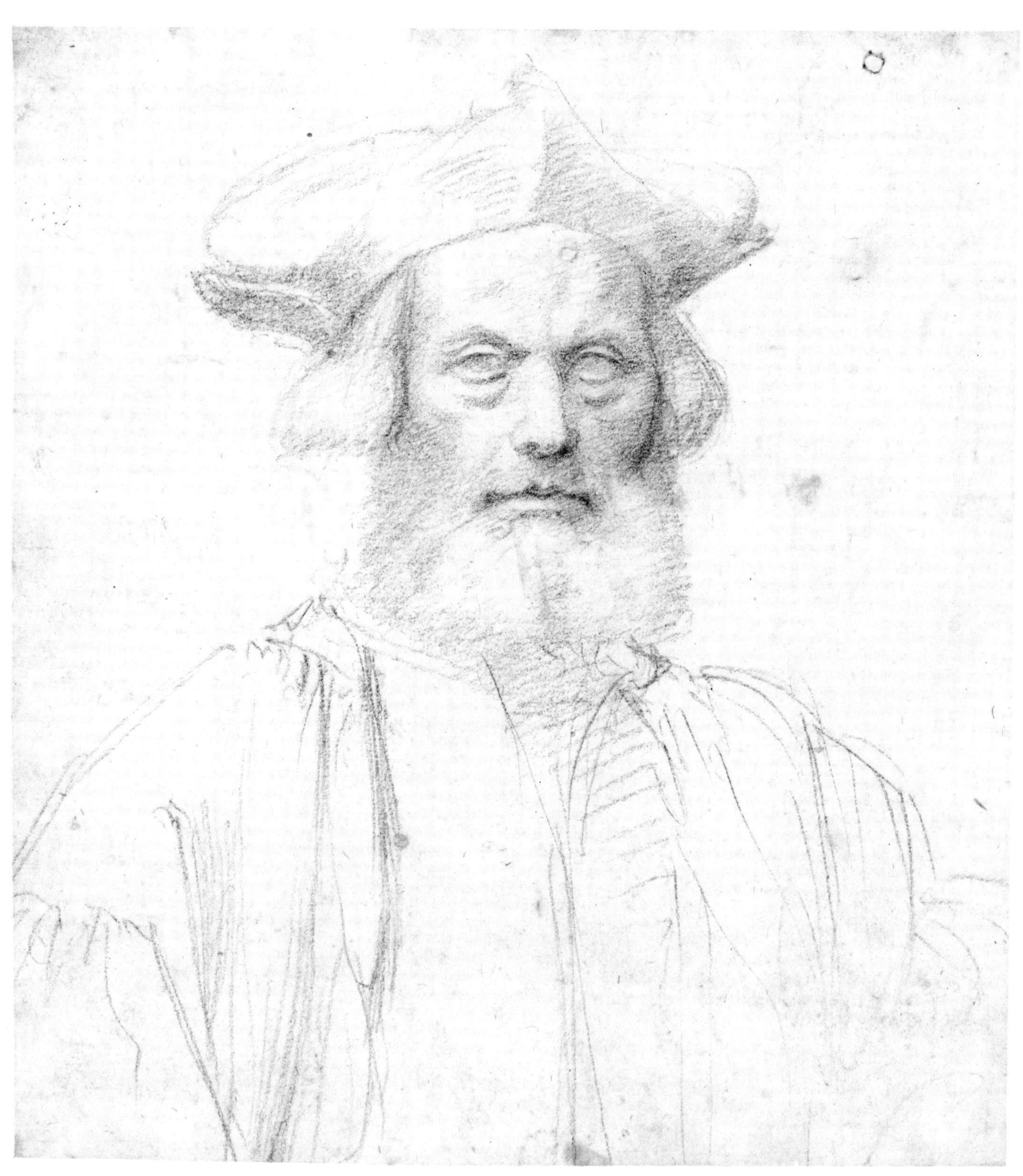

22. *Gianfrancesco Bembo (Cremonese, working 1514–1526).* BUST OF A MAN WEARING A BIRETTA.

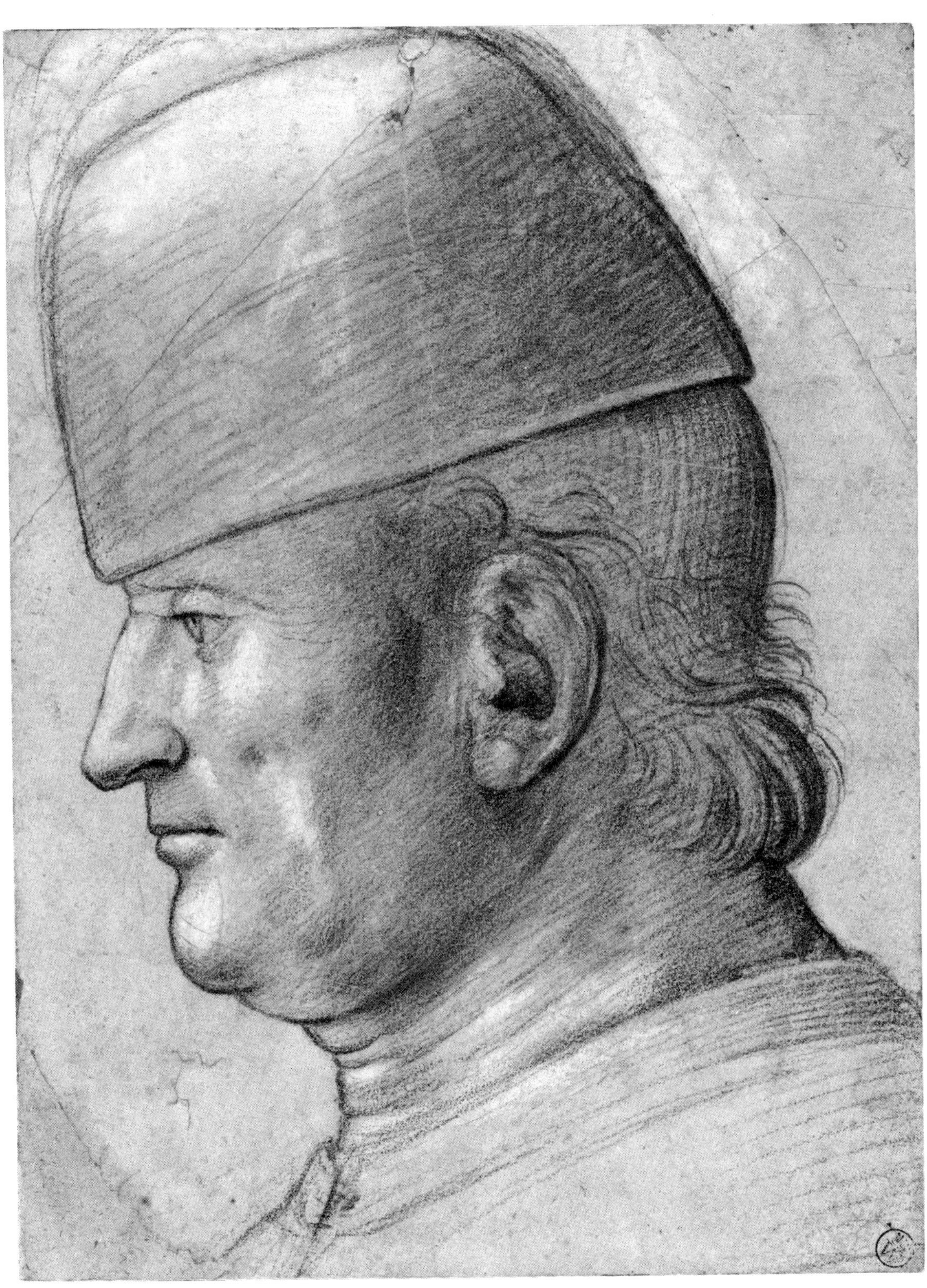

*23. Francesco Bonsignori (Veronese, about 1455–1519).* HEAD OF A MAN IN PROFILE.

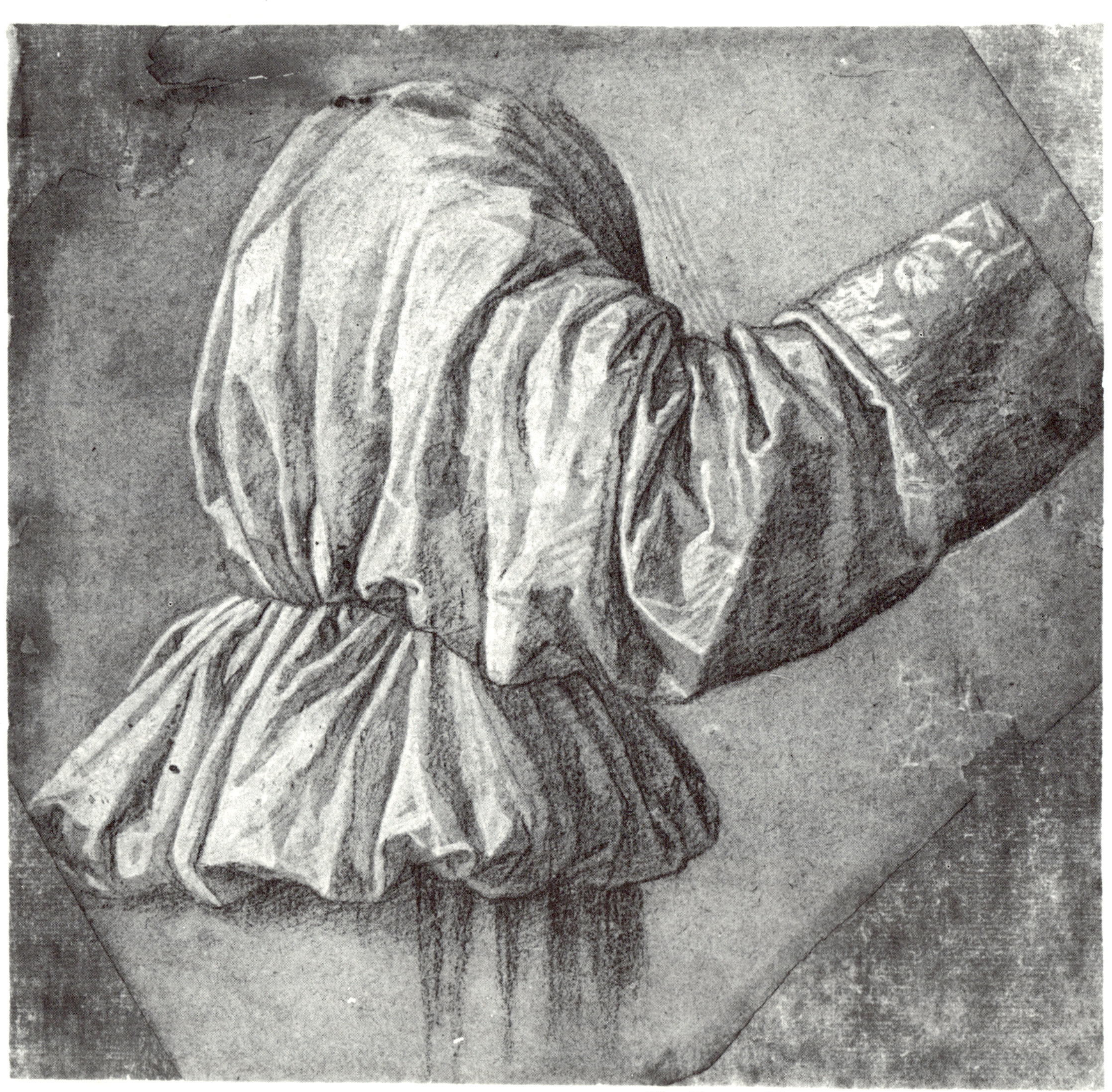

24. *Vincenzo Catena (Venetian, about 1470–1531).* DRAPERY STUDY. The Pierpont Morgan Library, Janos Scholz Collection

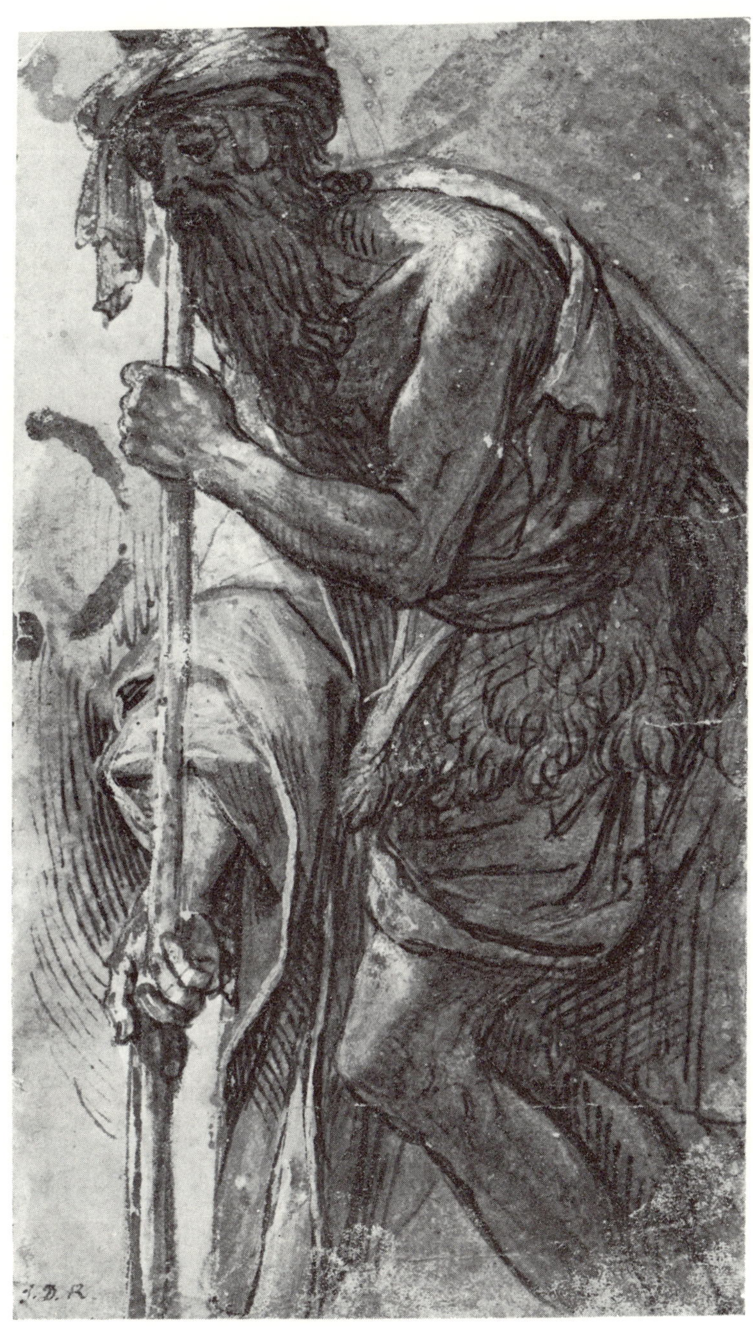

*25. Defendente Ferrari (Piedmontese, about 1470–1535).*
SHEPHERD, LEANING ON HIS STAFF.

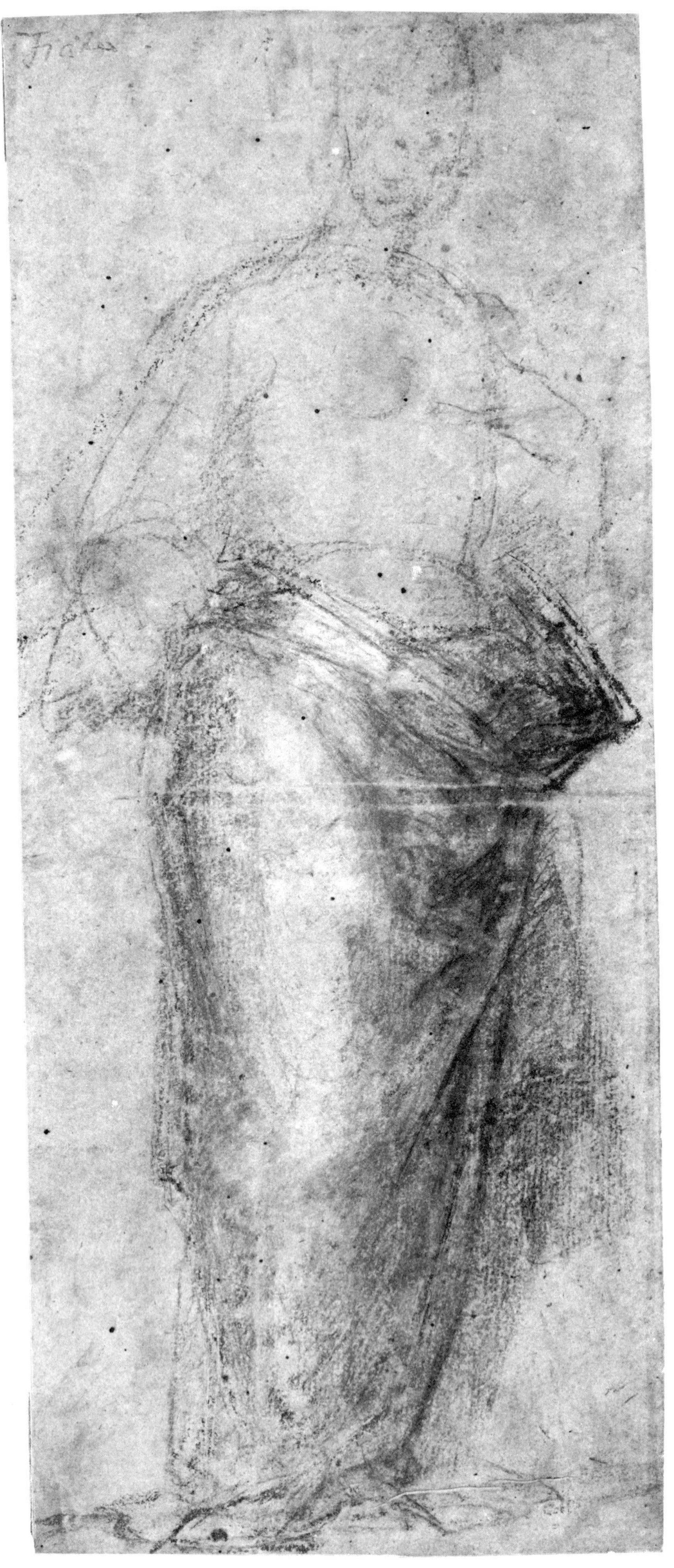

*26. Baccio Della Porta, called Fra Bartolomeo (Florentine, 1472–1517).* STANDING APOSTLE OR SAINT, HOLDING A BOOK.

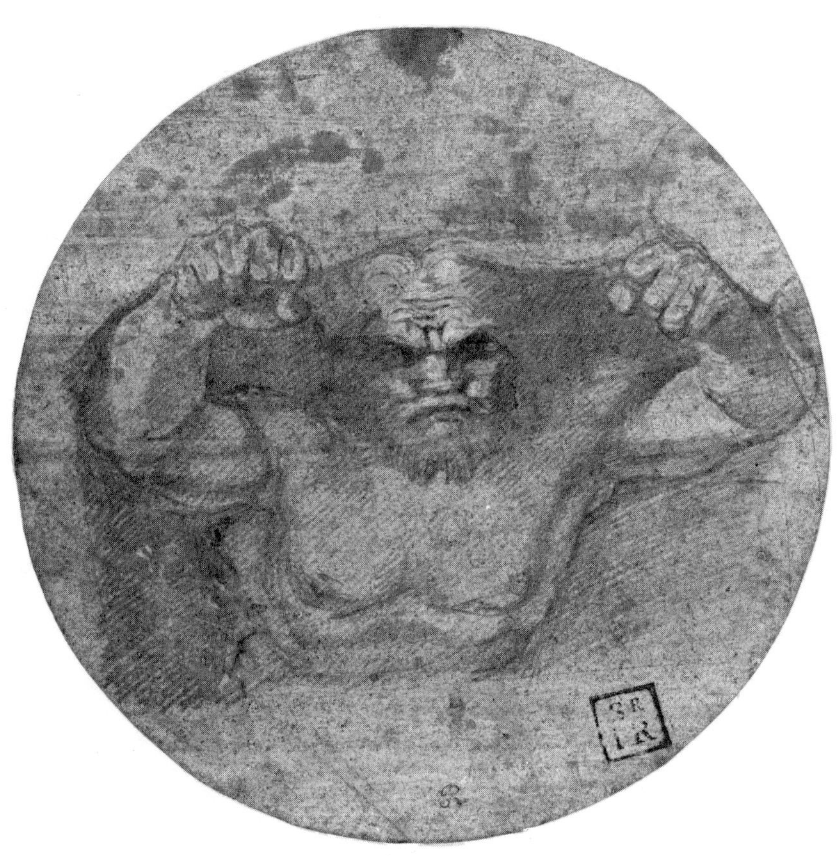

27. *Raffaelo Santi, called Raphael (Urbino-Rome, 1483–1520).*
MALE FIGURE SYMBOLIZING AN EARTHQUAKE.

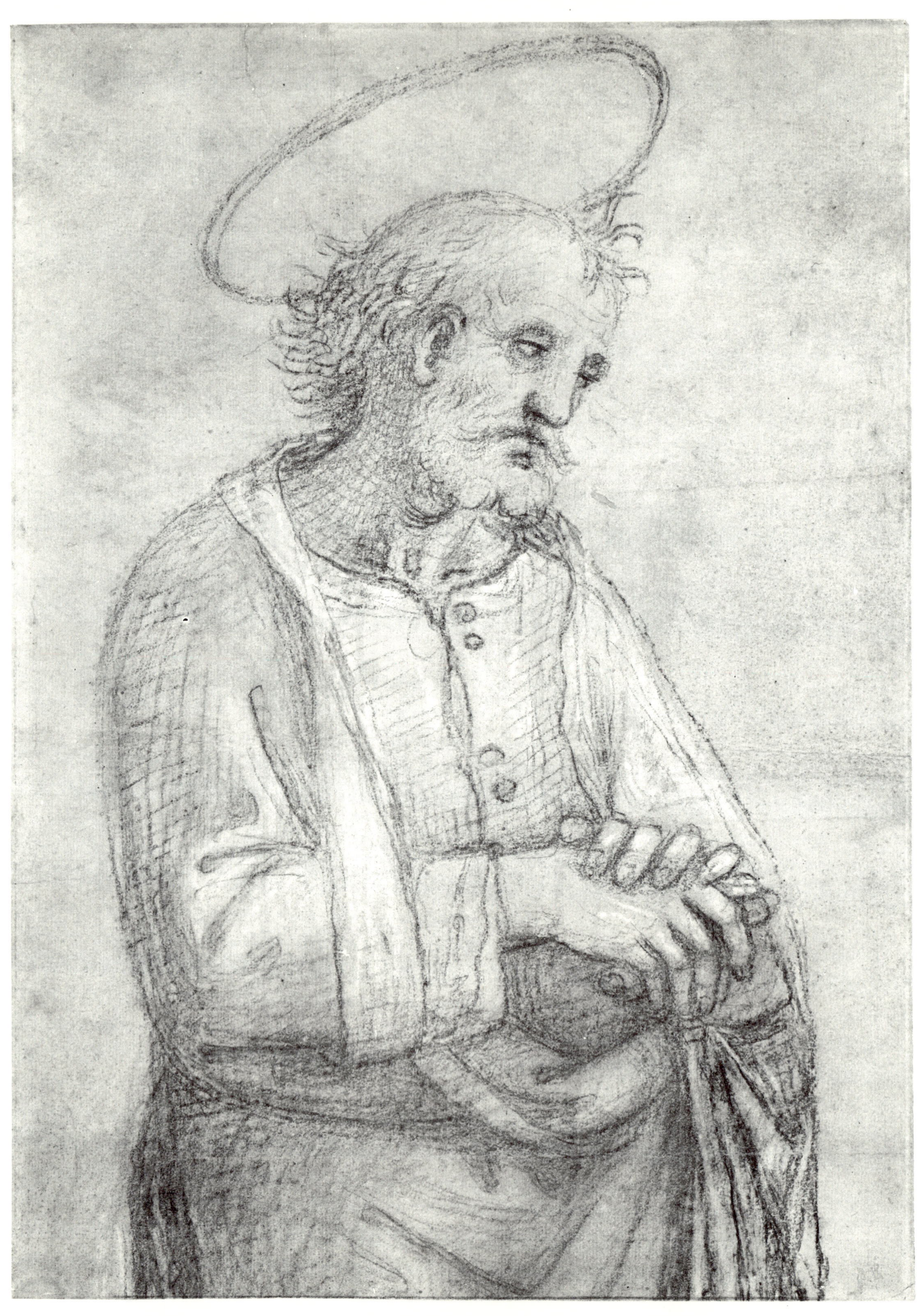

28. *Giannicola di Paolo Manni, called Lo Smica (Umbrian, about 1460–1544).* ST. ANTHONY ABBOT.

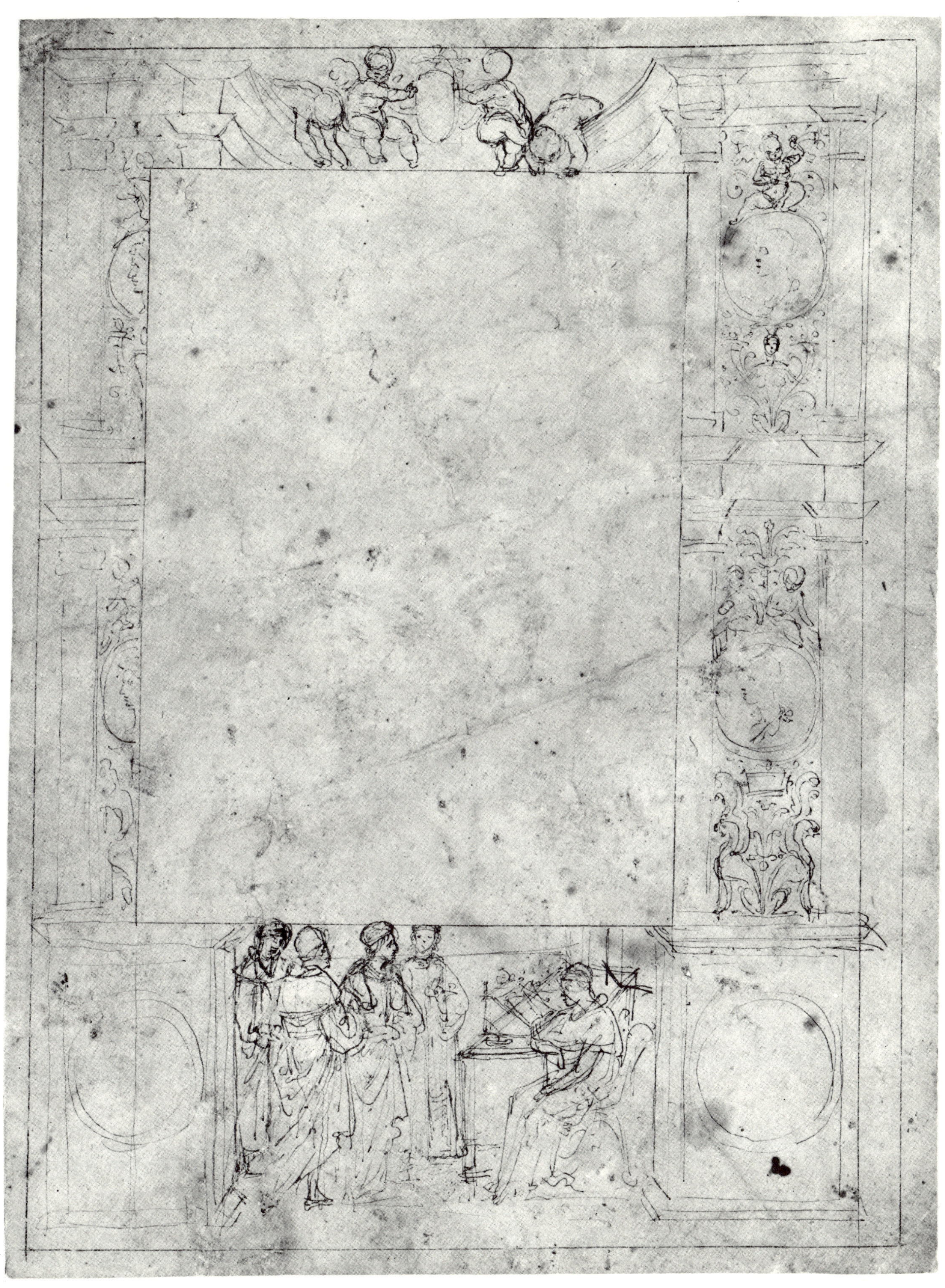

29. *Ferrarese master (about 1500).* DESIGN FOR AN ELABORATE TITLE PAGE.

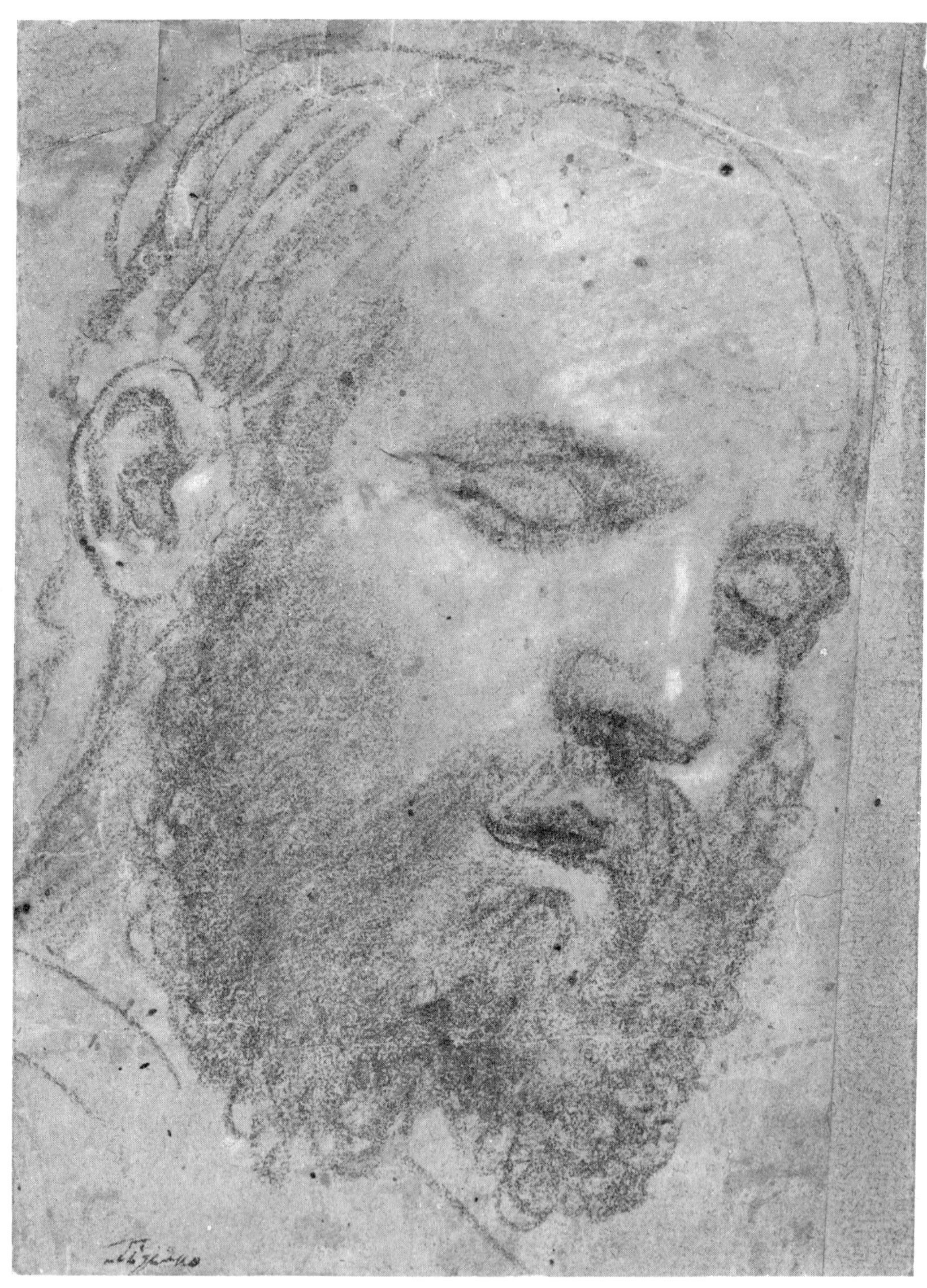

30. *Lorenzo Lotto (Venetian, about 1480–1536).* HEAD OF A BEARDED MAN.

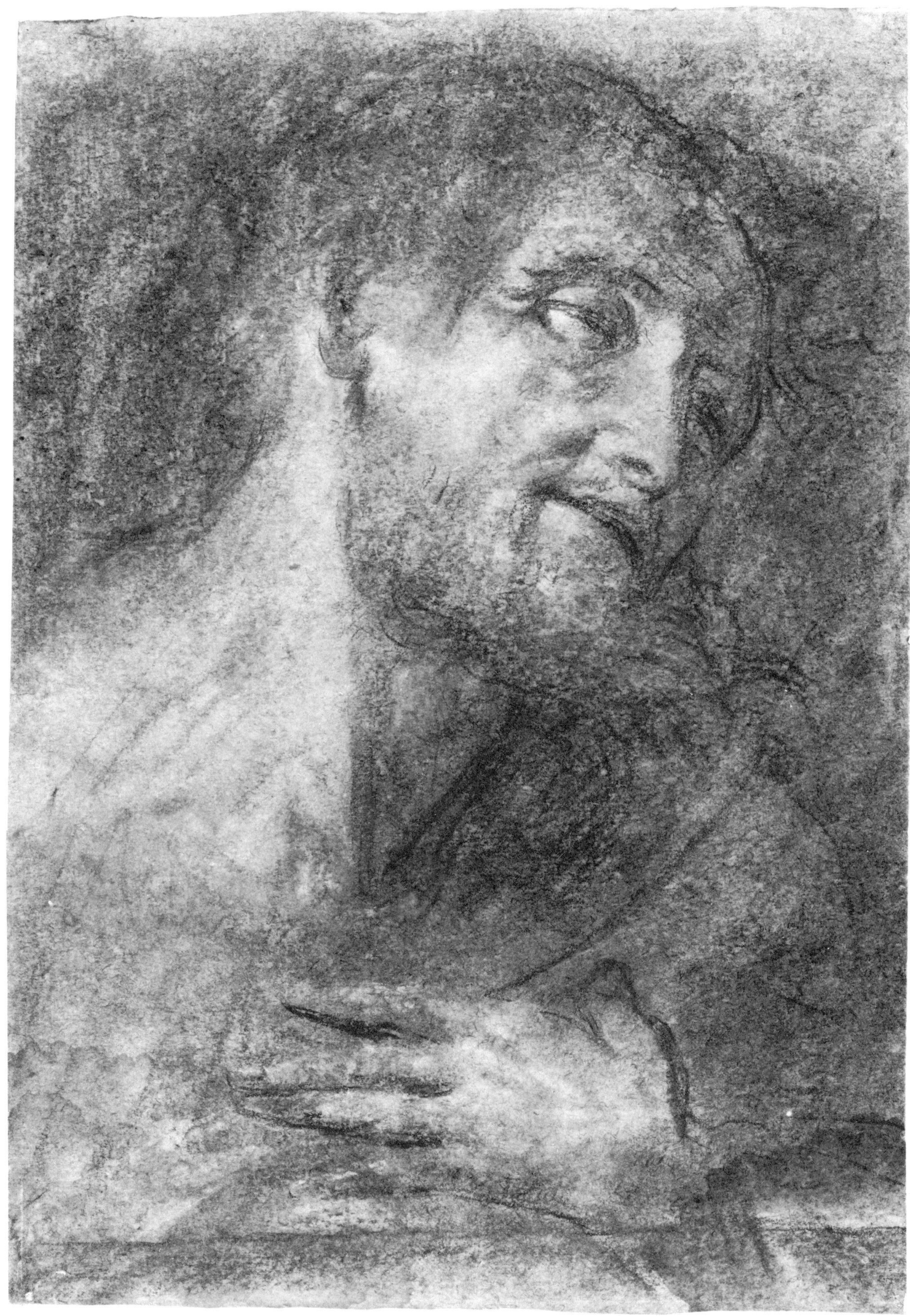

31. *Giovanni Girolamo Savoldo (Brescian, 1480–1548).* MAN'S HEAD AND HAND.

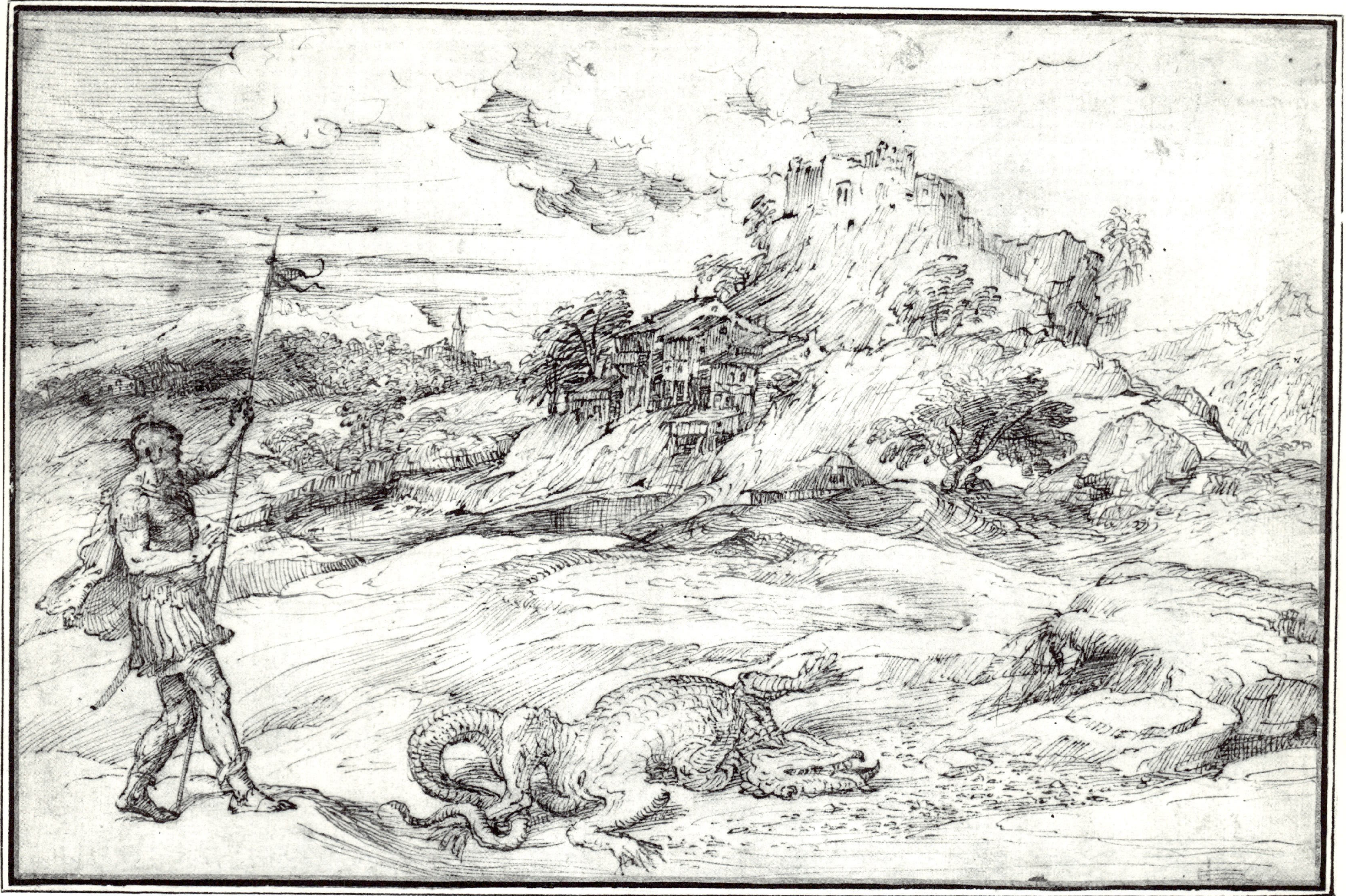

32. *Tiziano Vecellio, called Titian (Venetian, 1487–1576).* ST. THEODORE IN A LANDSCAPE.

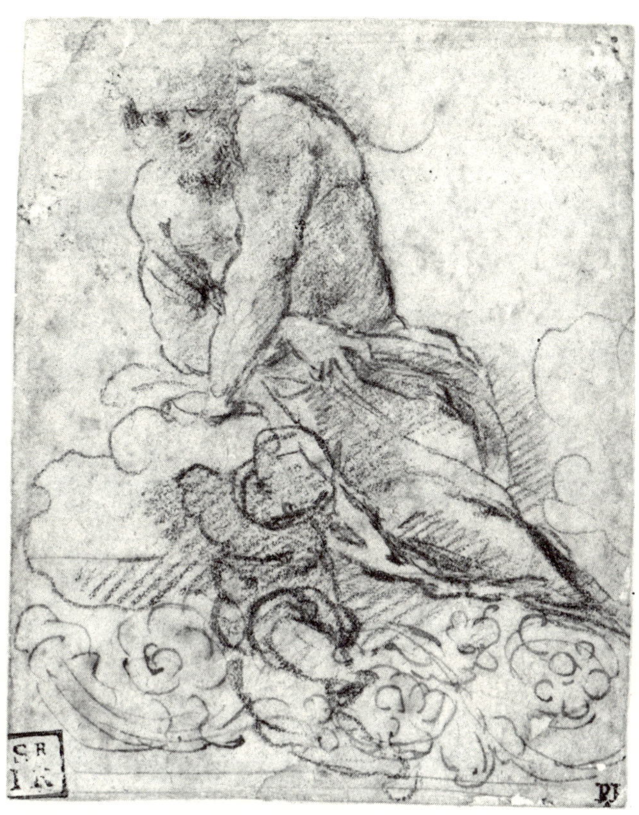

*33A. Antonio Allegri, called Correggio (Parma, 1489–1534).* STUDY OF A MALE FIGURE, A PUTTO AND A DECORATIVE FRIEZE.

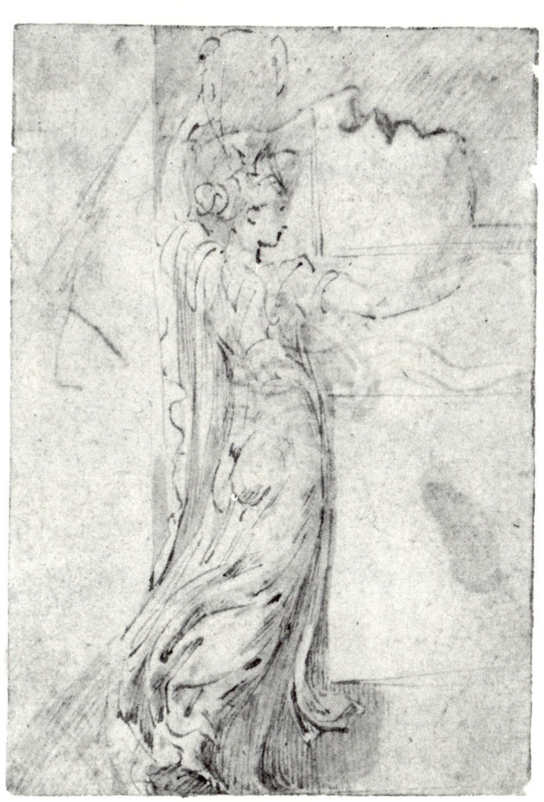

*33B. Francesco Mazzuola, called Parmigianino (Parma, 1503–1540).* STANDING FEMALE FIGURE, FACING RIGHT.

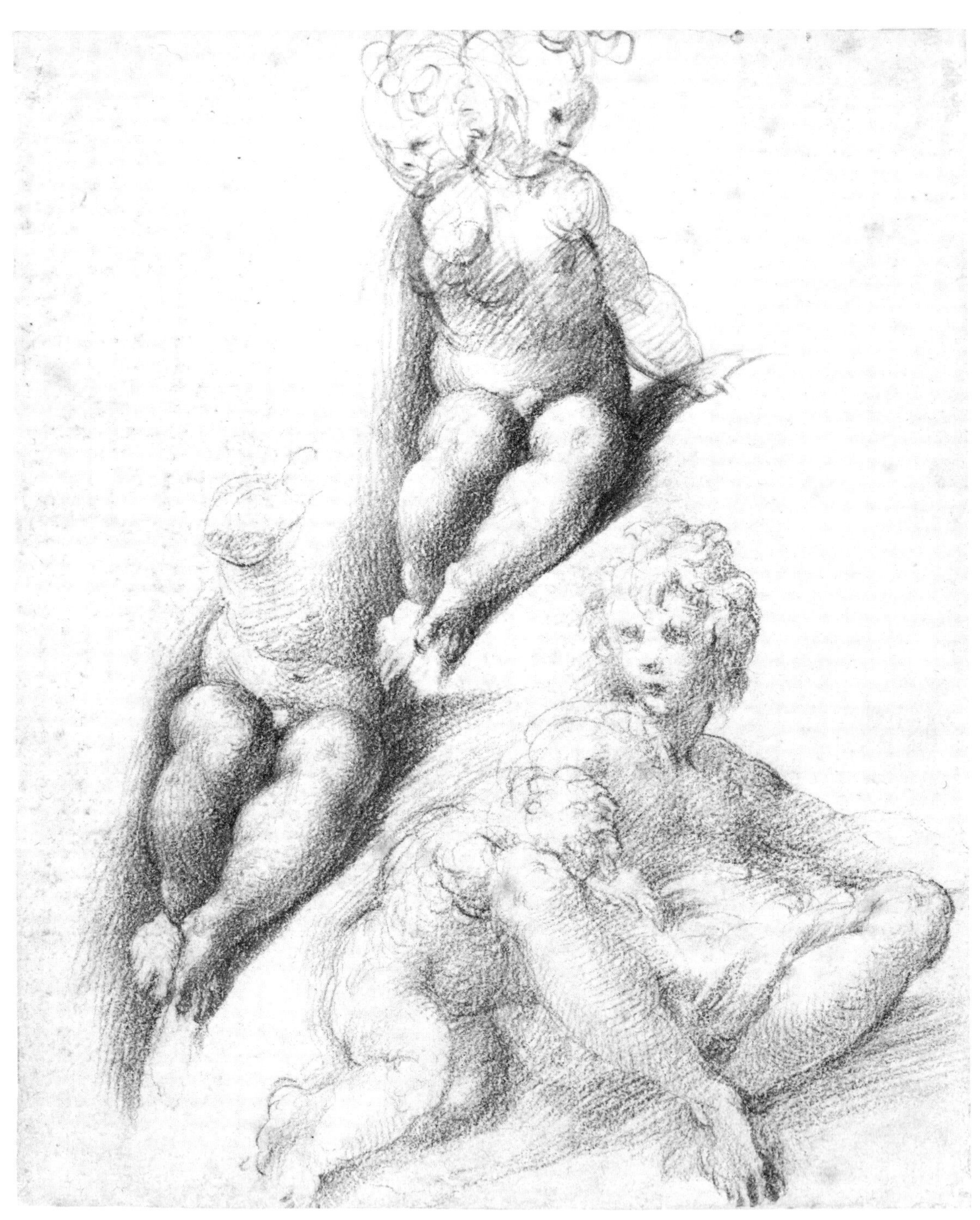

34. *Francesco Mazzuola, called Parmigianino.* STUDIES OF PUTTI AND A SEATED BOY.

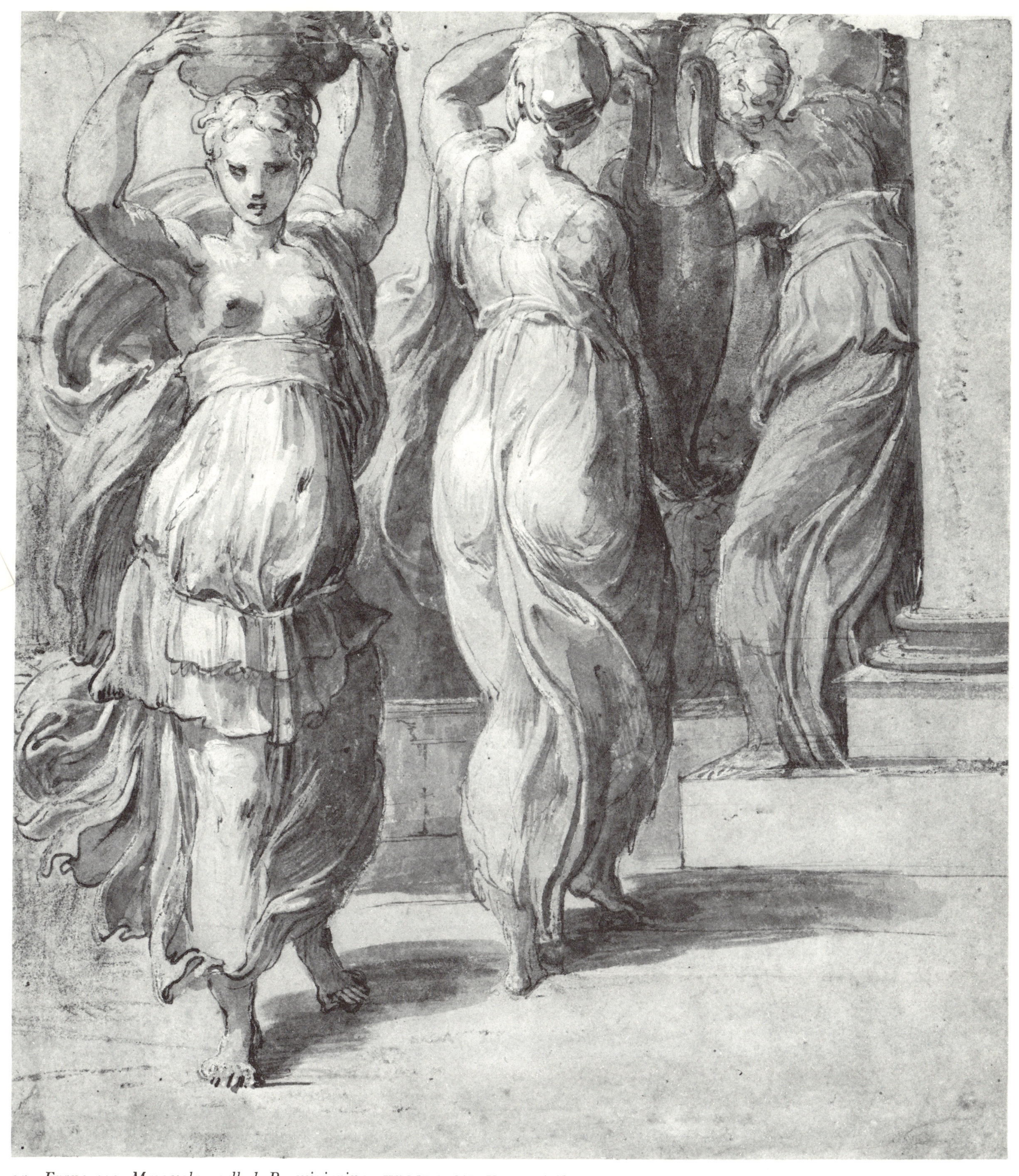

35. *Francesco Mazzuola, called Parmigianino.* WOMEN CARRYING BASKETS AND AMPHORAE.

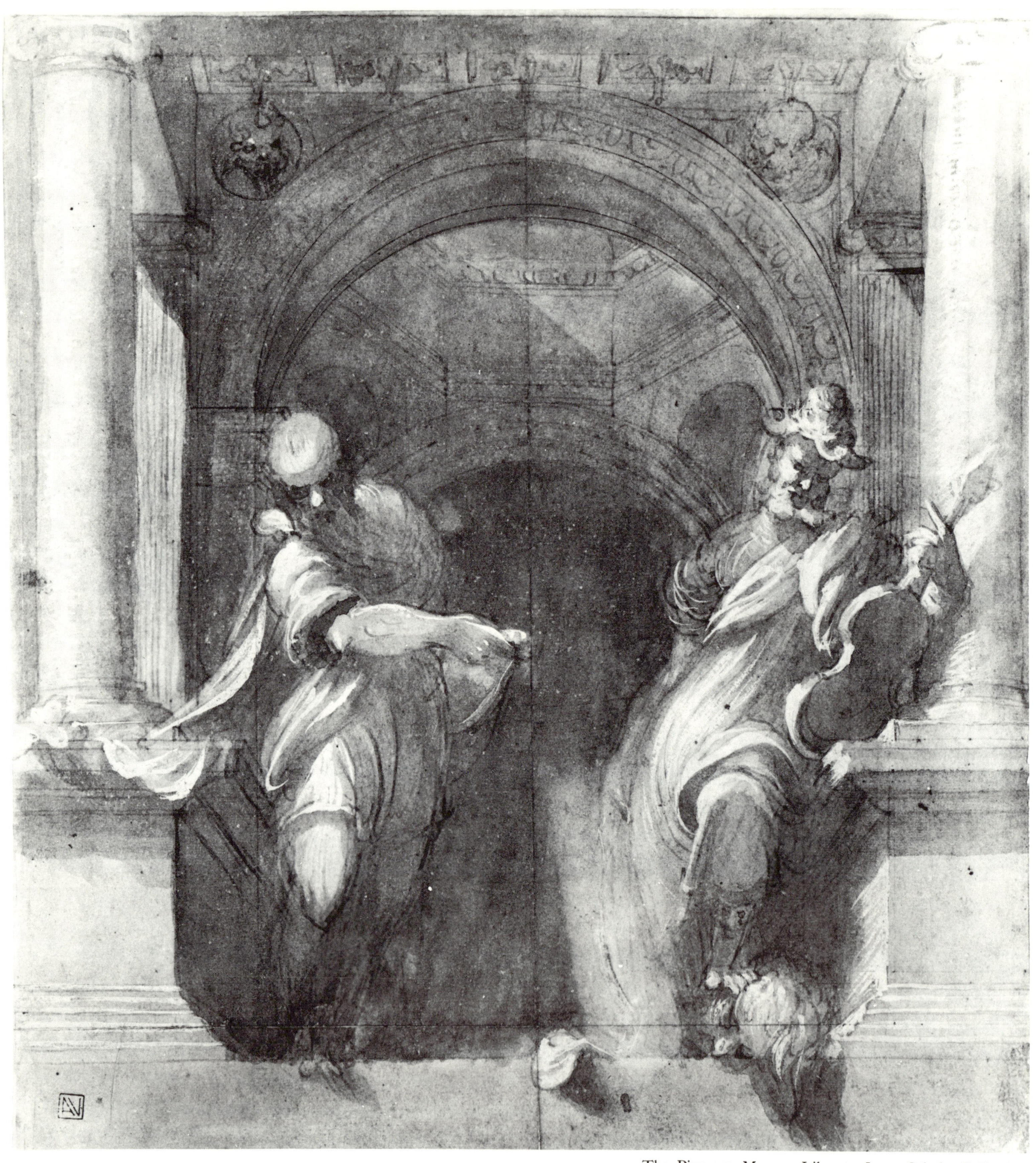

The Pierpont Morgan Library, Janos Scholz Collection

*36. Camillo Boccaccino (Cremonese, 1501–1546).* THE PROPHET ISAIAH AND KING DAVID.

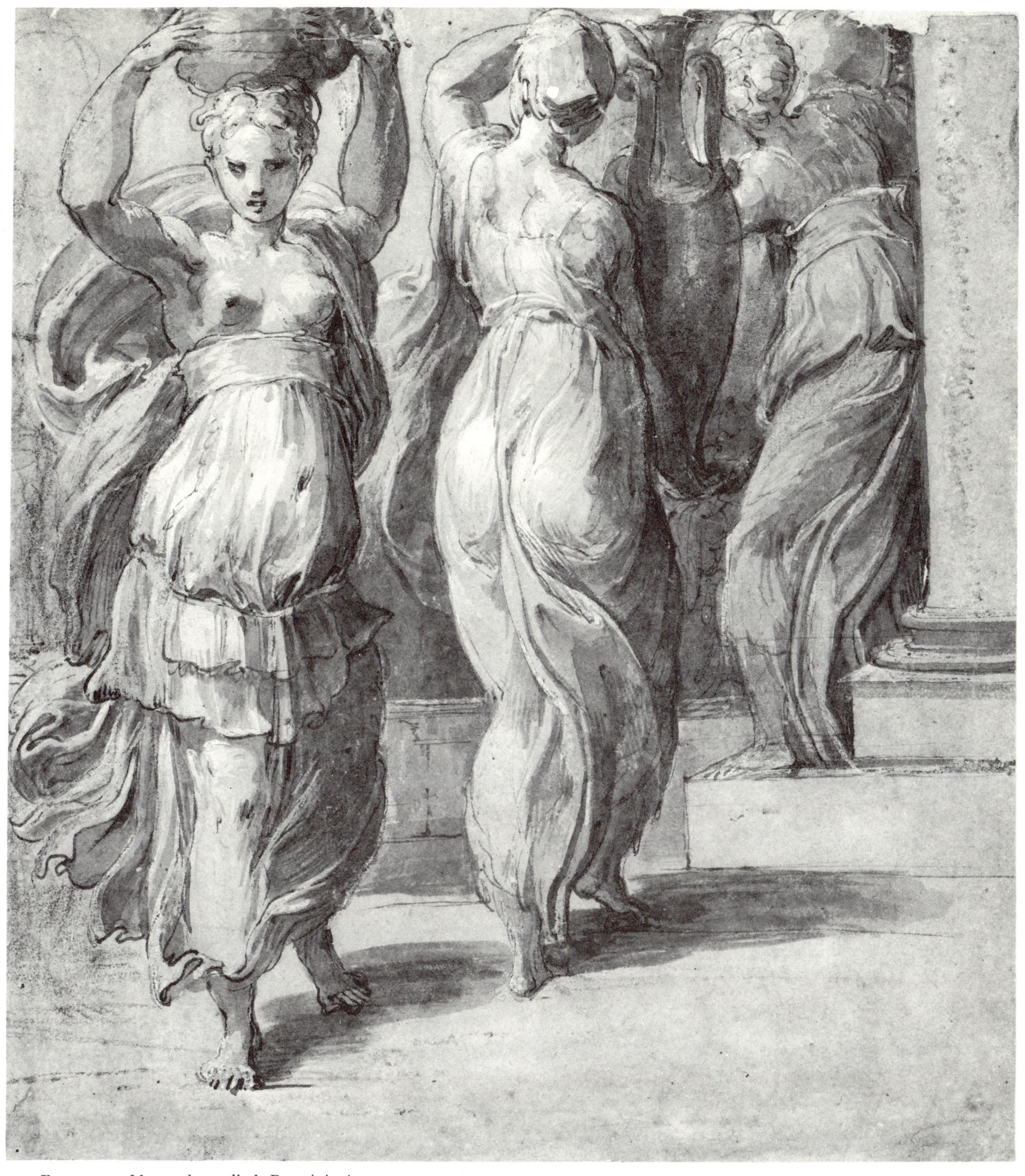

35. *Francesco Mazzuola, called Parmigianino.* WOMEN CARRYING BASKETS AND AMPHORAE.

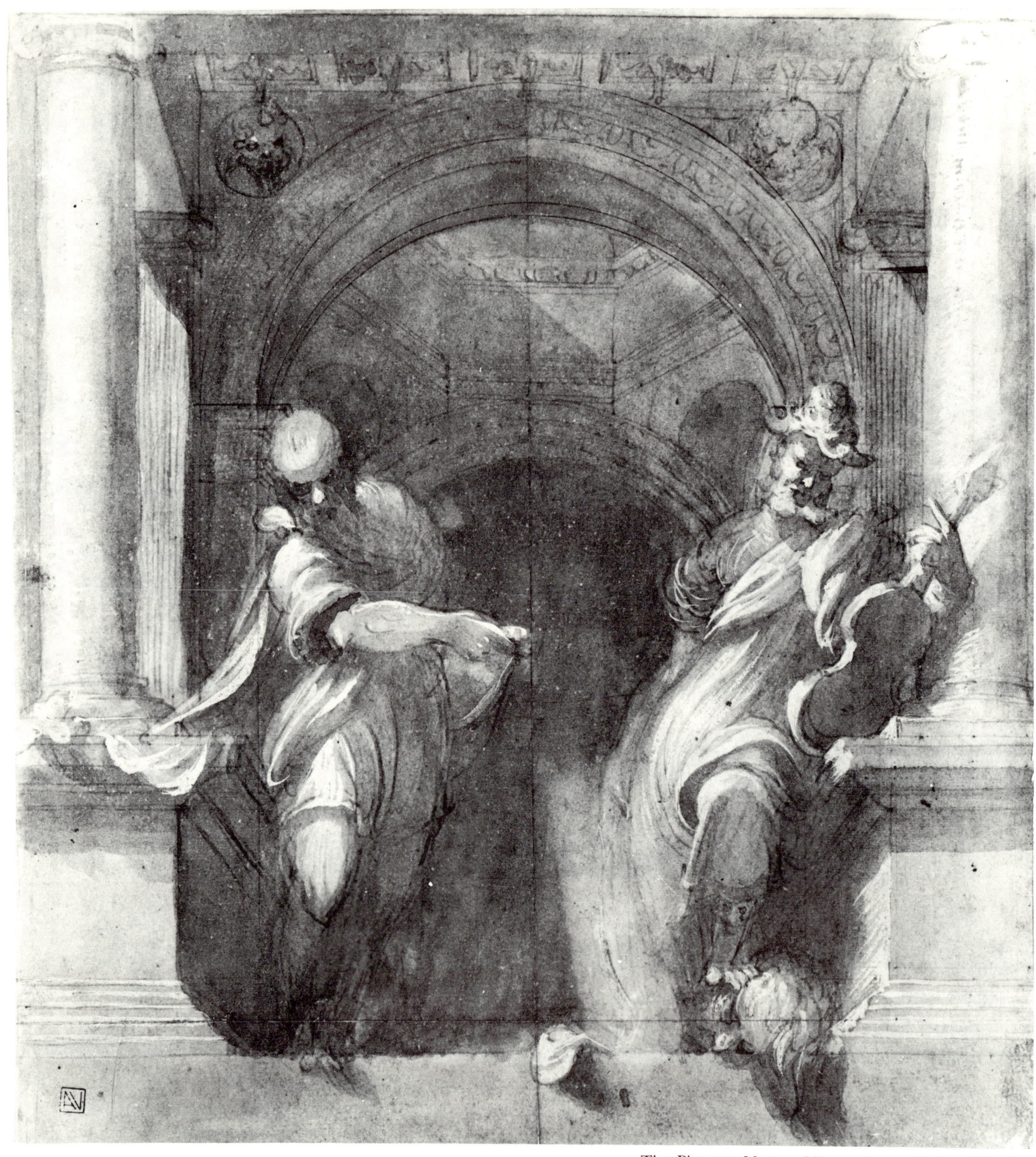

The Pierpont Morgan Library, Janos Scholz Collection

36. *Camillo Boccaccino (Cremonese, 1501–1546).* THE PROPHET ISAIAH AND KING DAVID.

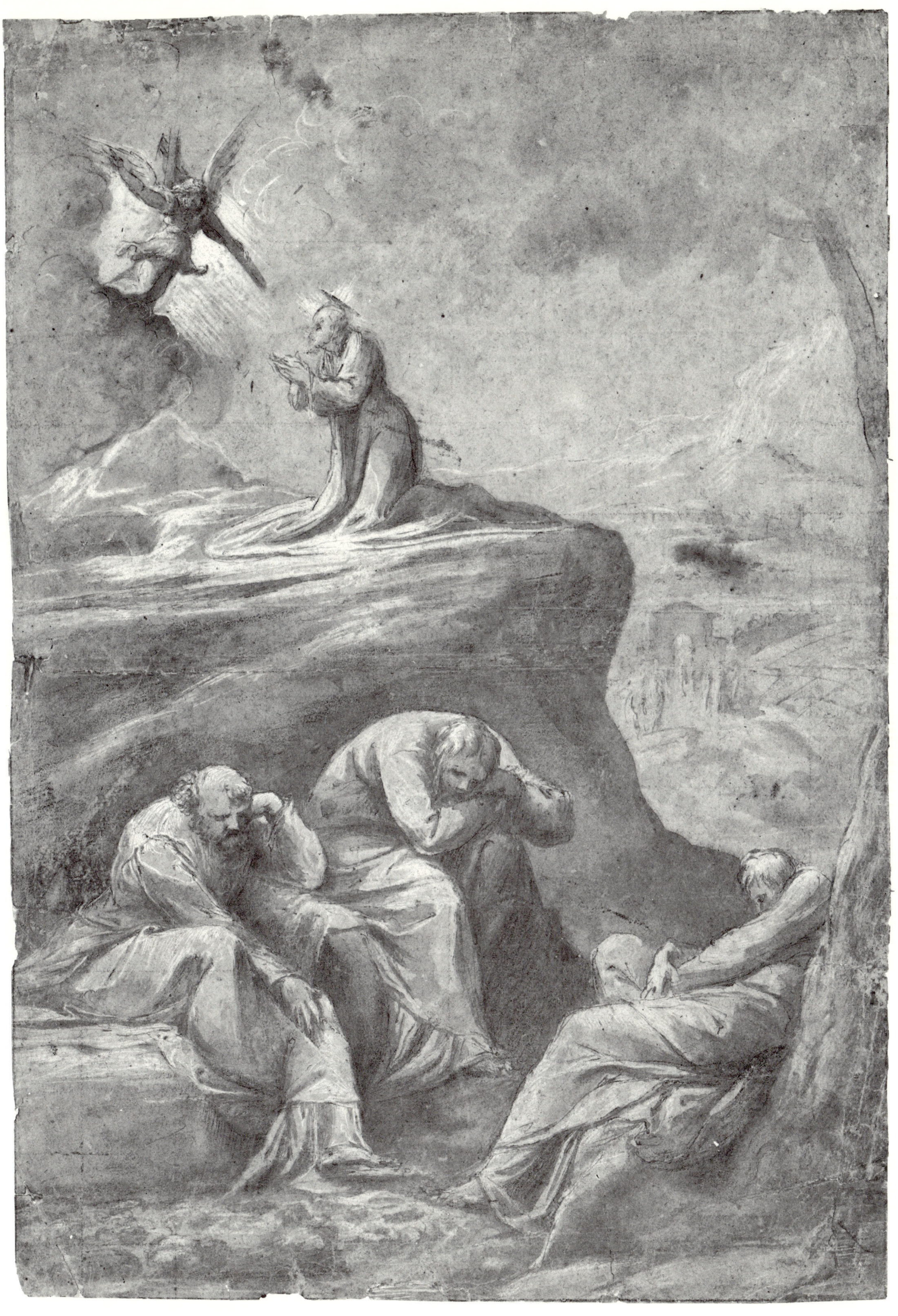

37. *Polidoro Caldara, called Polidoro da Caravaggio (Roman, about 1500–1543).* CHRIST ON THE MOUNT OF OLIVES.

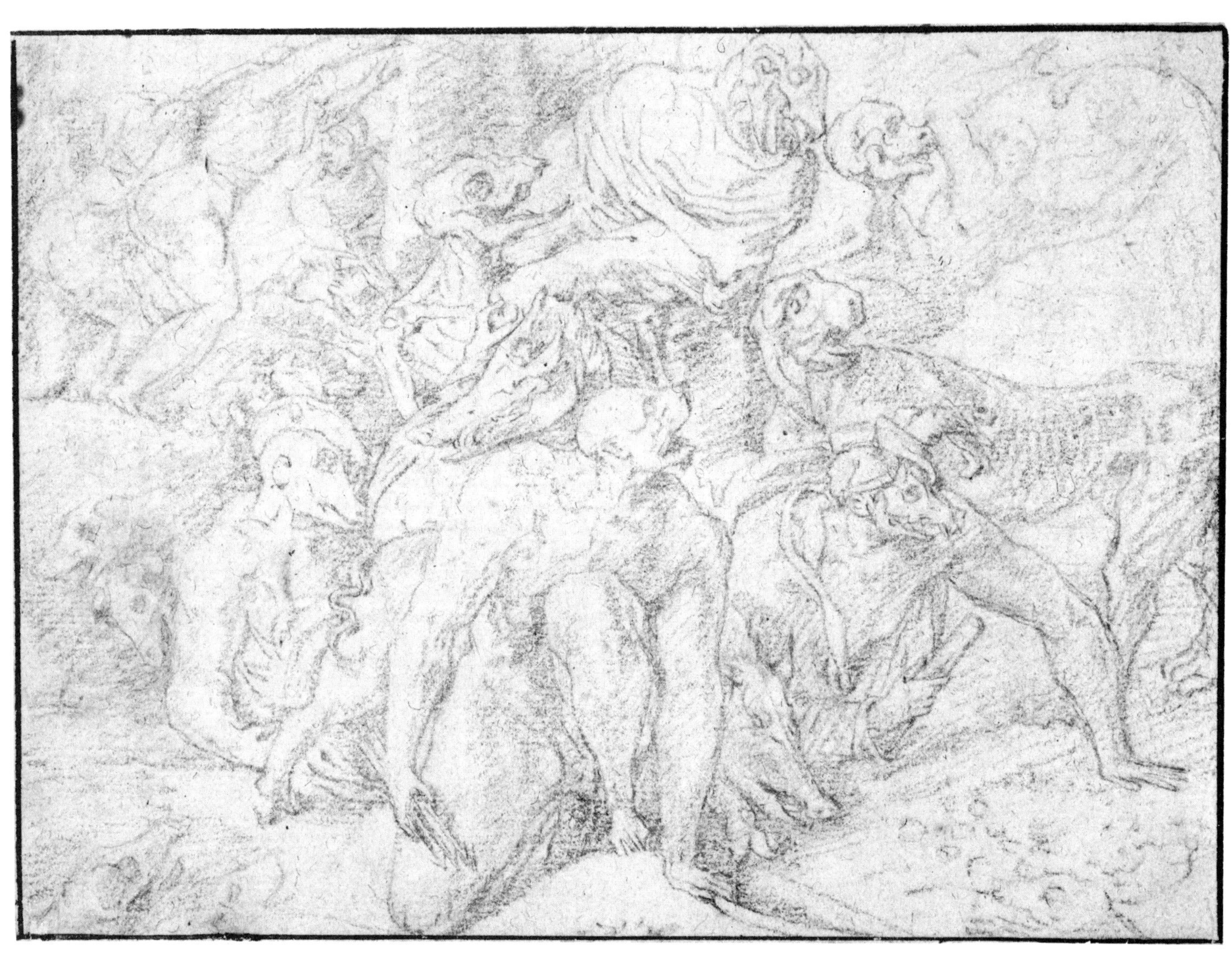

38. *Francesco Primaticcio (Bolognese, 1504–1570).* CIRCE CHANGING THE COMPANIONS OF ULYSSES INTO SWINE.

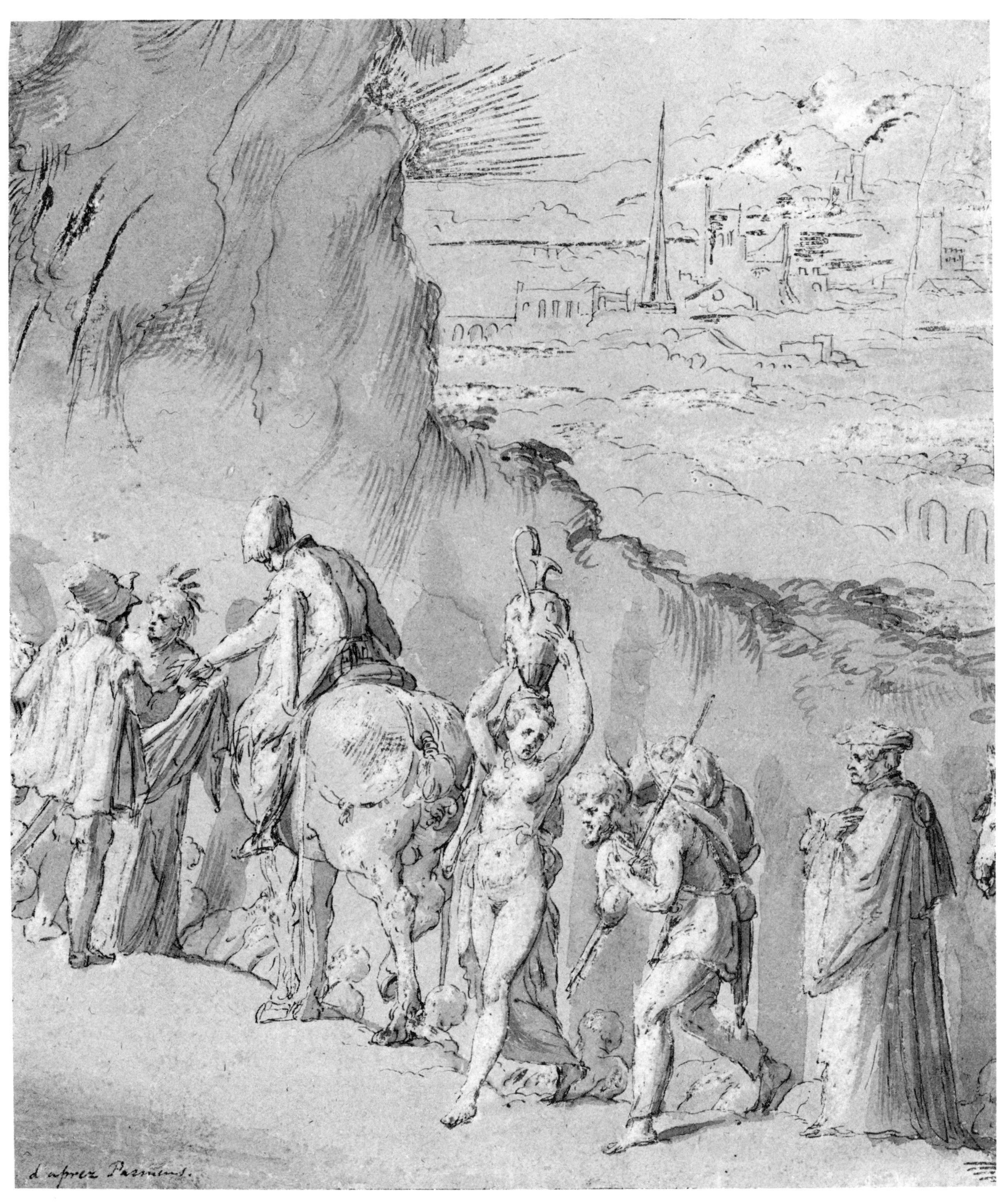

*39. Nicolò dell'Abbate (Modena, about 1512–1571).* PEOPLE WALKING IN A LANDSCAPE; IN THE DISTANCE, IDEALISTIC VIEW OF ROME.

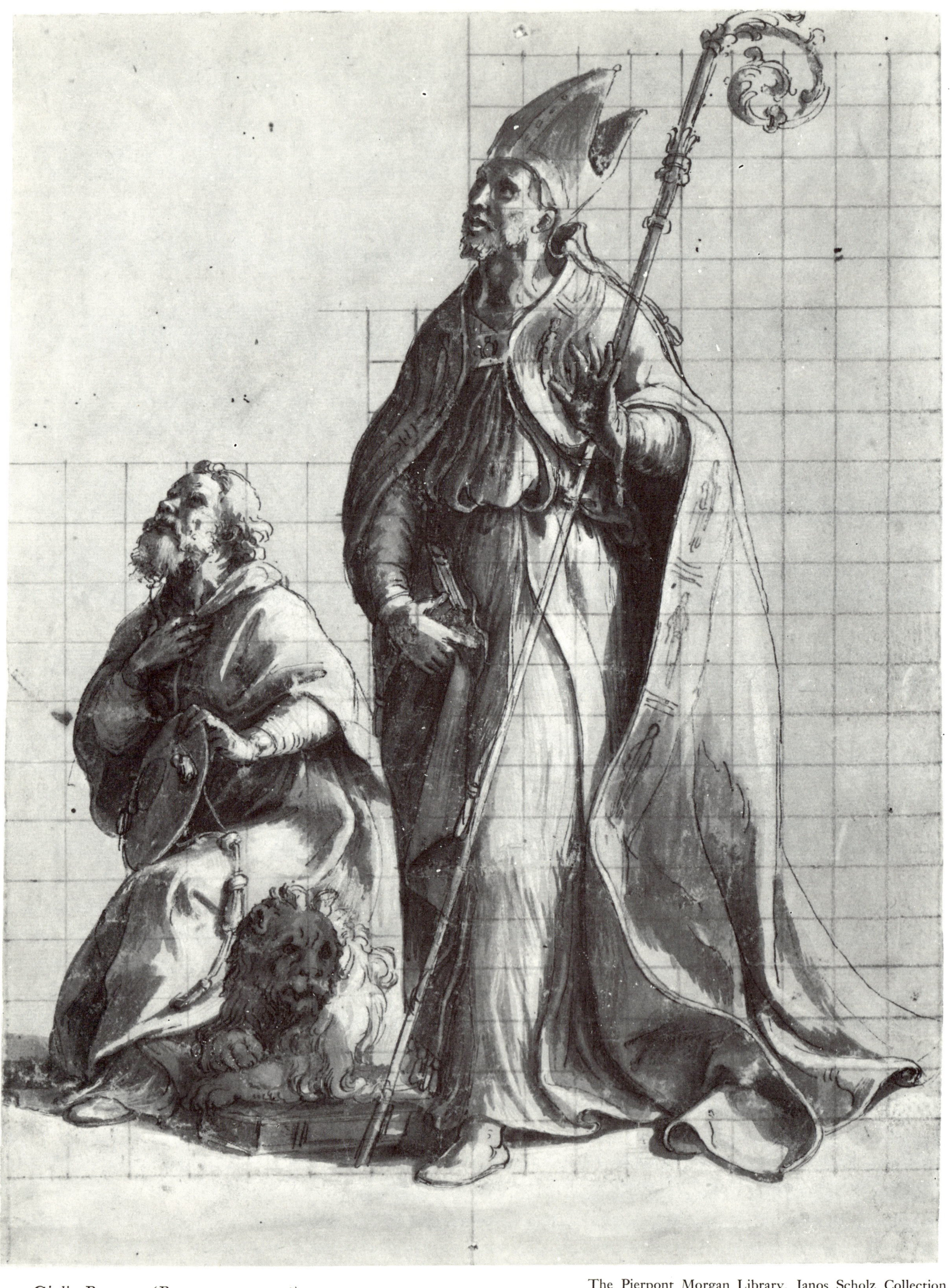

40. *Giulio Romano (Roman, 1493–1546).* ST. JEROME AND ST. AUGUSTINE.

The Pierpont Morgan Library, Janos Scholz Collection

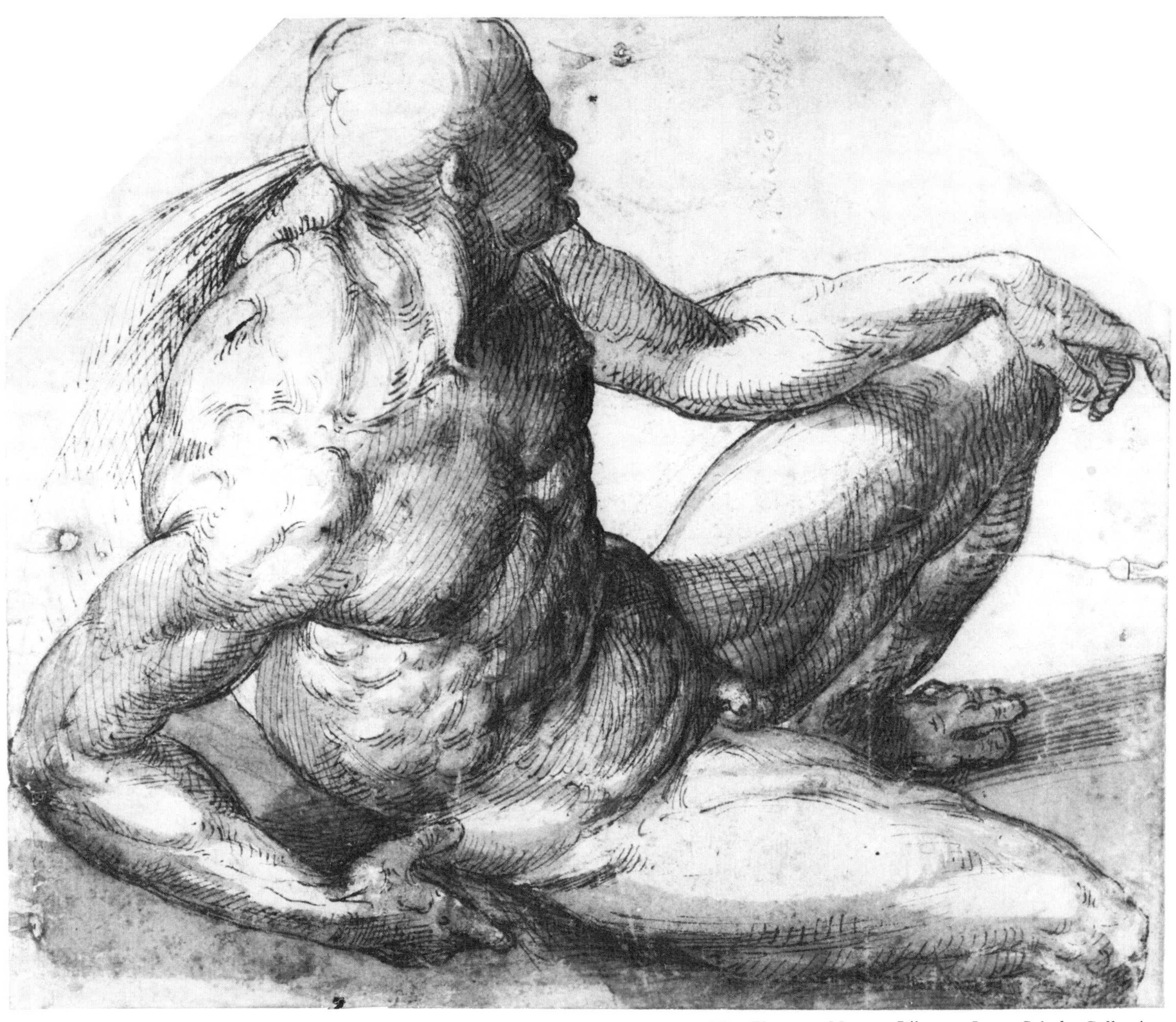

The Pierpont Morgan Library, Janos Scholz Collection

41. *Domenico Beccafumi (Sienese, 1484/86–1551).* SEATED MALE FIGURE.

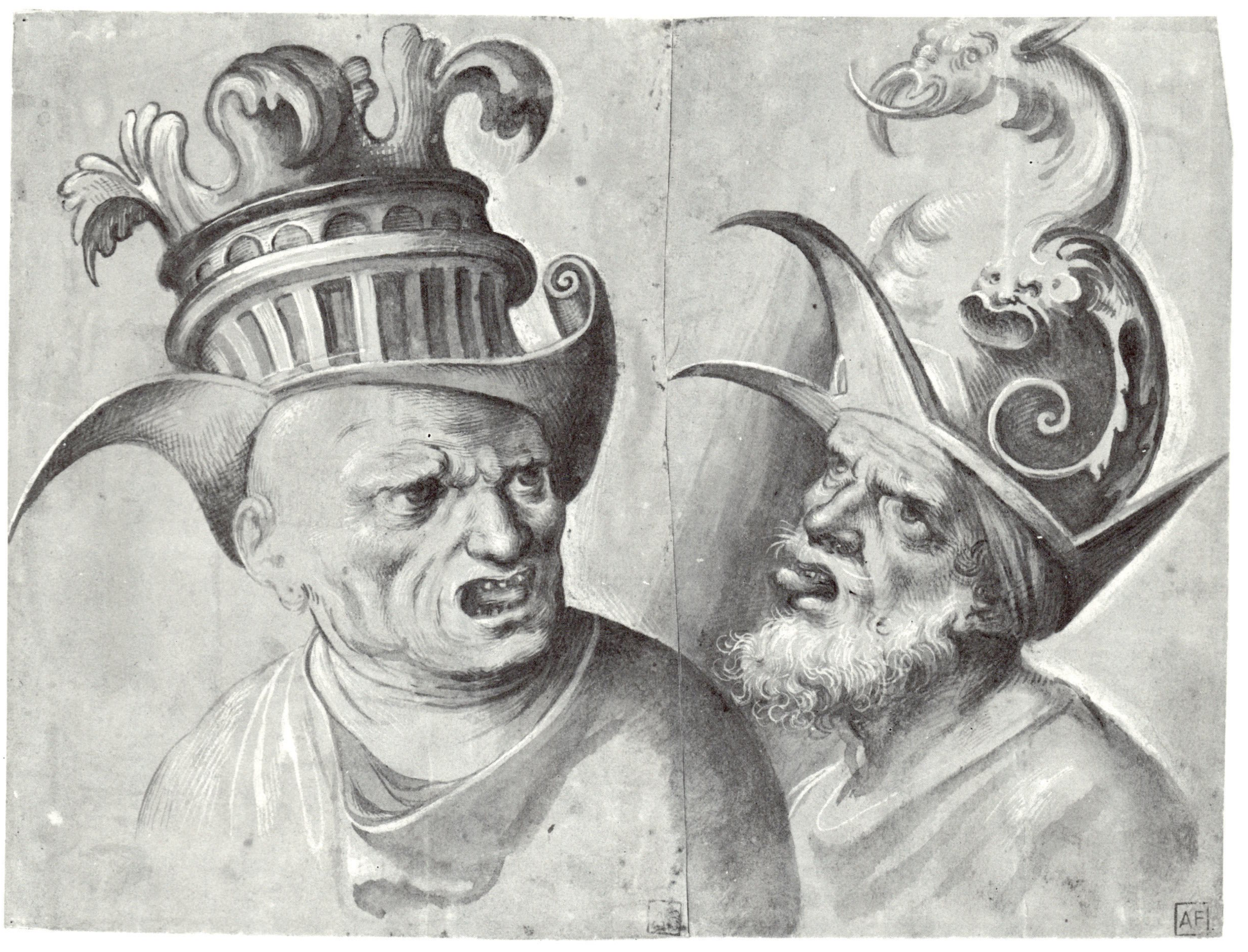

42. *Jacopo Ripanda (Ferrarese, working about 1490–1530).* TWO GROTESQUE HEADS.

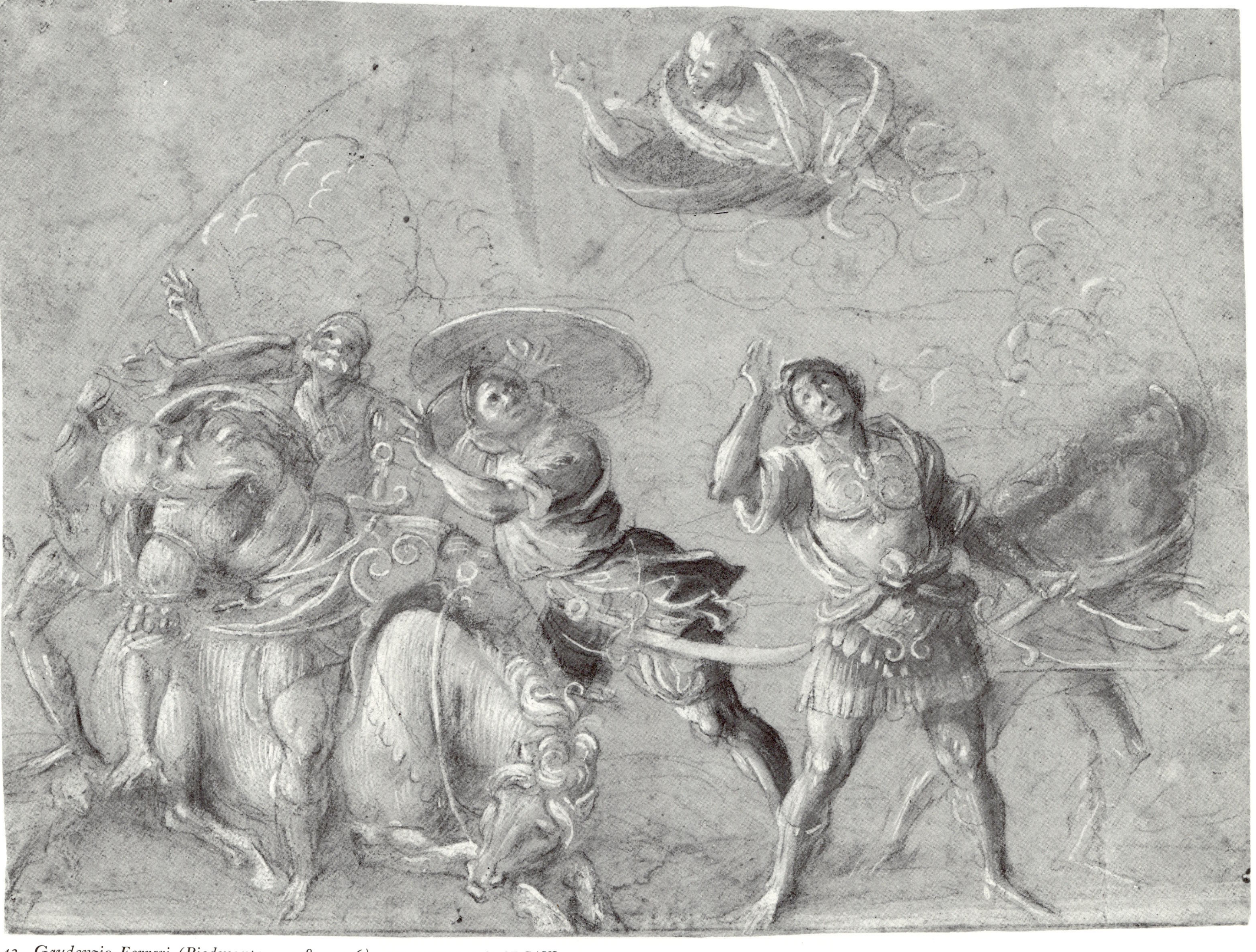

43. *Gaudenzio Ferrari (Piedmontese, 1480–1546).* THE CONVERSION OF PAUL.

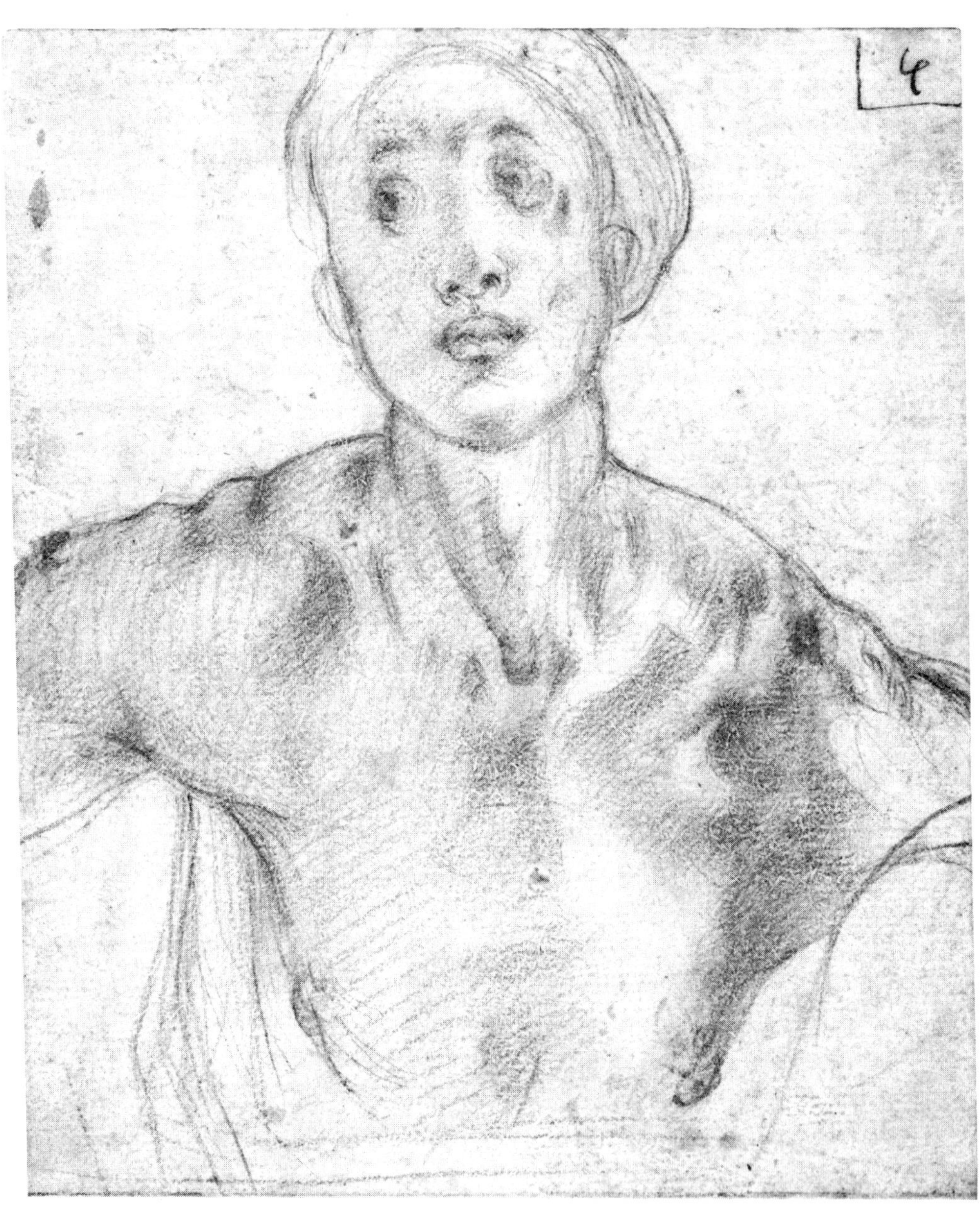

44. *Jacopo da Pontormo (Florentine, 1494–1557).*
HALF-LENGTH FIGURE OF A YOUTH.

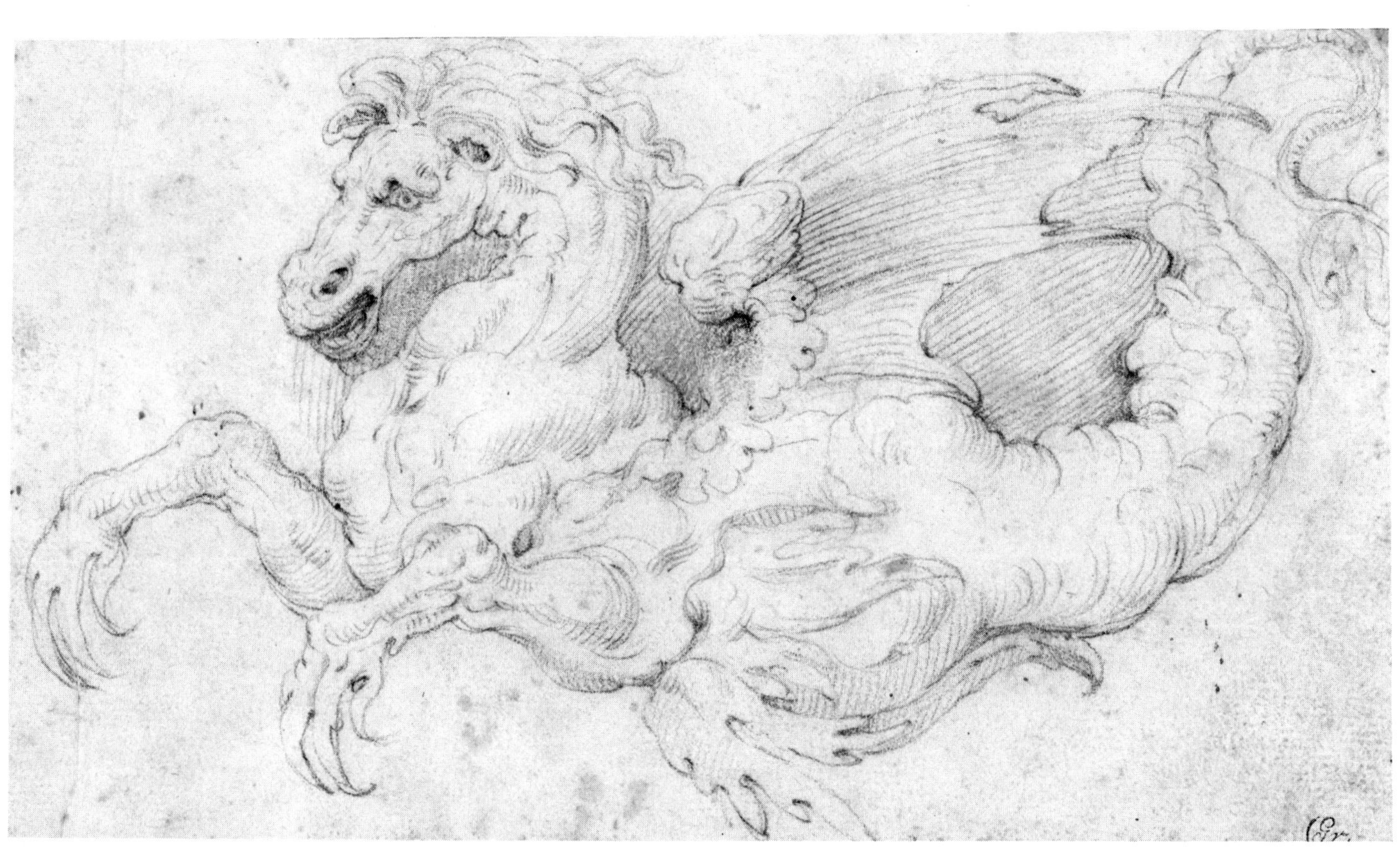

*45. Francesco Salviati (Florentine, 1510–1563).* A MONSTER.

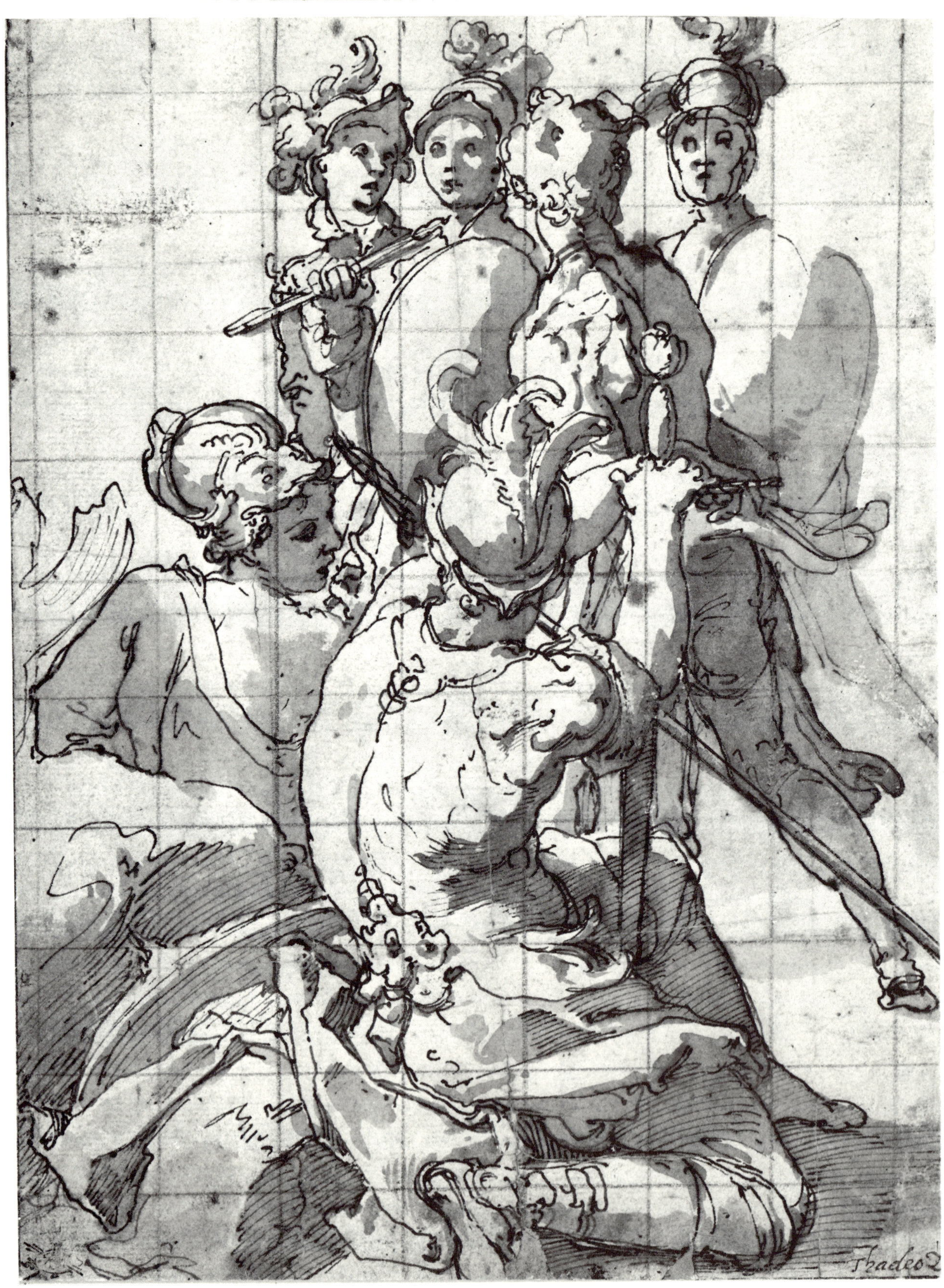


46. *Taddeo Zuccaro (Tuscan, 1529–1566).* GROUP OF WARRIORS.

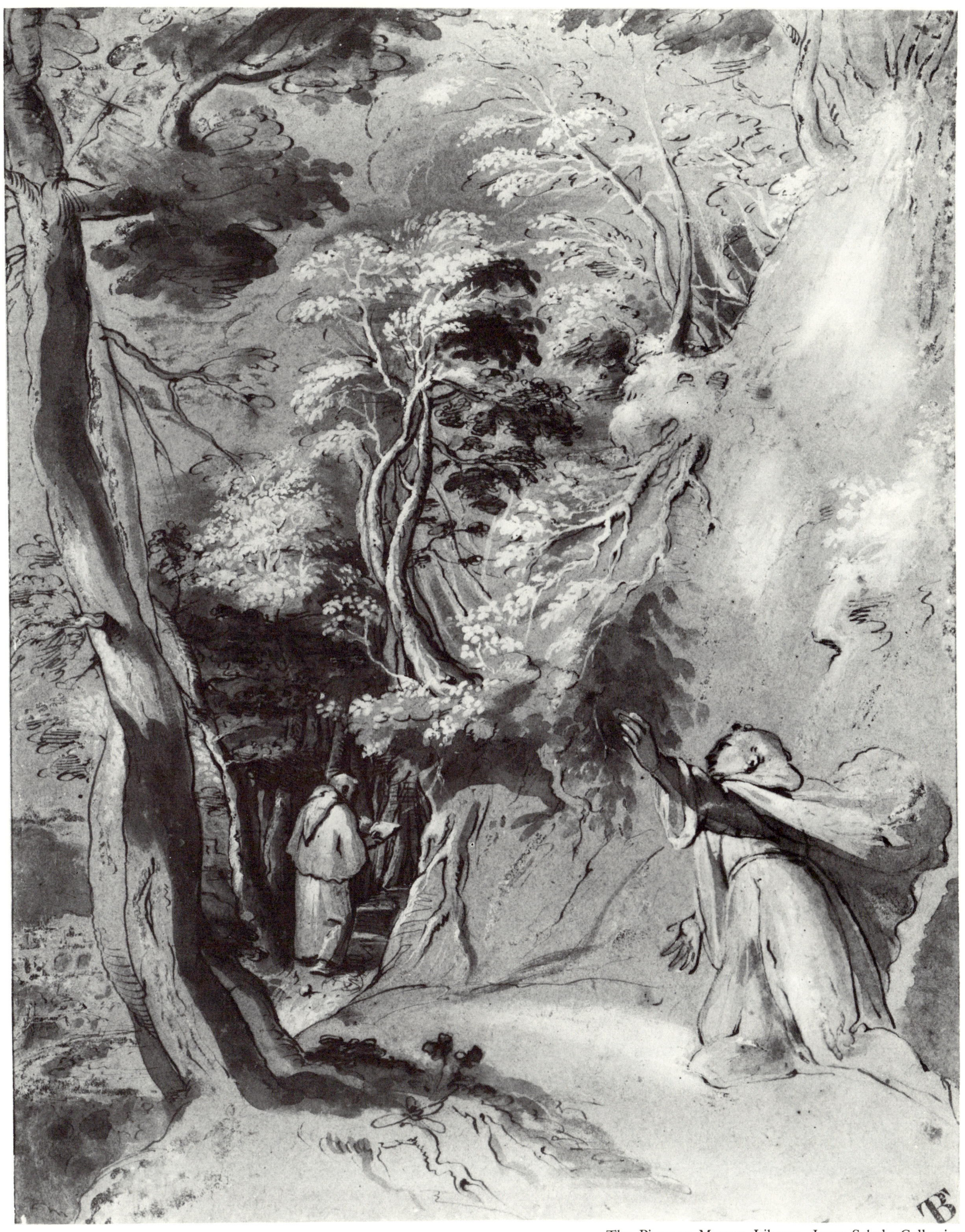

The Pierpont Morgan Library, Janos Scholz Collection

47. *Federigo Barocci (Urbino, 1526–1612).* ST. FRANCIS RECEIVING THE STIGMATA.

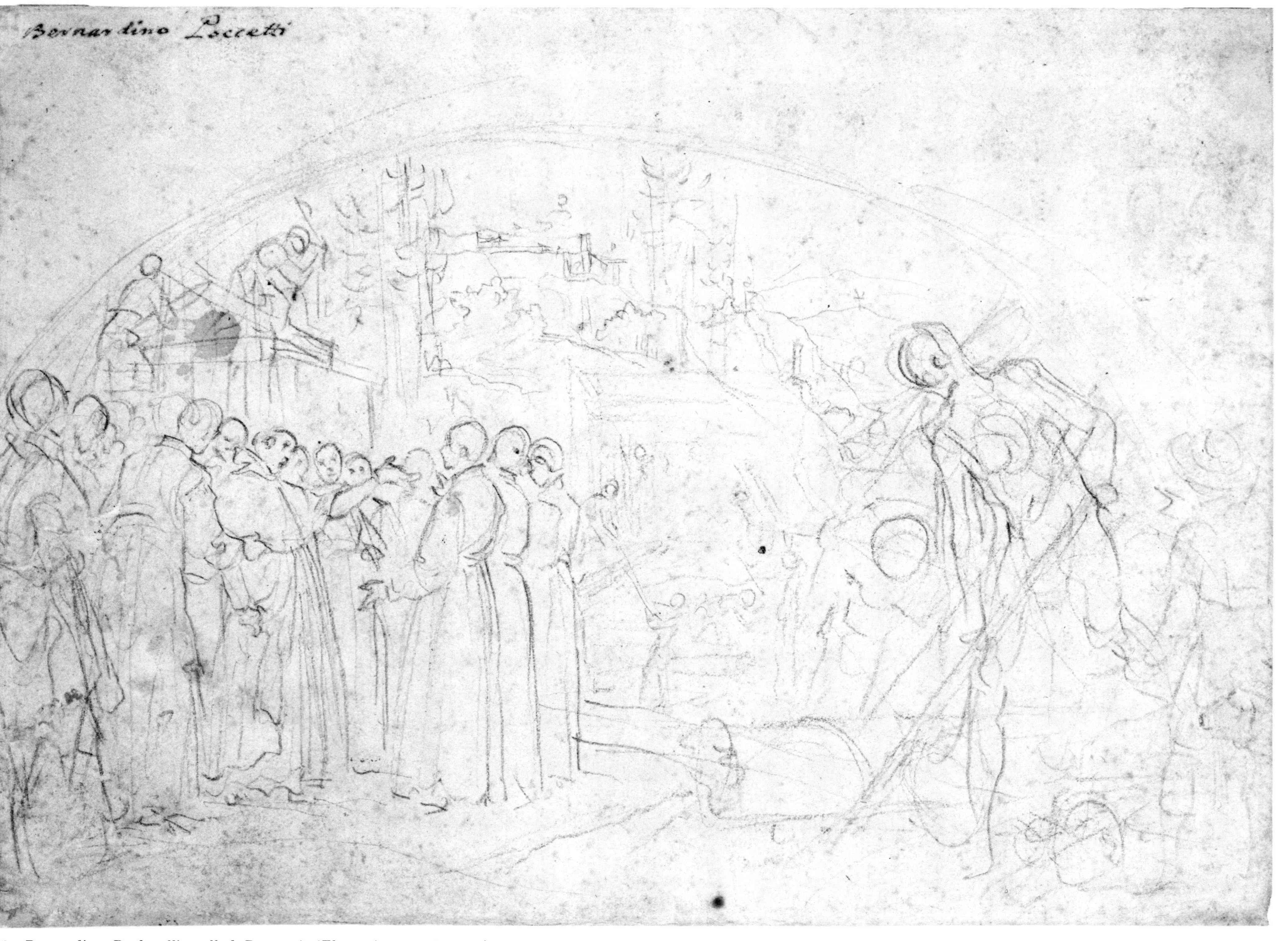


*48. Bernardino Barbatelli, called Poccetti (Florentine, 1548–1612).* THE SEVEN SAINTLY FOUNDERS SUPERVISING THE BUILDING OF THE MONASTERY OF MONTE SENARIO IN 1234.

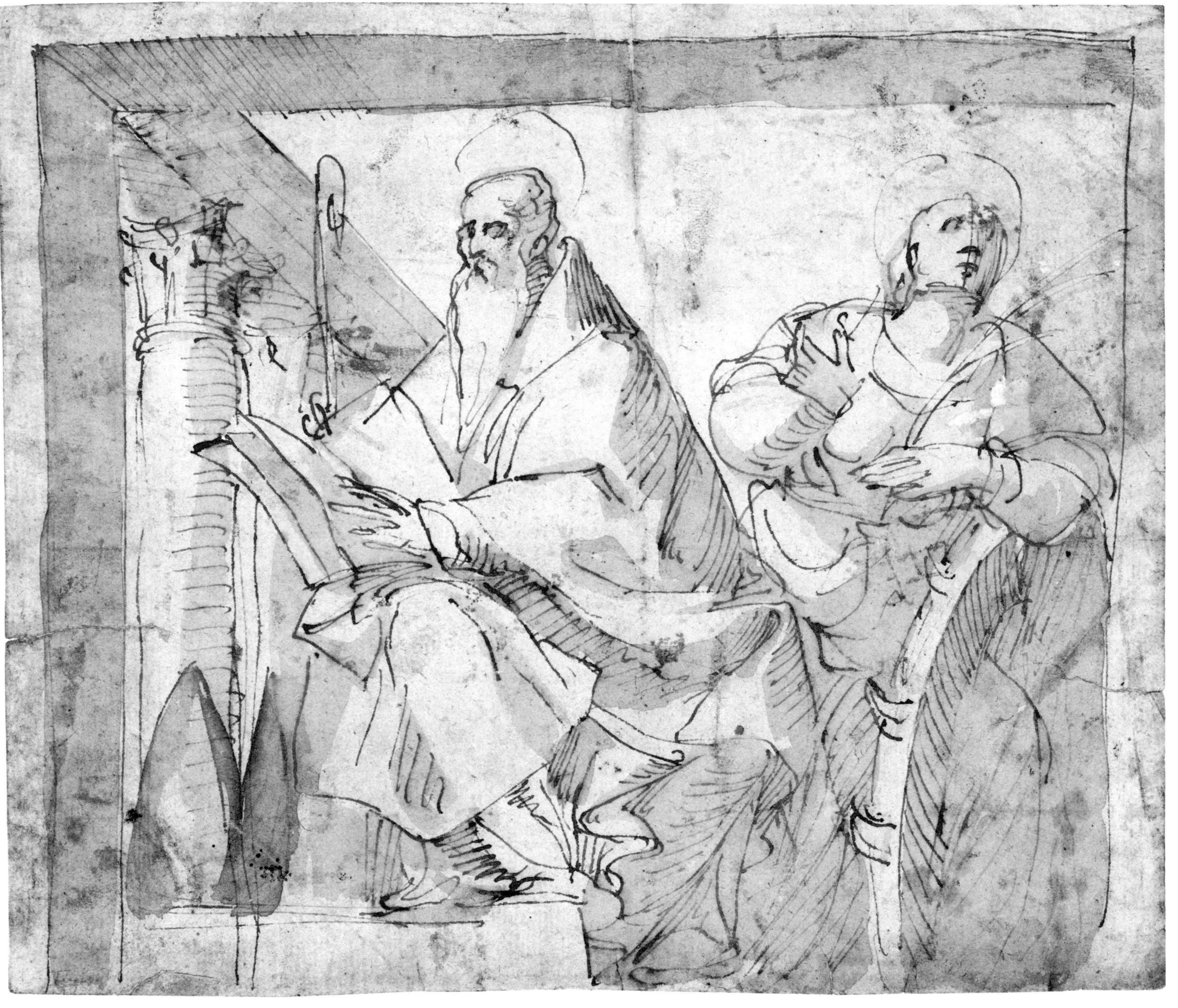

49. *Moretto da Brescia (Brescian, about 1498–1554).* ST. AUGUSTINE AND ST. CATHERINE.

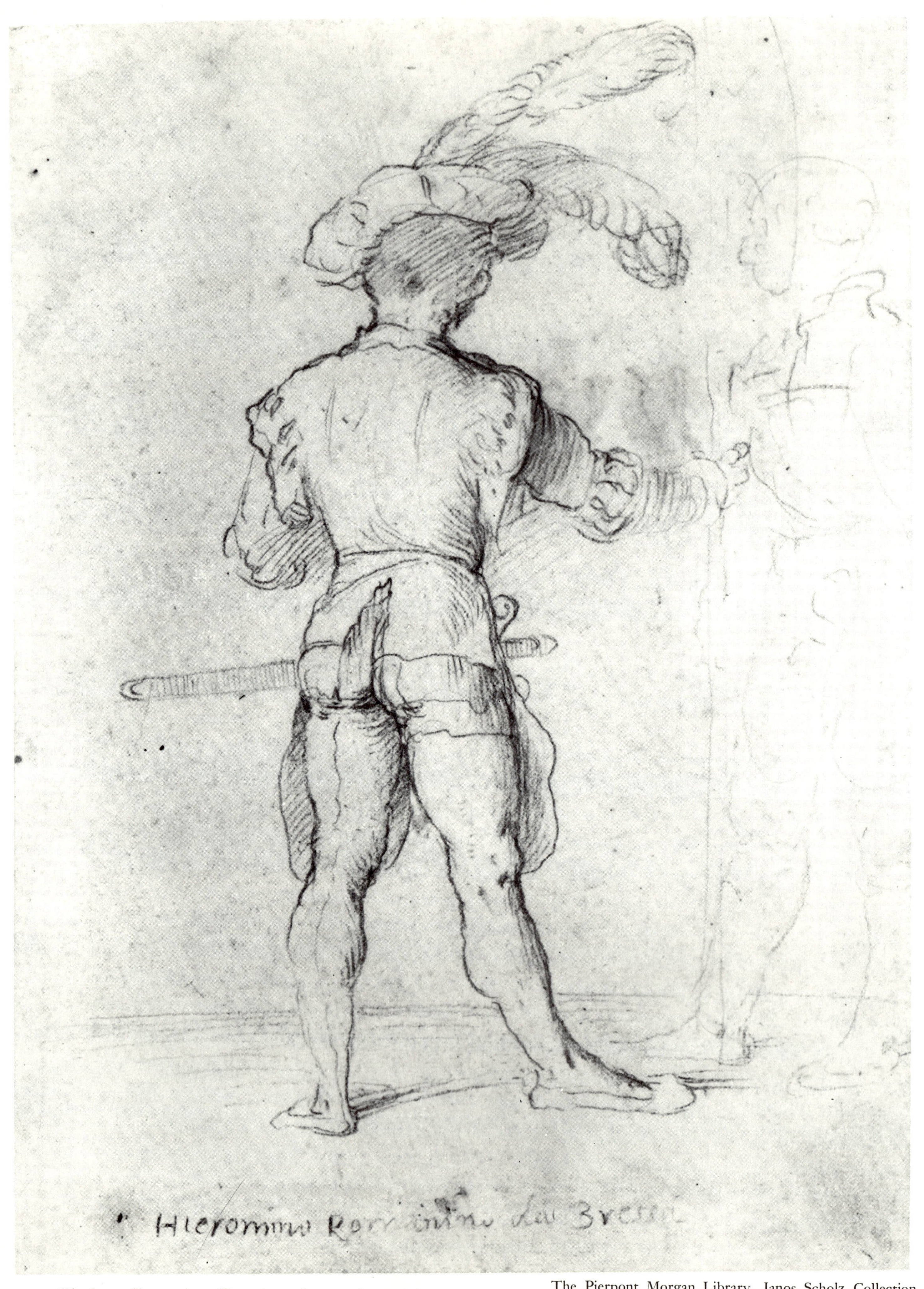

*50. Girolamo Romanino (Brescian, about 1485–1561).*
STANDING SOLDIERS.

The Pierpont Morgan Library, Janos Scholz Collection

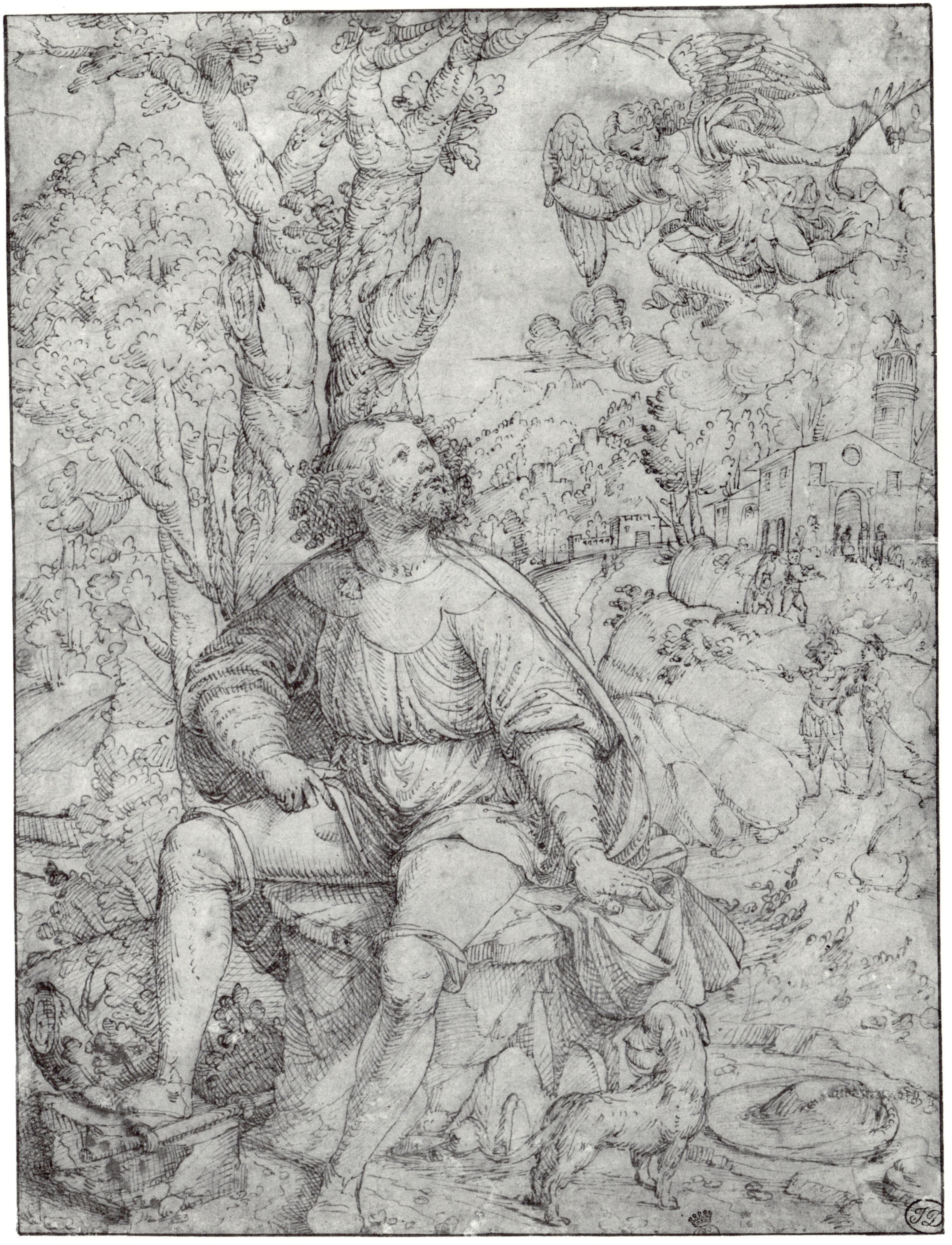

51. *Giulio Campi (Cremonese, about 1502–1572).* ST. ROCH, SEATED IN A LANDSCAPE.

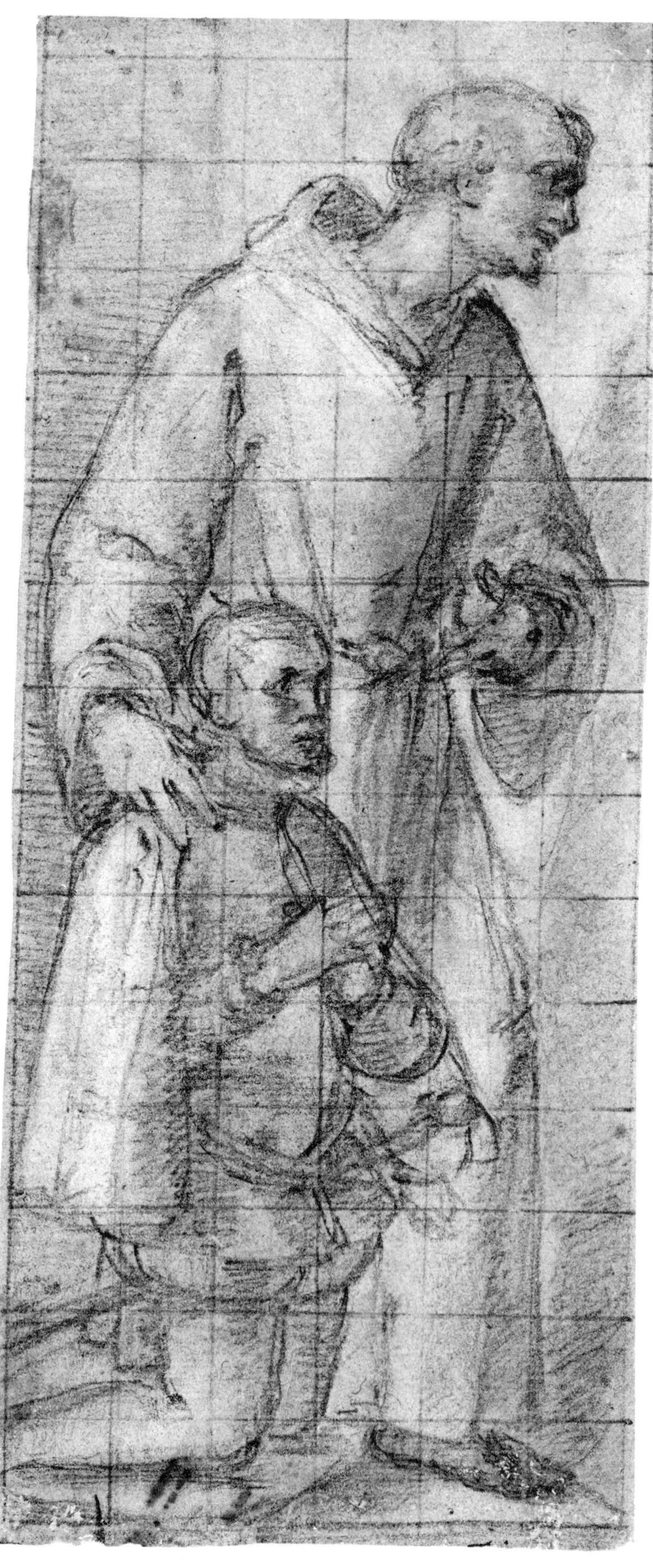

52. *Bernardino Campi (Cremonese, about 1522–1590/95).*
MONK STANDING, WITH A KNEELING MAN.

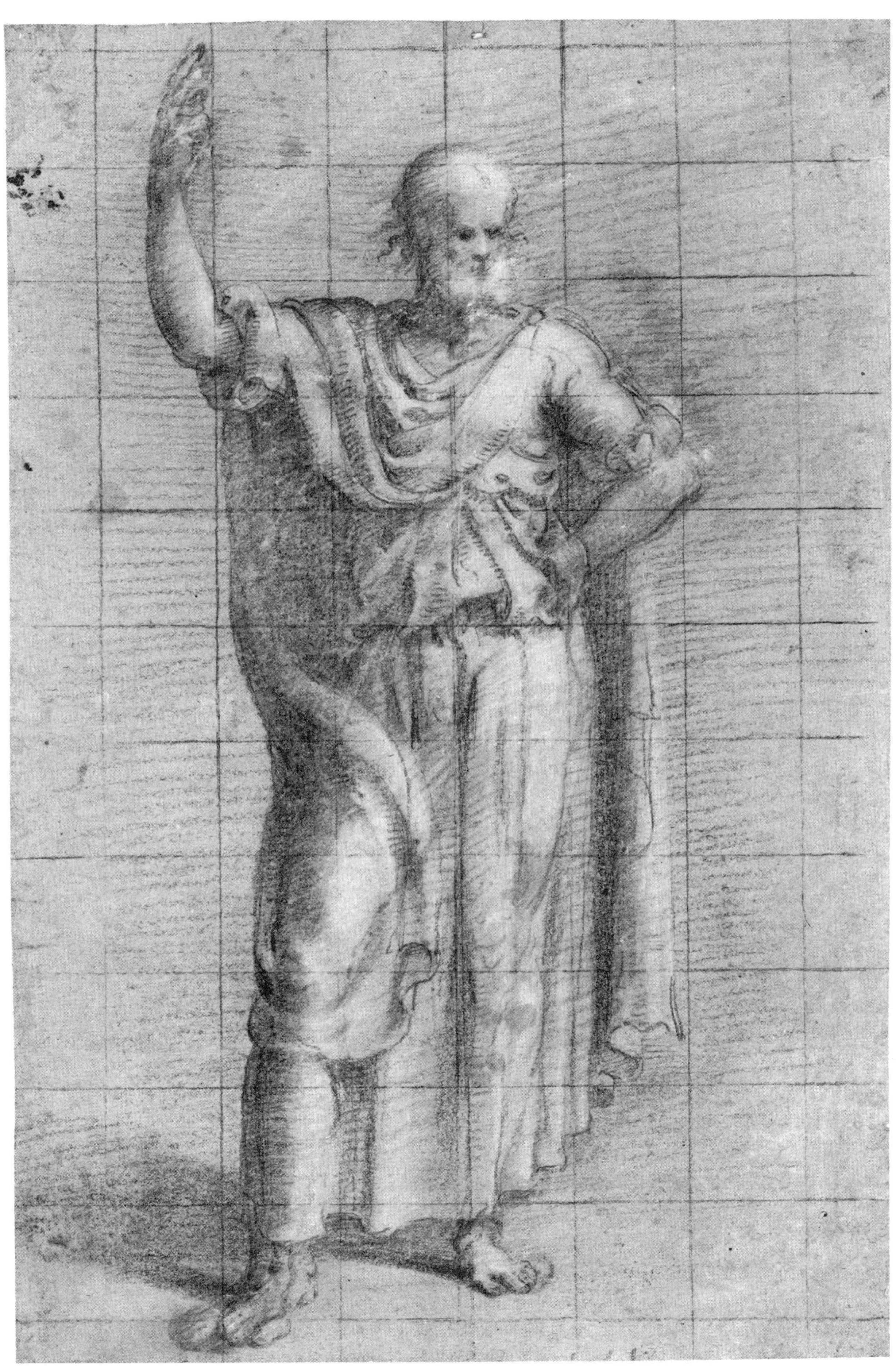

53. *Antonio Campi (Cremonese, died 1591).* STANDING MALE FIGURE.

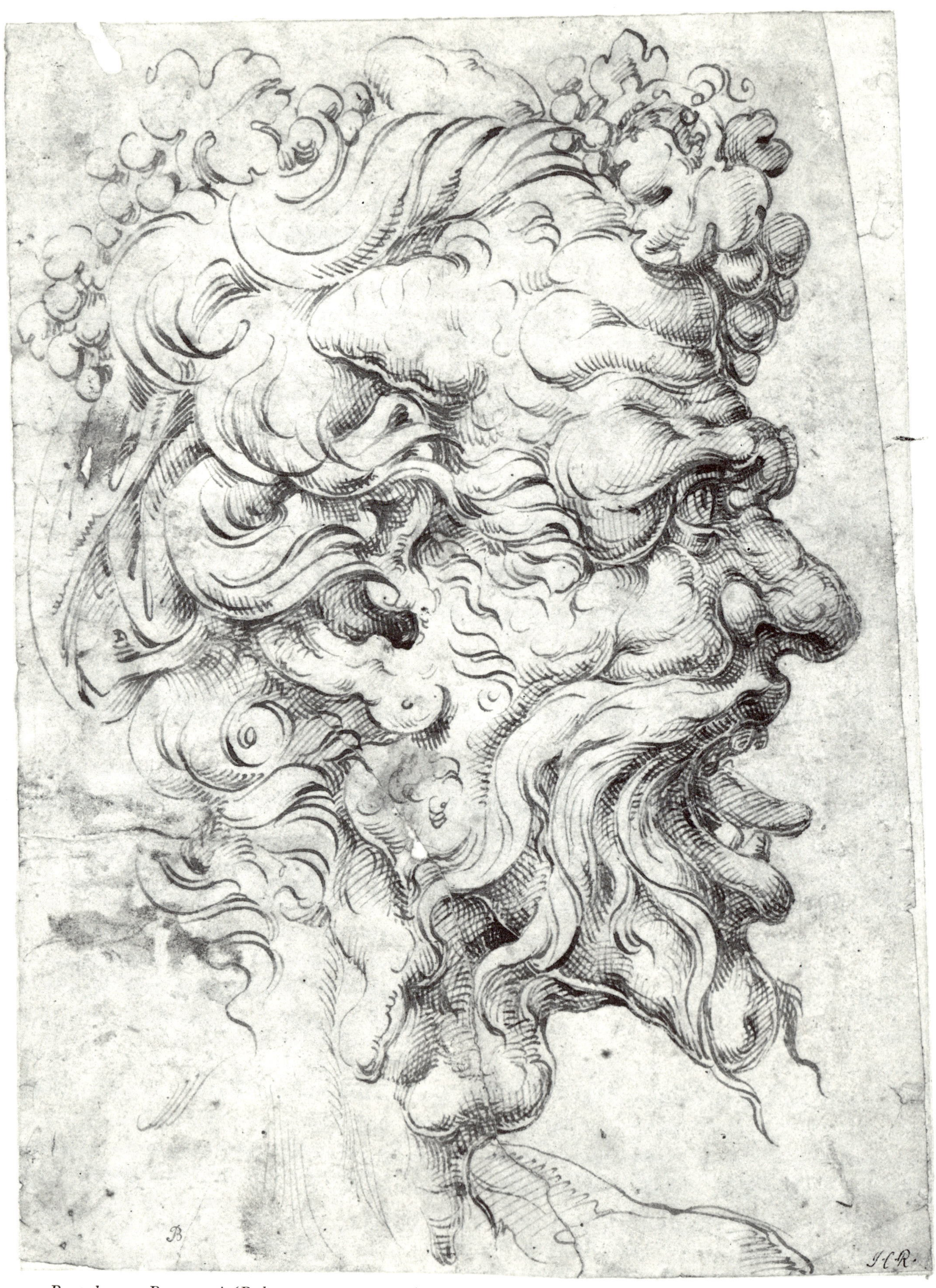

54. *Bartolomeo Passarotti (Bolognese, 1529–1592).* GROTESQUE HEAD.

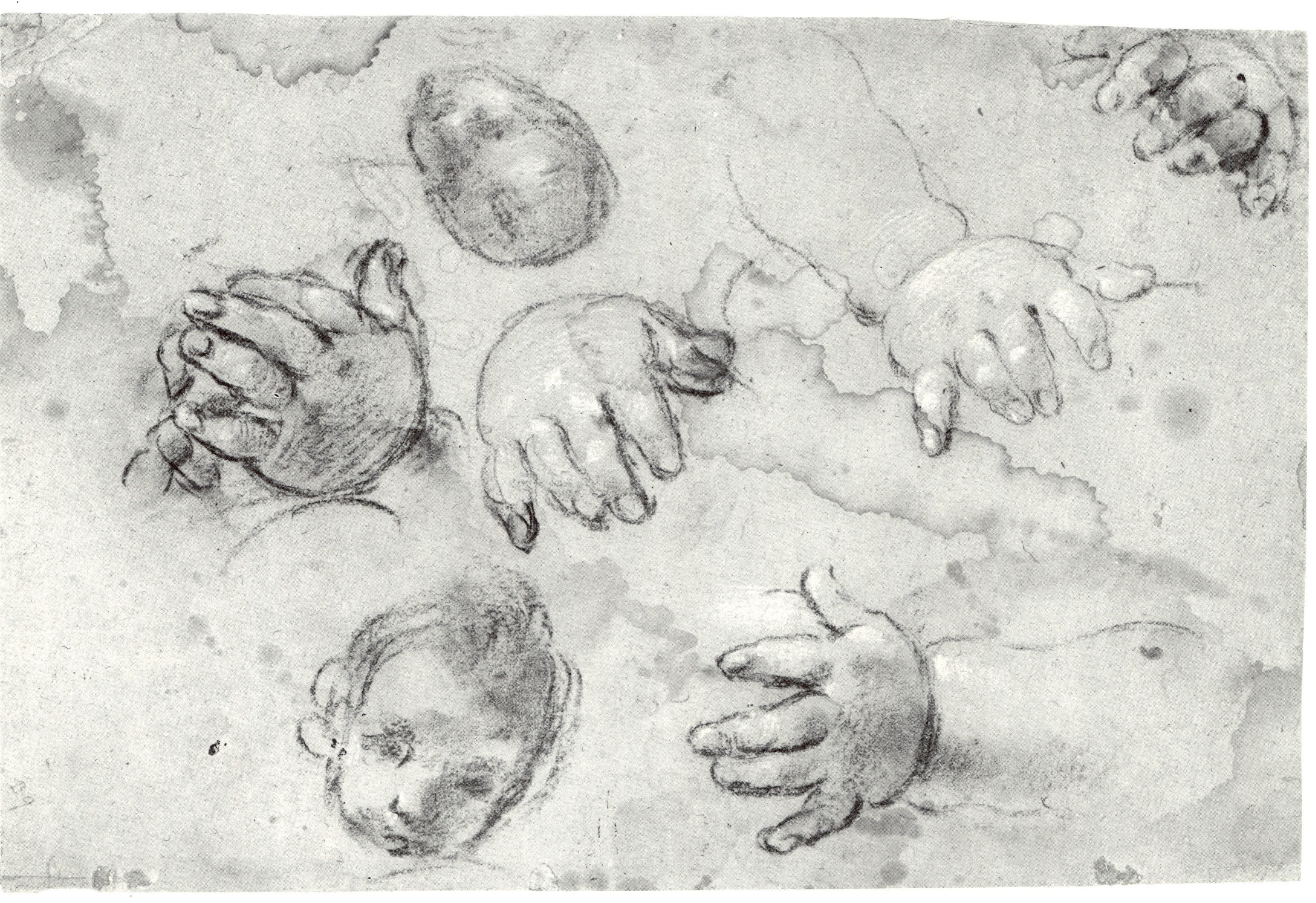

55. *Bartolomeo Schedone (Modena, 1578–1615).* HANDS AND HEADS.

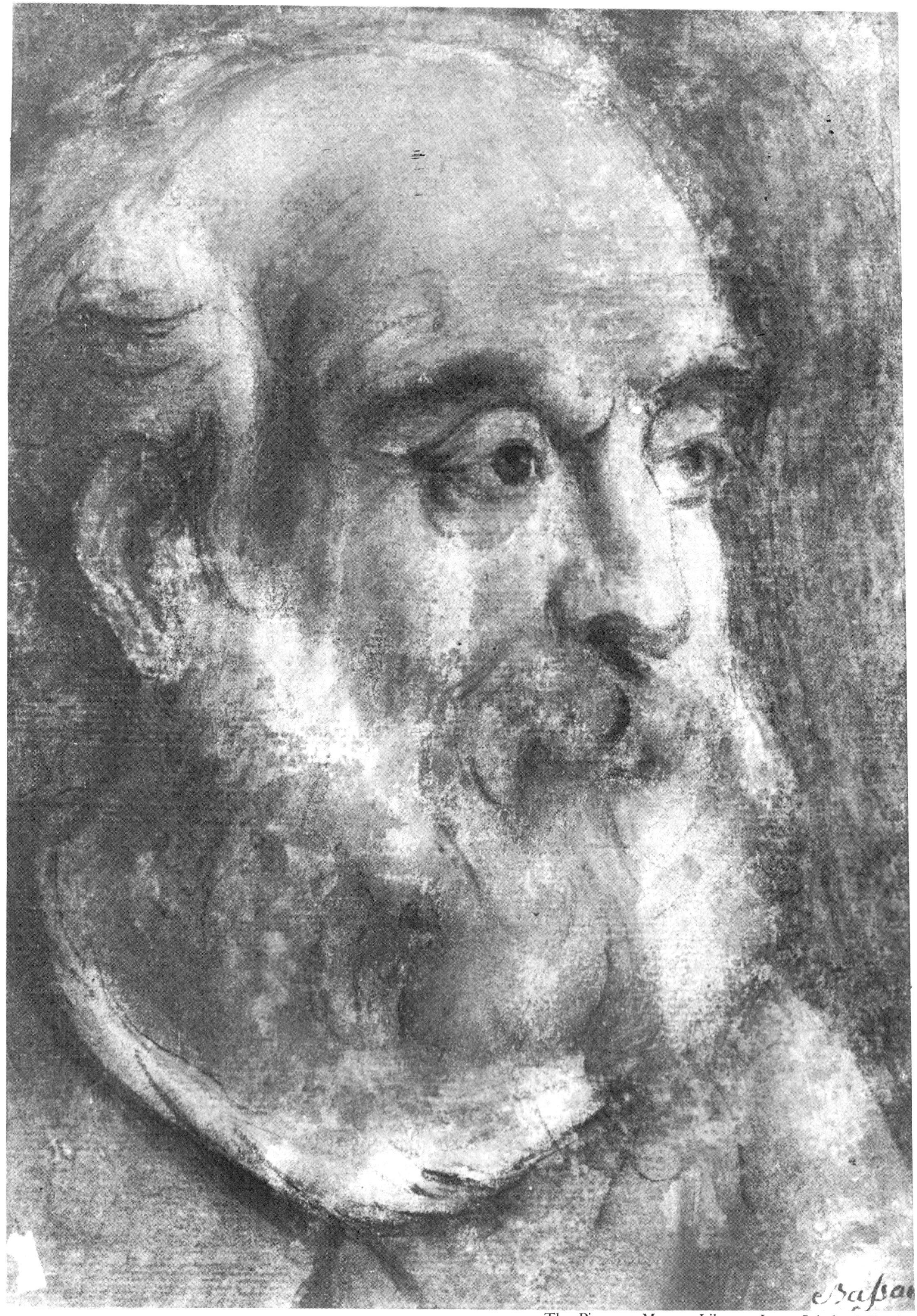

The Pierpont Morgan Library, Janos Scholz Collection

56. *Jacopo da Ponte, called Jacopo Bassano (Bassano, 1517/18–1592).*
HEAD OF A BEARDED OLD MAN.

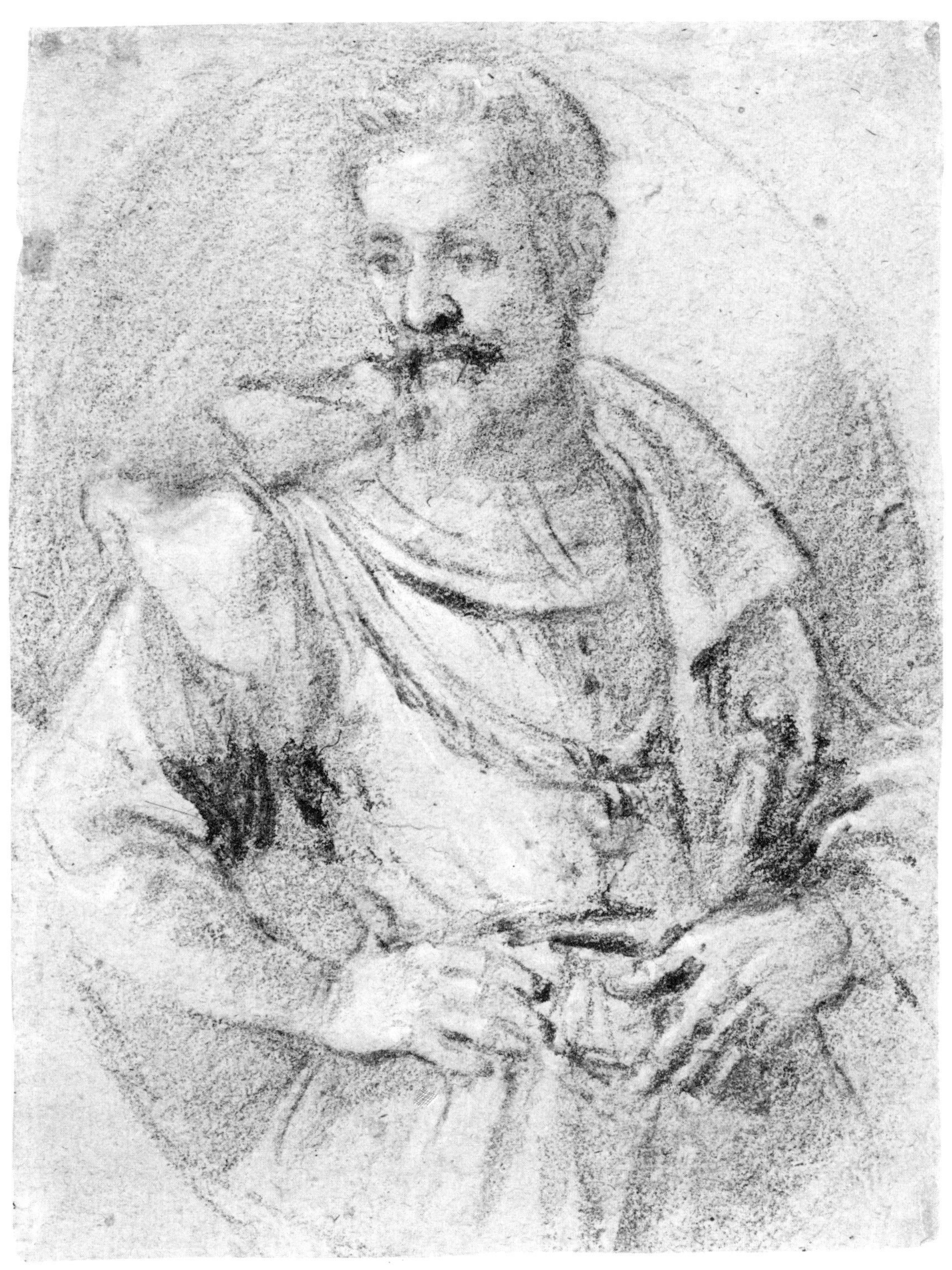

57. *Leandro da Ponte, called Leandro Bassano (Bassano, 1557–1622).*
HALF-LENGTH FIGURE OF A CAVALIER.

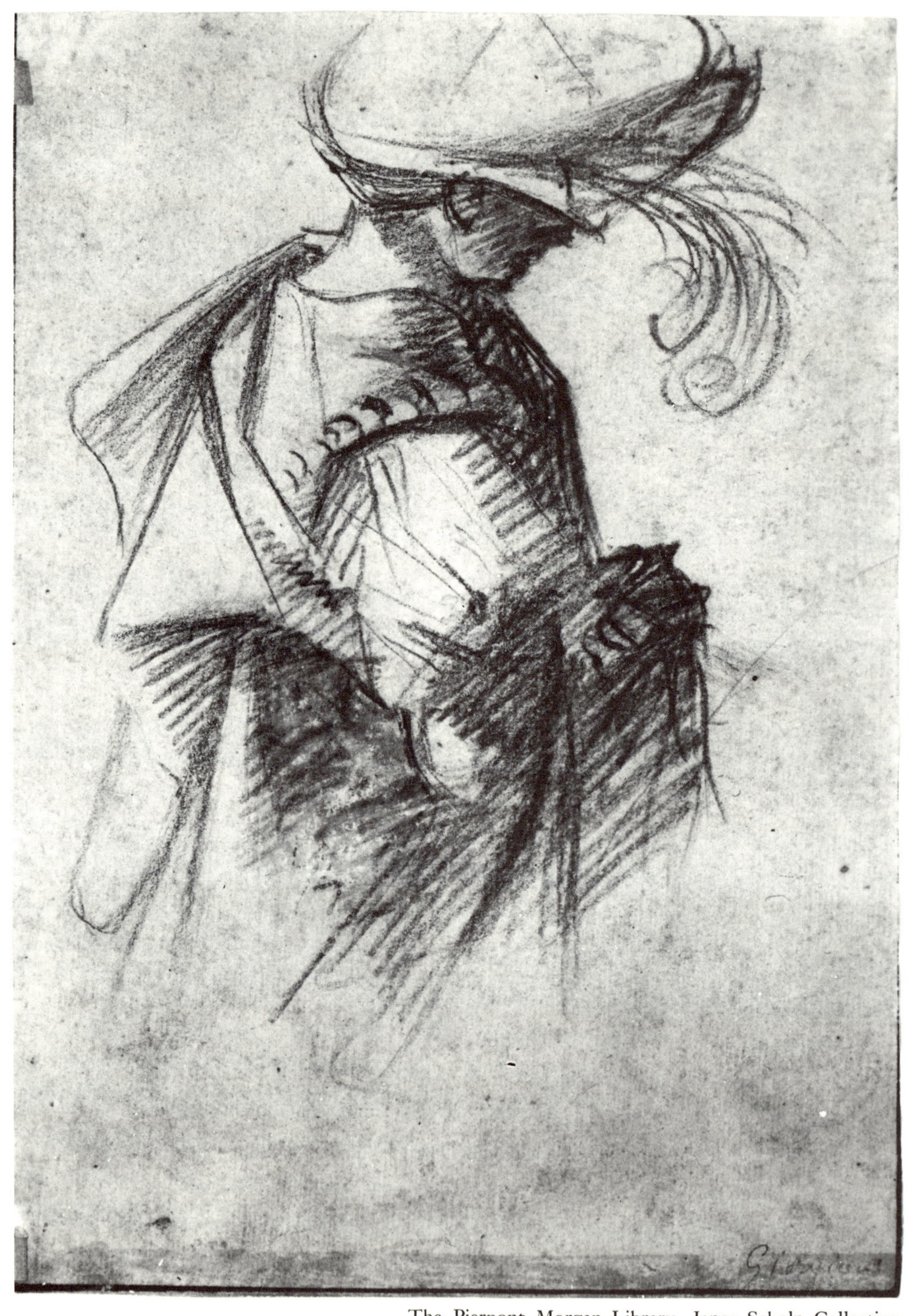

The Pierpont Morgan Library, Janos Scholz Collection

*58. Giovanni Antonio da Pordenone (Venetian, 1484–1539).*

HALF-LENGTH FIGURE OF A MAN WEARING A PLUMED HAT.

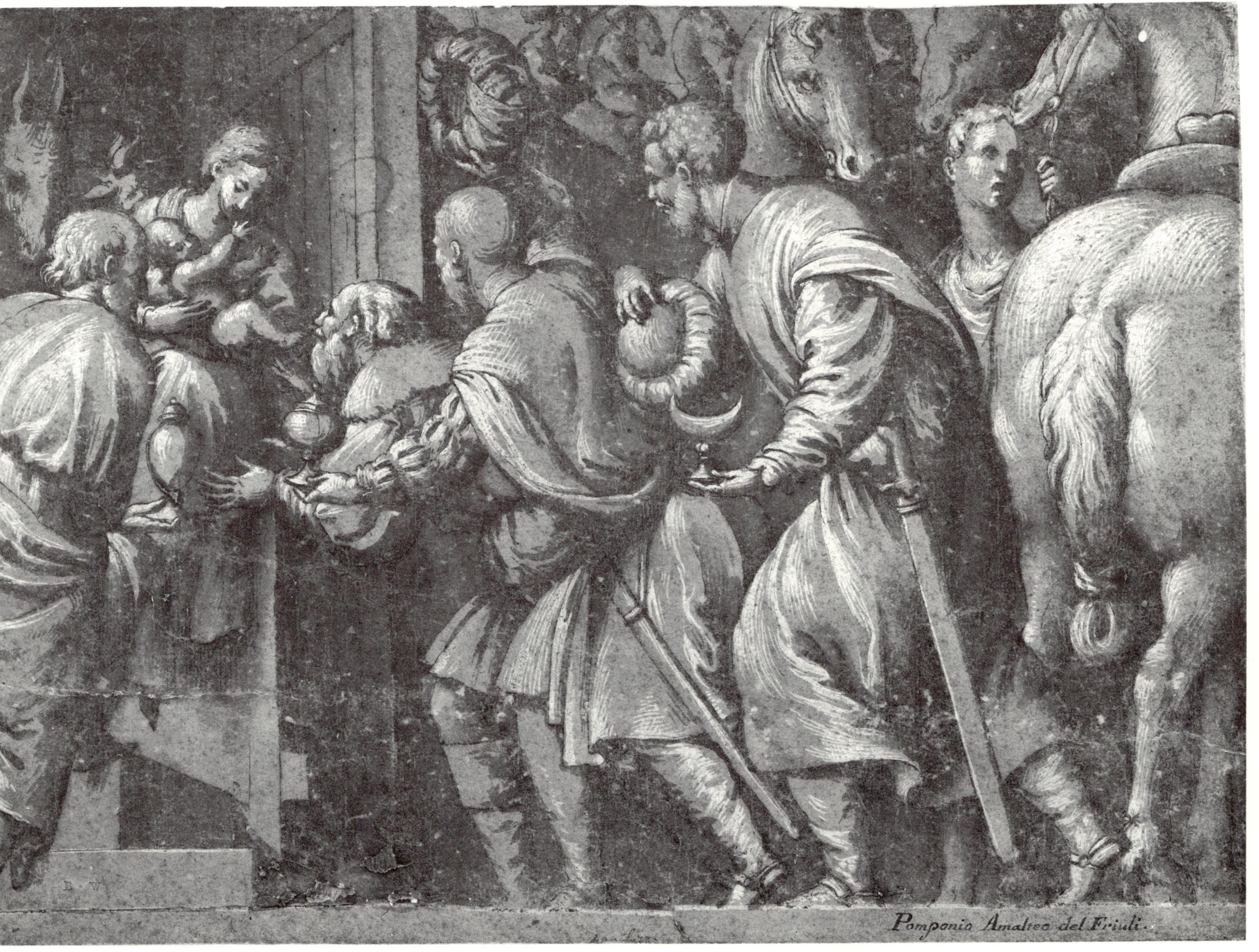


59. *Giovanni Antonio da Pordenone.* THE ADORATION OF THE MAGI.

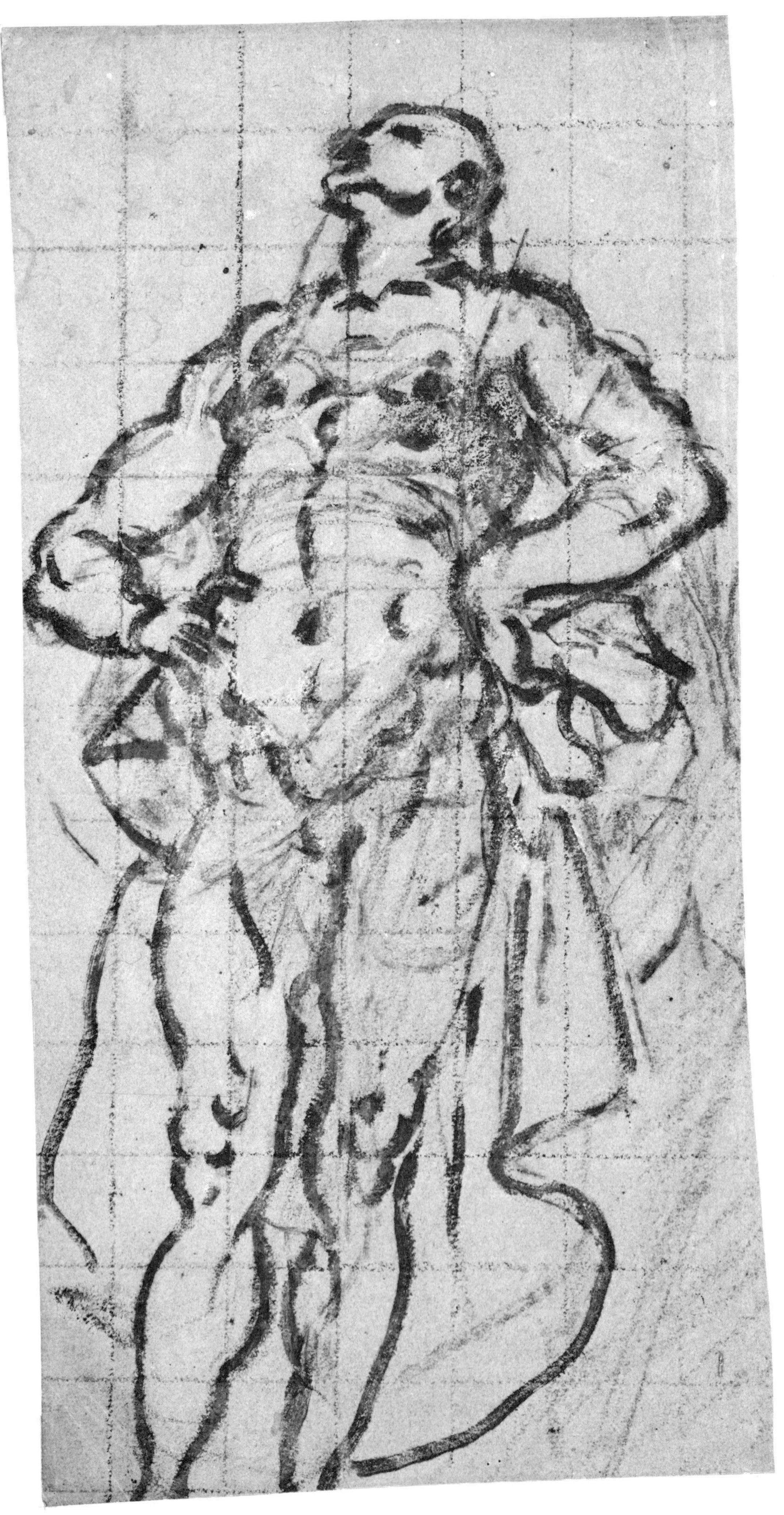

60. *Jacopo Tintoretto (Venice, 1518–1594).* STANDING MAN.

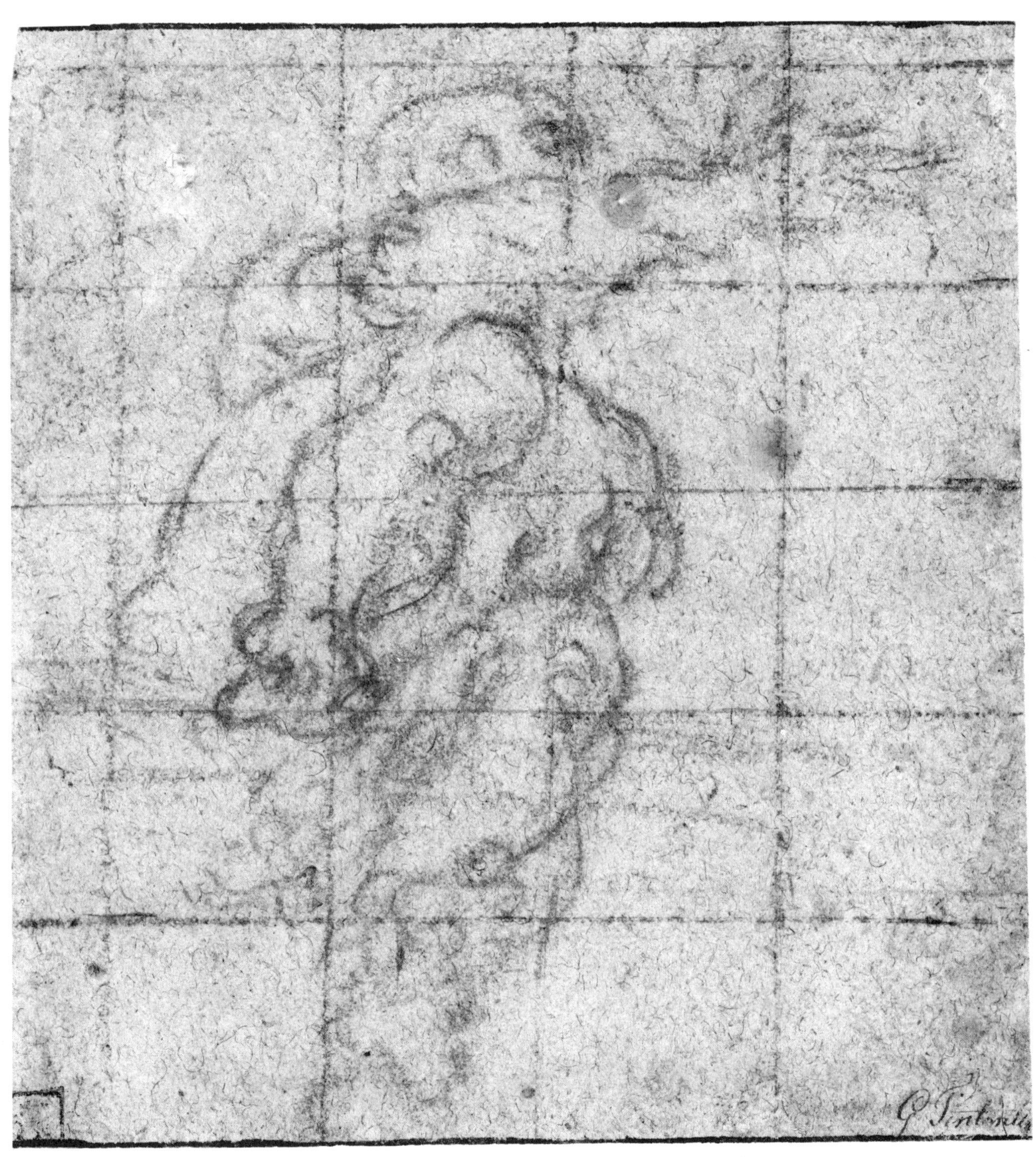

*61. Jacopo Tintoretto.* CROUCHING MAN.

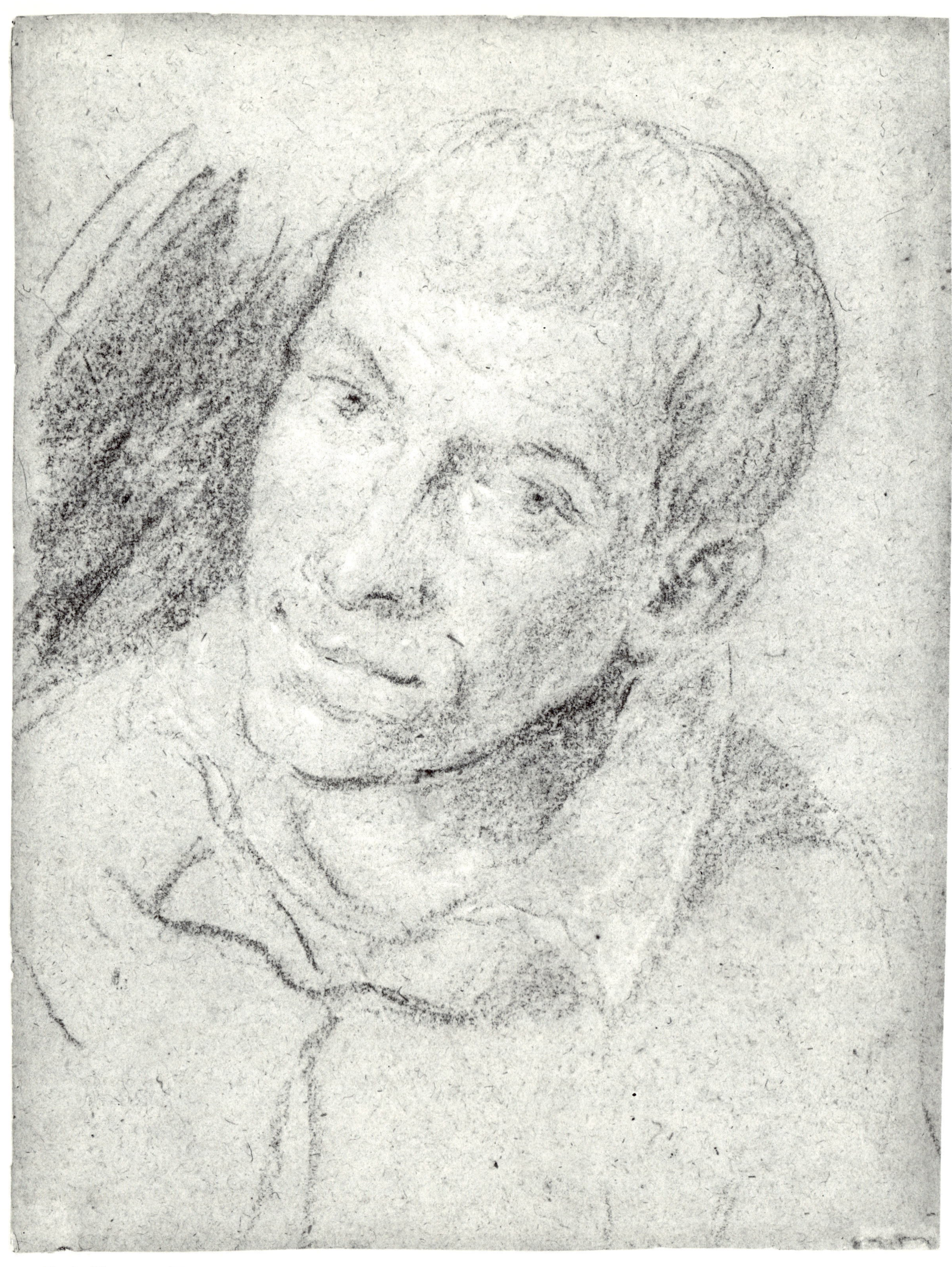

62. *Paolo Veronese (Verona-Venice, 1528–1588).* HEAD OF A MAN.

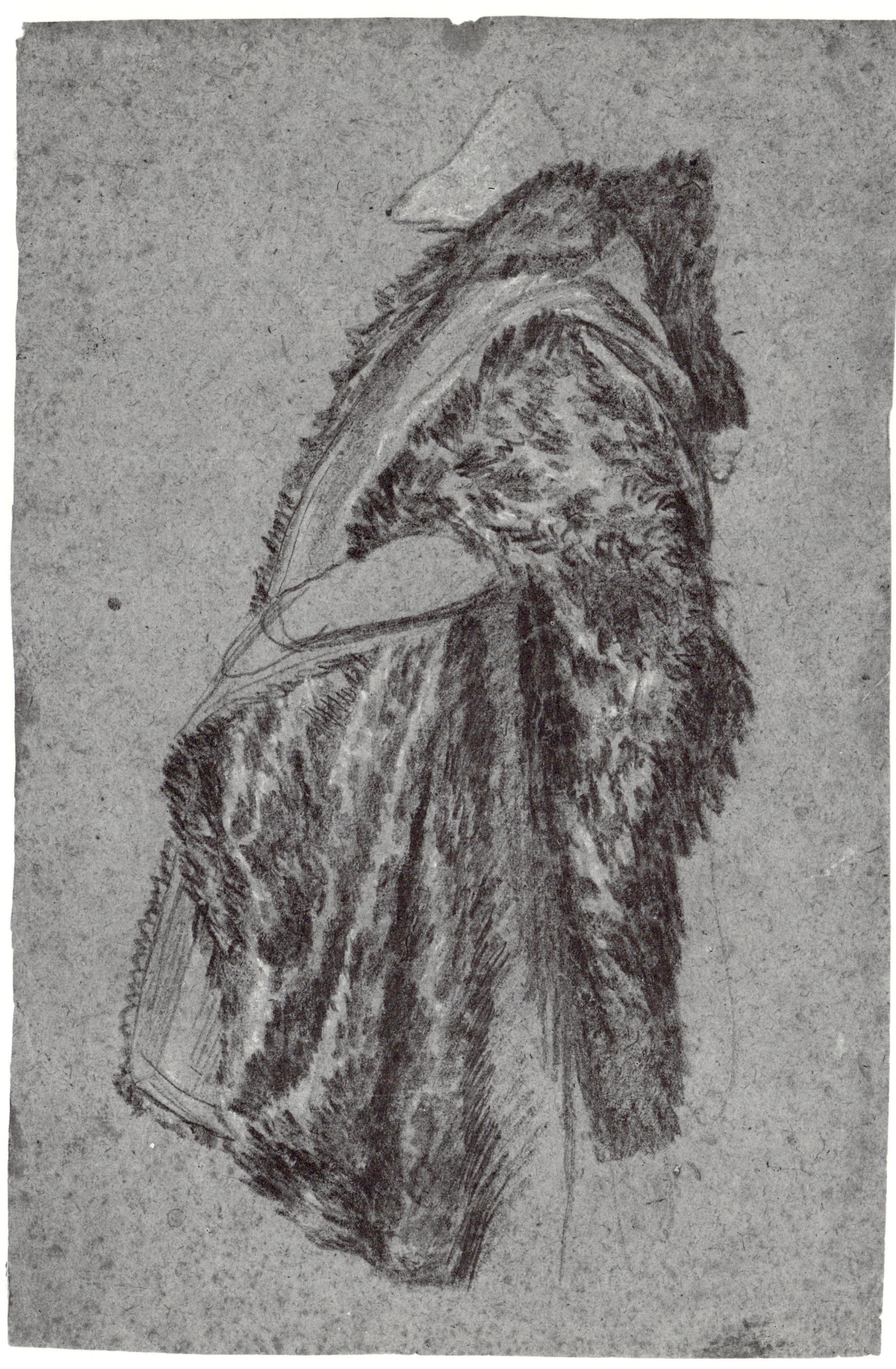

63. *Paolo Veronese.* STUDY OF A FUR CAPE.

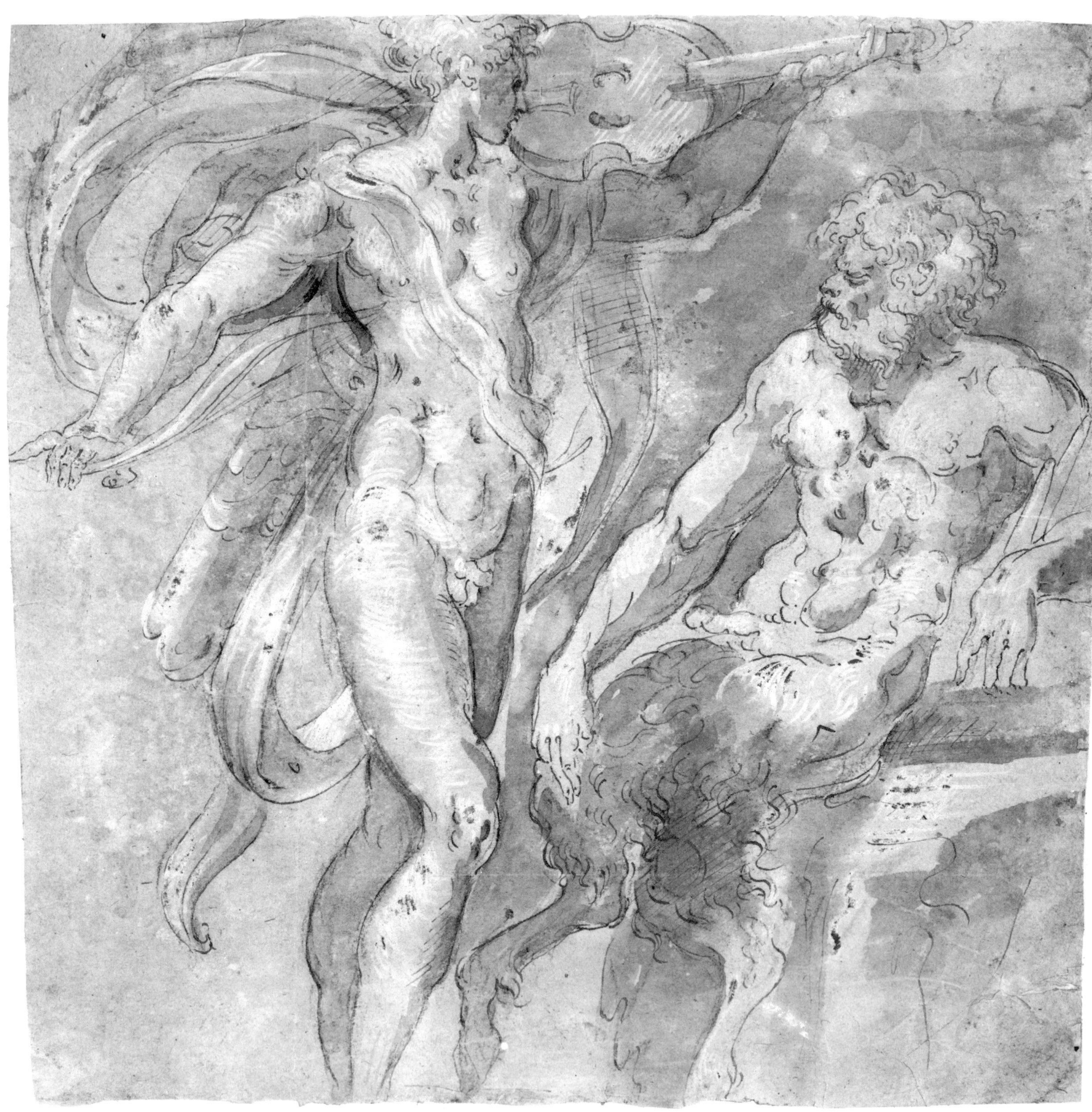

64. *Andrea Meldolla, called Schiavone (Venetian, 1522–1563).* APOLLO AND MARSYAS.

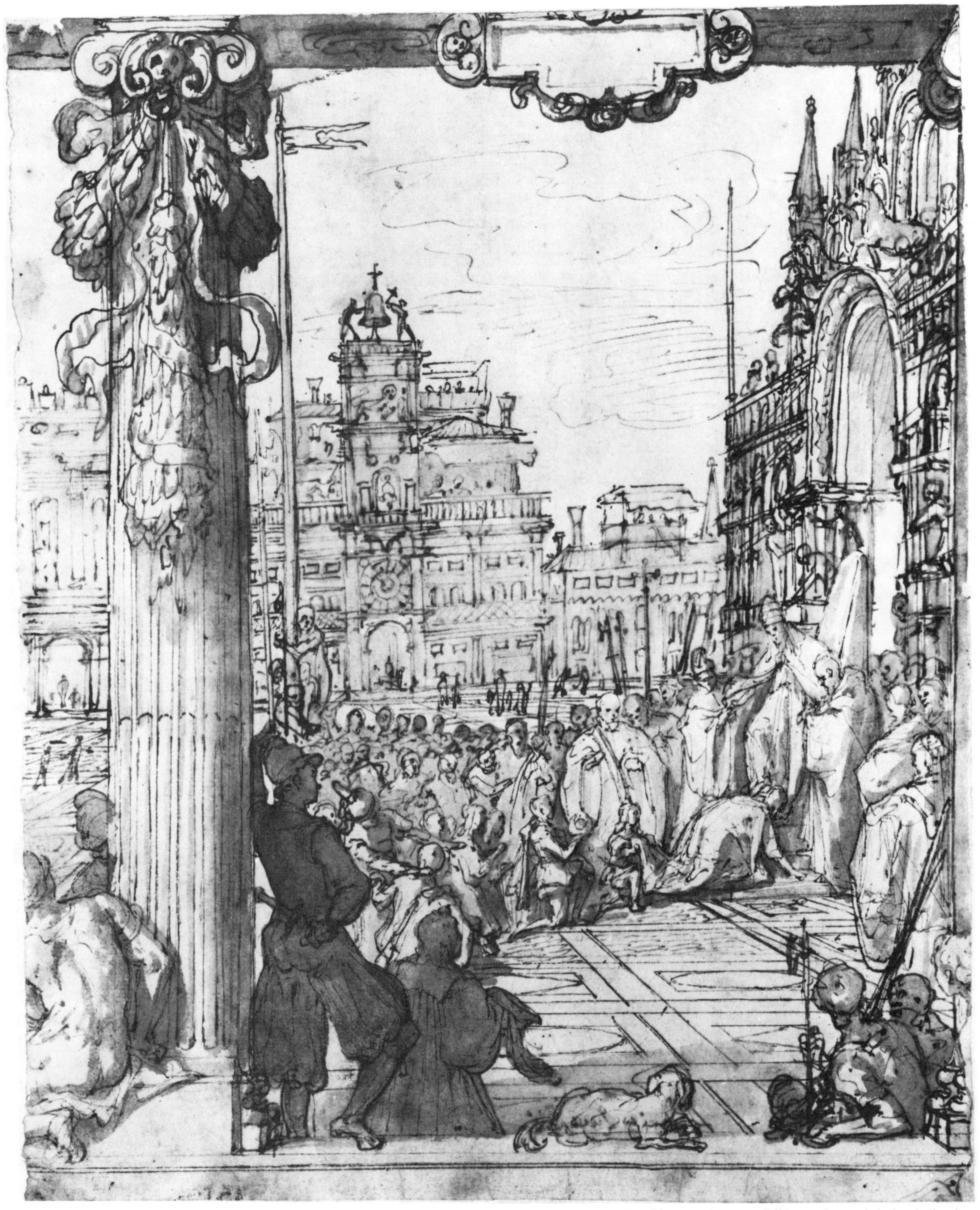

The Pierpont Morgan Library, Janos Scholz Collection

*65. Federigo Zuccaro (Tuscan, 1540/41–1609).*
EMPEROR FREDERIC BARBAROSSA BEFORE POPE ALEXANDER III.

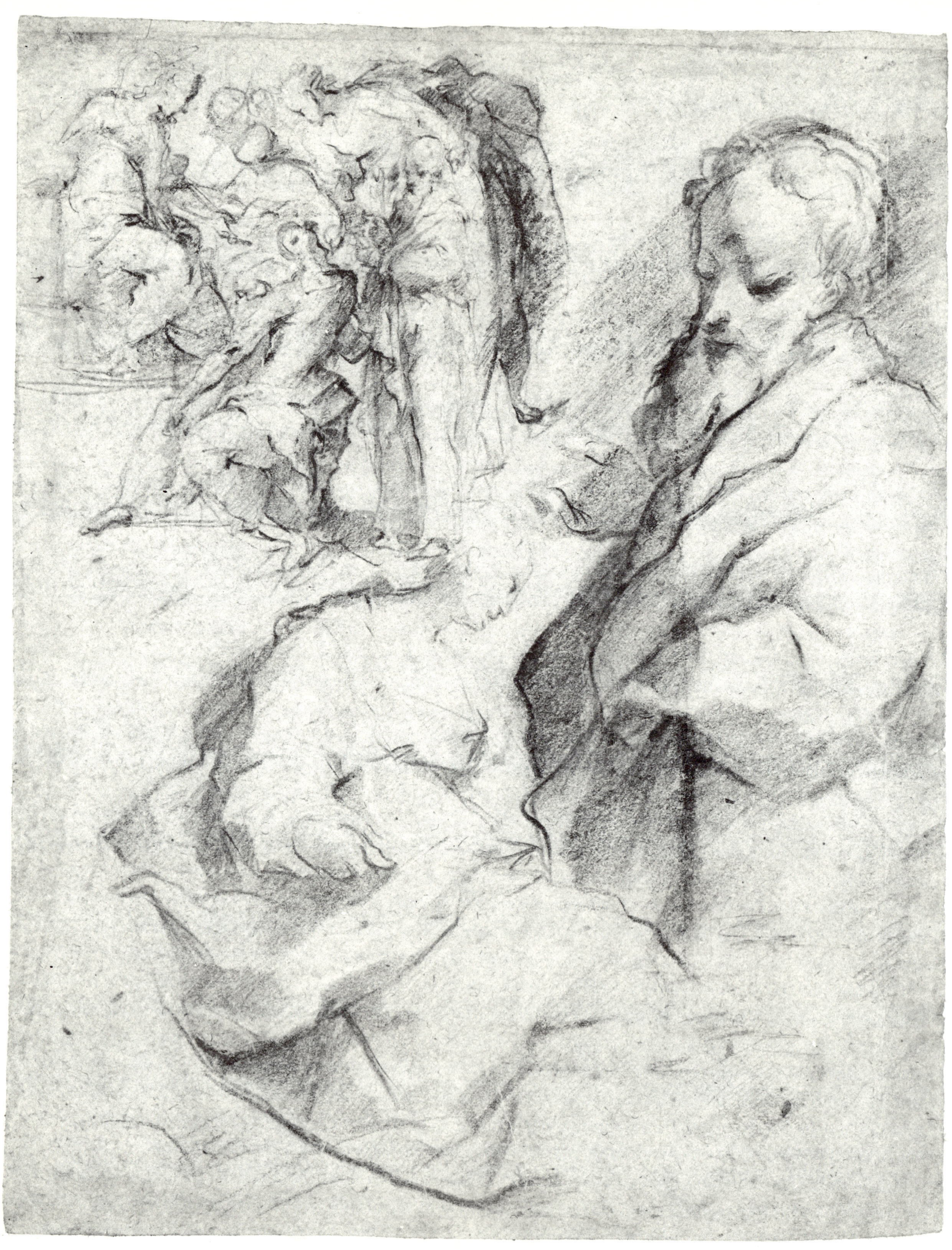

66. *Francesco Vanni (Siena, 1563–1610).* SCENES FROM THE LIFE OF ST. CATHERINE OF SIENA.

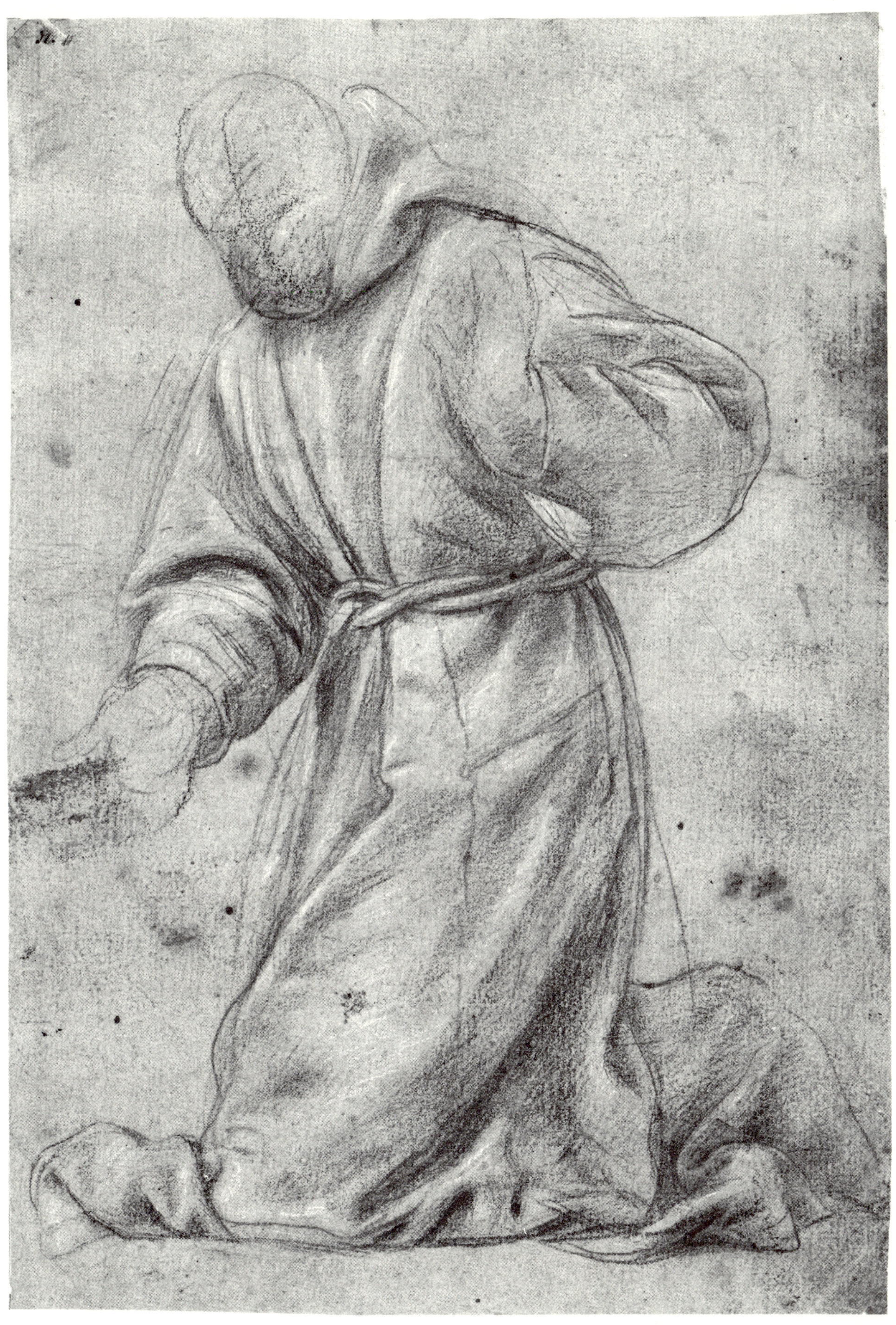

67. *Antonio d'Enrico, called Tanzio da Varallo (Lombard, 1574/81–1635).* KNEELING MONK.

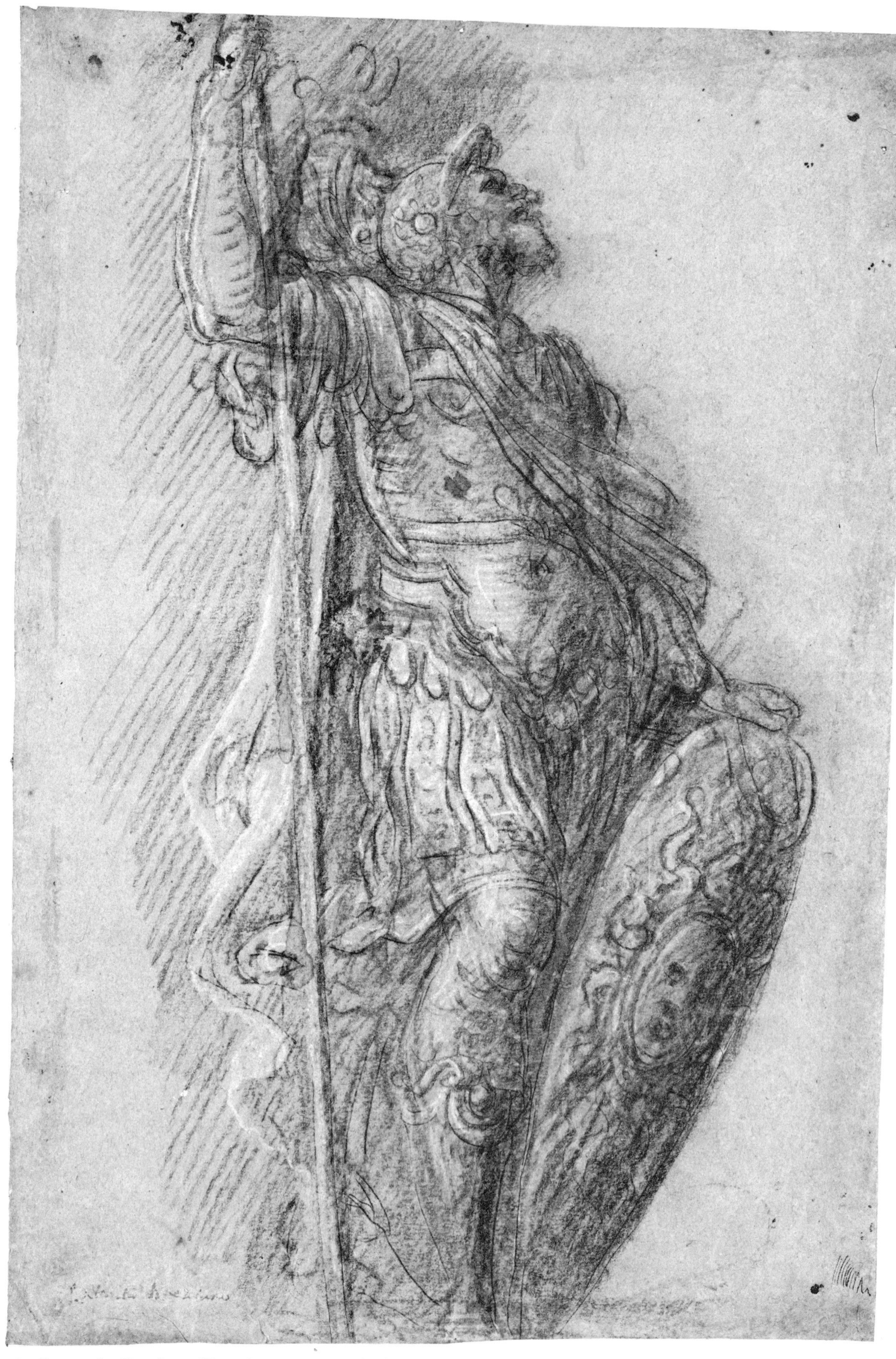

68. *Lattanzio Gambara (Brescian, 1530–1573/74).* JOSHUA, STANDING.

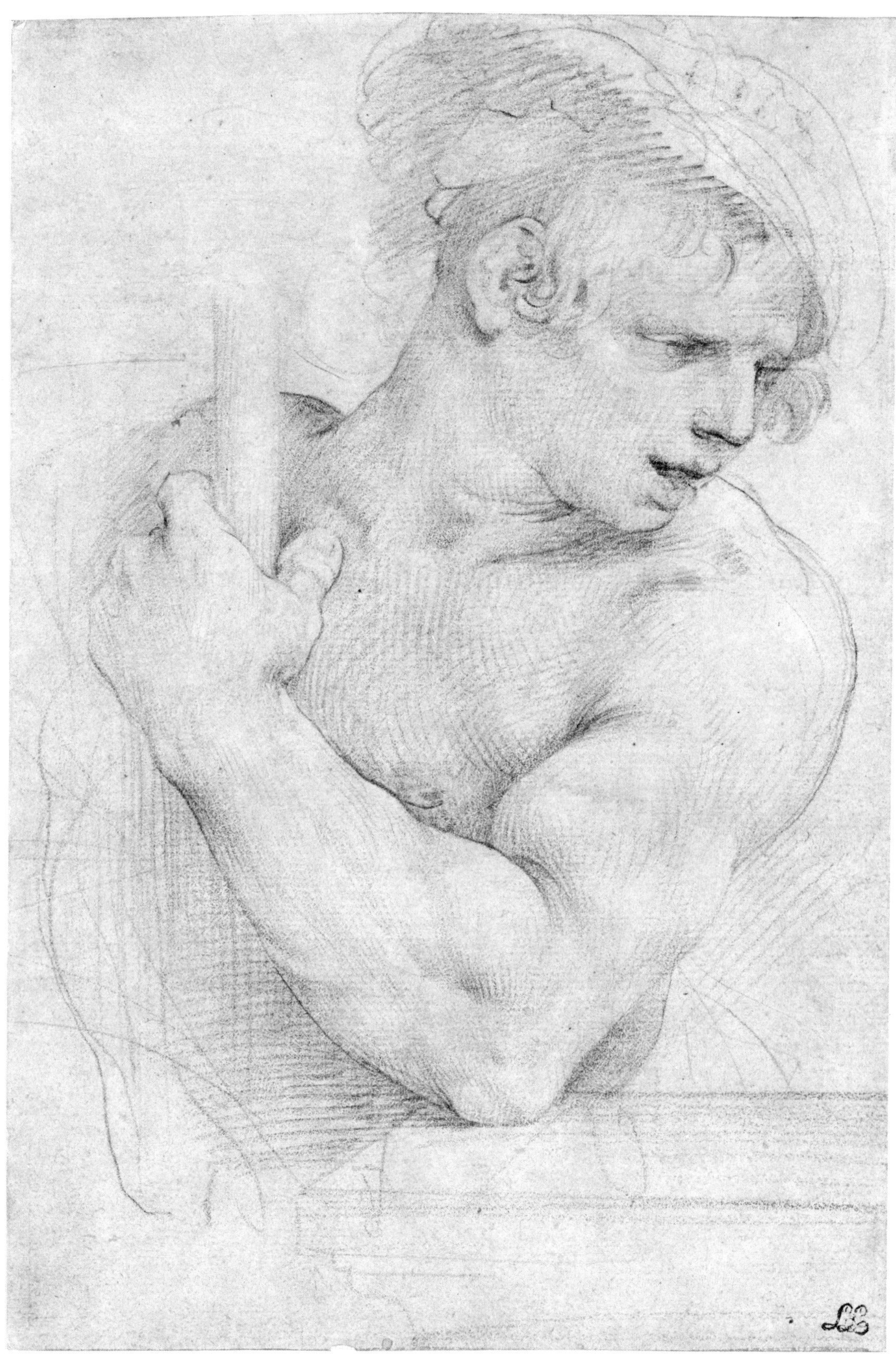

*69. Giuseppe Cesari, called Cavaliere d'Arpino (Roman, 1568–1640).*
HALF-LENGTH FIGURE OF A MAN HOLDING A BANNER.

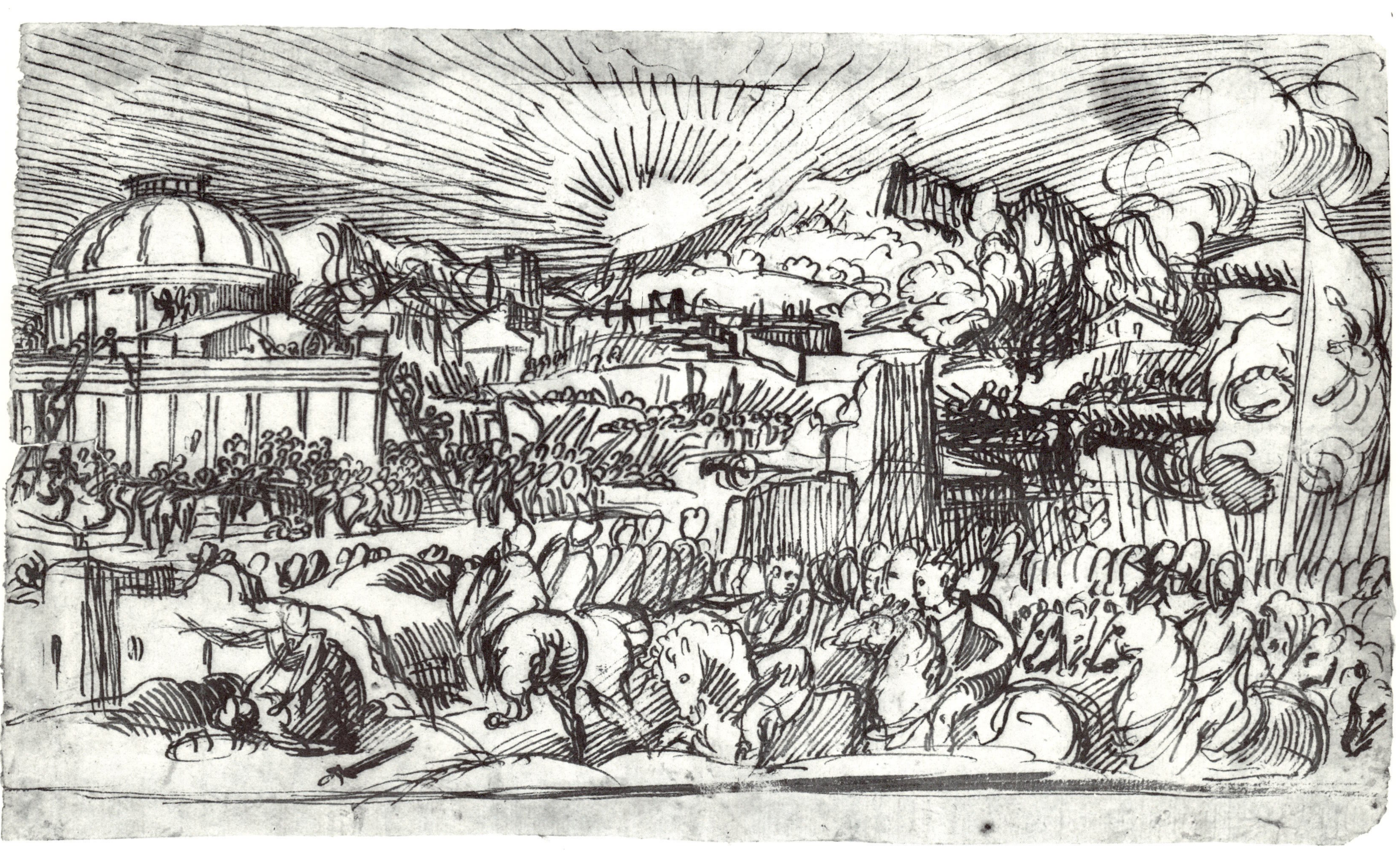

70. *Paolo Farinato (Veronese, 1524–1606).* SIEGE OF A TOWN.

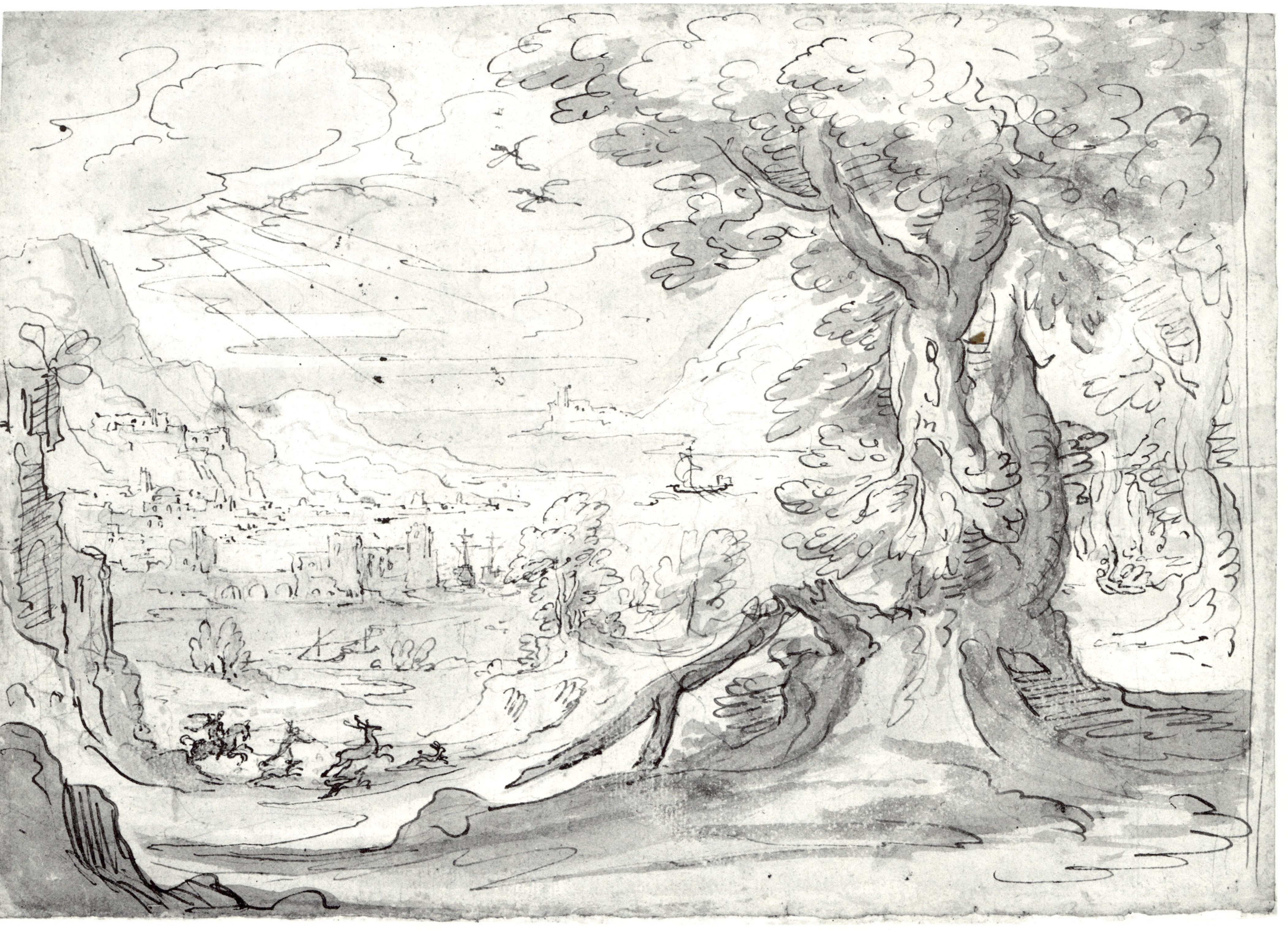

71. *Lodewyck Toeput, called Pozzoserrato (Antwerp-Treviso, about 1550–1603/05).* LANDSCAPE WITH A STAG HUNT.

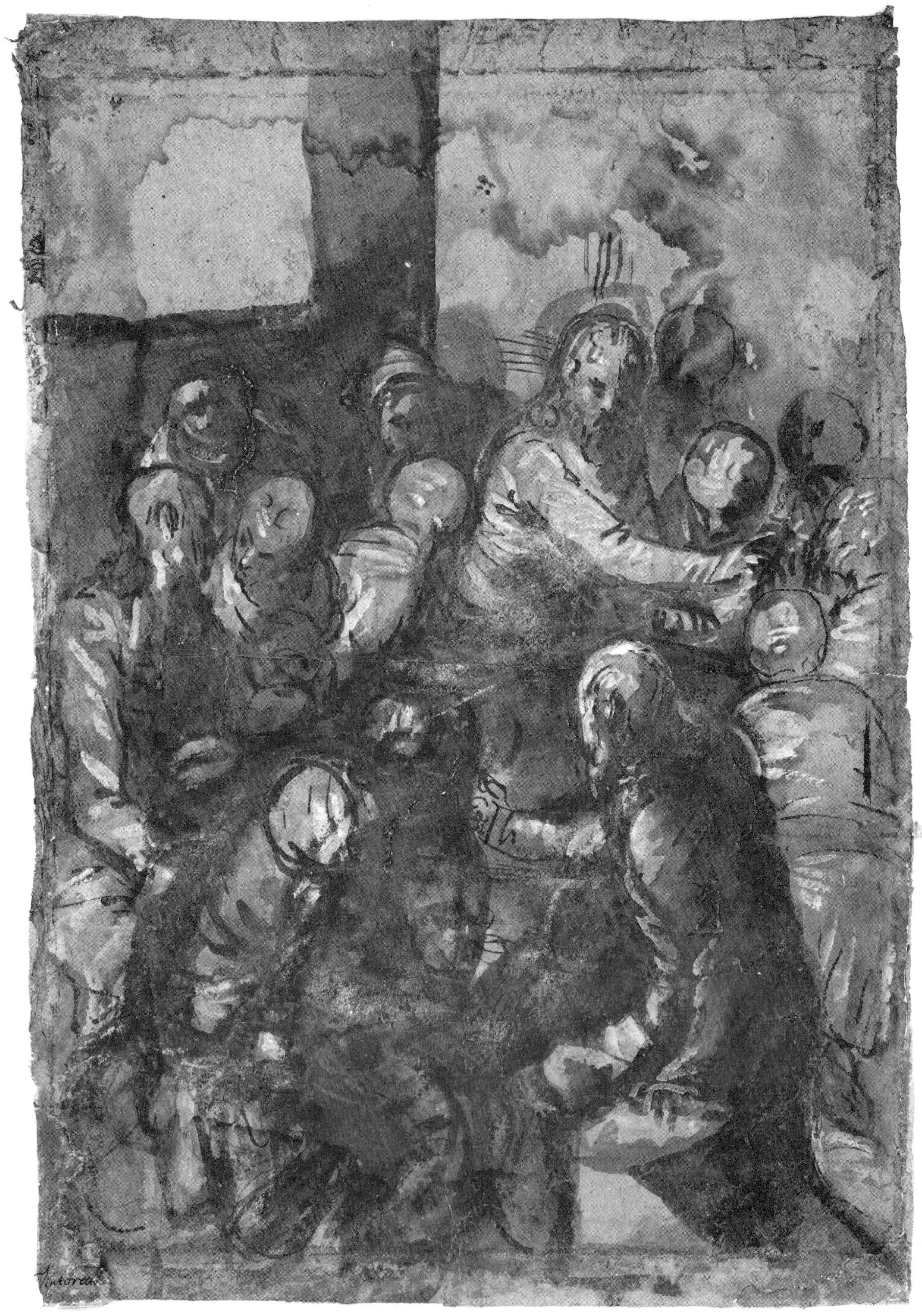

72. *Jacopo Negretti, called Palma Giovane (Venice, 1544–1628).* CHRIST AND HIS DISCIPLES.

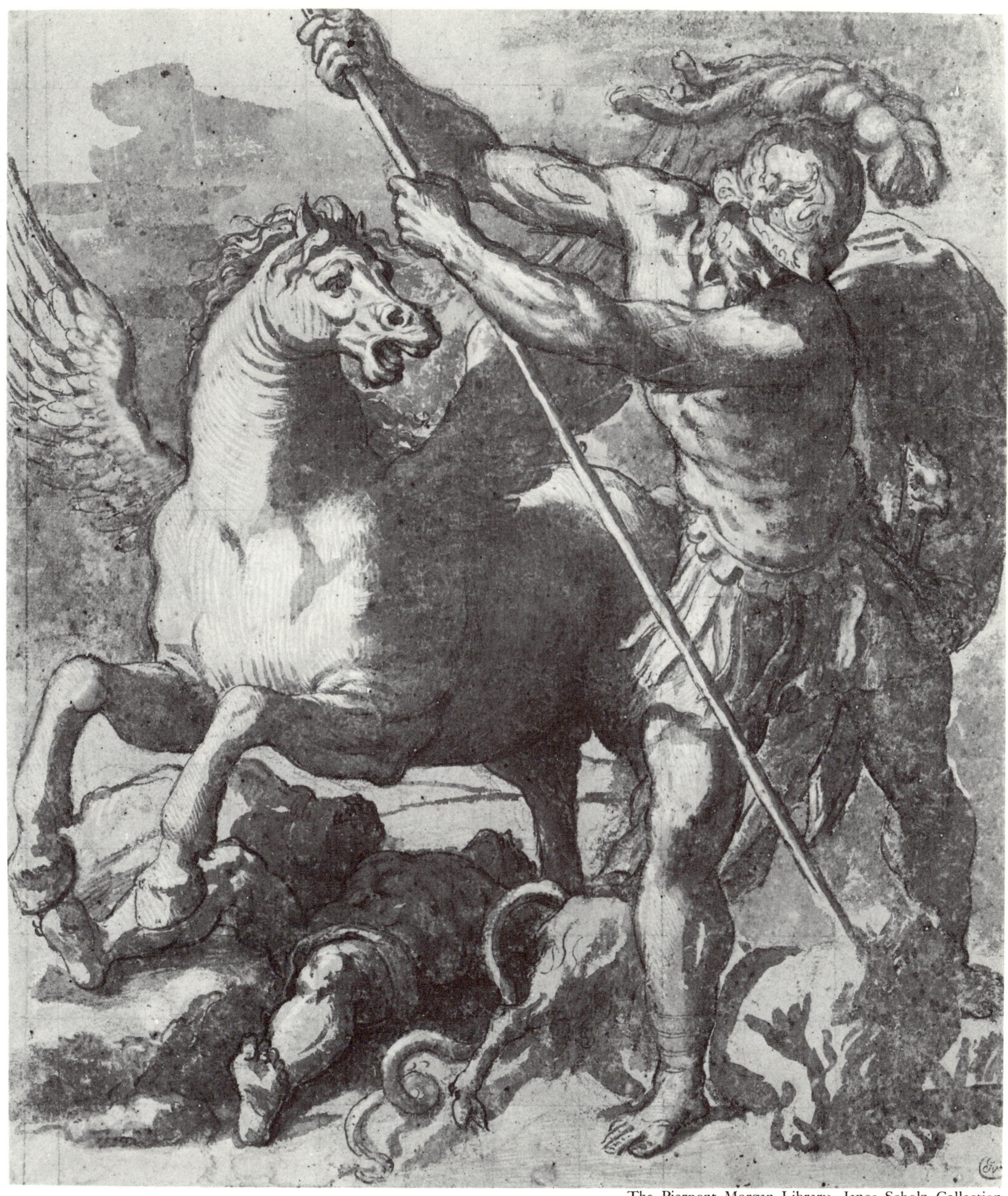

The Pierpont Morgan Library, Janos Scholz Collection

73. *Giuseppe Porta, called Salviati (Venetian, about 1520–1575).*
BELLEROPHON KILLING THE CHIMERA.

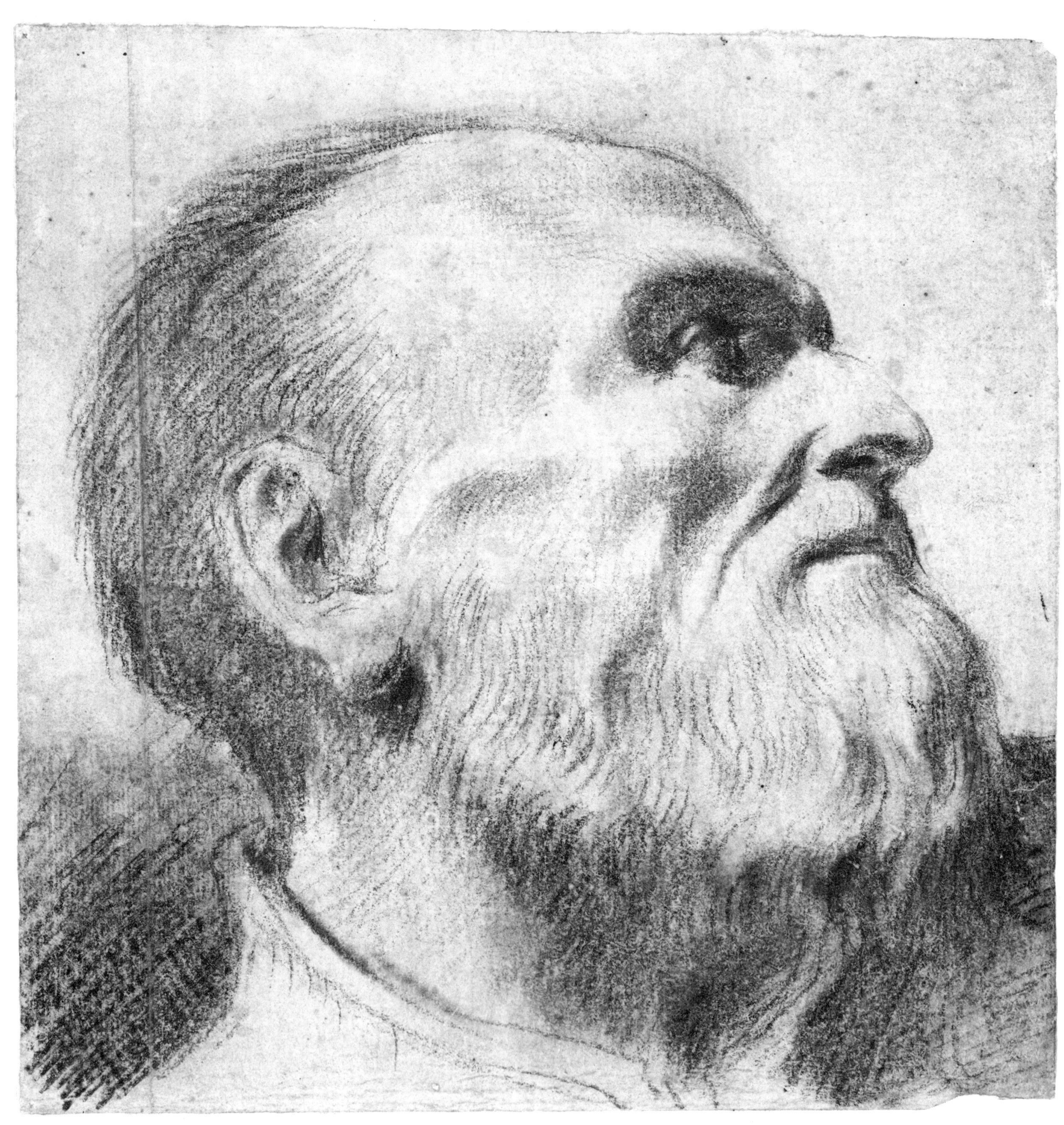

74. *Pietro Faccini (Bolognese, 1562–1602).* HEAD OF S. FILIPPO NERI.

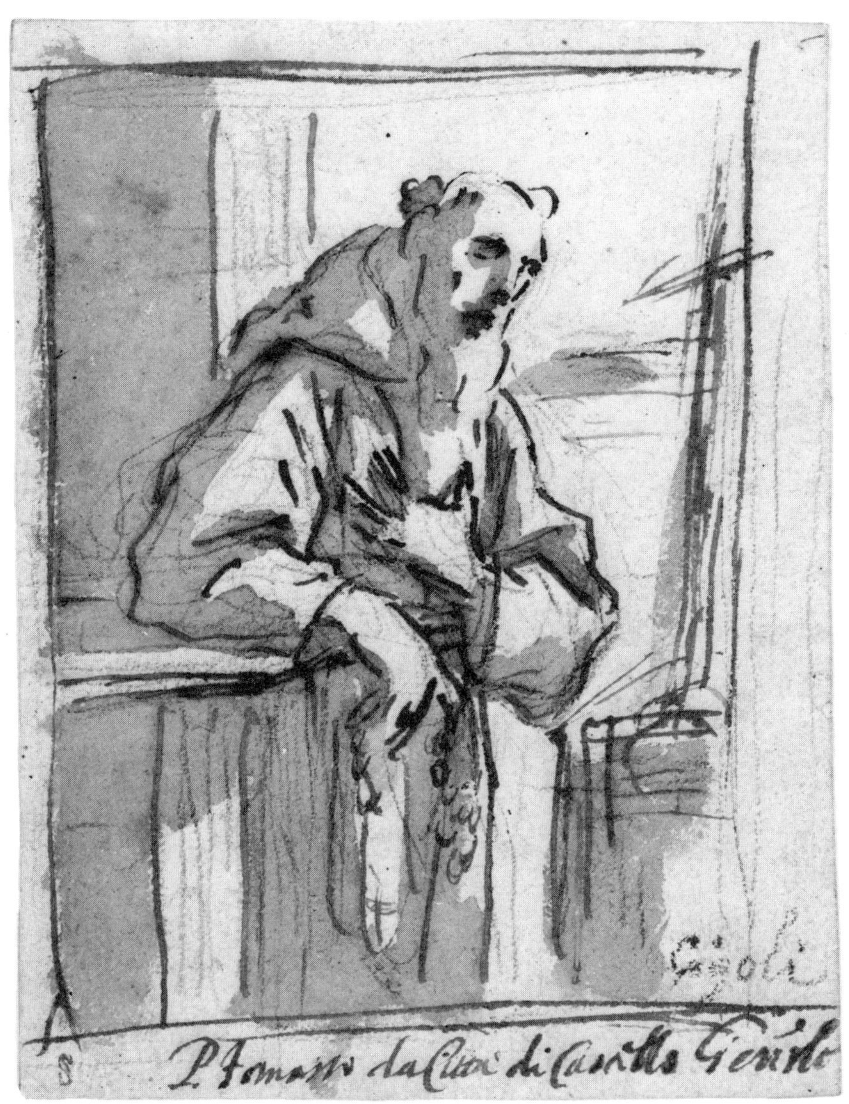


75. *Lodovico Cardi, called Il Cigoli (Florentine, 1559–1613).*
MONK IN PRAYER BEFORE THE CROSS.

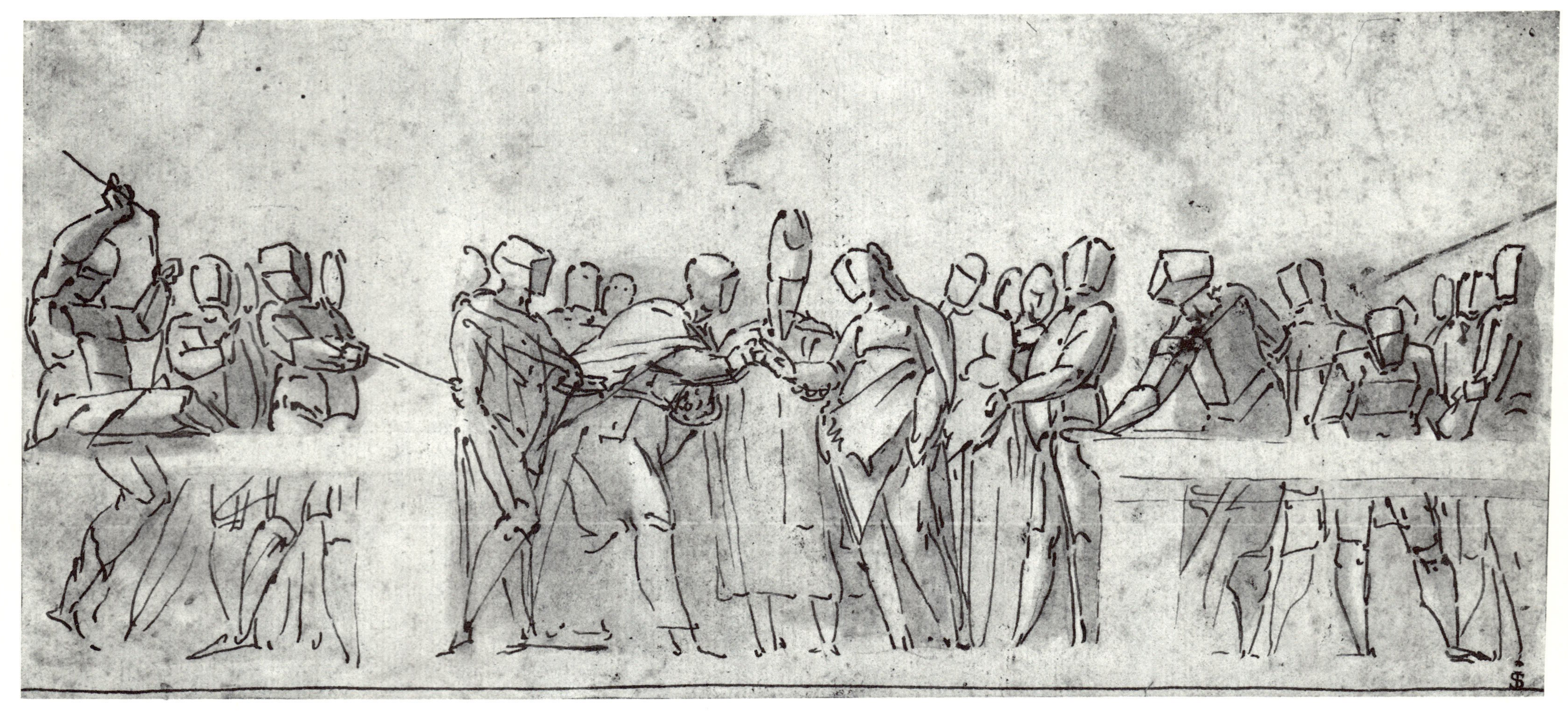

76. *Luca Cambiaso (Genoese, 1527–1585).* MARRIAGE OF THE VIRGIN.

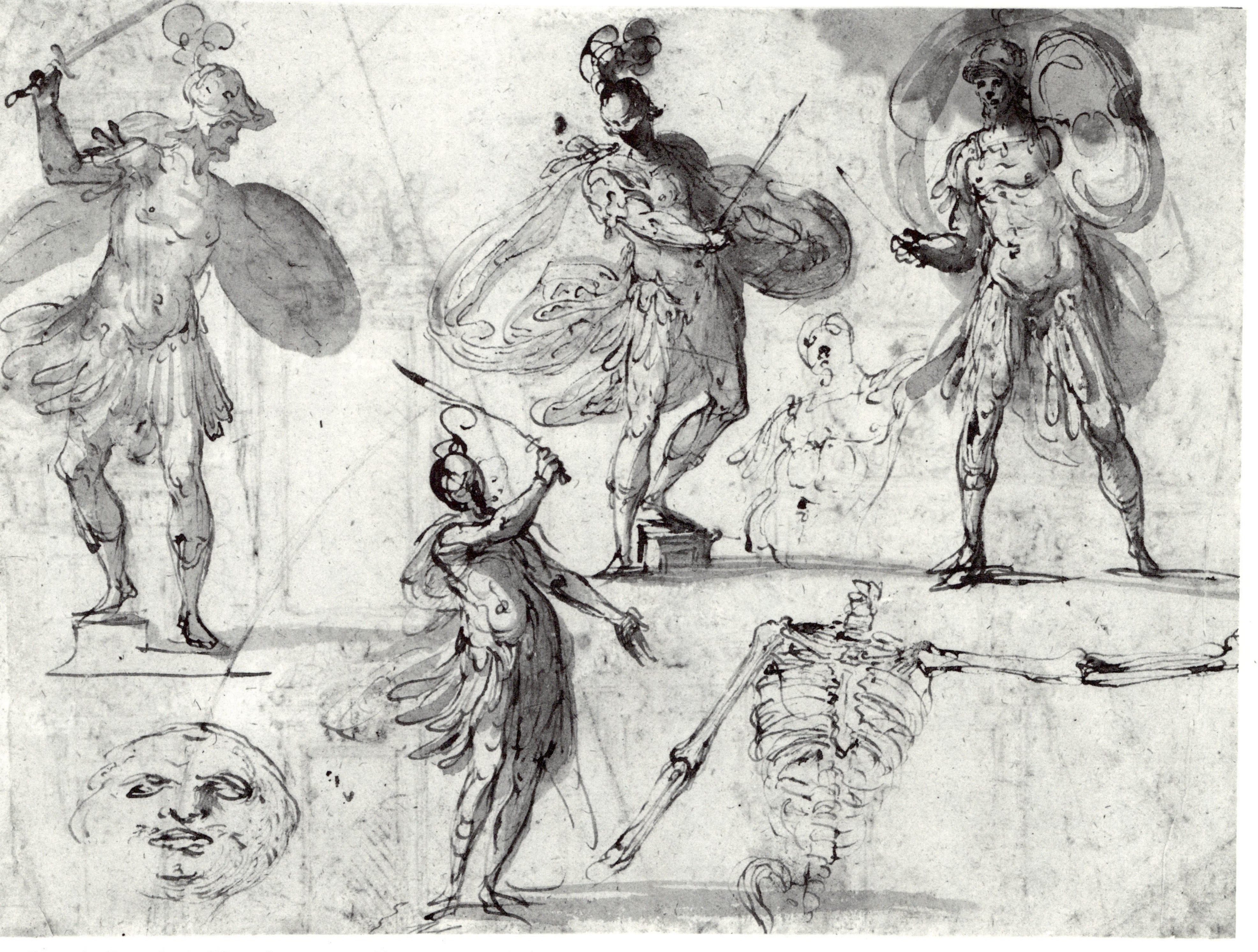

77. *Bernardo Buontalenti (Florentine, 1536–1608).* SKETCHES FOR THEATRICAL COSTUMES.

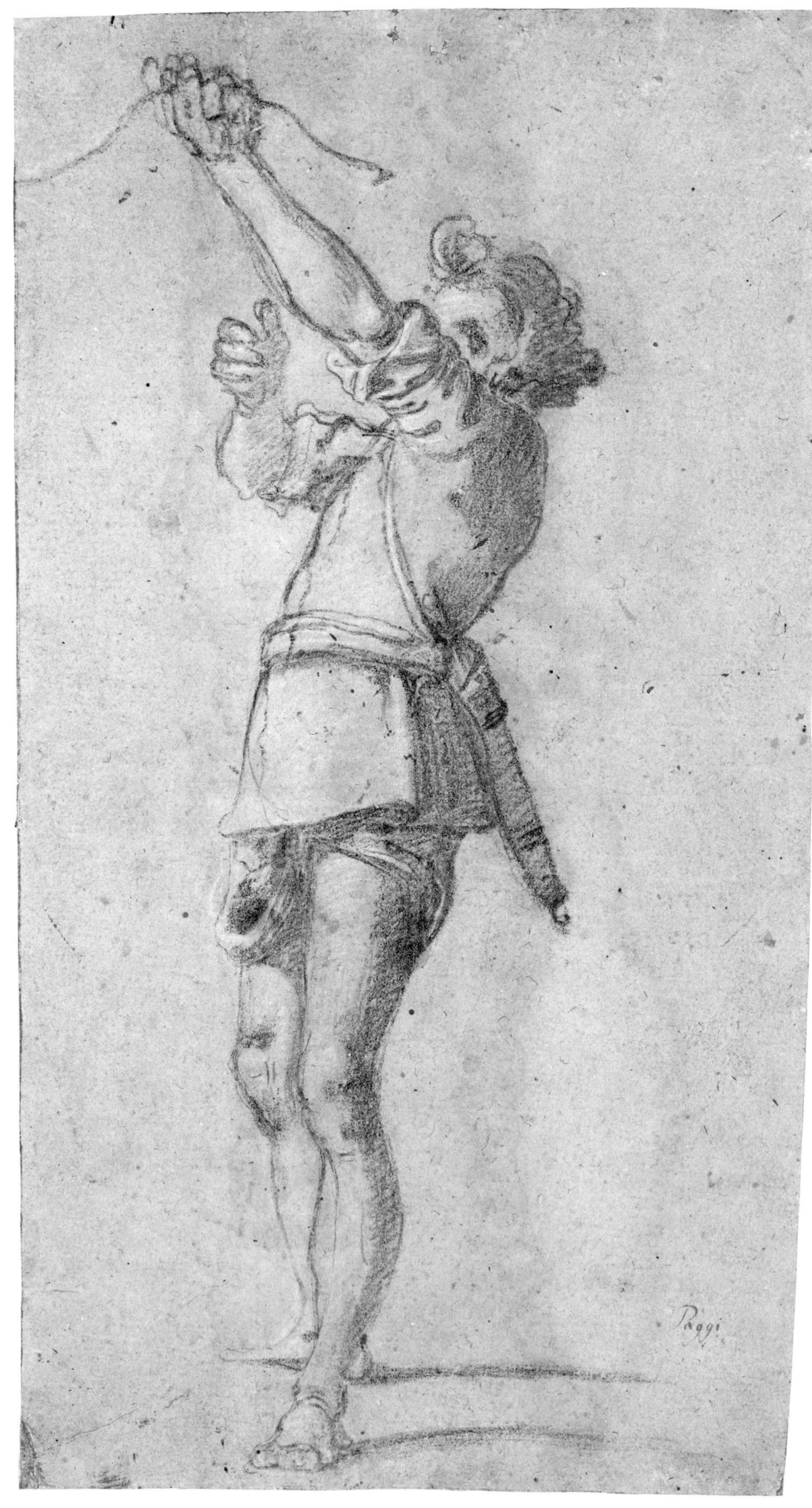


78. *Giovanni Battista Paggi (Genoese, 1554–1627).* AN ARCHER.

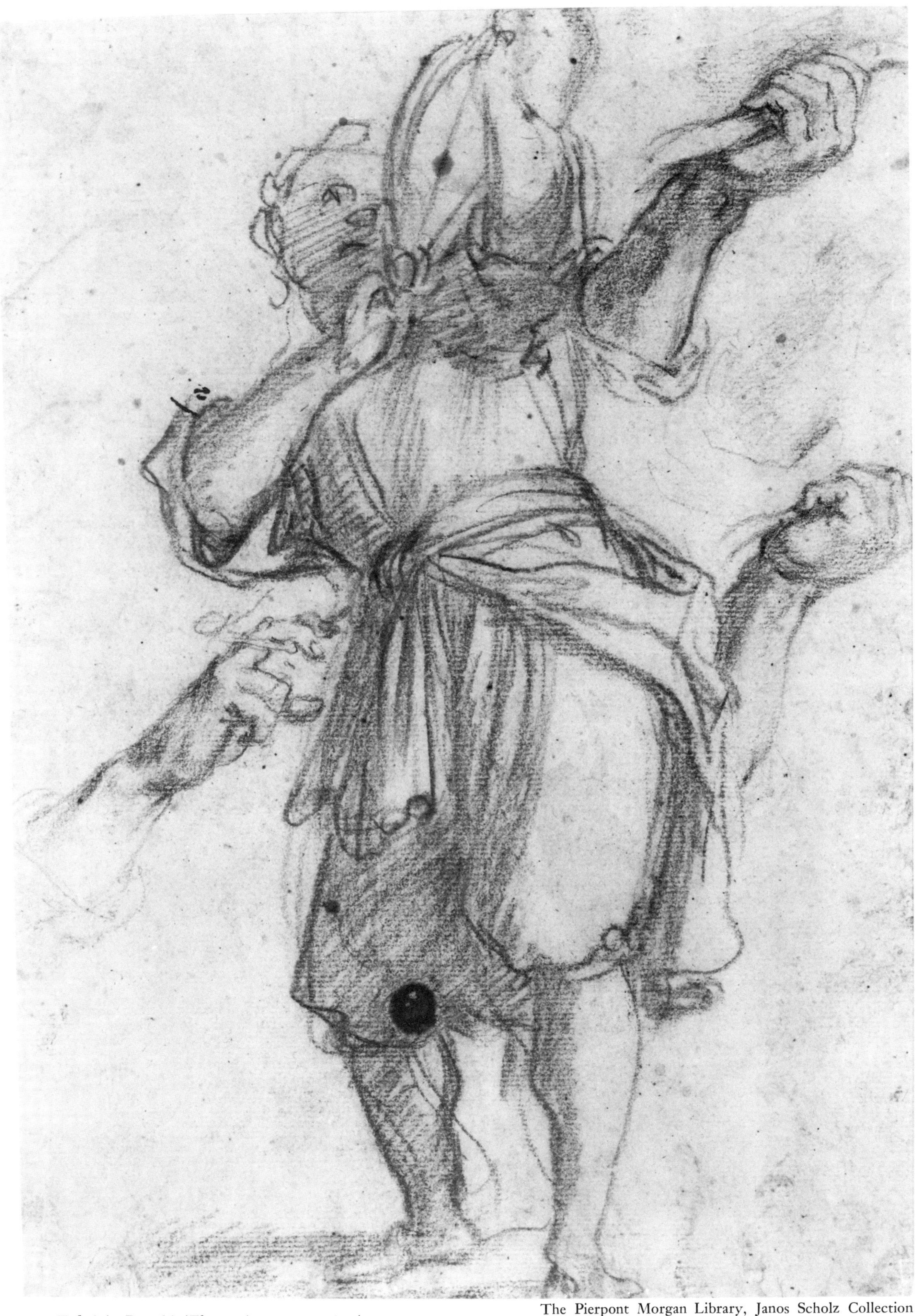

The Pierpont Morgan Library, Janos Scholz Collection

79. *Fabrizio Boschi (Florentine, 1570–1642).* AN ARCHER.

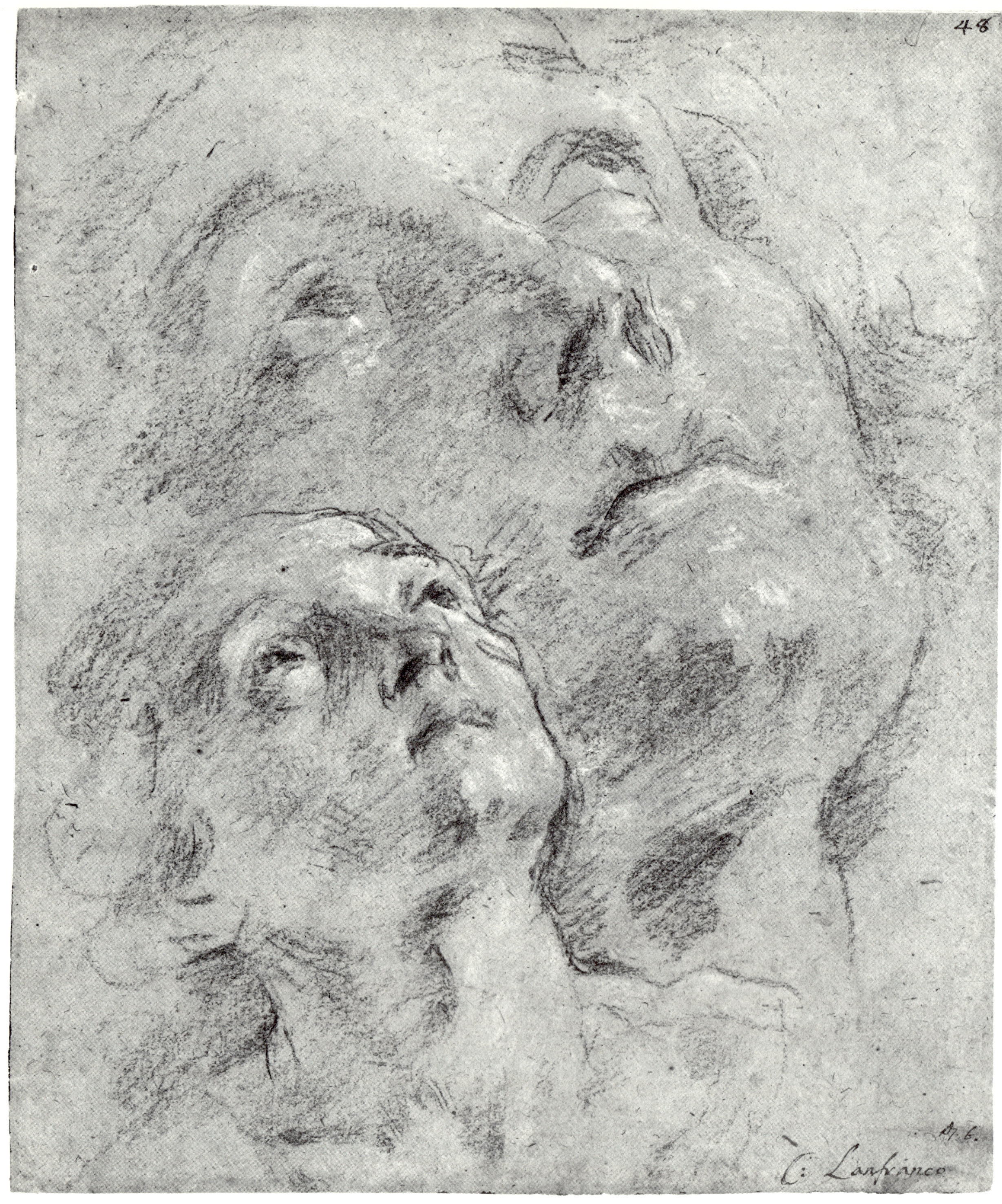

80. *Giovanni Lanfranco (Parma-Rome, 1582–1647).* STUDIES FOR THE HEAD OF A YOUTH.

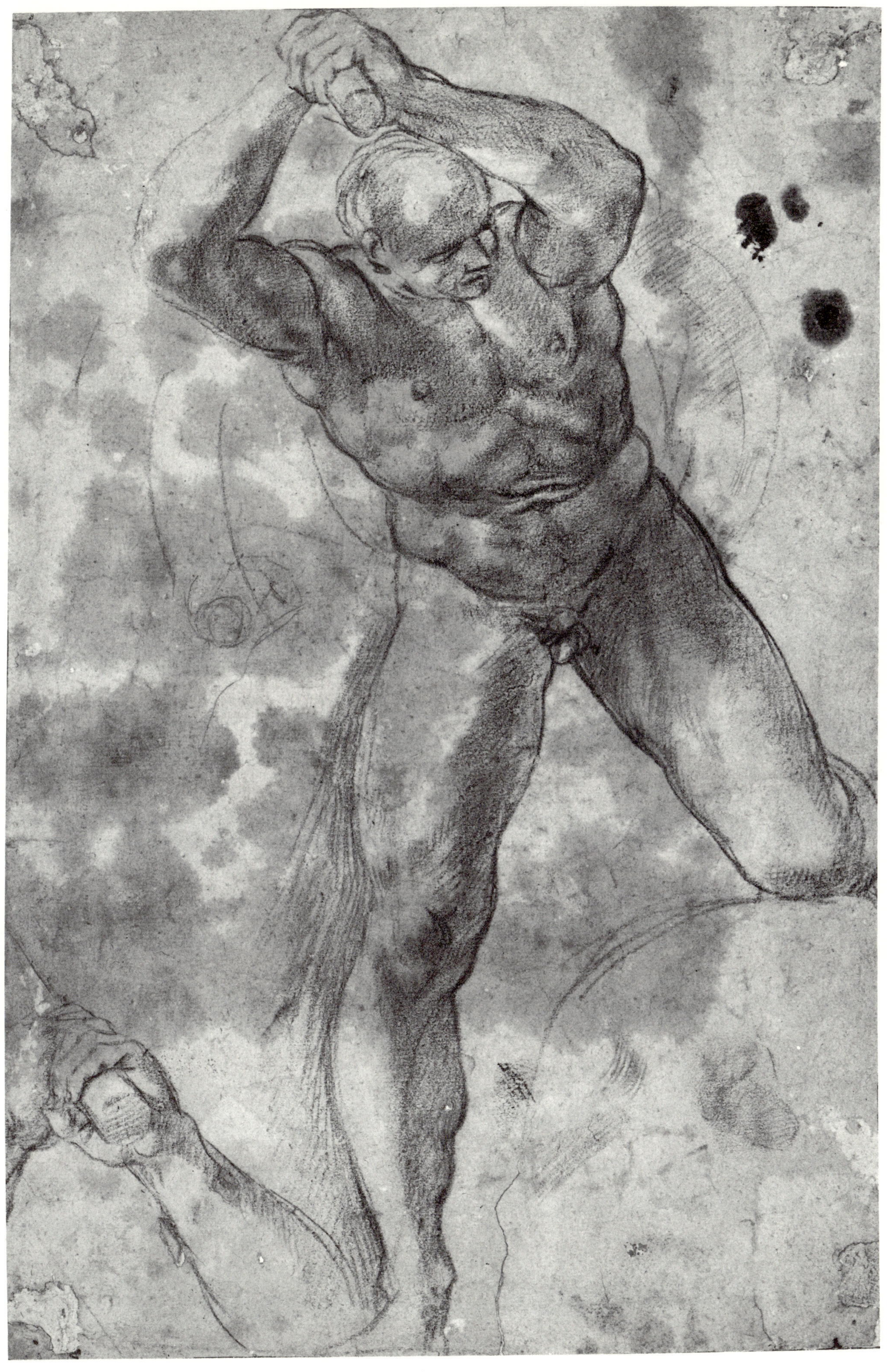

81. *Annibale Carracci (Bolognese, 1560–1609).* NUDE MAN STRIKING WITH A CLUB.

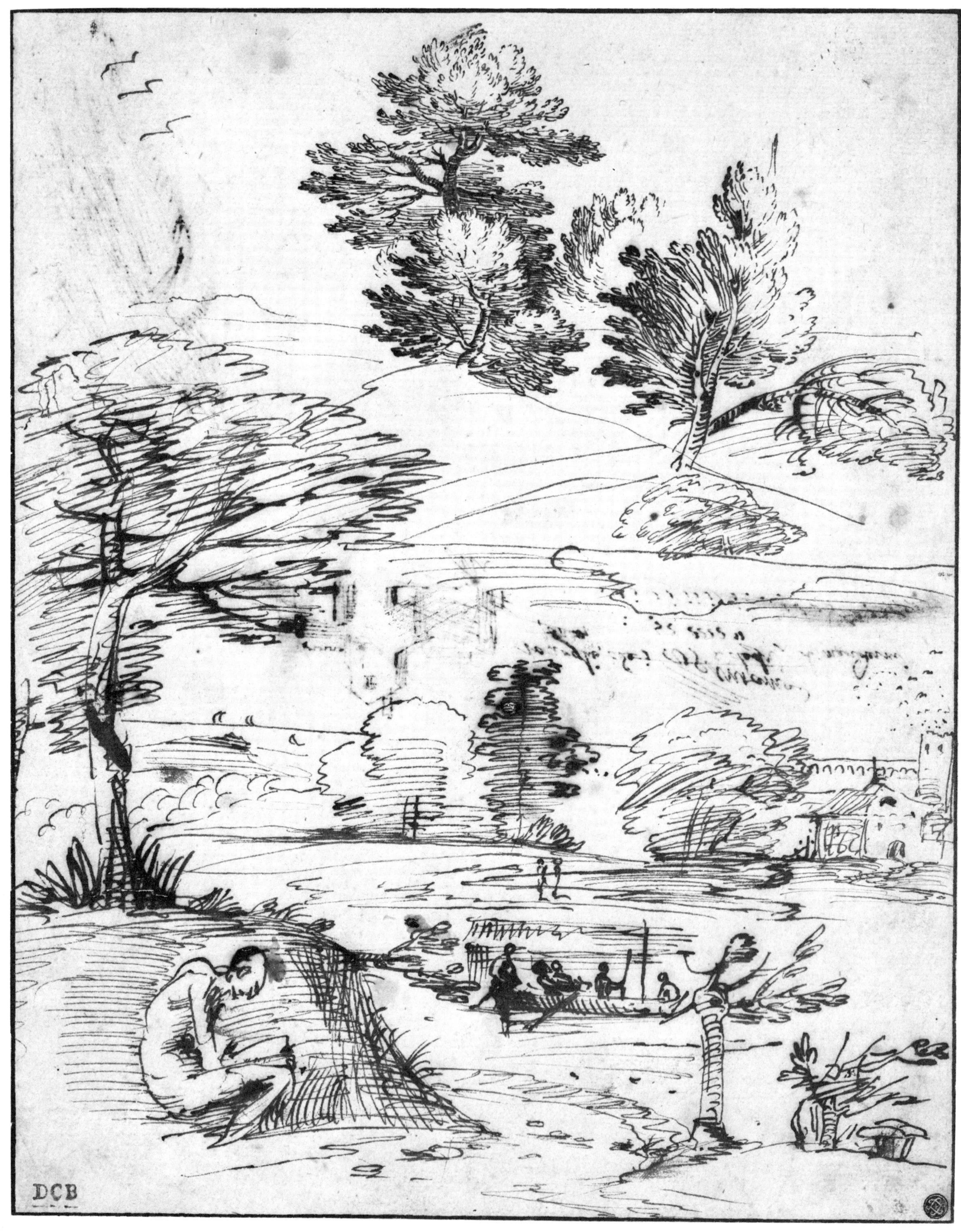


82. *Annibale Carracci.* LANDSCAPE WITH FIGURES.

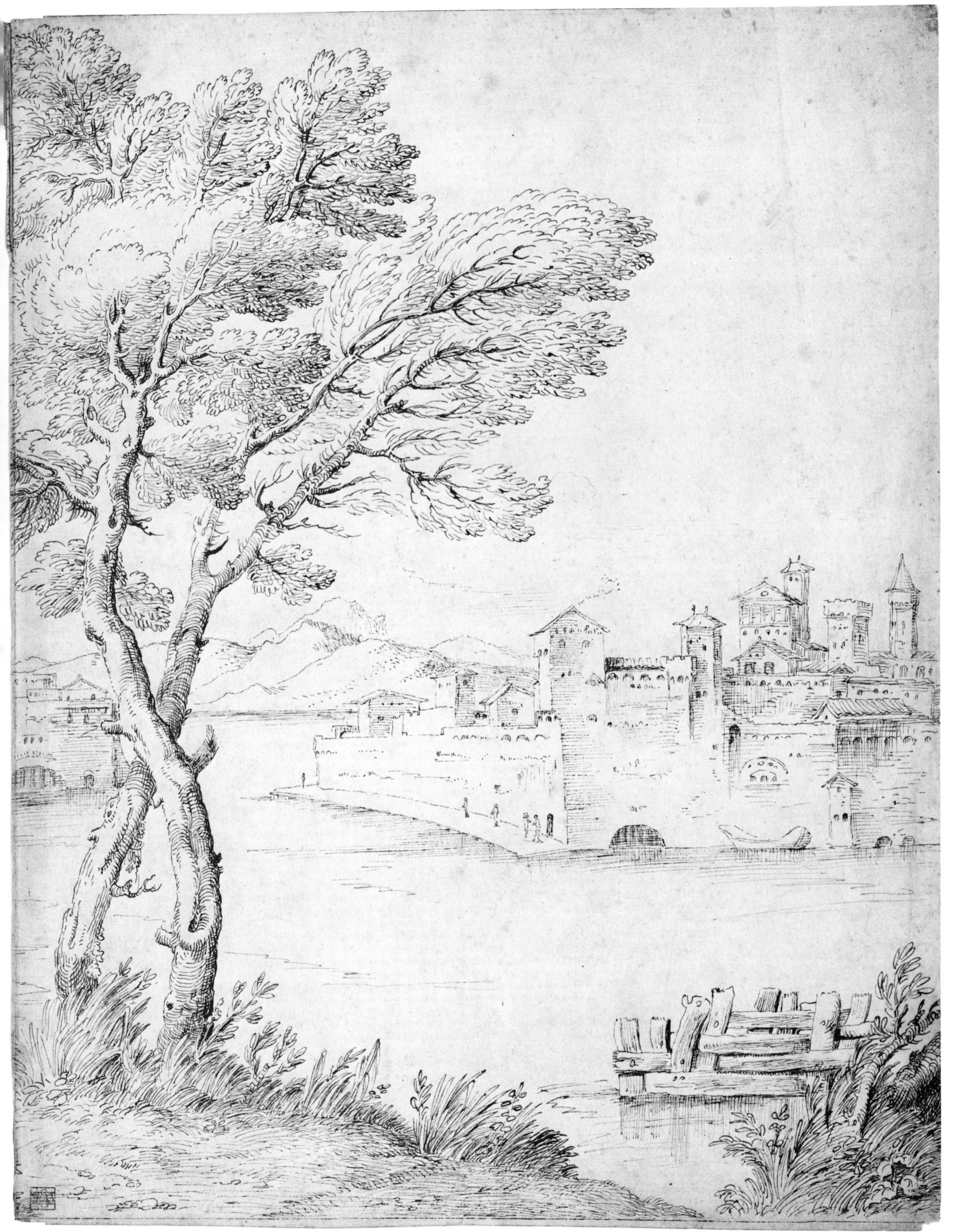

83. *Domenico Zampieri, called Domenichino (Bolognese, 1581–1641).* LANDSCAPE WITH A FORTIFIED TOWN IN A LAKE.

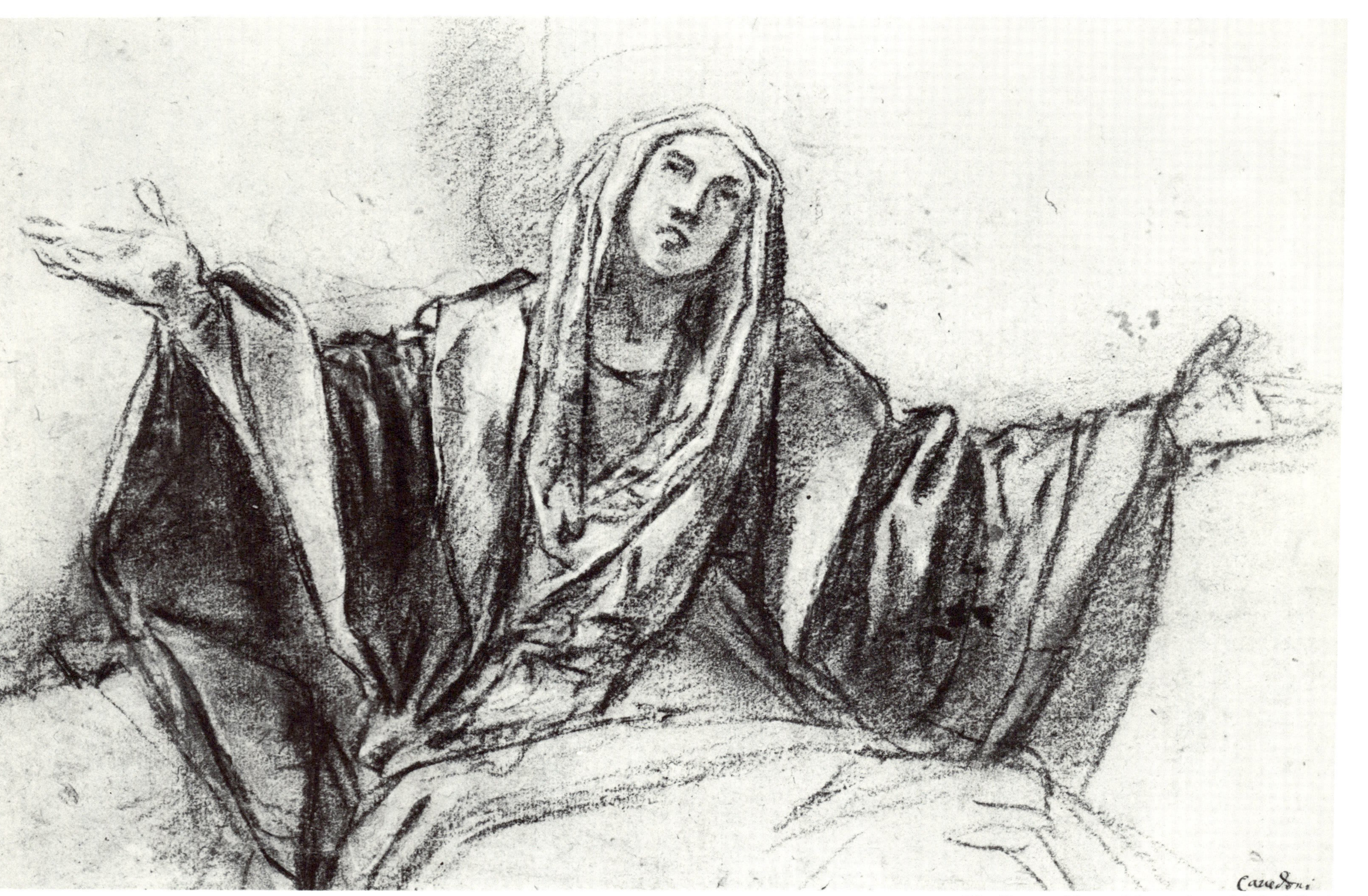


The Pierpont Morgan Library, Janos Scholz Collection

*84. Giacomo Cavedone (Bolognese, 1577–1660).* THE VIRGIN UNDER THE CROSS.

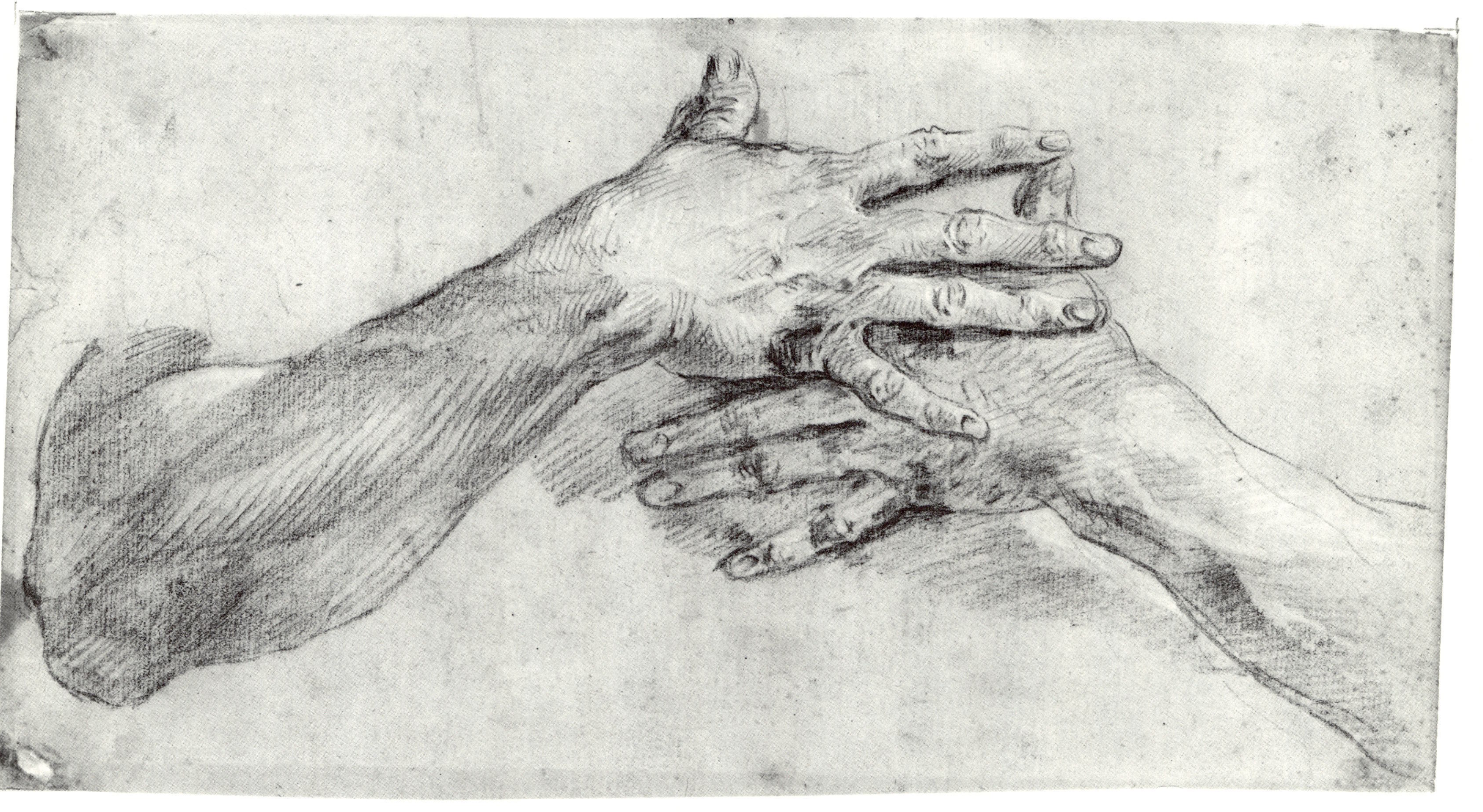

85. *Guido Reni (Bolognese, 1575–1642).* HAND AND ARM STUDIES.

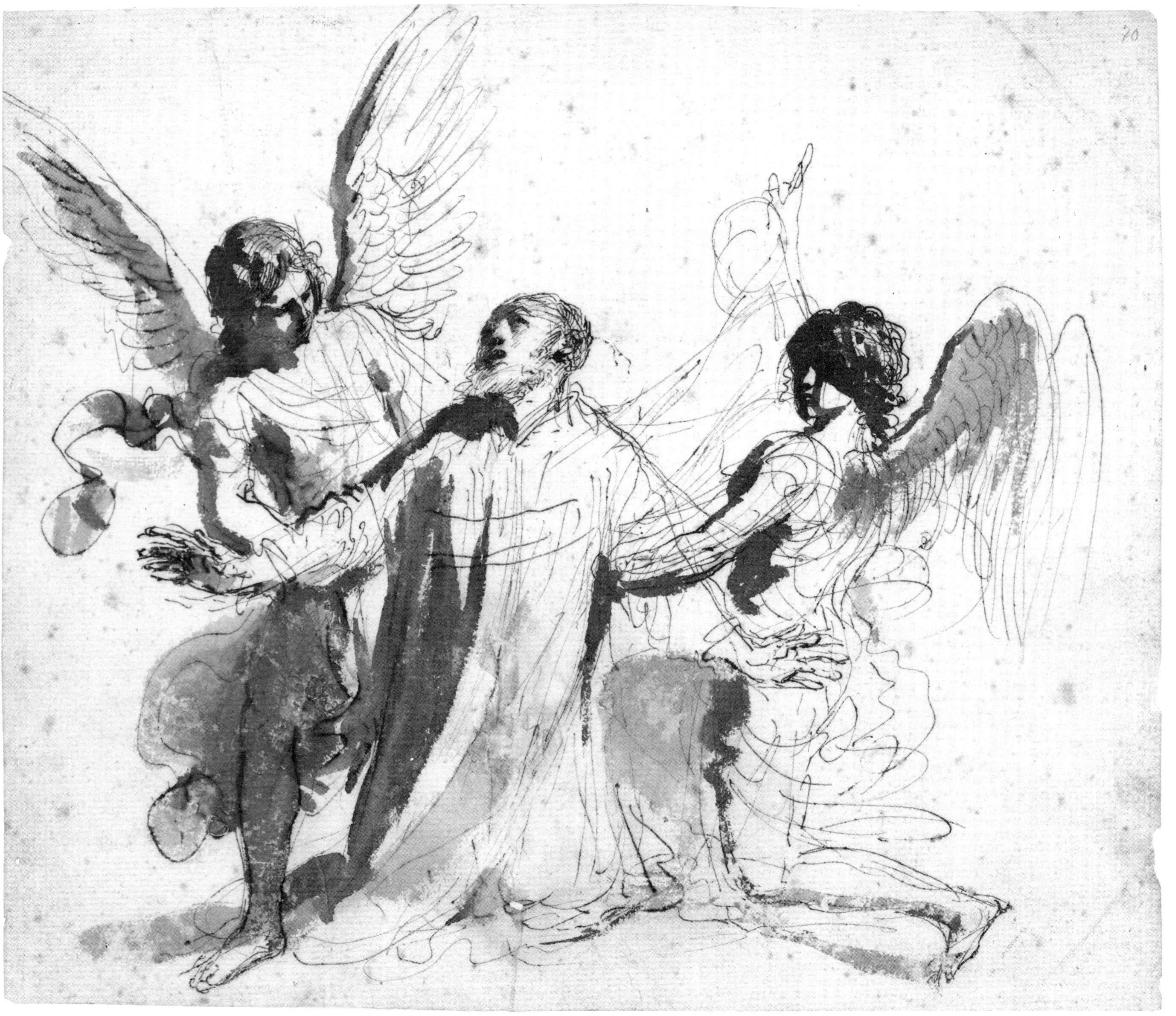

86. *Giovanni Francesco Barbieri, called Guercino (Bolognese, 1591–1666).* DEATH OF S. FILIPPO NERI.

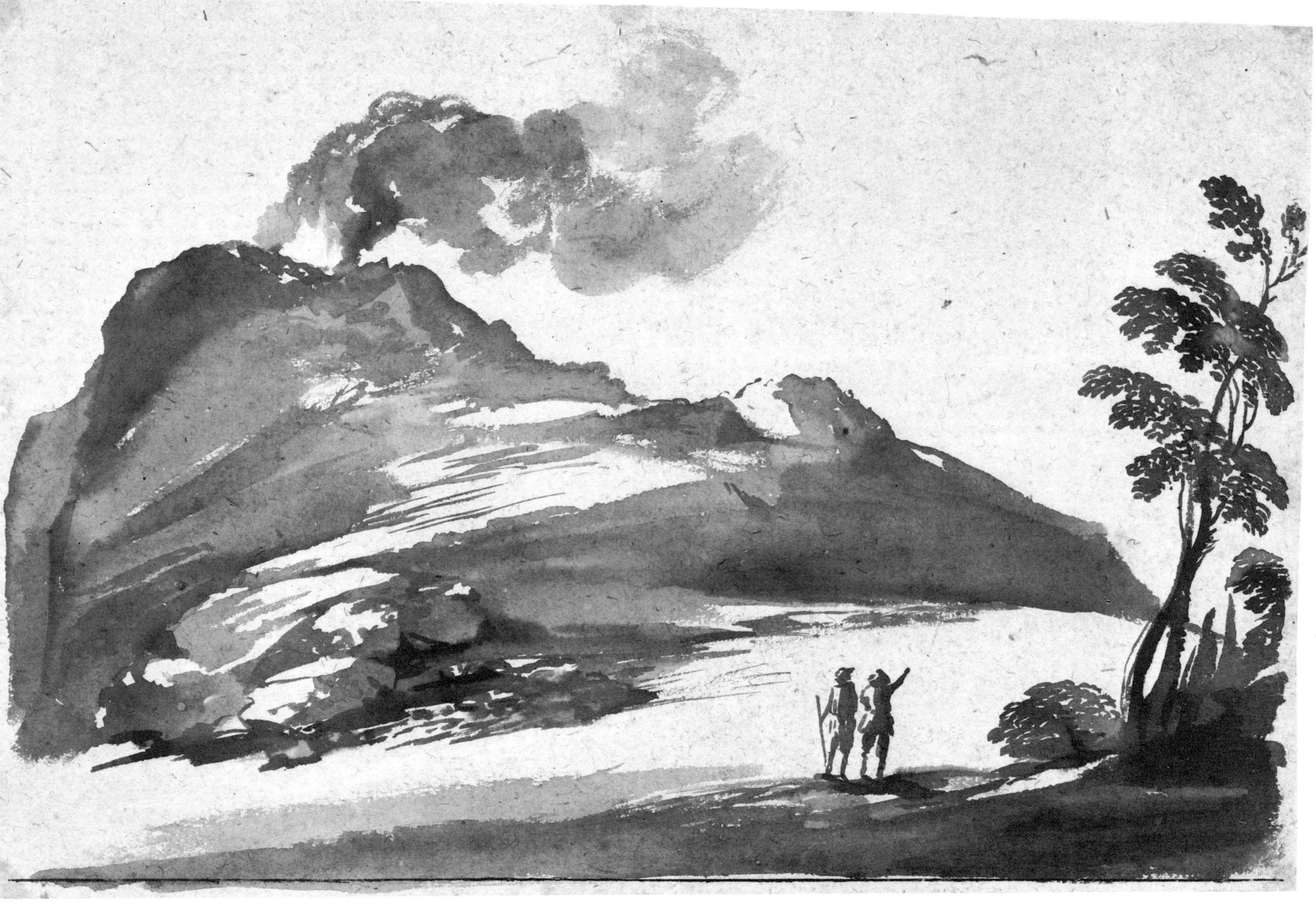

87. *Giovanni Francesco Barbieri, called Guercino.* LANDSCAPE WITH VOLCANO.

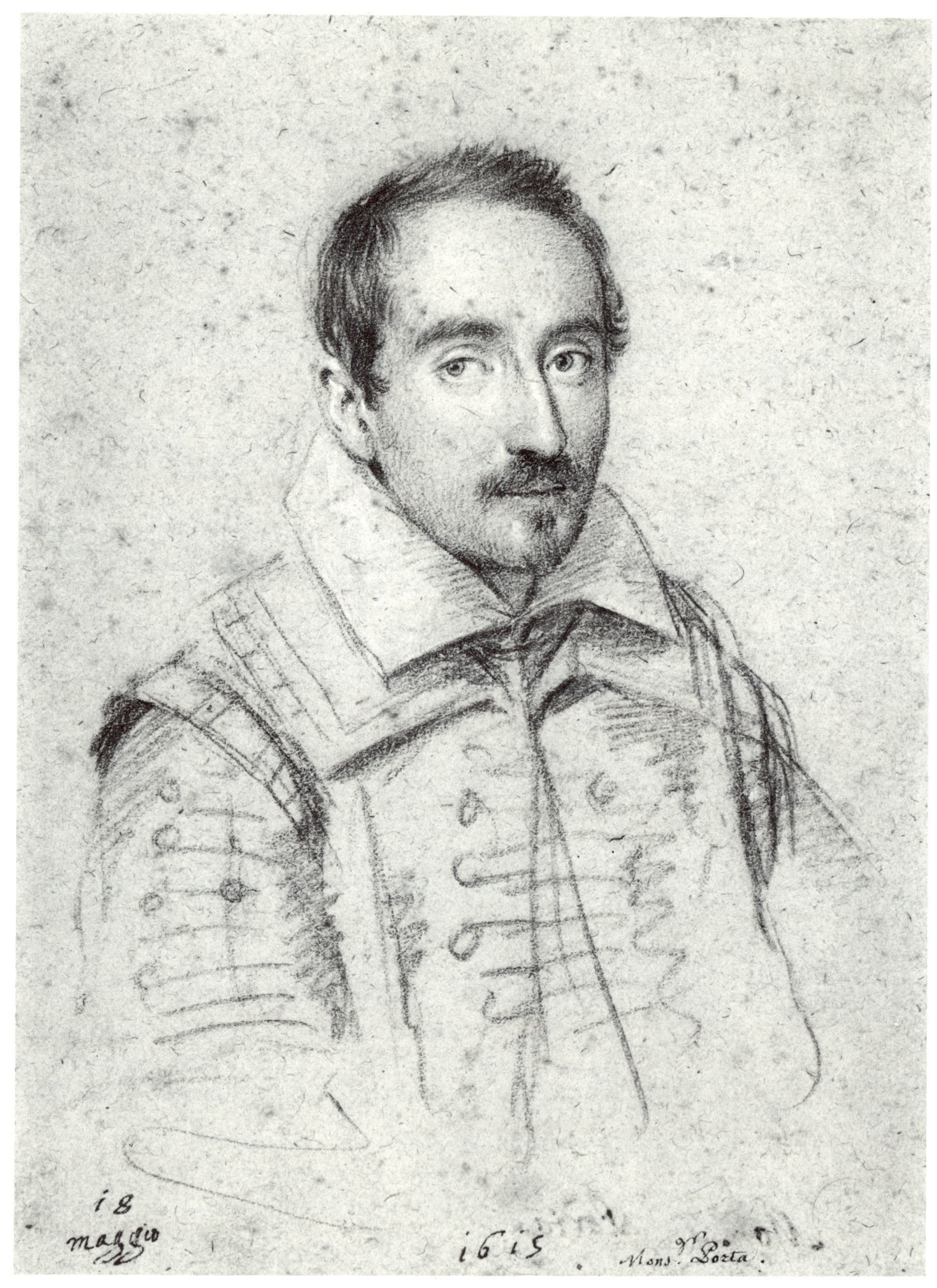


88. *Ottavio Leoni (Paduan, 1578–1630).* PORTRAIT OF MONSIGNOR PORTA.

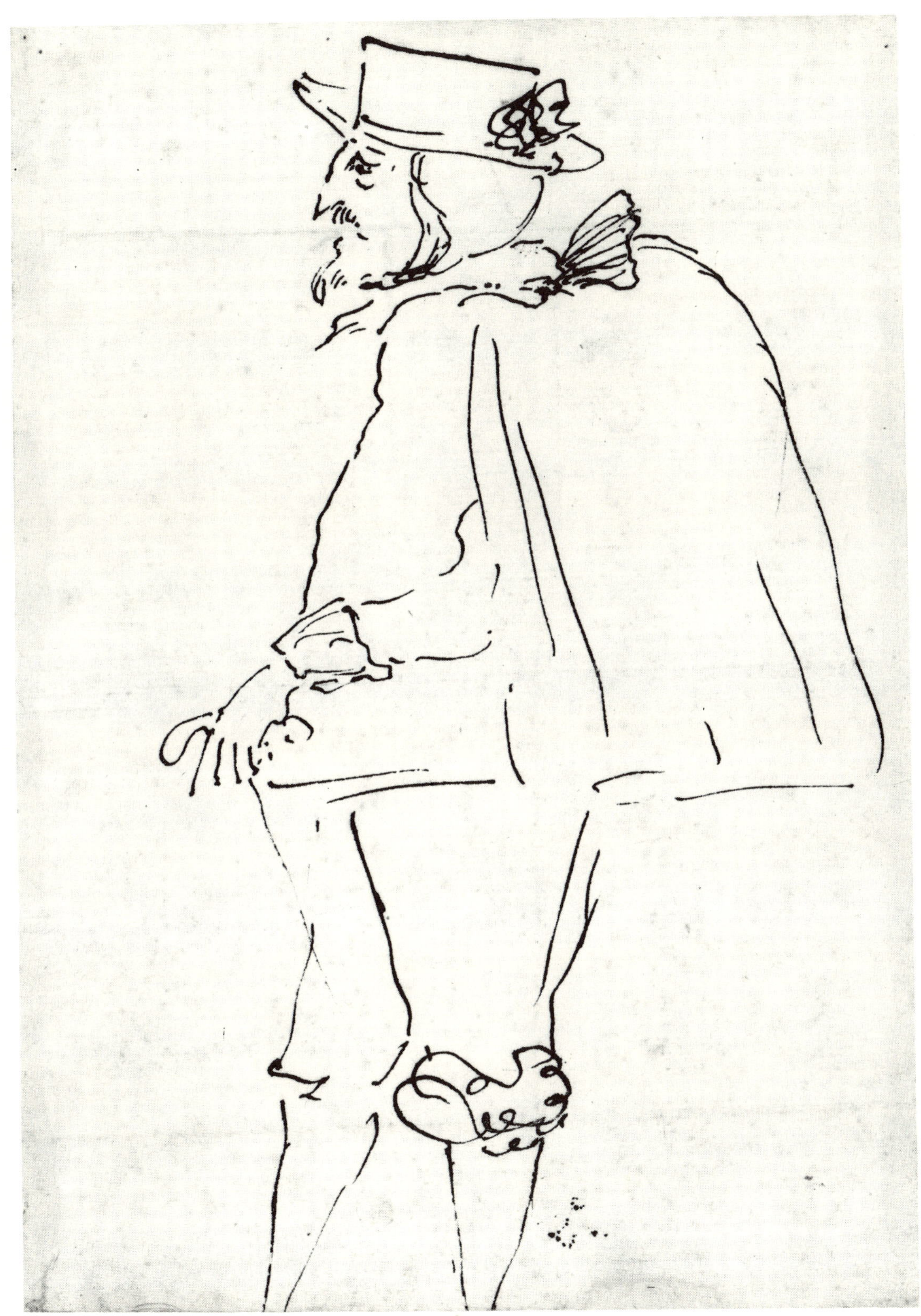

89. *Giovanni Lorenzo Bernini (Roman, 1598–1680).* CARICATURE OF A CAVALIER.

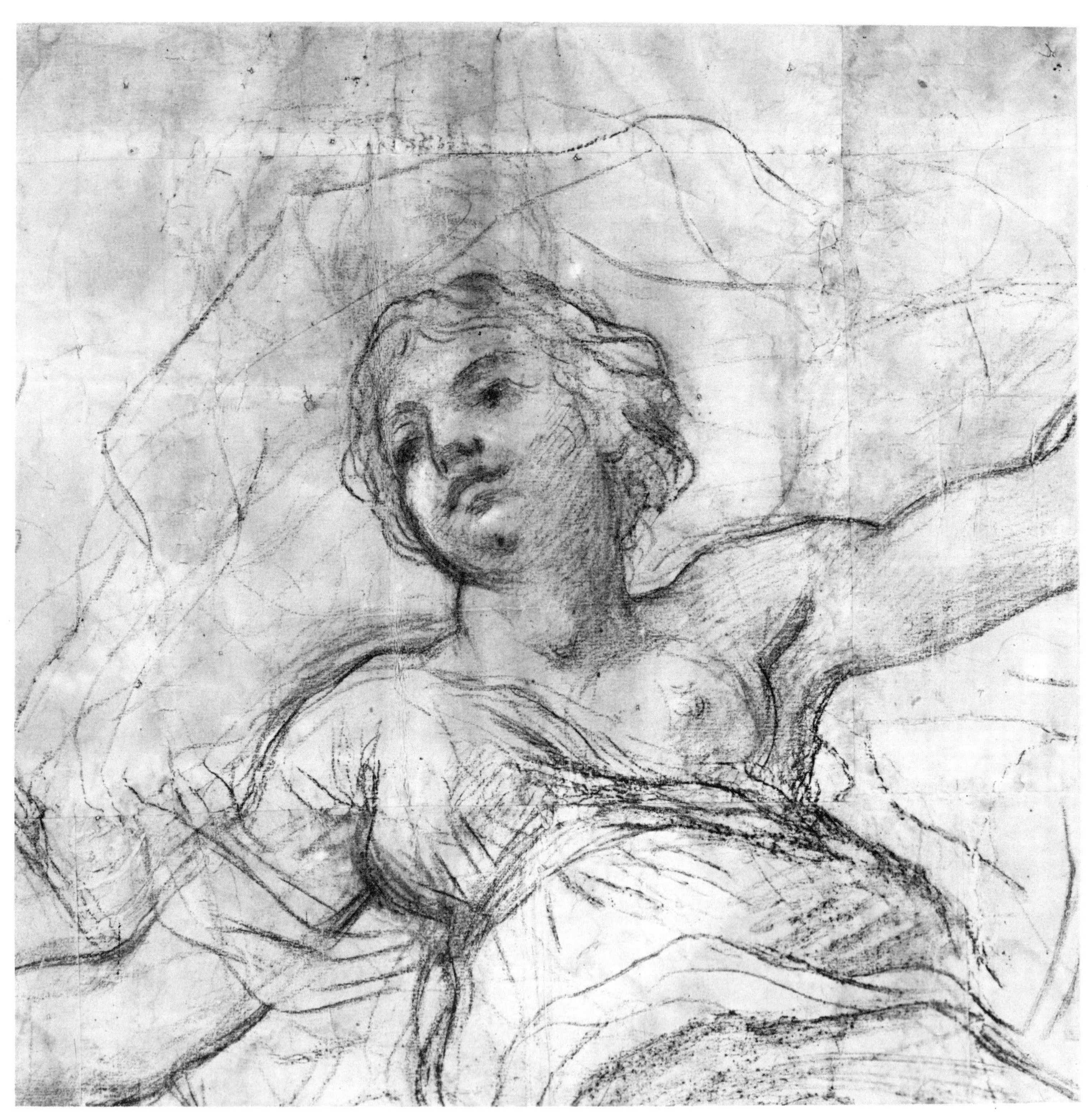

90. *Pietro Berettini, called Pietro da Cortona (Roman, 1596–1669).* HALF-LENGTH FIGURE OF A WOMAN.

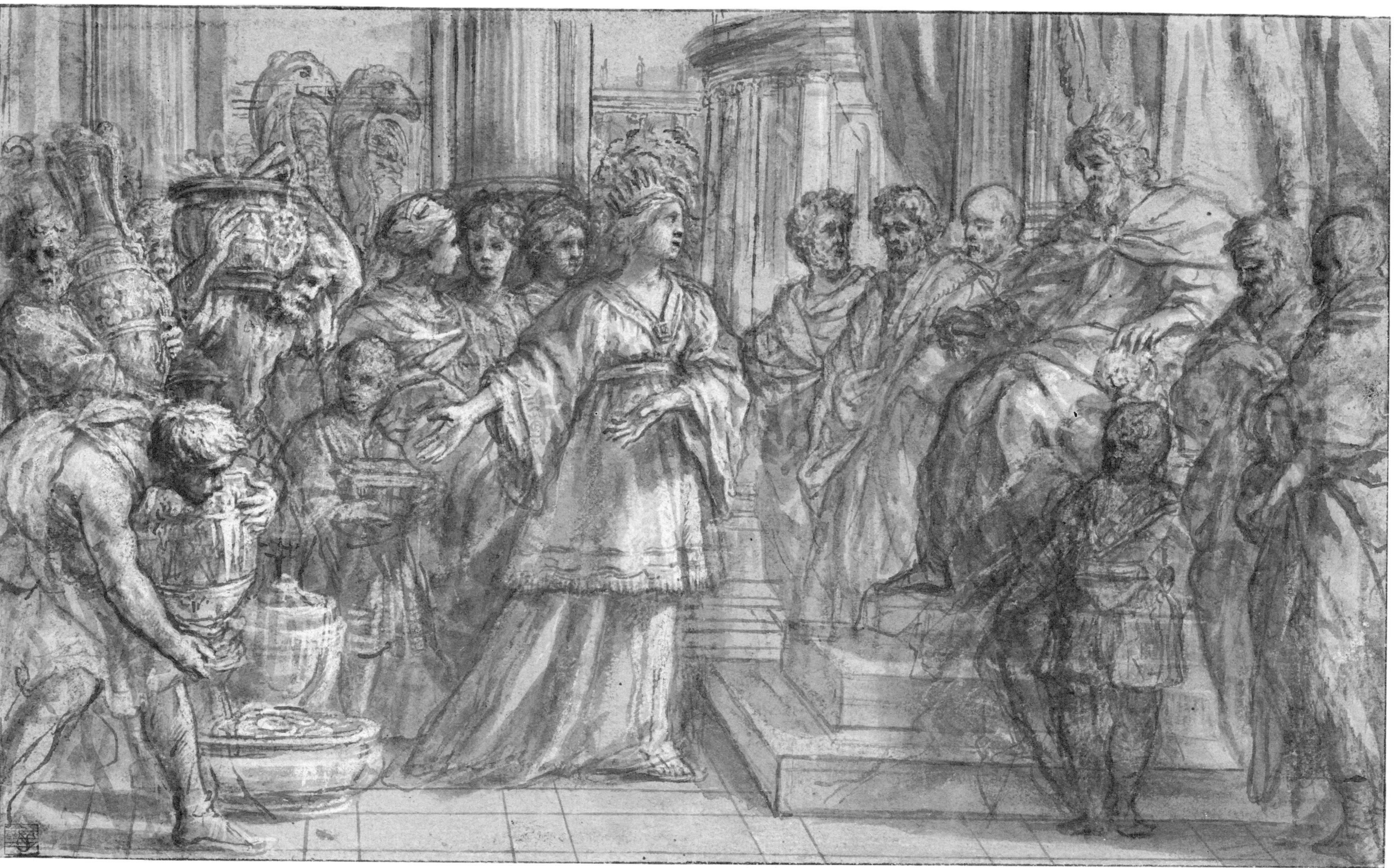

91. *Pietro Berettini, called Pietro da Cortona.* THE QUEEN OF SHEBA BEFORE SOLOMON.

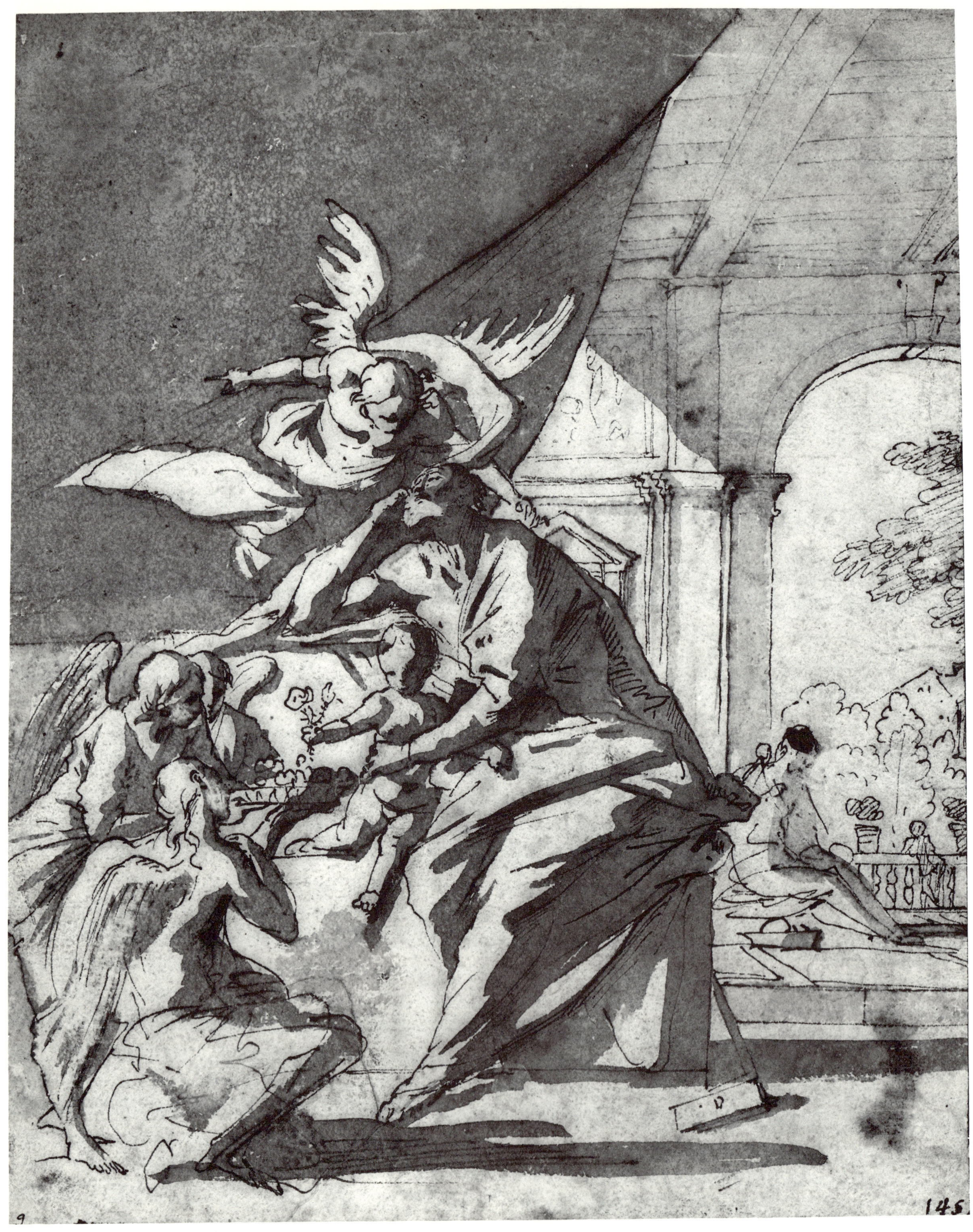


92. *Pietro Testa (Roman, 1611–1650).* THE DREAM OF JOSEPH.

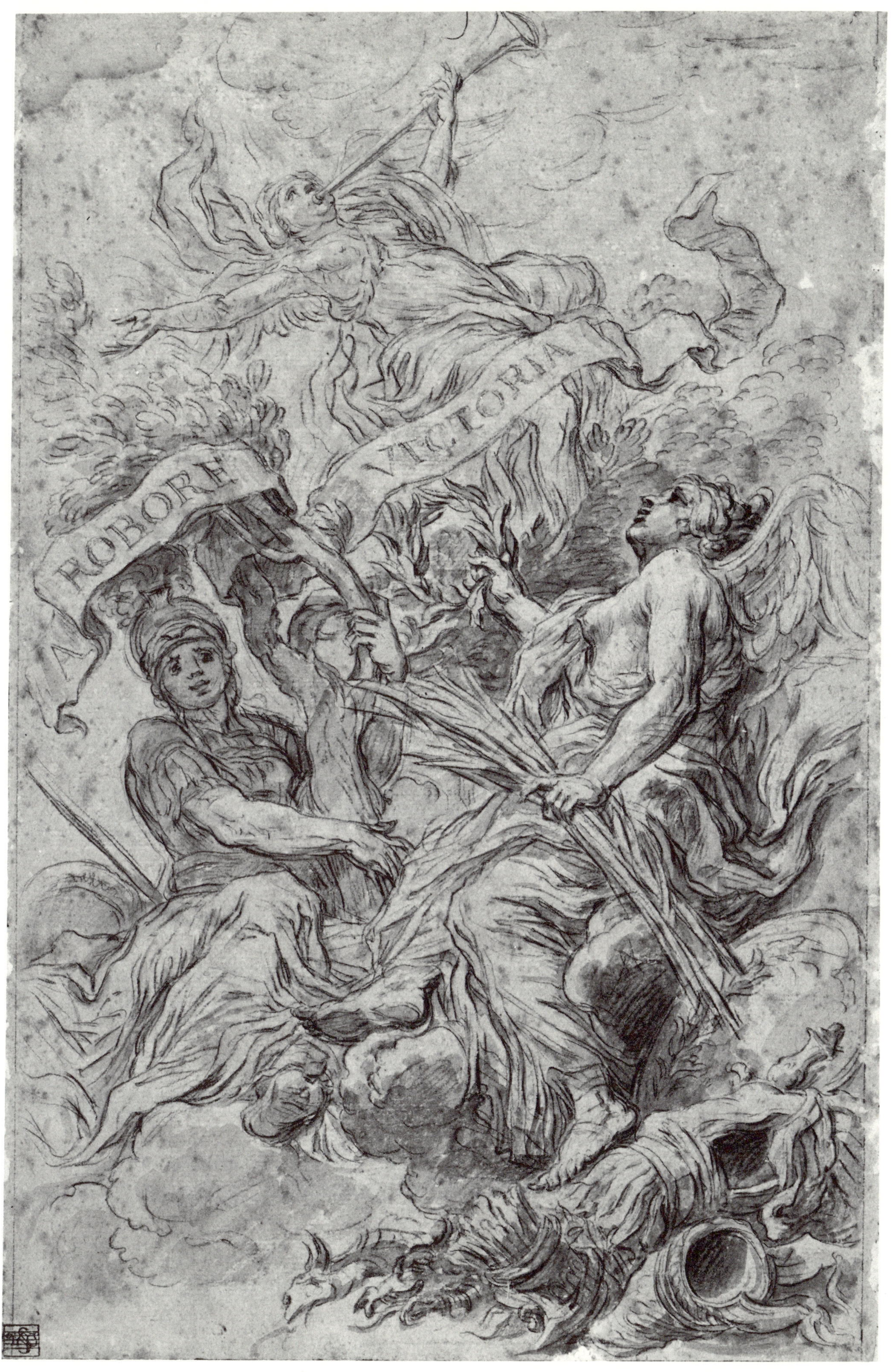


93. *Baldassare Franceschini, called Il Volterrano (Florentine, 1611–1689).*
TRIUMPH OF THE ROVERE.

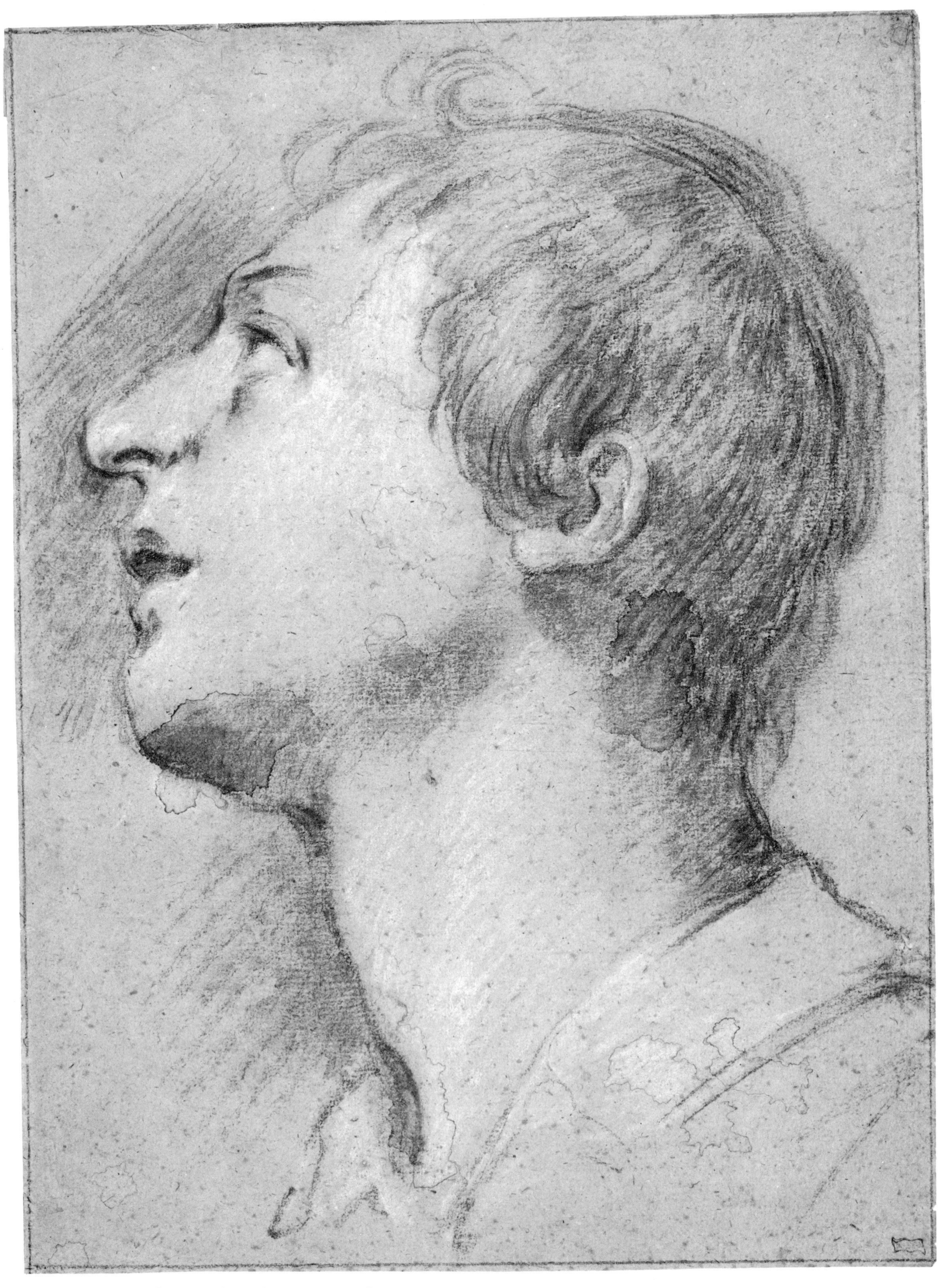

94. *Orazio Gentileschi (Florentine, 1562–1657).* HEAD OF A YOUTH.

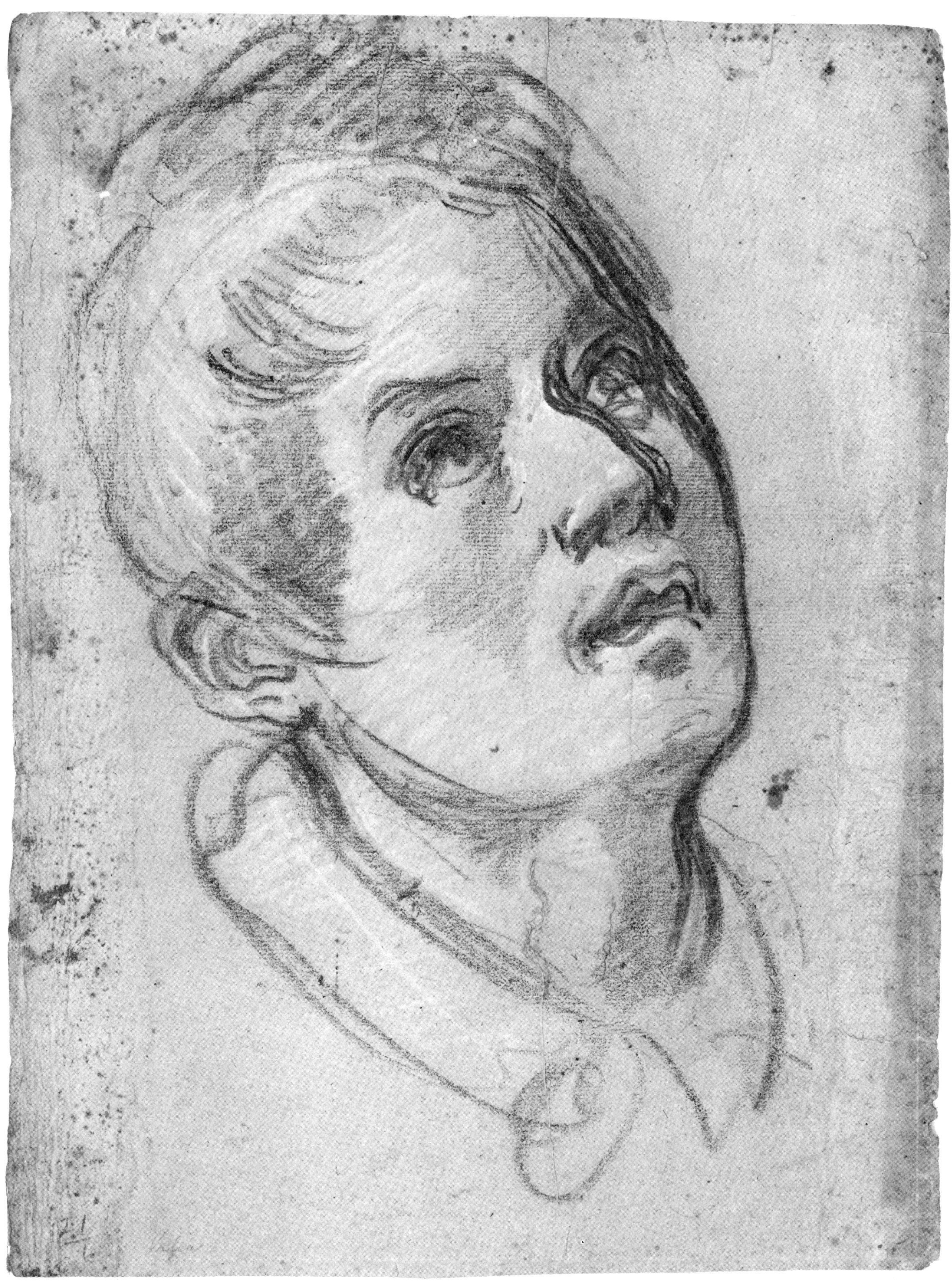

95. *Jacopo Chimenti, called Jacopo da Empoli (Florentine, 1551–1640).* HEAD OF A YOUTH.

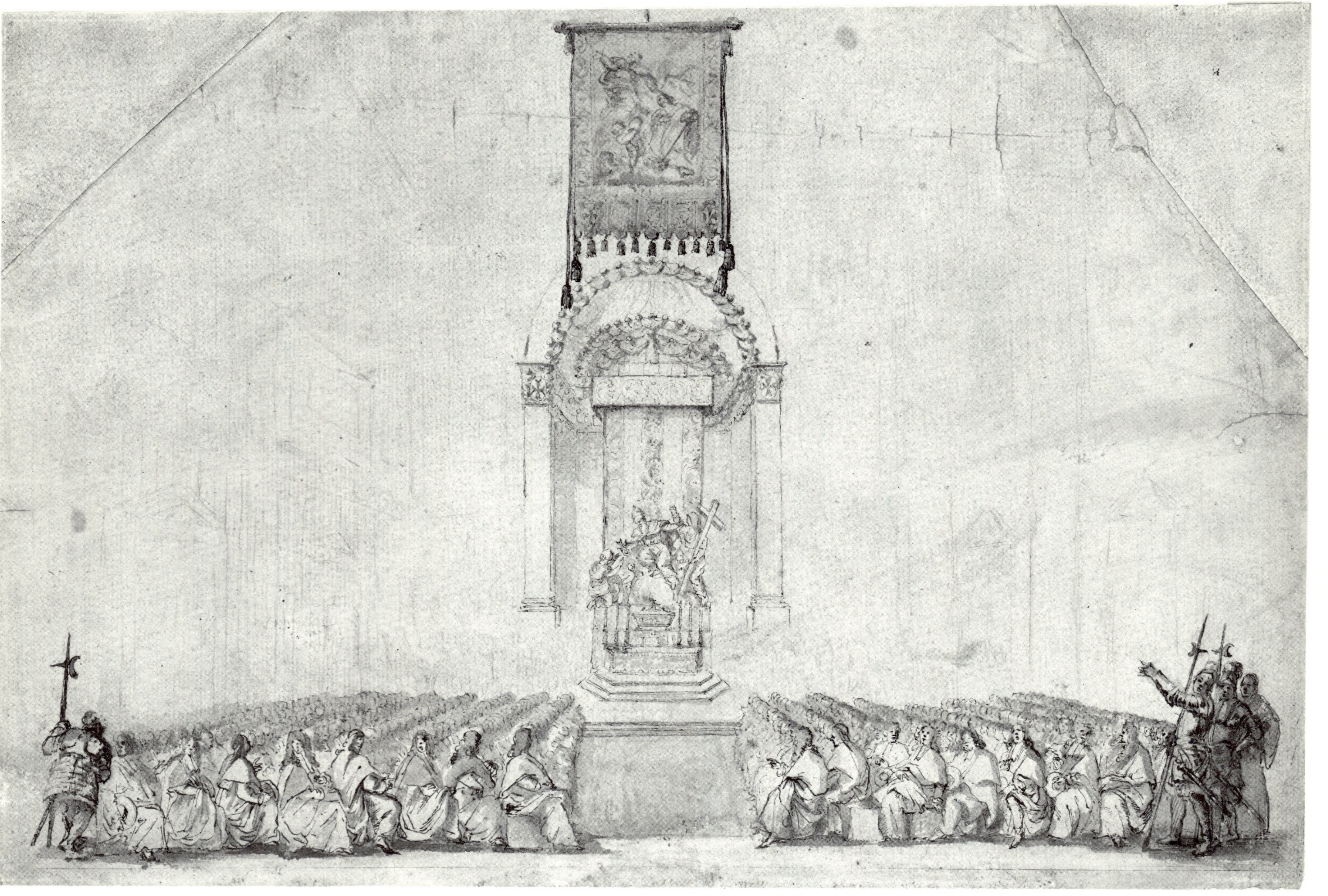

96. *Stefano della Bella (Florentine, 1610–1664).* CONVENTION IN A CHURCH.

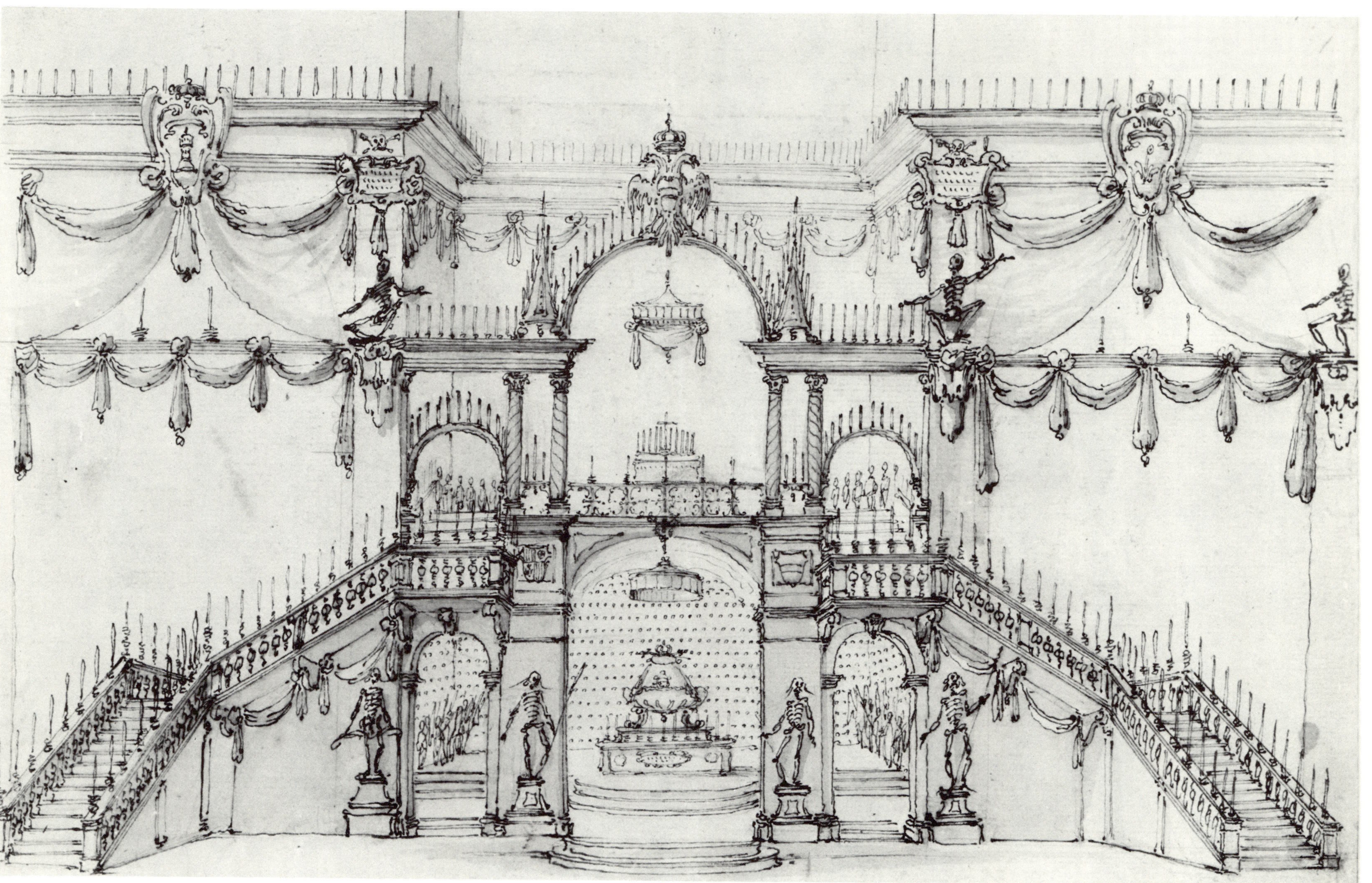

97. *Alfonso Parigi (Florentine, died 1656).* PROJECT FOR FUNERARY DECORATIONS.

The Pierpont Morgan Library, Janos Scholz Collection

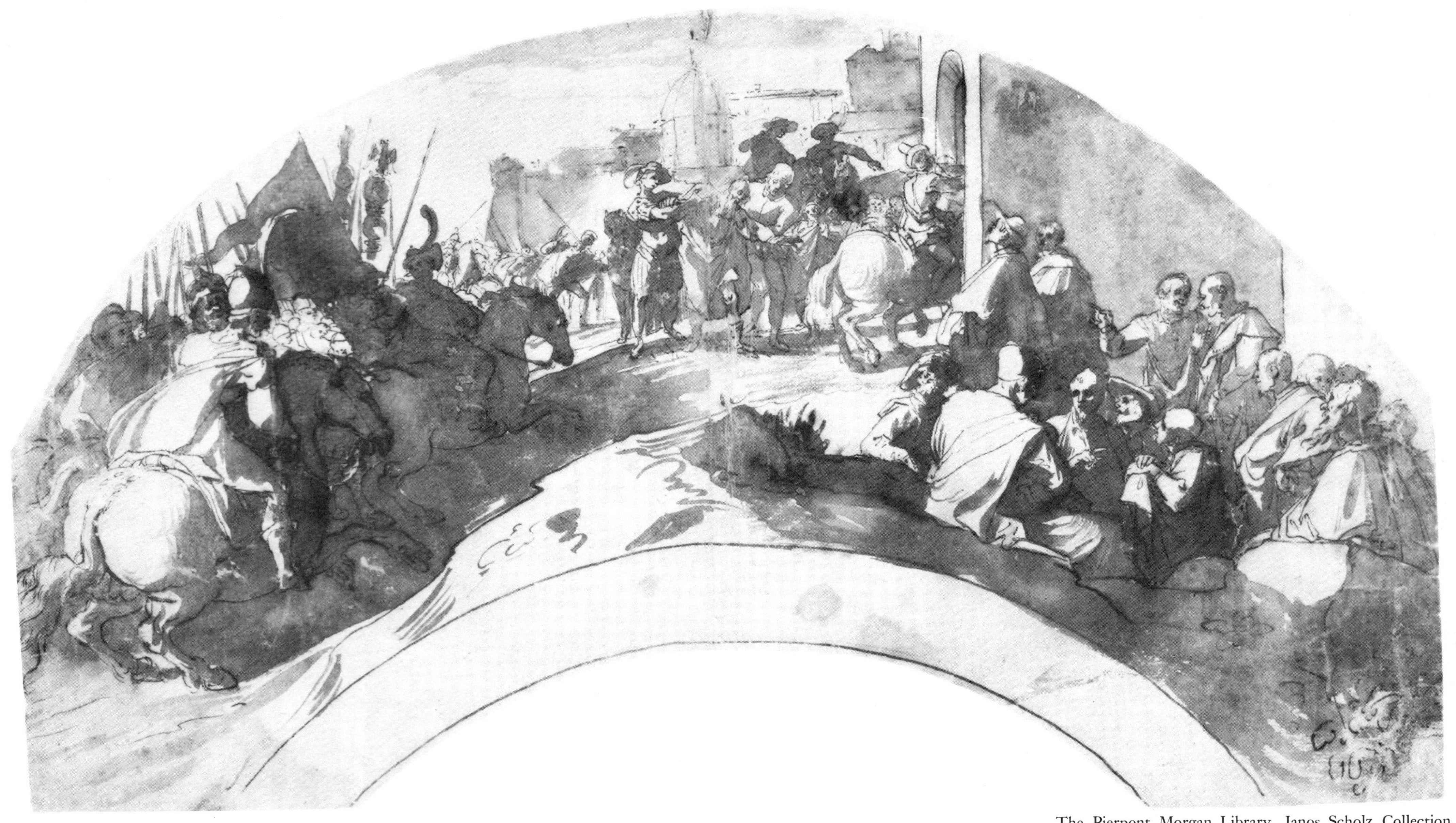

The Pierpont Morgan Library, Janos Scholz Collection

98. *Giovanni Manozzi, called Giovanni da San Giovanni (Florentine, 1592–1636).*
ST. PAUL LED INTO DAMASCUS.

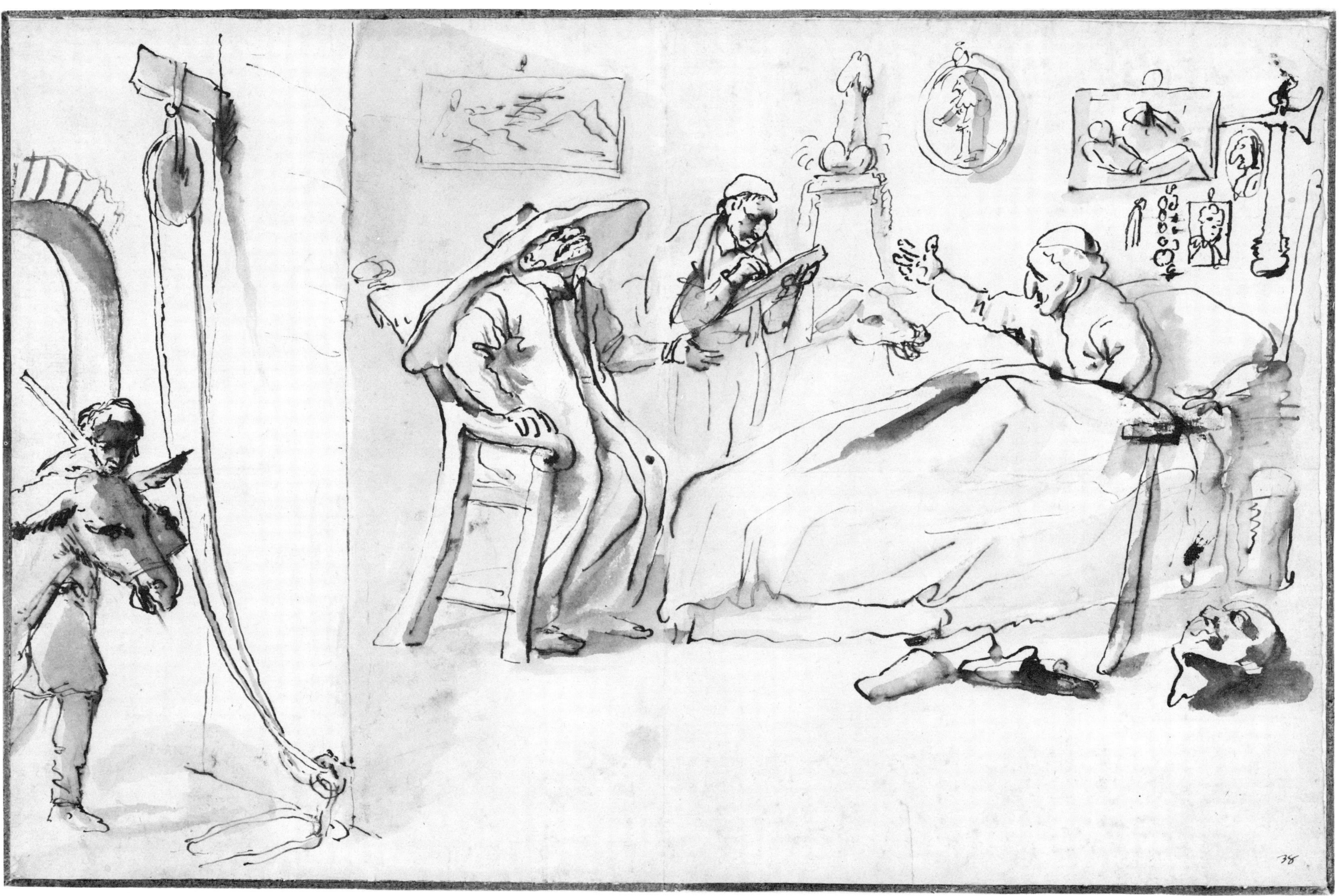


99. *Pierfrancesco Mola (Coldrerio-Rome, 1612–1660).* MAN DICTATING HIS WILL.

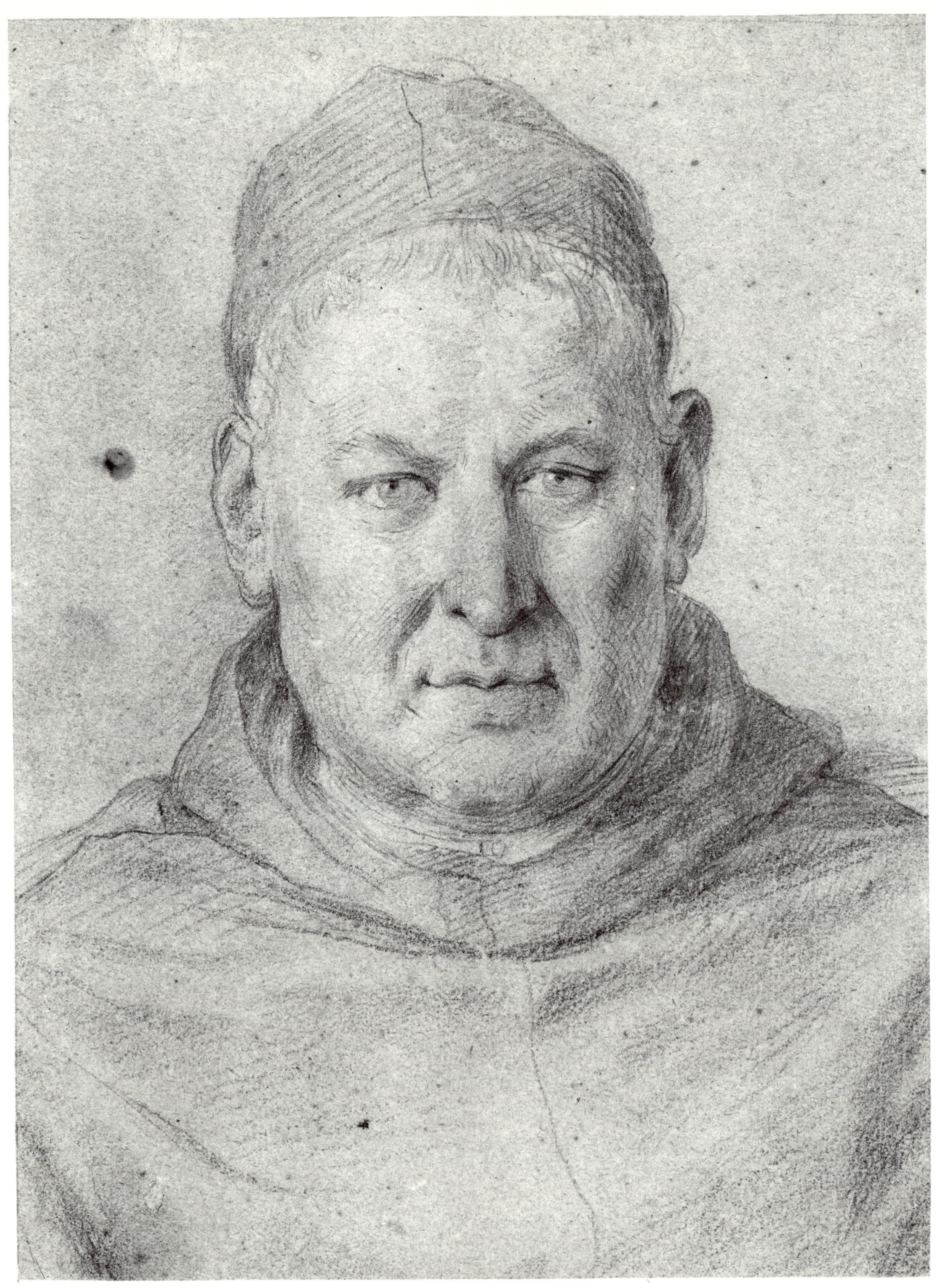

100. *Giovanni Battista Salvi, called Sassoferrato (Roman, 1609–1685).* PORTRAIT OF A CLERIC.

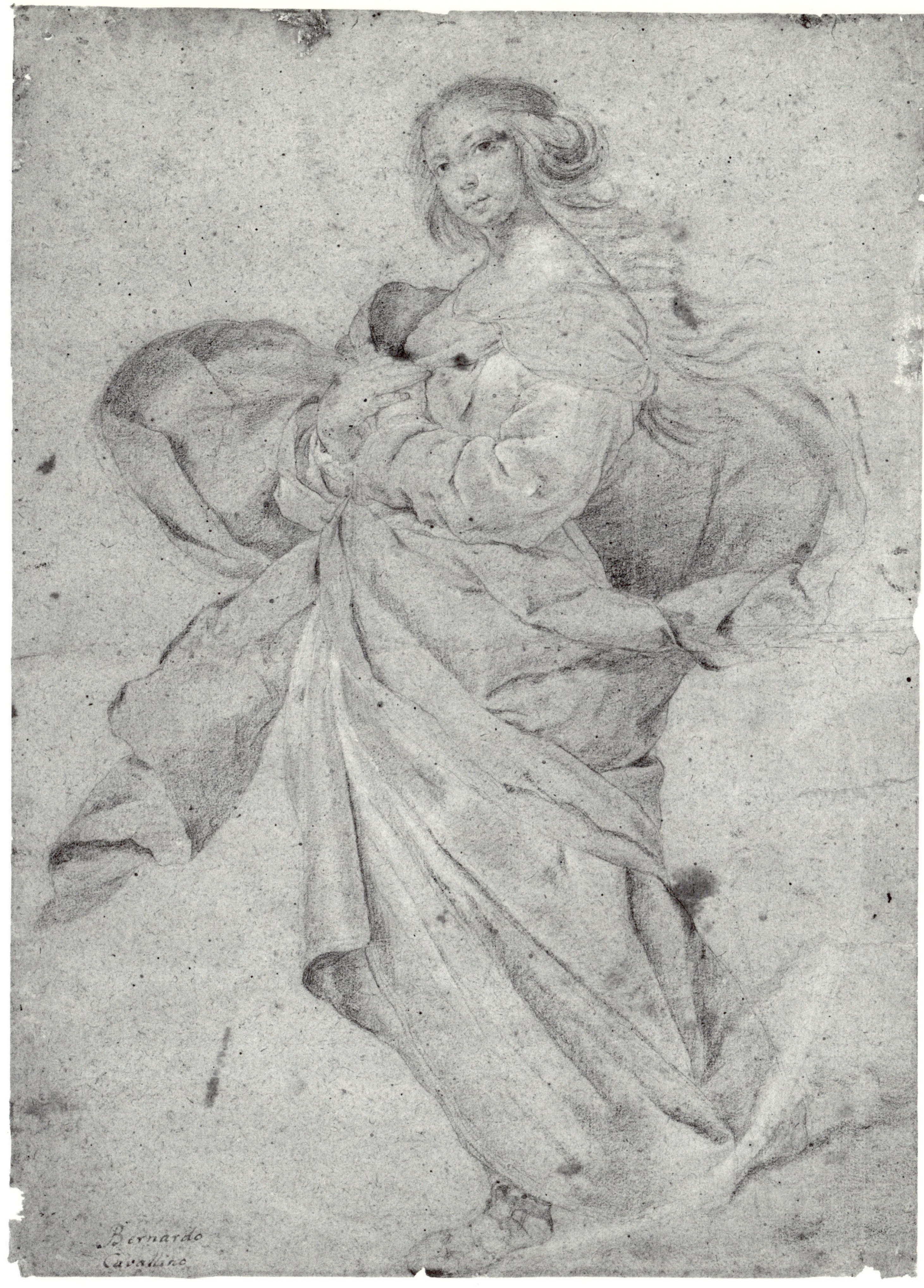


101. *Bernardo Cavallino (Neapolitan, 1616–1654).* STUDY OF A WOMAN WALKING.

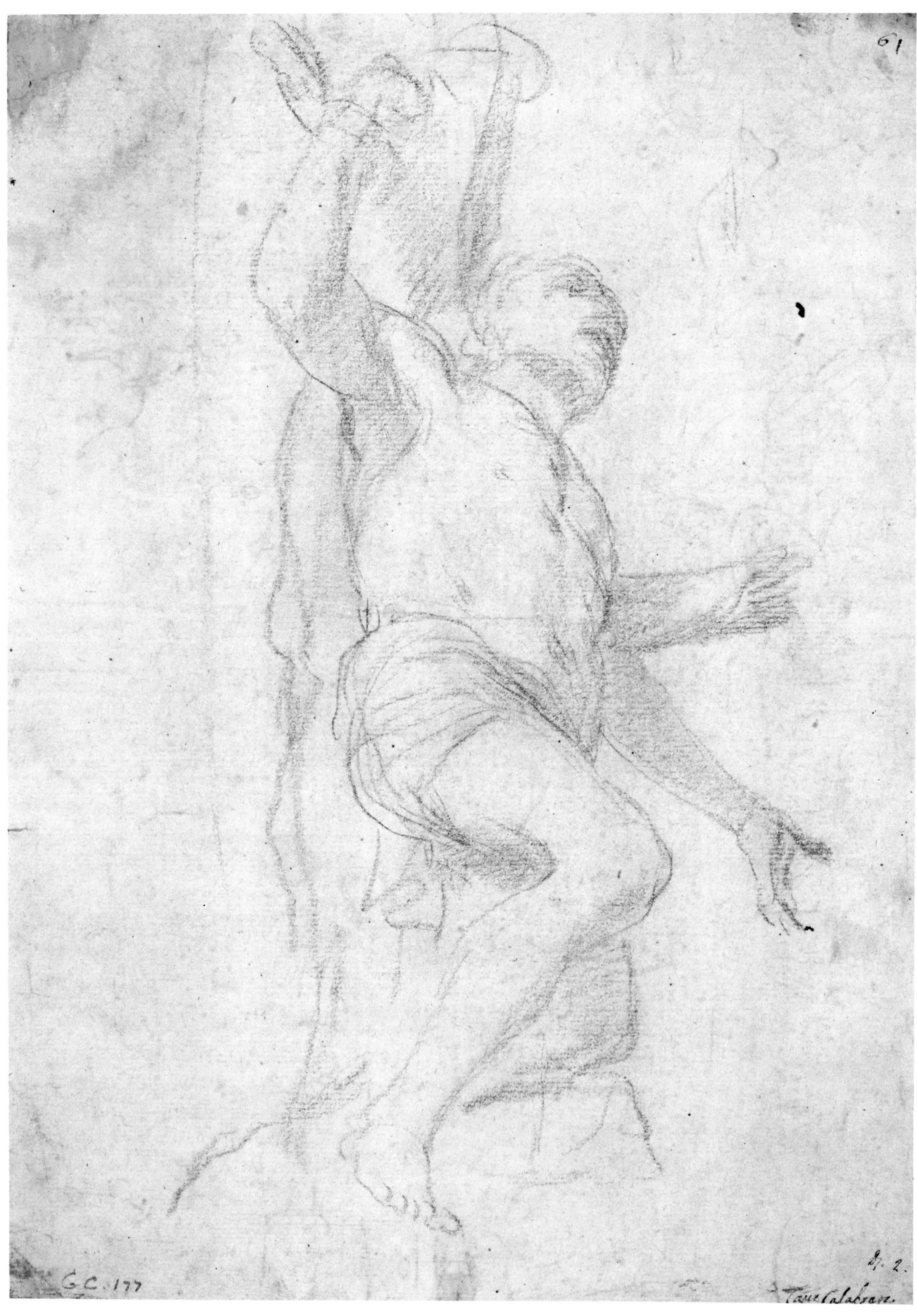

102. *Mattia Preti (Rome-Naples, 1613–1699).* ST. SEBASTIAN.

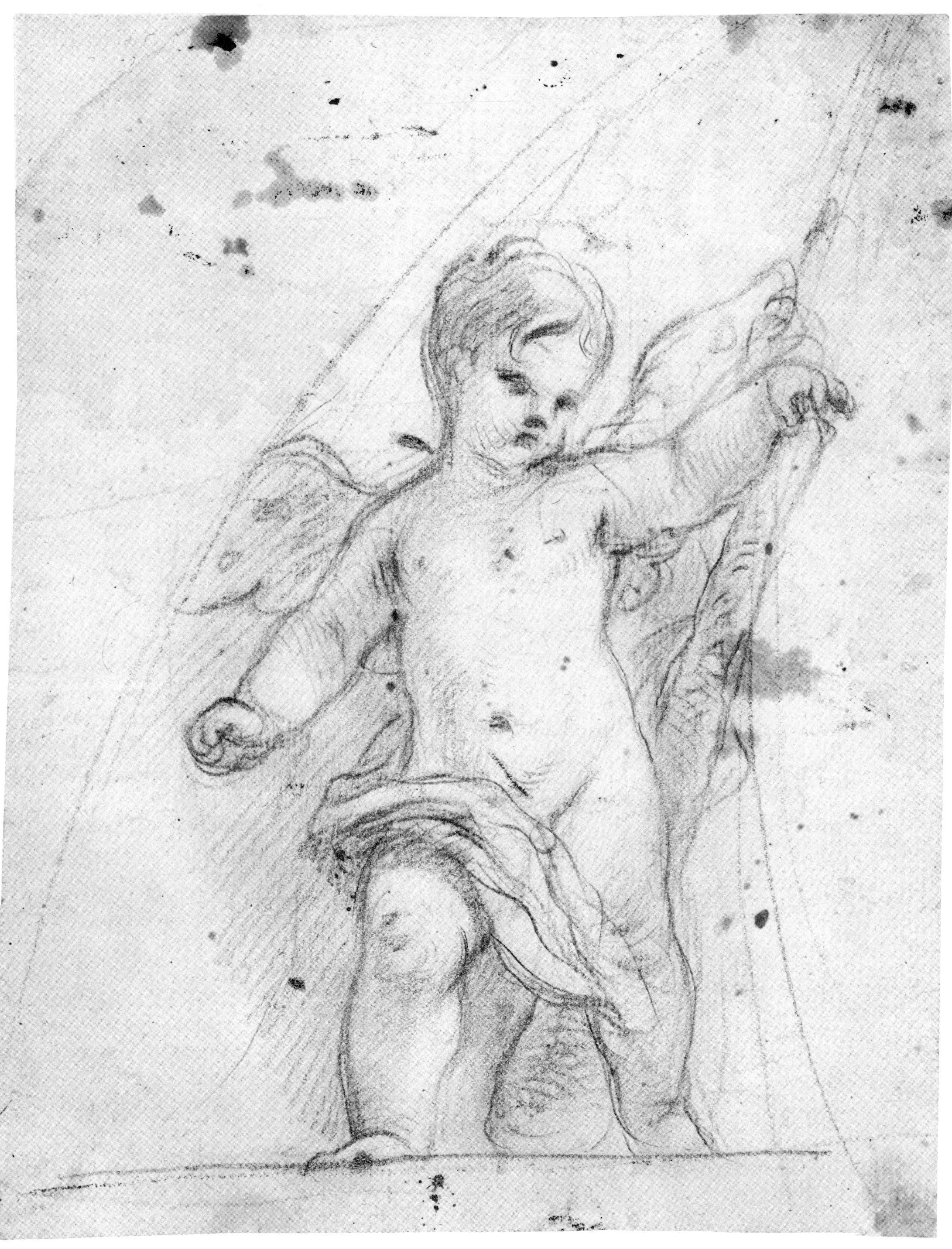

*103. Luca Giordano (Neapolitan, 1632–1705).* STANDING CHERUB HOLDING A CLUB.

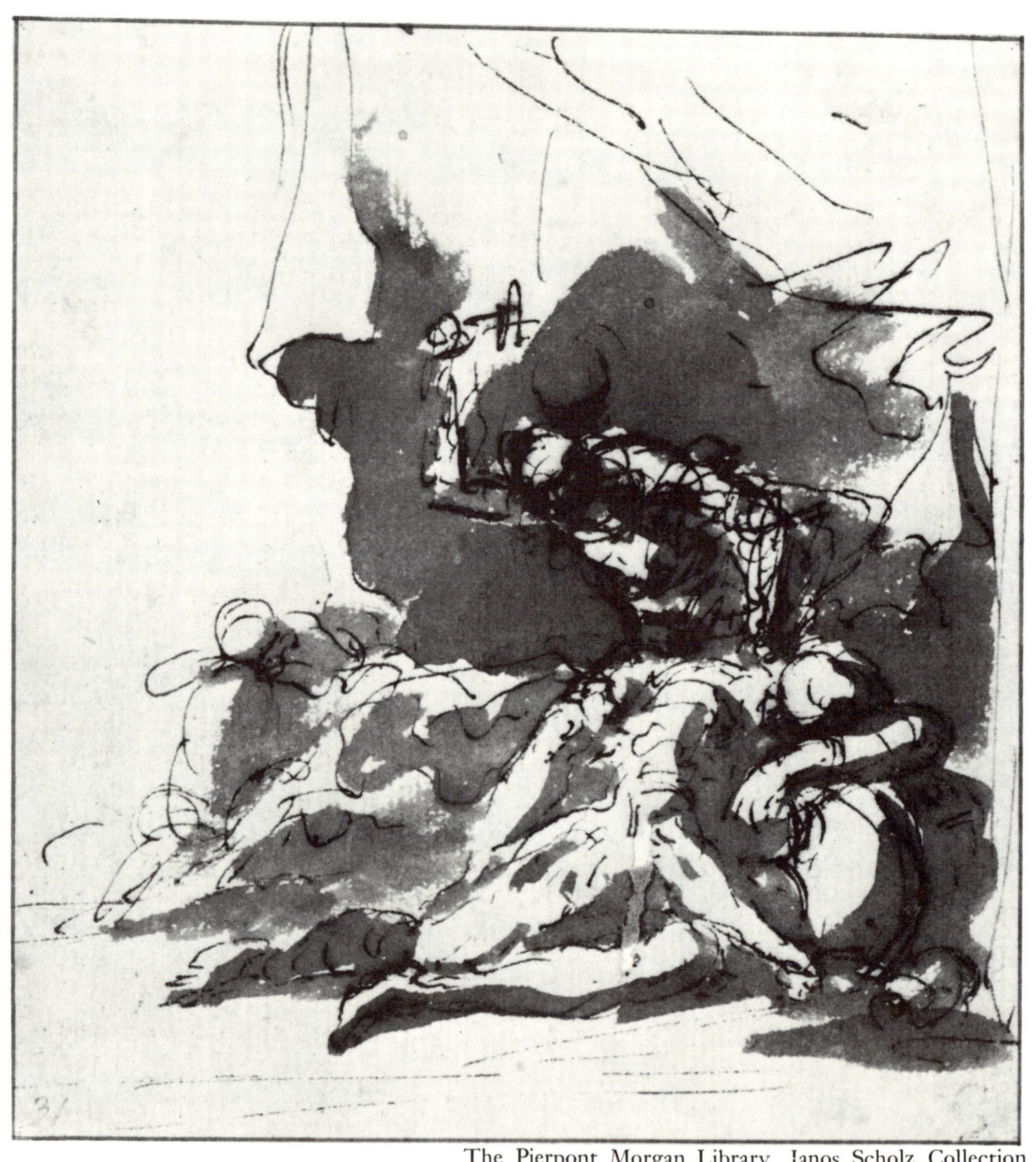

The Pierpont Morgan Library, Janos Scholz Collection

*104. Salvator Rosa (Naples-Rome, 1615–1673).* JAEL AND SISERA.

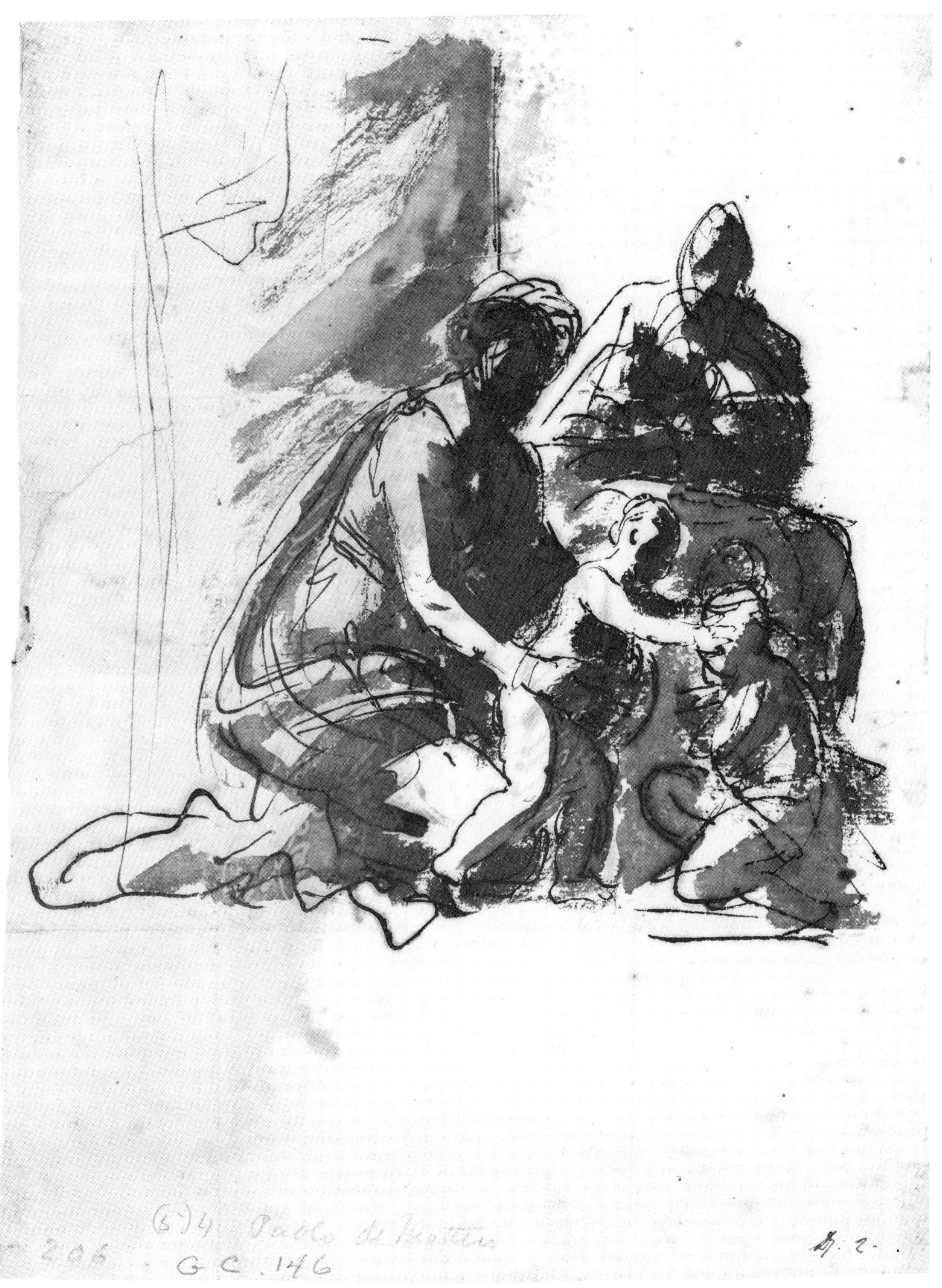


*105. Paolo de Matteis (Neapolitan, 1662–1729).* THE HOLY FAMILY AND ST. JOHN.

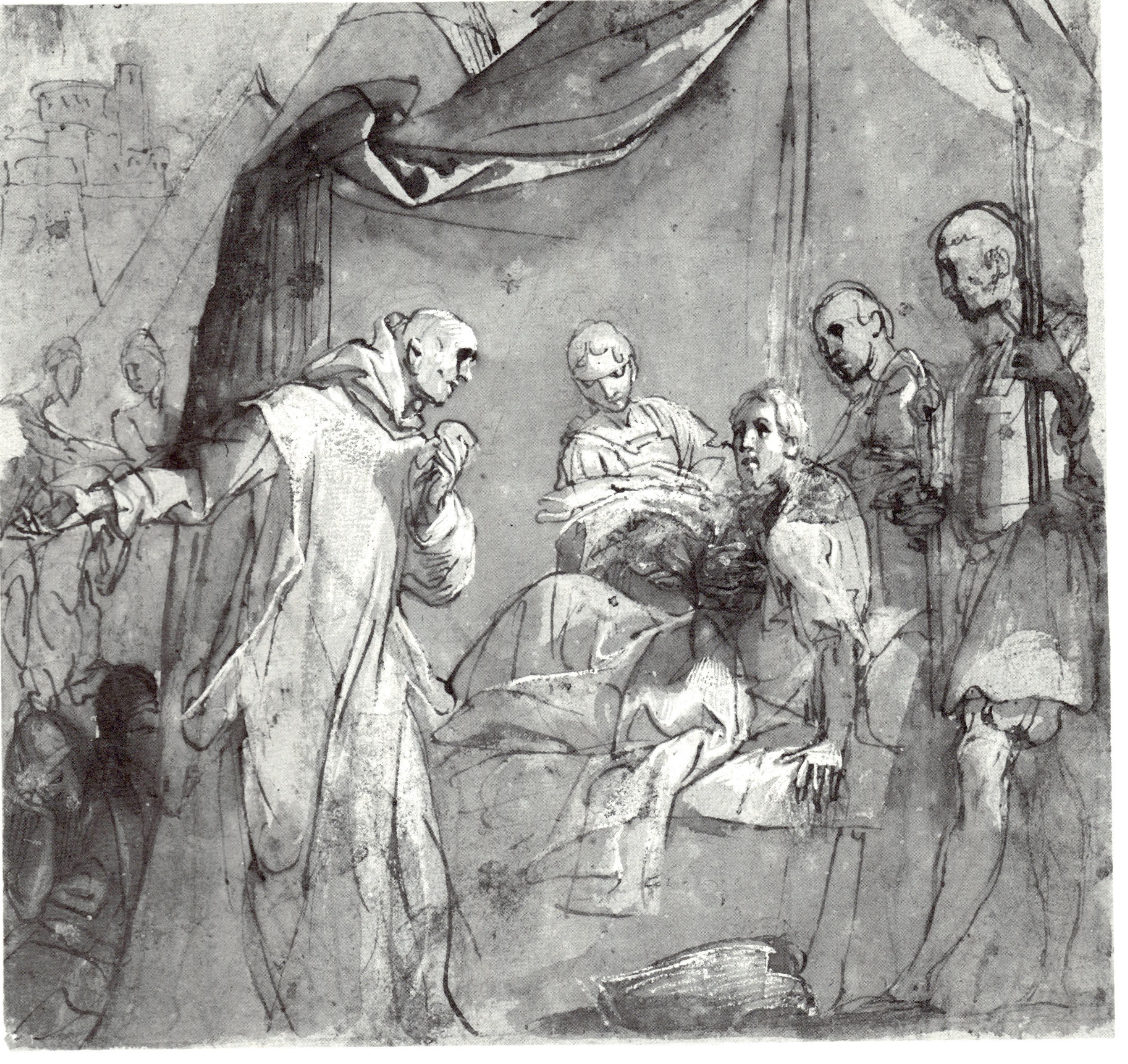

106. *Daniele Crespi (Lombard, 1590/95–1630).* ST. BRUNO AND COUNT ROGER OF CALABRIA.

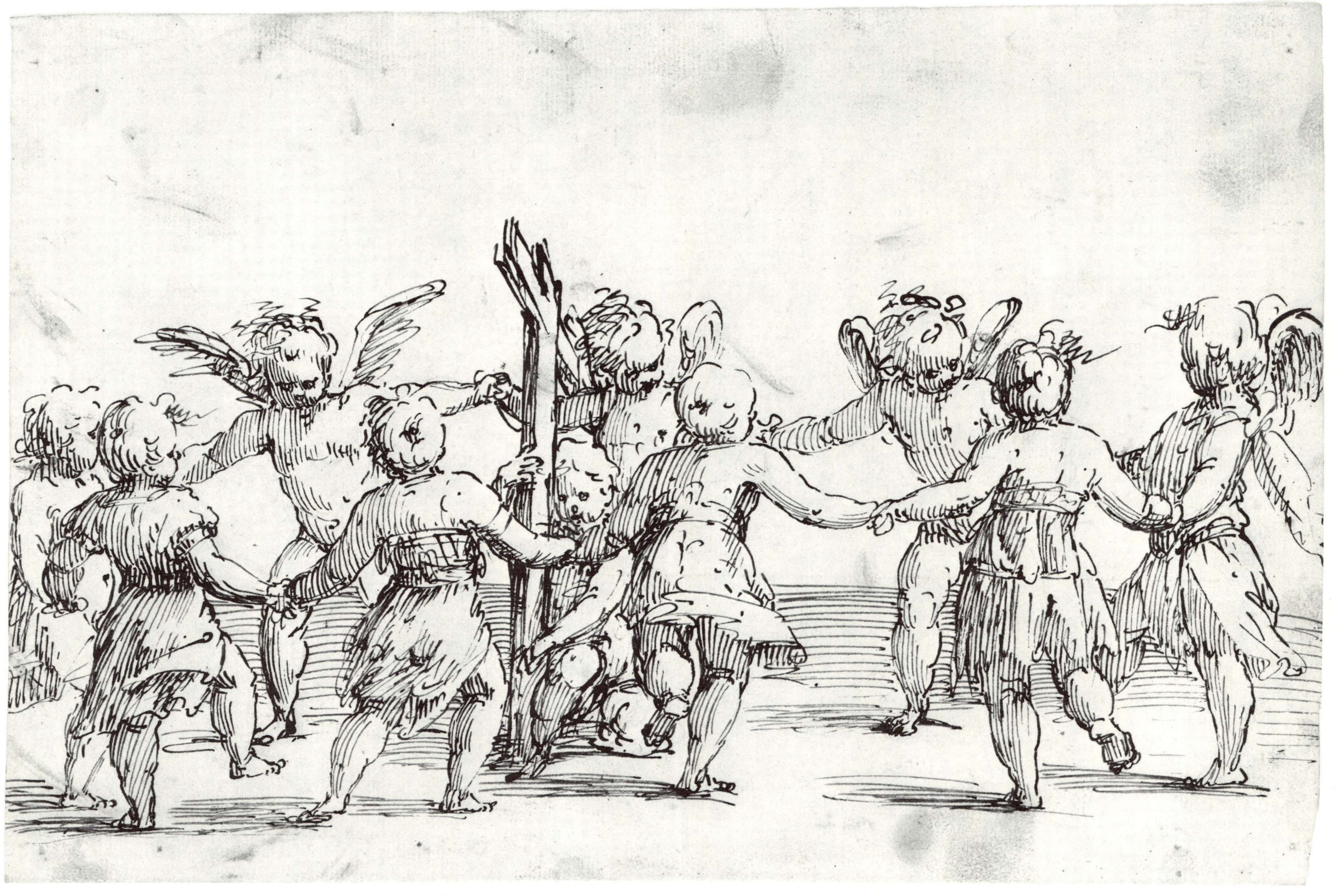

107. *Bernardo Strozzi (Genoese, 1581–1644).* CHERUBS DANCING AROUND THE CHRIST CHILD, WHO HOLDS THE CROSS.

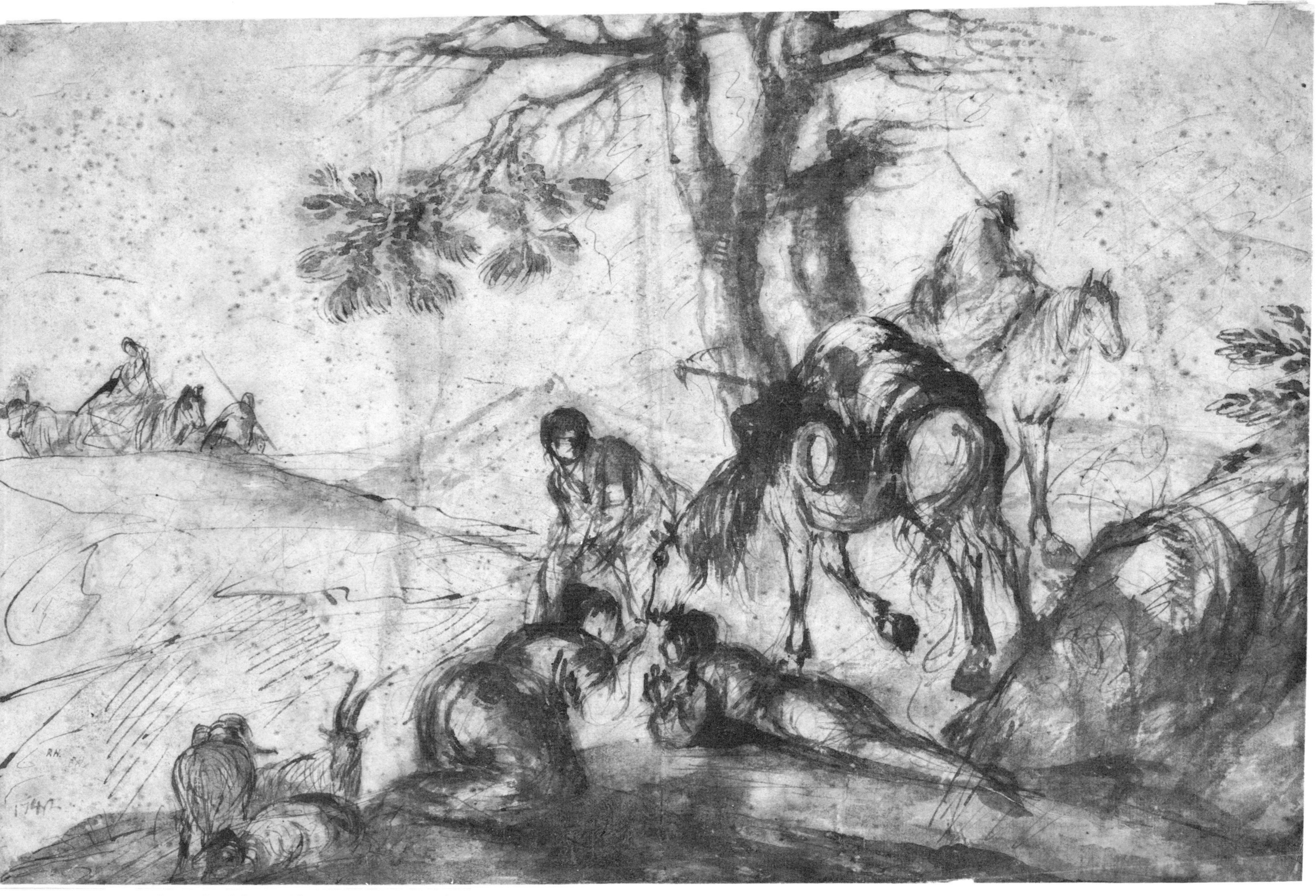

108. *Giovanni Benedetto Castiglione (Genoese, 1616–1670).* TRAVELERS RESTING UNDER A TREE.

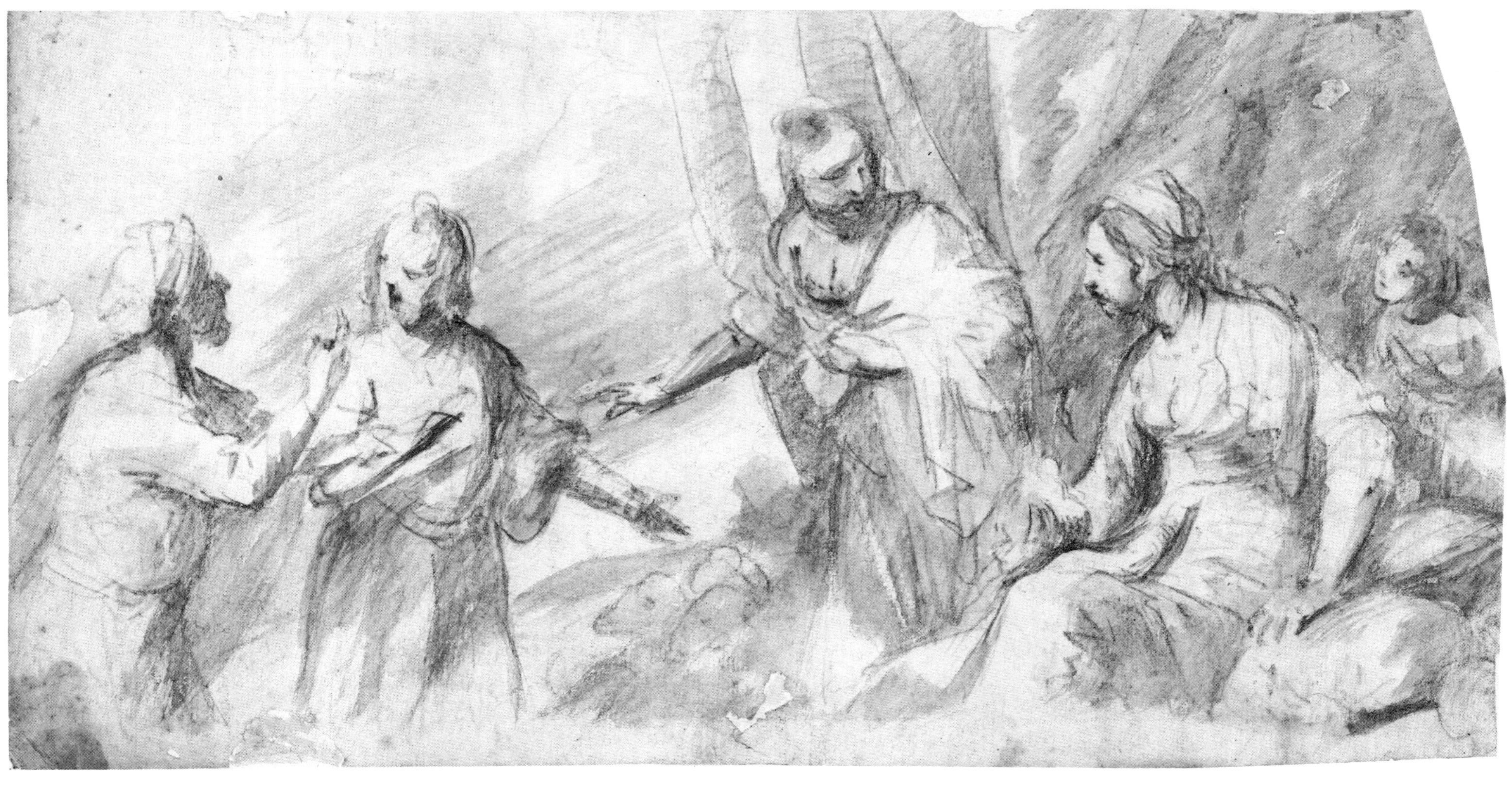

109. *Giovanni Andrea de' Ferrari (Genoese, 1598–1669).* JACOB PROMISING LABAN SEVEN YEARS OF SERVICE.

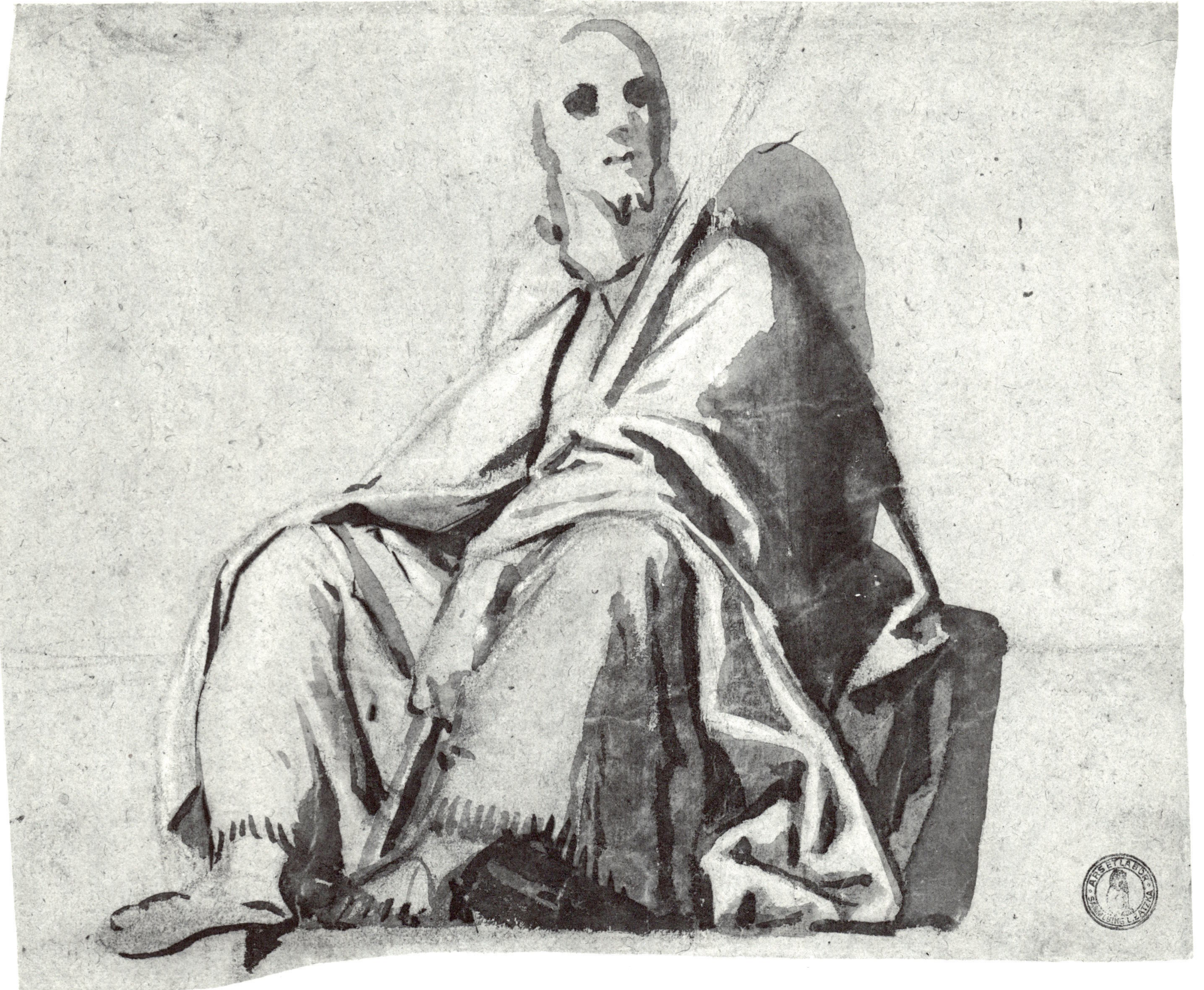

110. *Pierfrancesco Mazzucchelli, called Il Morazzone (Lombard, 1571/73–1626),* SEATED MALE FIGURE.

The Pierpont Morgan Library, Janos Scholz Collection

111. *Giovanni Battista Benaschi (Turin-Naples, 1636–1688).* TRUMPETERS.

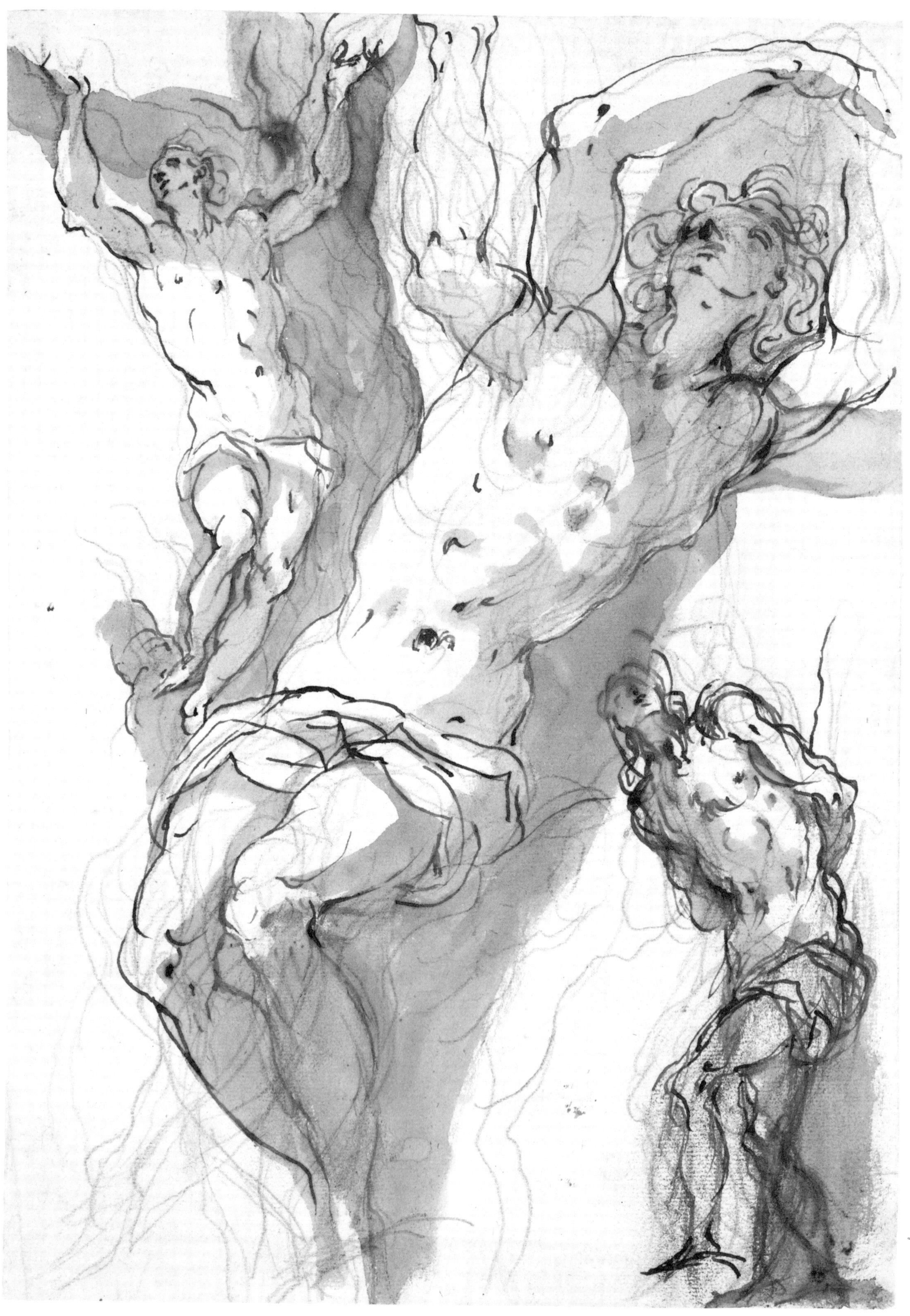

*112. Alessandro Maganza (Vicenza, 1556–about 1640).* STUDIES FOR A ST. SEBASTIAN.

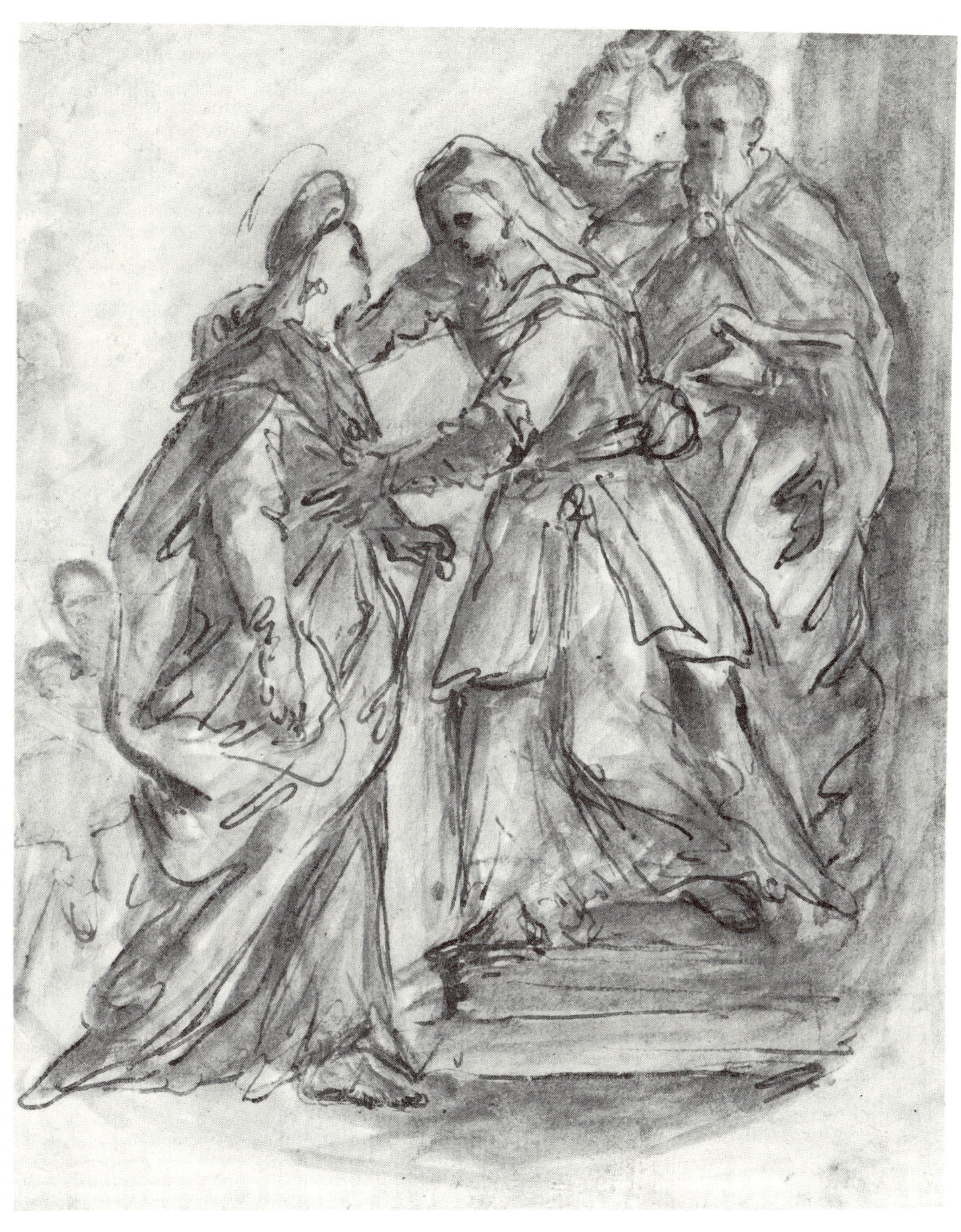

*113. Francesco Maffei (Venetian, 1606–1660).* THE VISITATION.

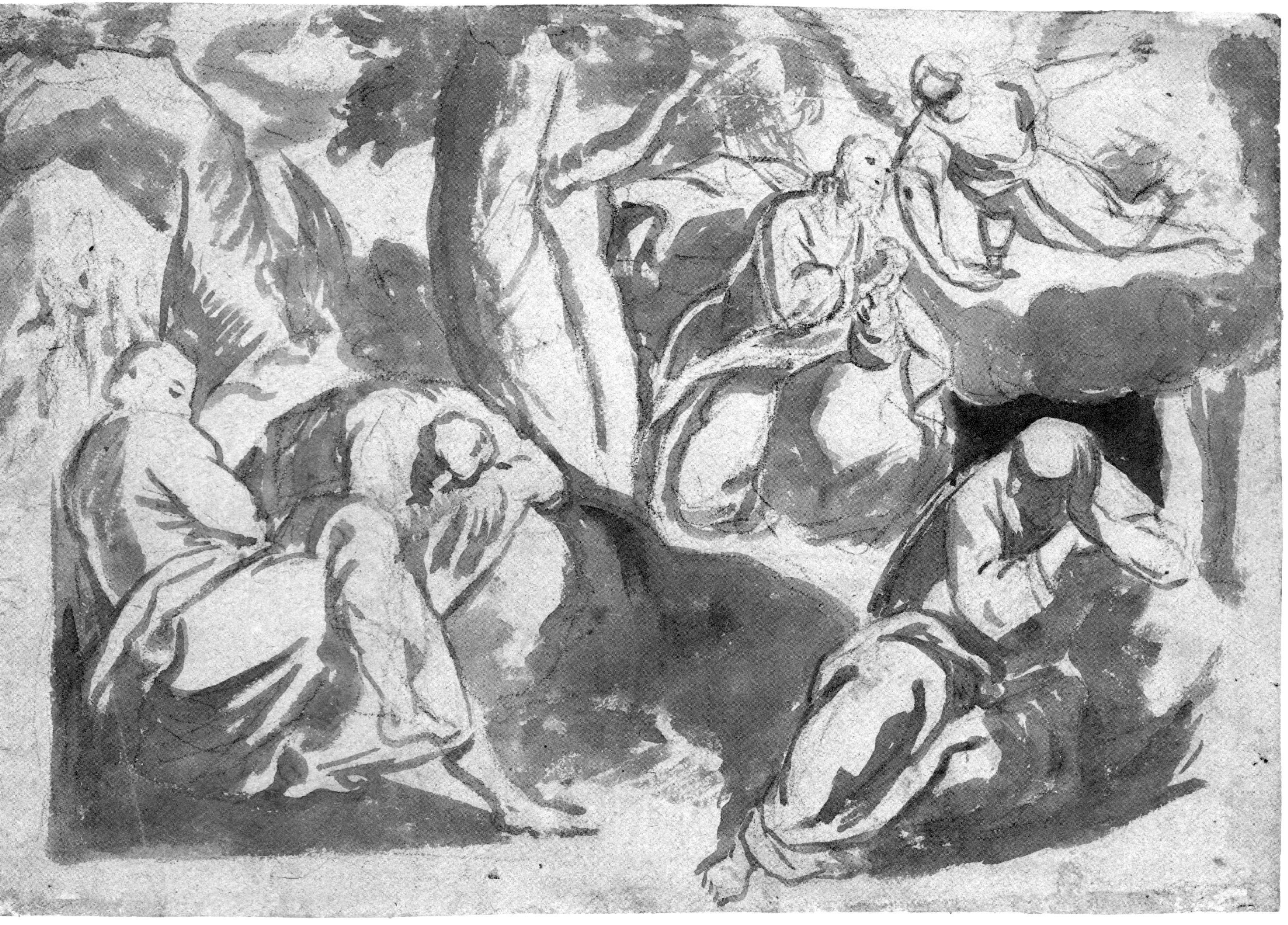

114. *Domenico Tintoretto (Venice, 1560–1635).* CHRIST ON THE MOUNT OF OLIVES.

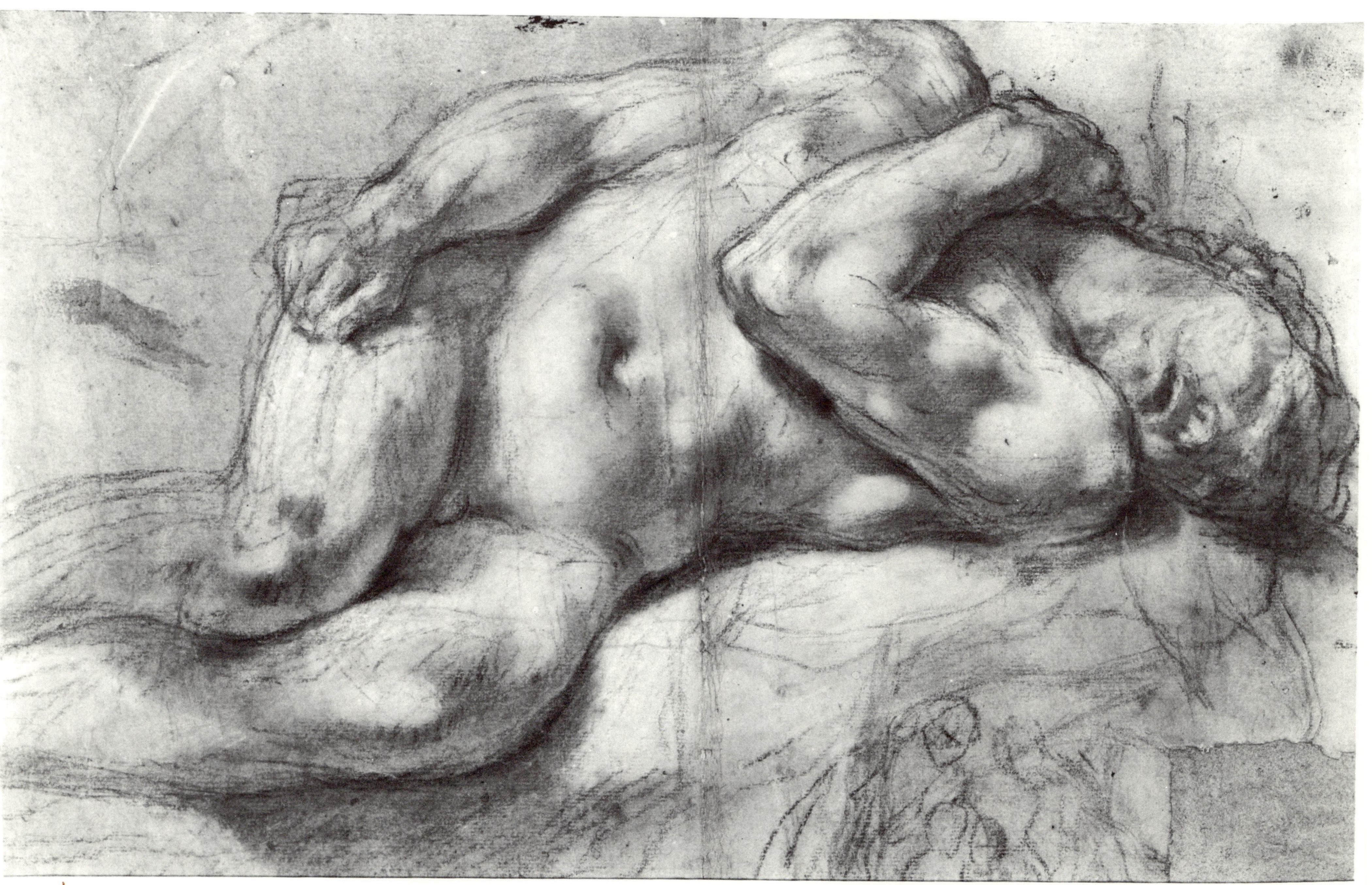

115. *Domenico Maria Canuti (Bolognese, 1620–1684).* STUDY OF A DEAD OR SLEEPING MAN.

The Pierpont Morgan Library, Janos Scholz Collection

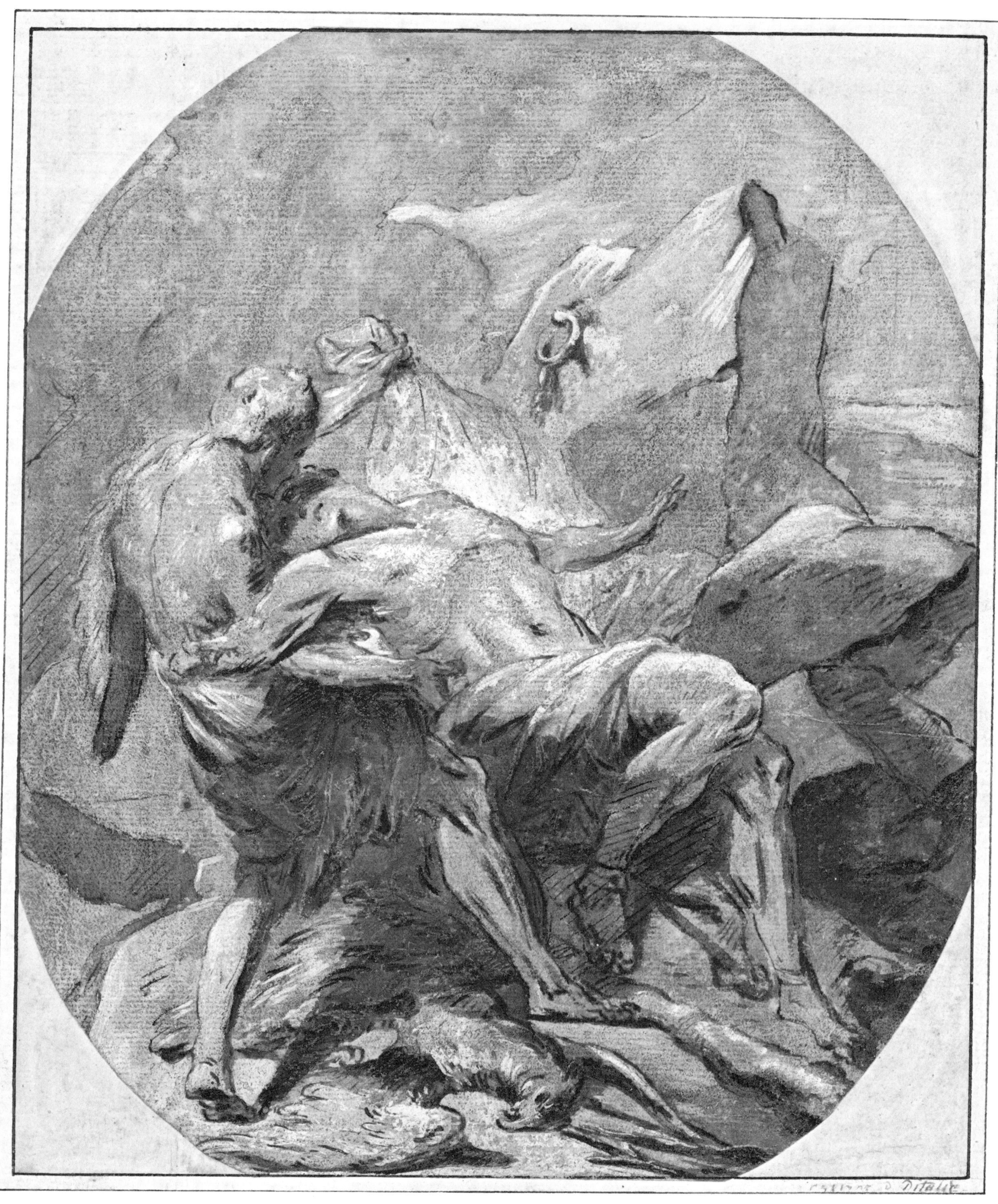

*116. Federico Bencovich (Venetian, about 1677–1753).* HERCULES FREEING PROMETHEUS.

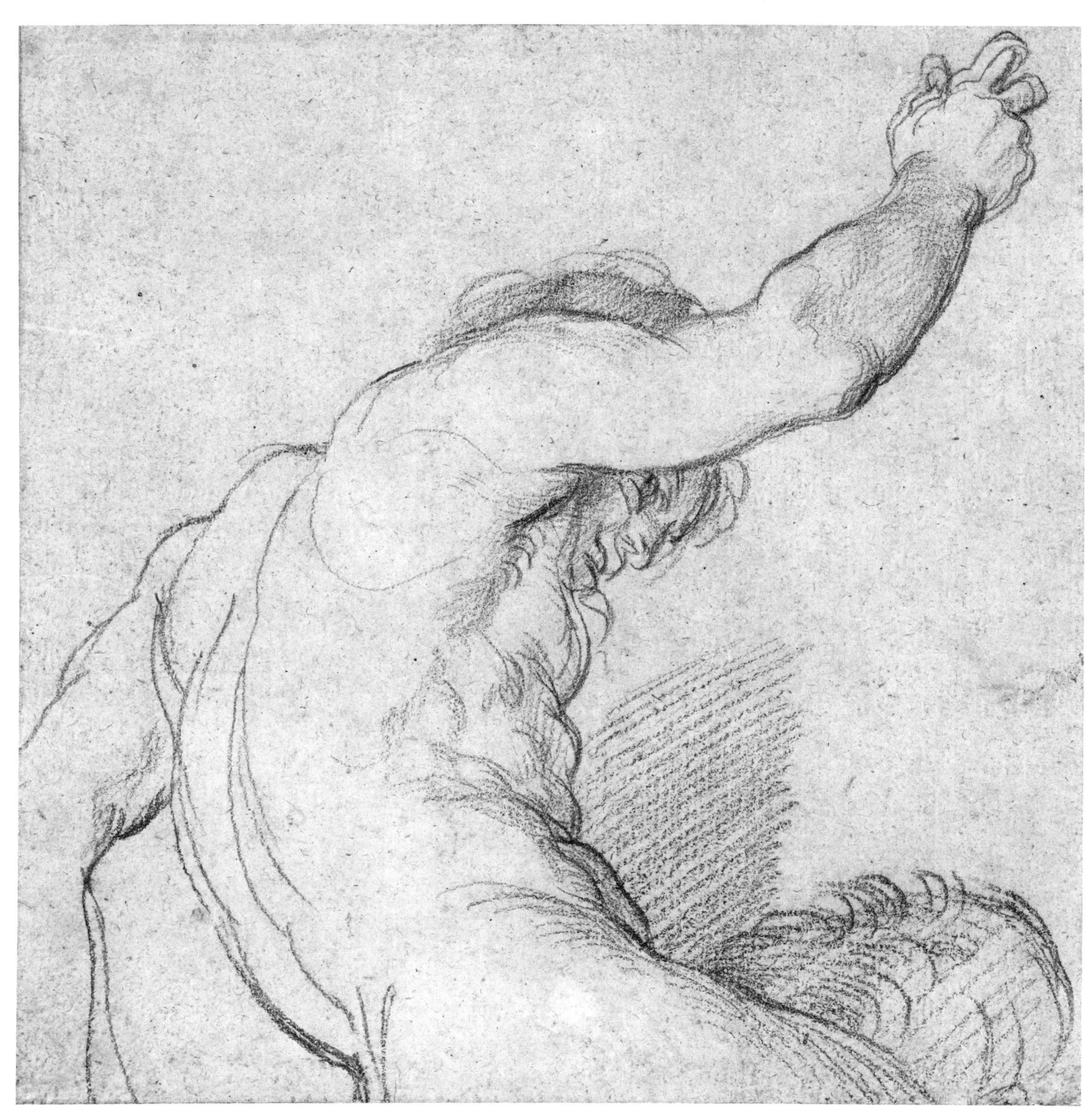

*117. Carlo Maratta (Roman, 1625–1713).* HALF-LENGTH FIGURE OF A FAUN.

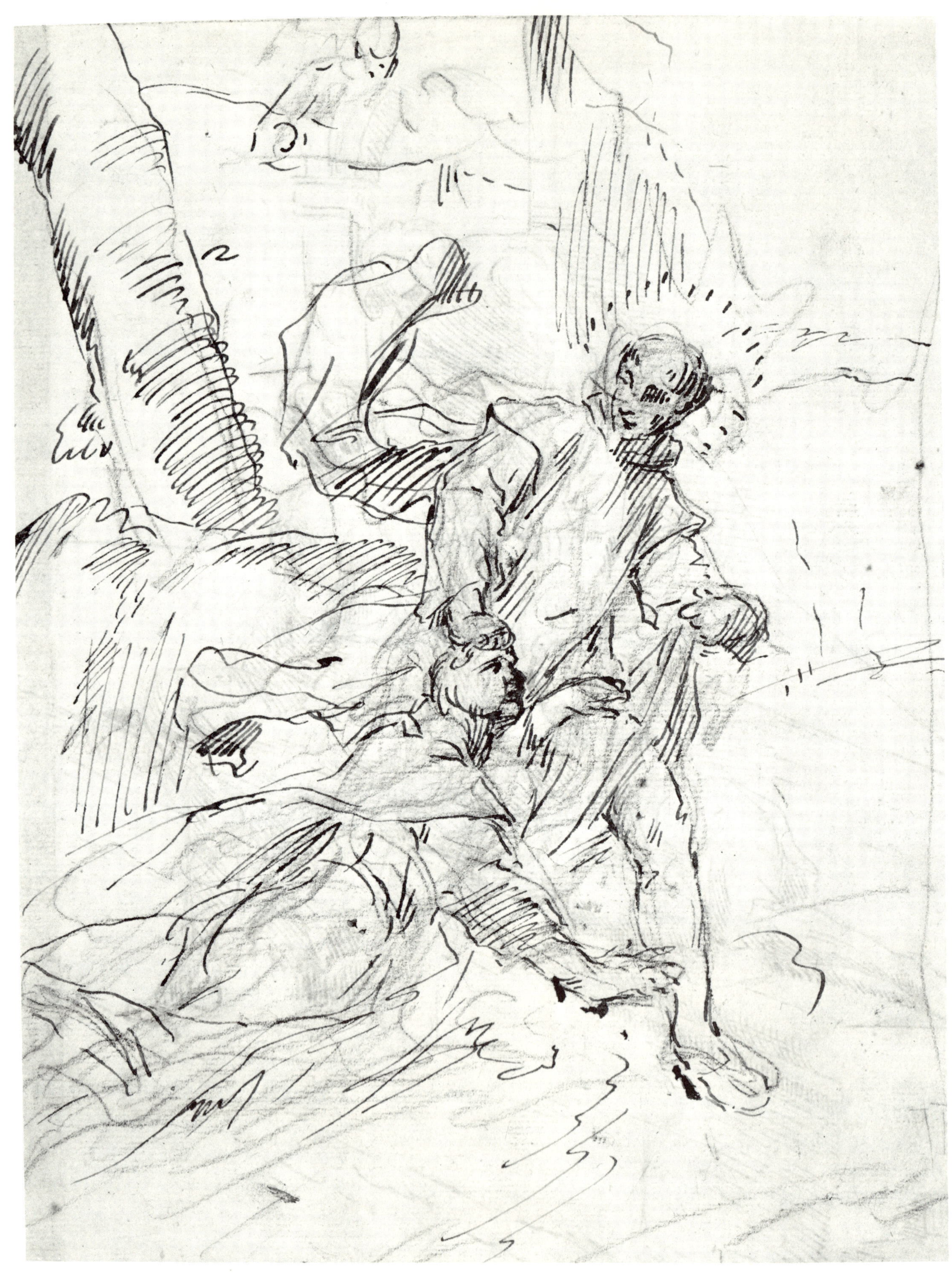

118. *Andrea Sacchi (Roman, 1599–1661).* EPISODE FROM THE LIFE OF A SAINT.

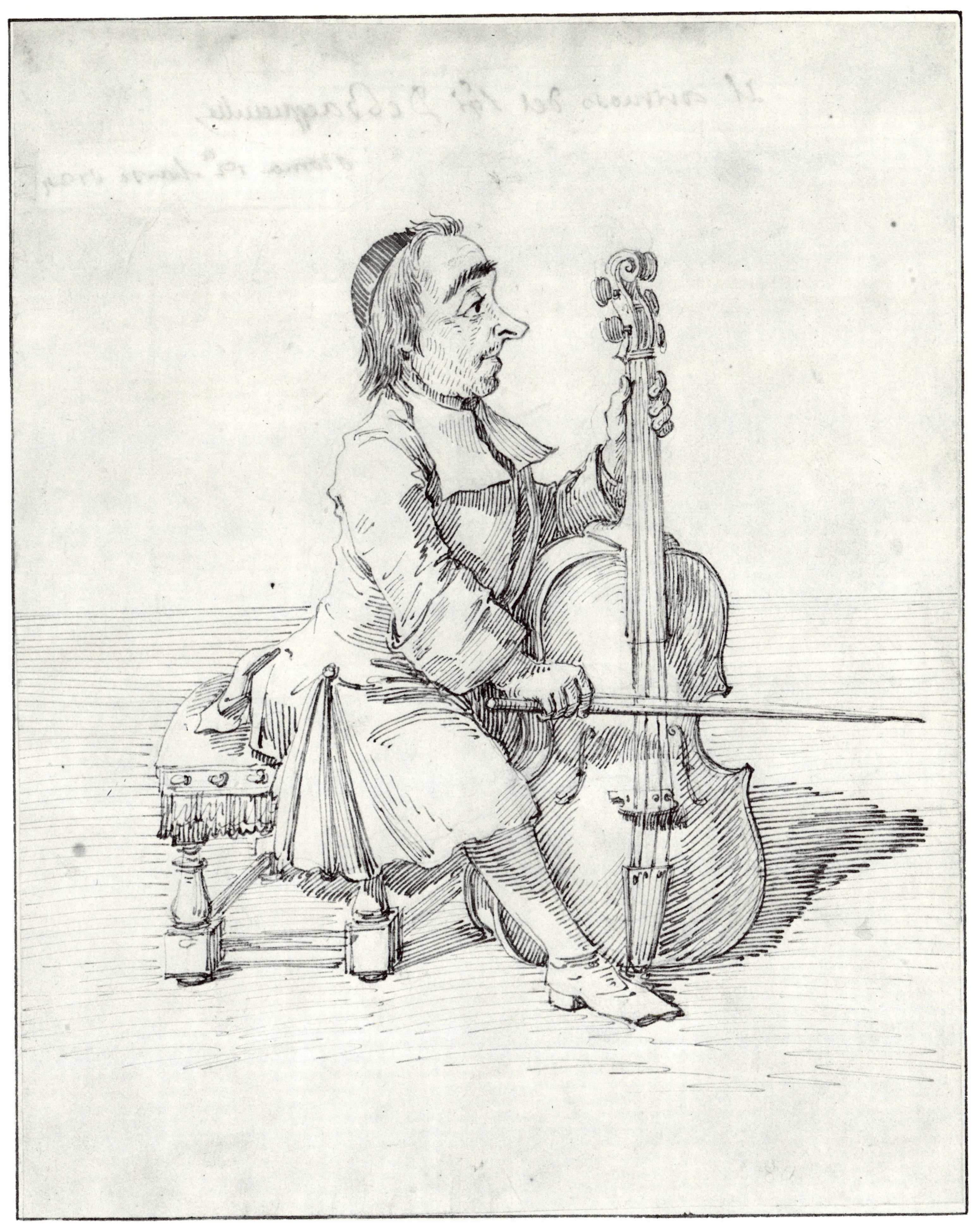

*119. Pierleone Ghezzi (Roman, 1674–1755).* VIOLONCELLIST PLAYING HIS INSTRUMENT.

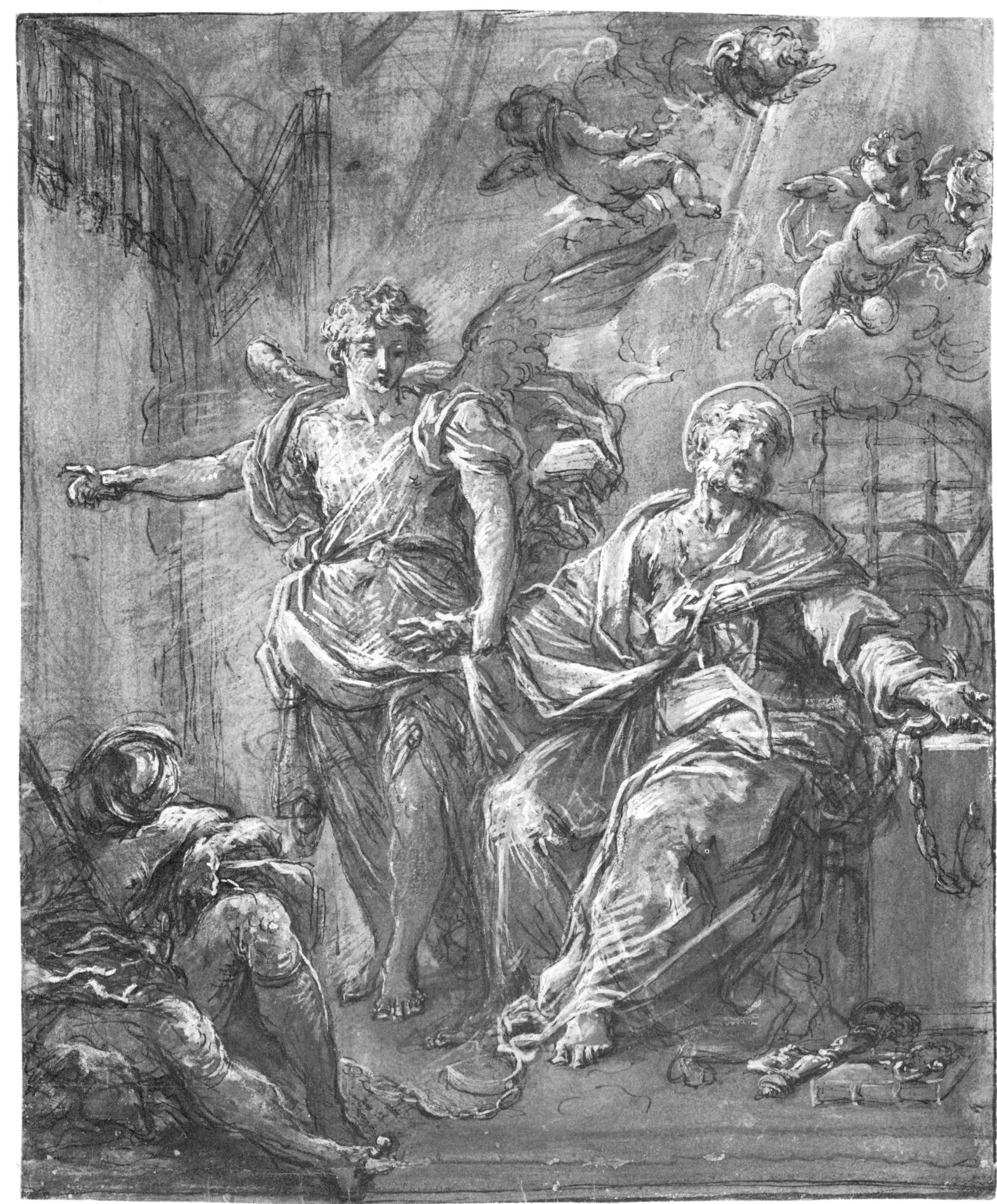

*120. Giuseppe Passeri (Roman, 1654–1714).* ST. PETER FREED FROM PRISON.

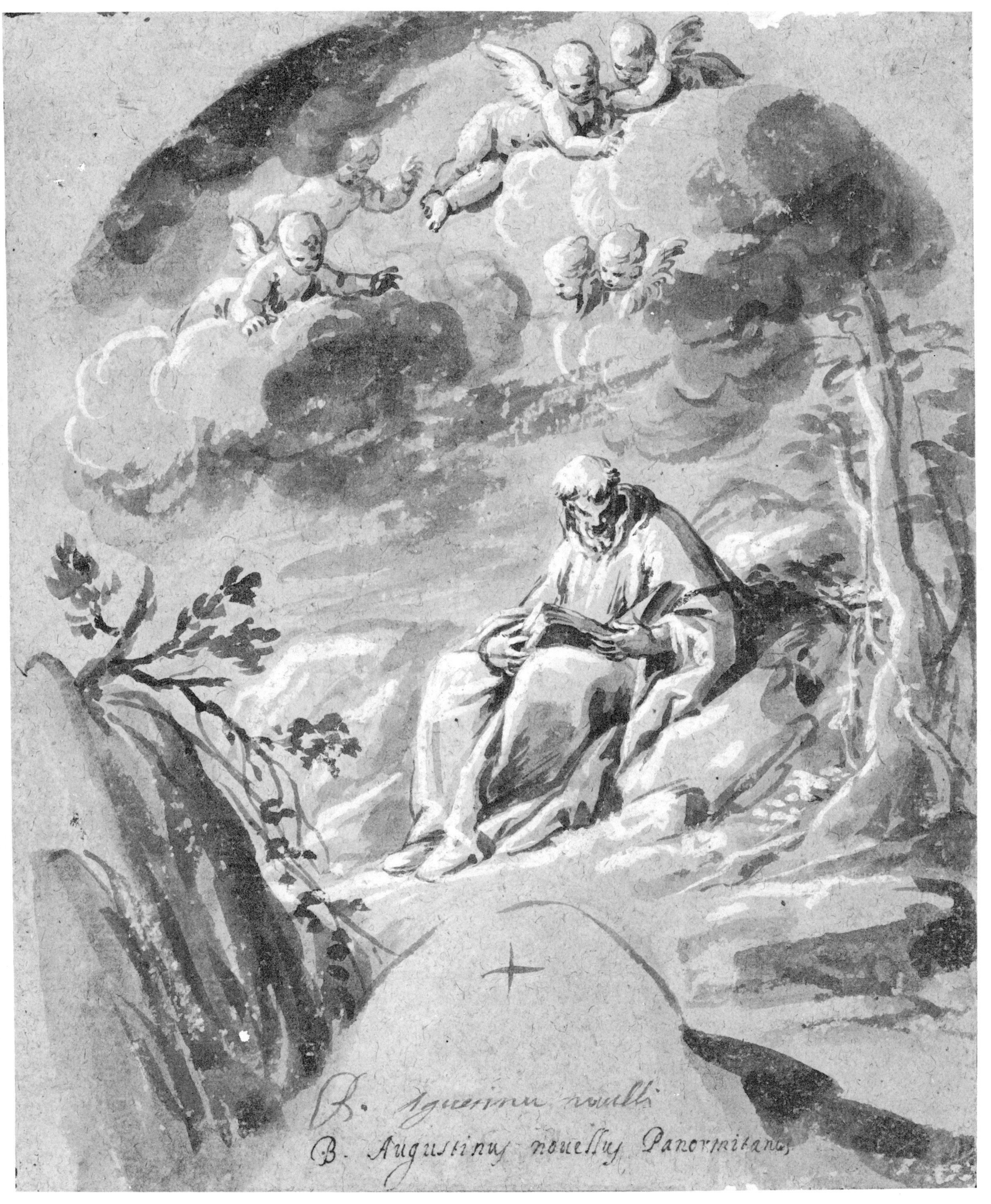


*121. Alessandro Magnasco (Genoese, about 1667–1749).* SEATED MONK IN A LANDSCAPE.

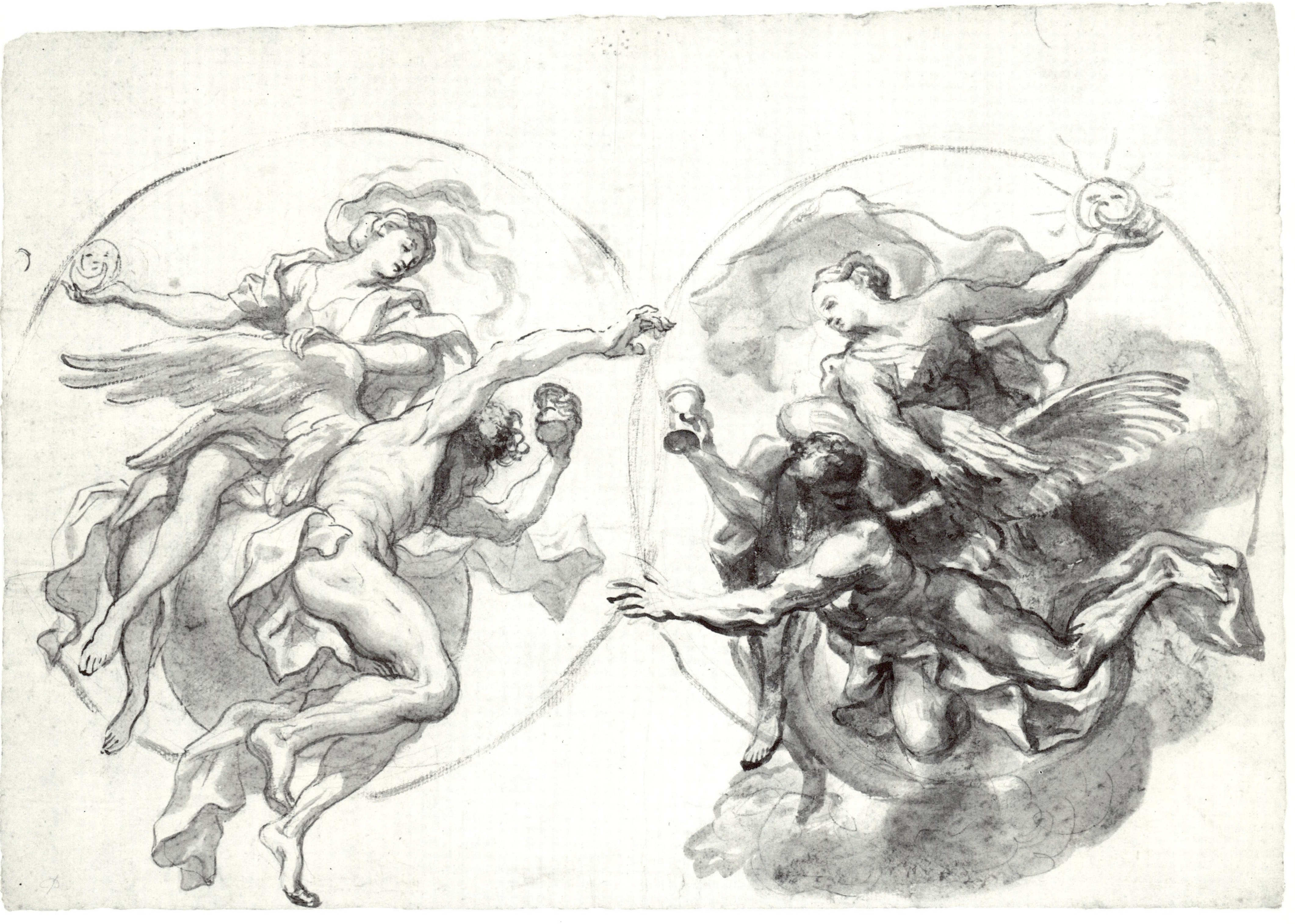

122. *Domenico Piola (Genoese, 1627–1703).* ALLEGORY OF THE SOLSTICE.

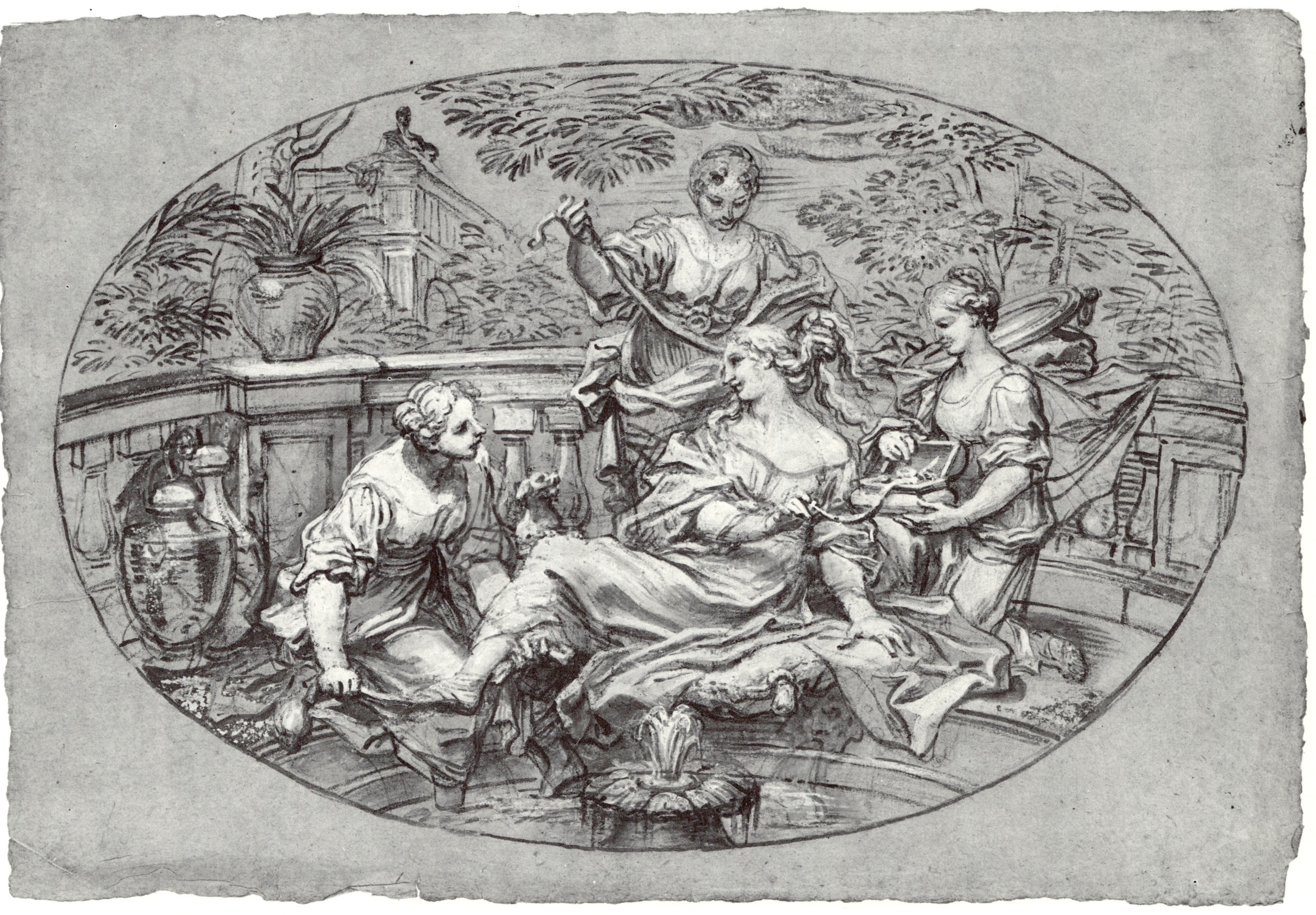

123. *Paolo Girolamo Piola (Genoese, 1666–1724).* THE TOILET OF BATHSHEBA.

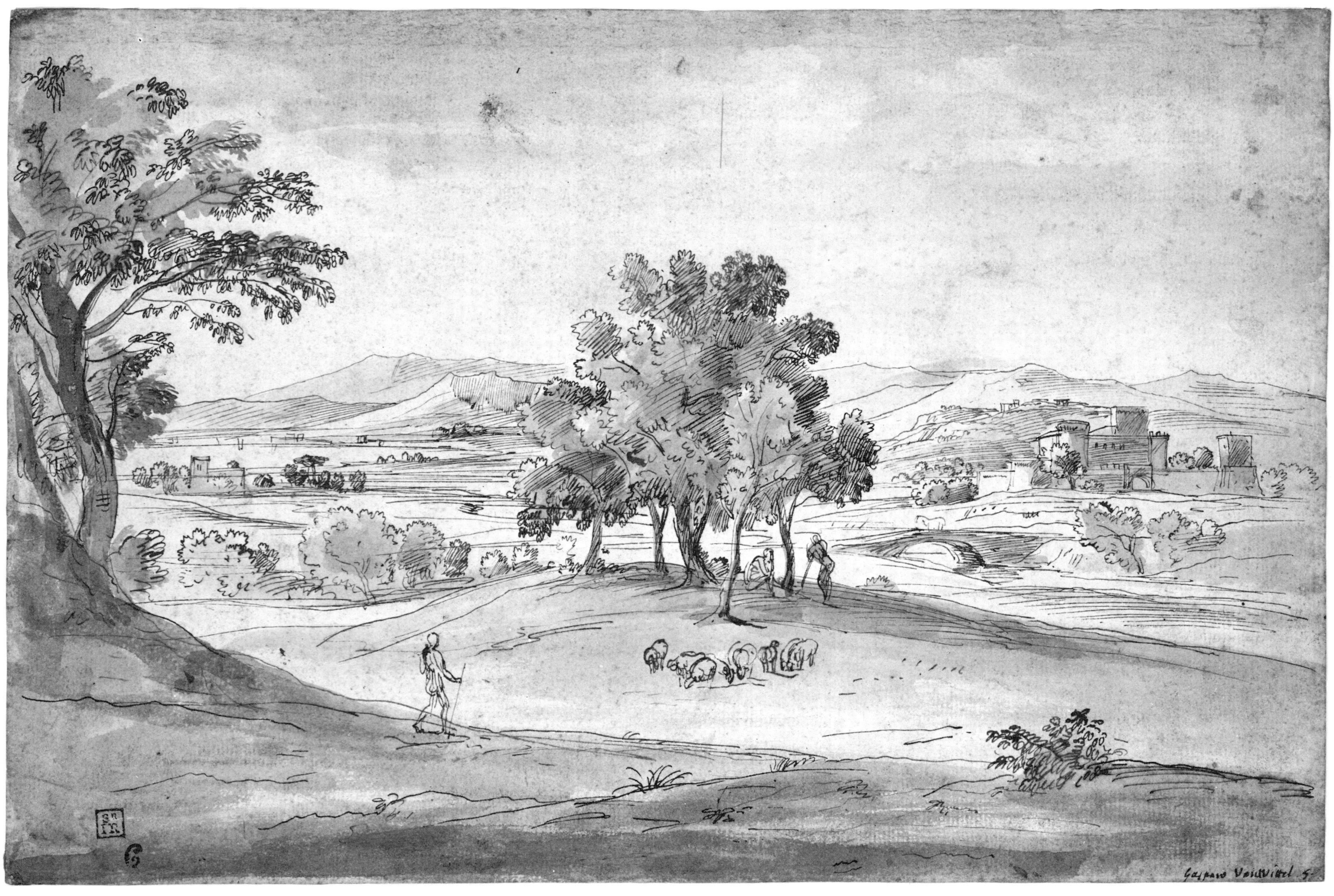

124. *Gaspare Vanvitelli (Utrecht-Rome, 1647–1736).* THE ROMAN CAMPAGNA.

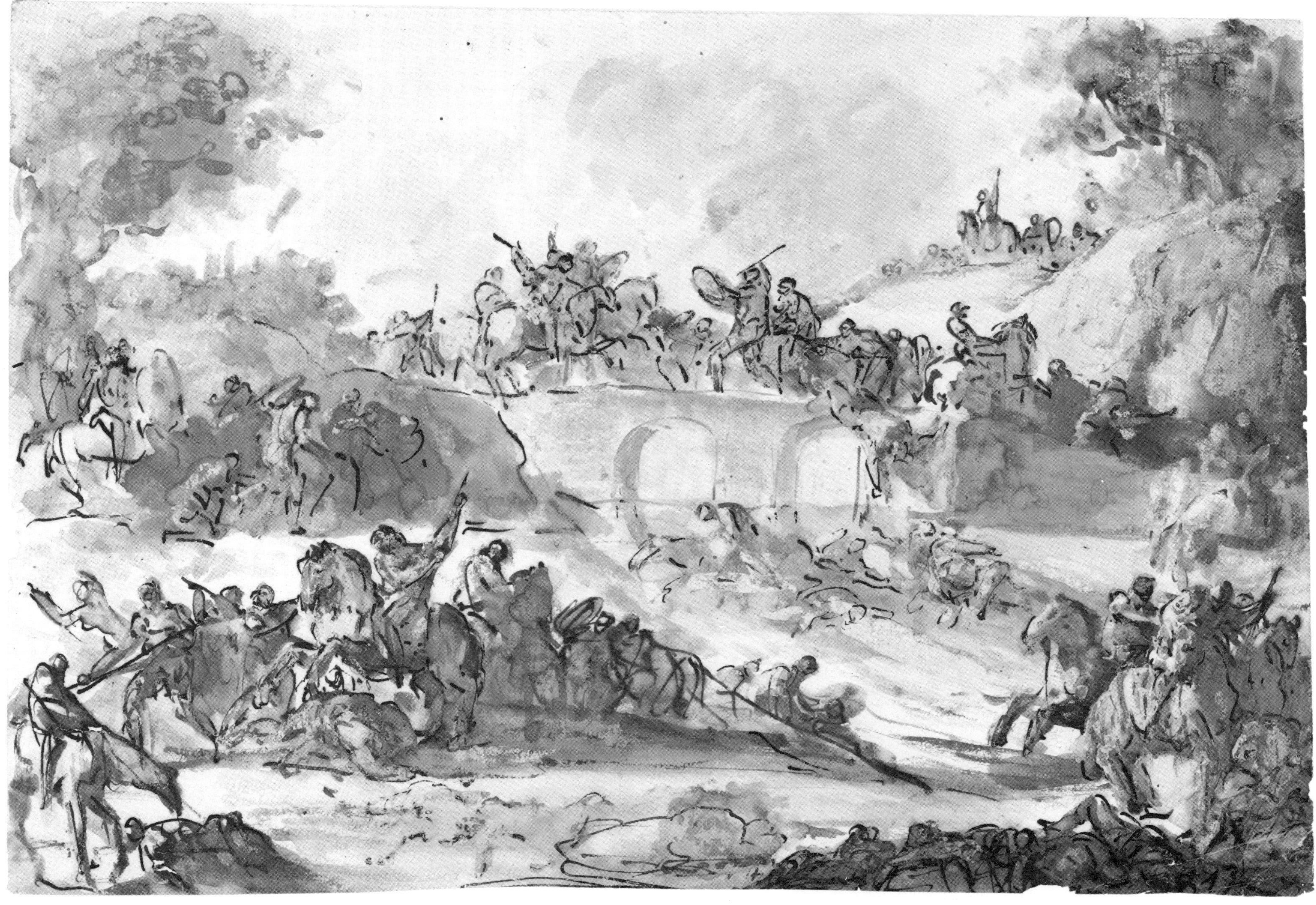

125. *Domenico del Mondo (Neapolitan, 1717–1806).* HORATIUS COC ES DEFENDING THE BRIDGE.

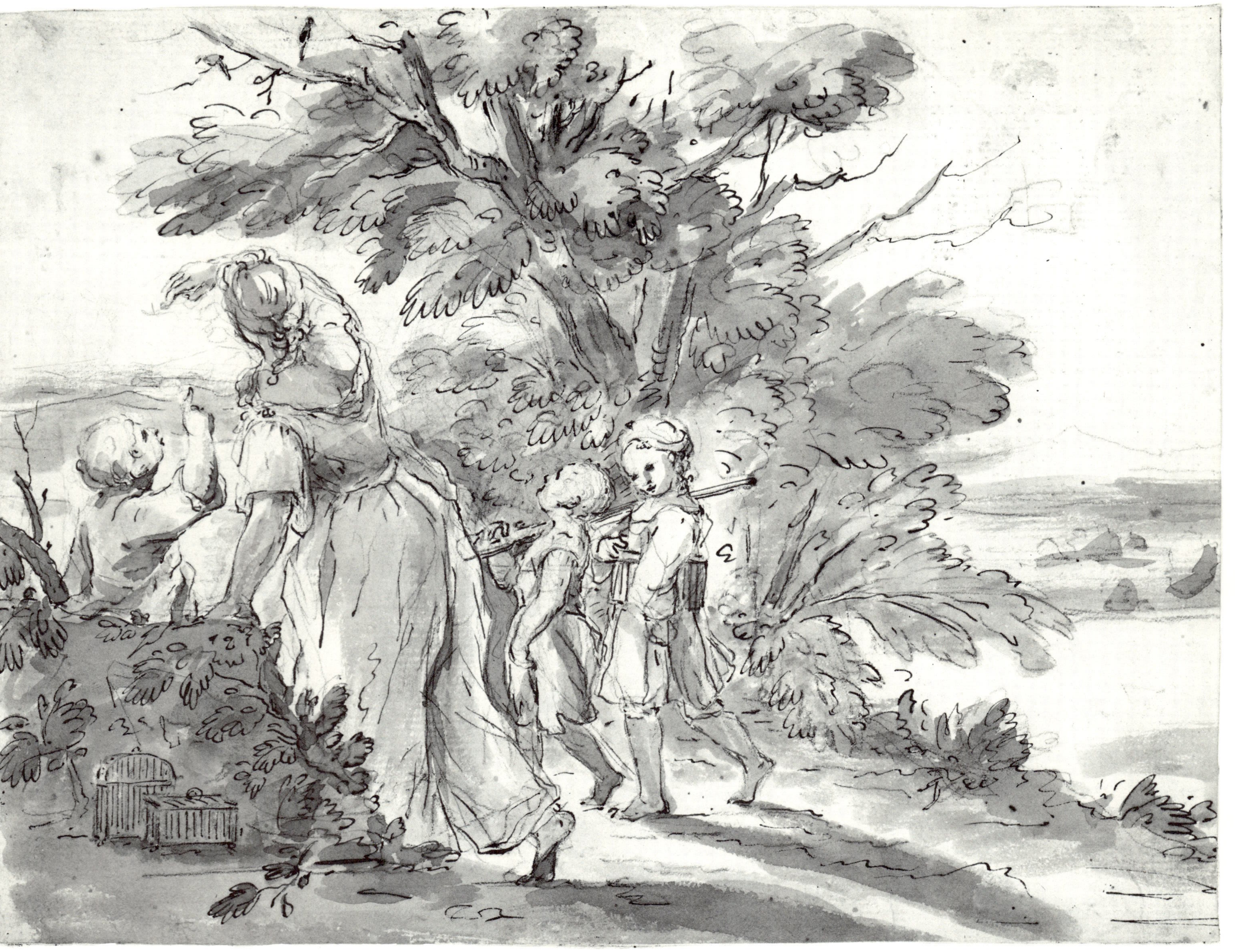

126. *Gian Gioseffo dal Sole (Bolognese, 1654–1719).* THE BIRD CATCHERS.

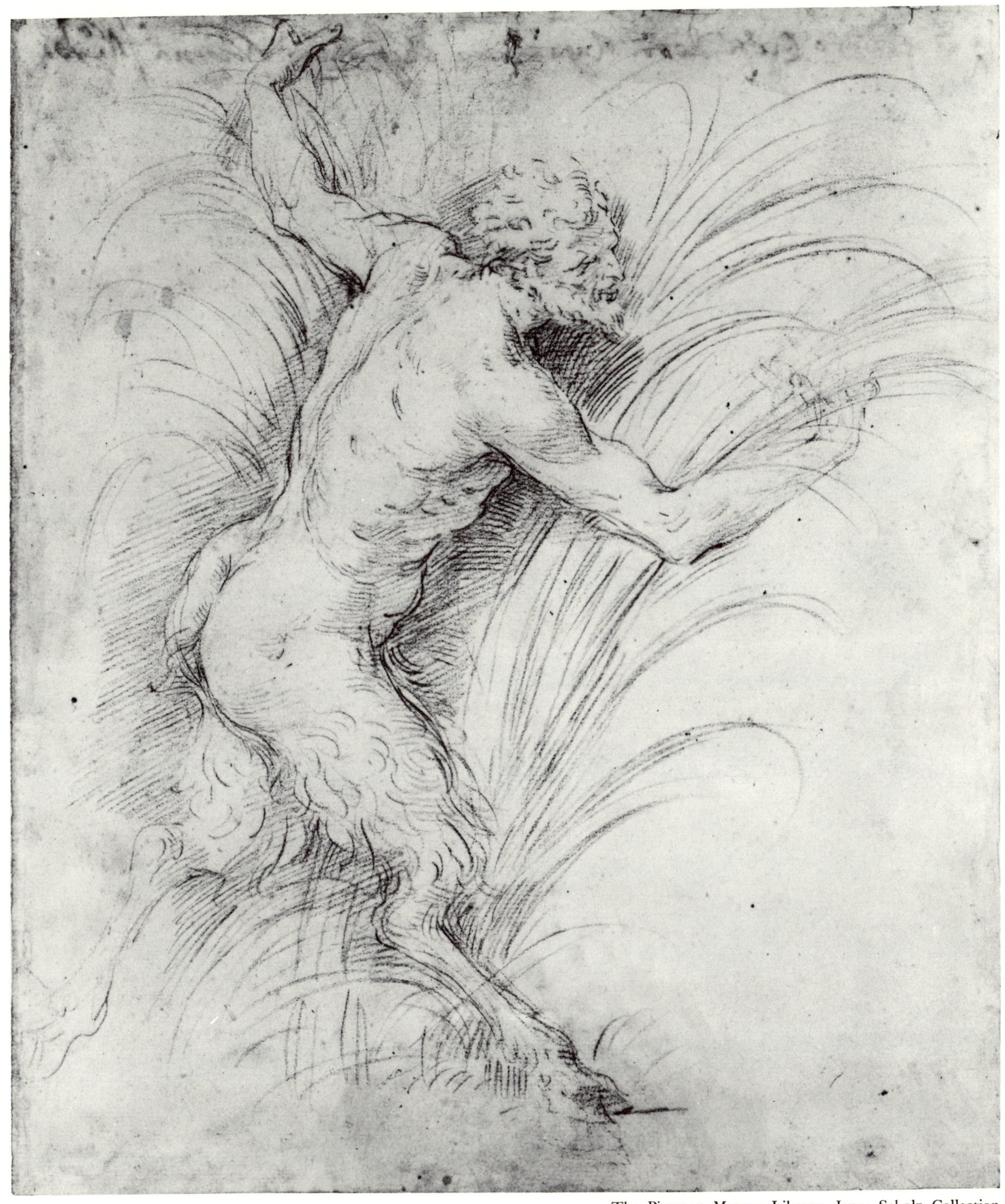

The Pierpont Morgan Library, Janos Scholz Collection

*127. Donato Creti (Bolognese, 1671–1749).* SATYR.

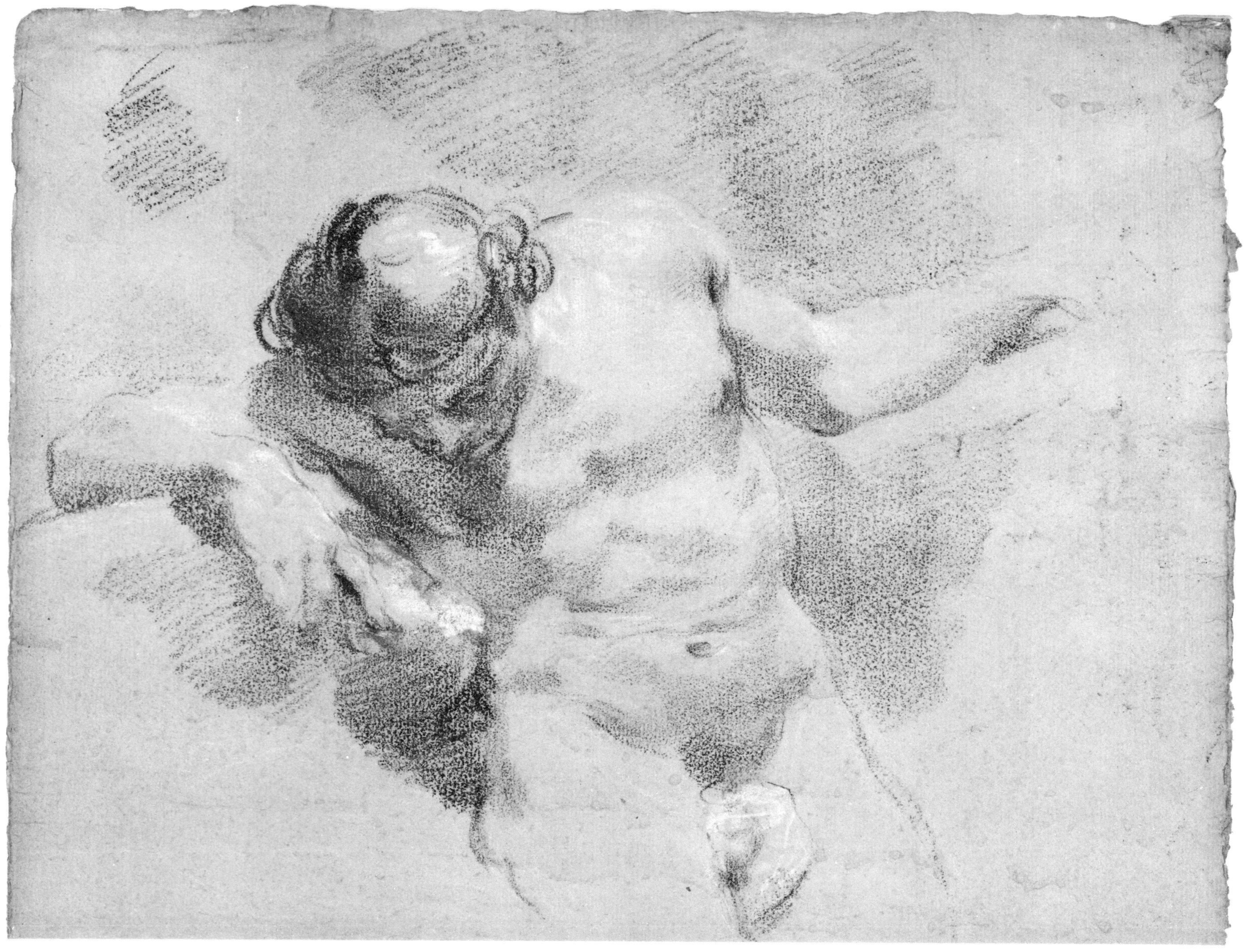

128. *Gaetano Gandolfi (Bolognese, 1734–1802).* THE DEAD CHRIST.

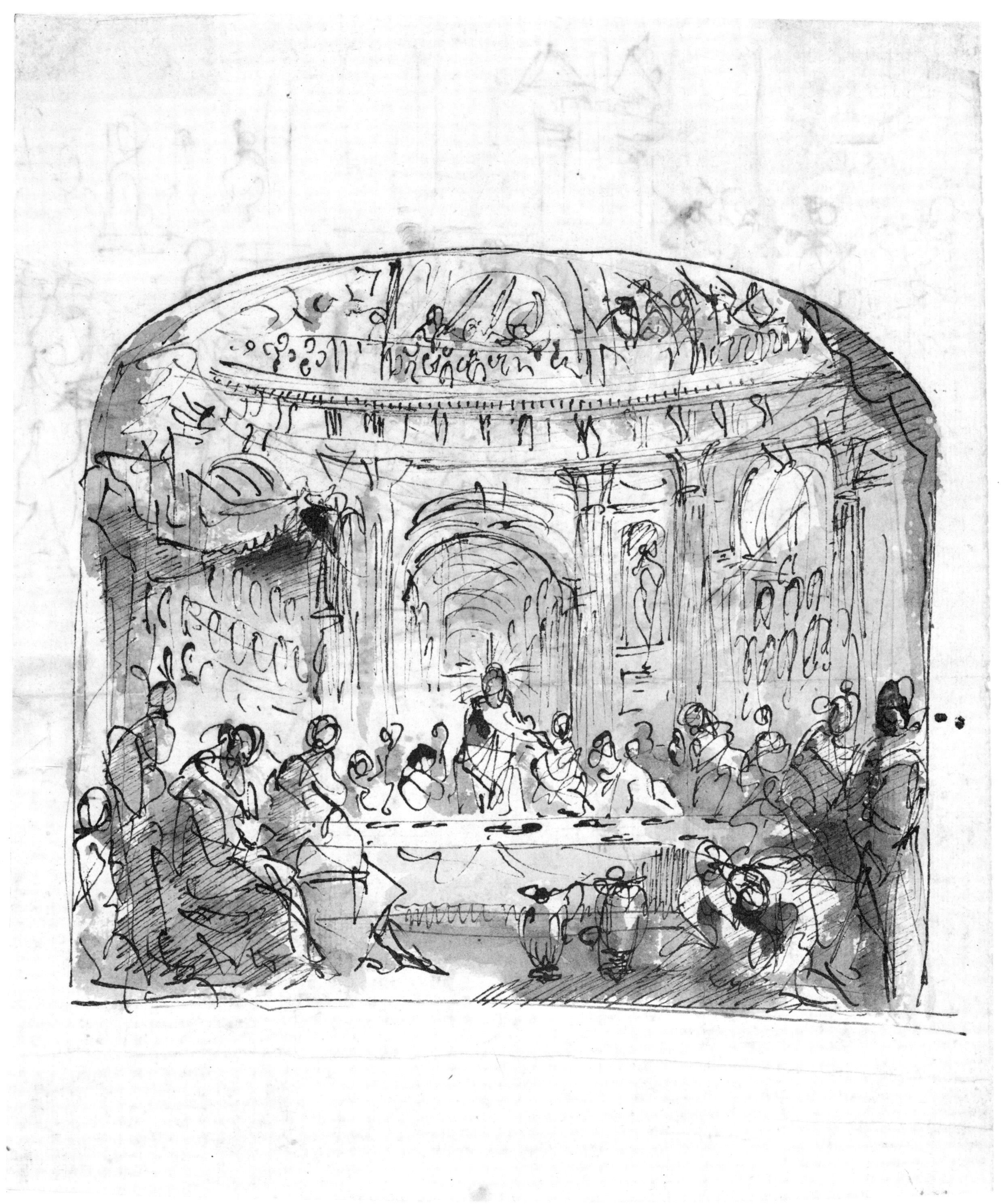

129. *Gaetano Gandolfi.* THE MARRIAGE FEAST AT CANA.

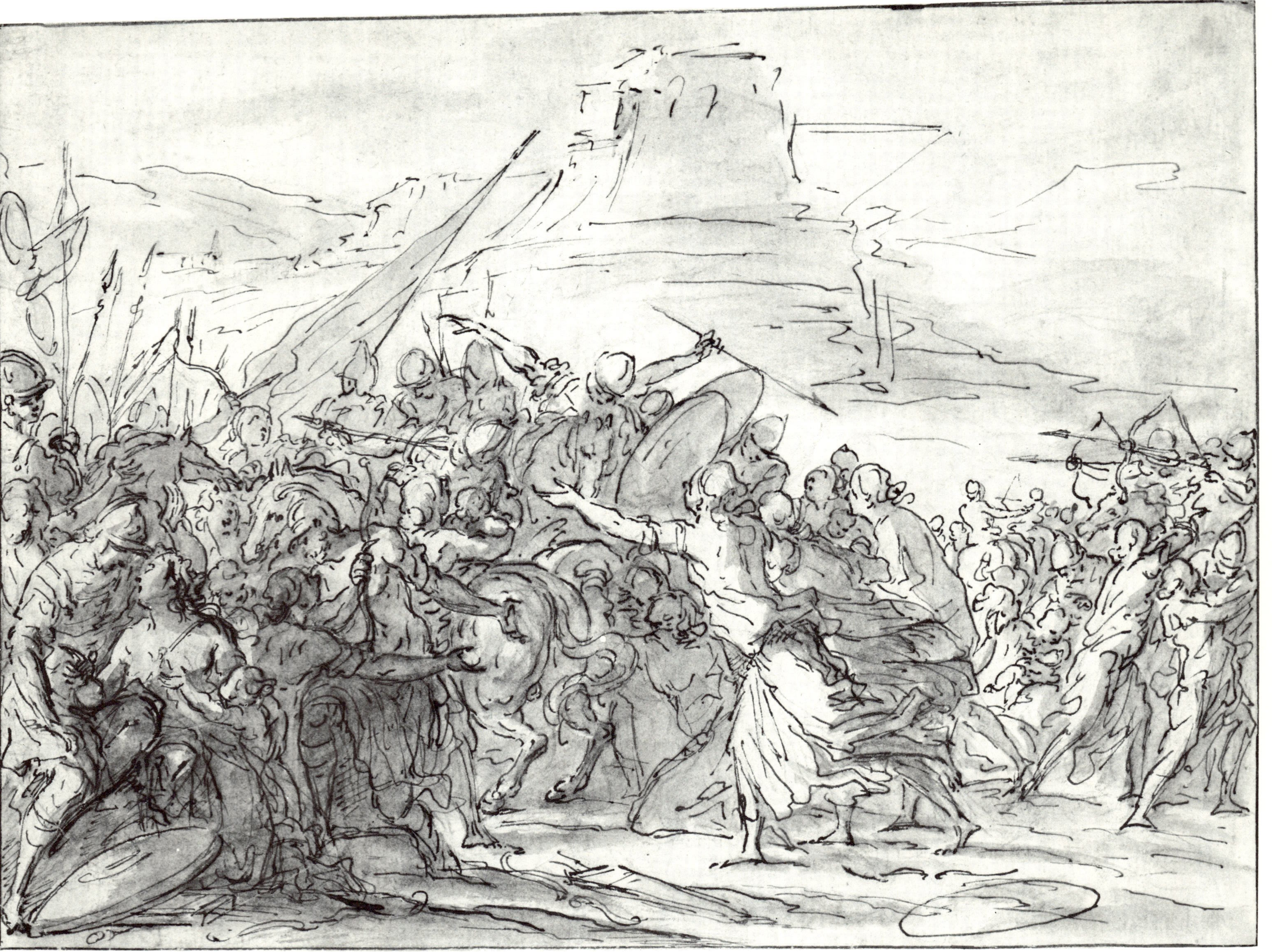

130. *Sebastiano Ricci (Venetian, 1659–1734).* ROMAN BATTLE.

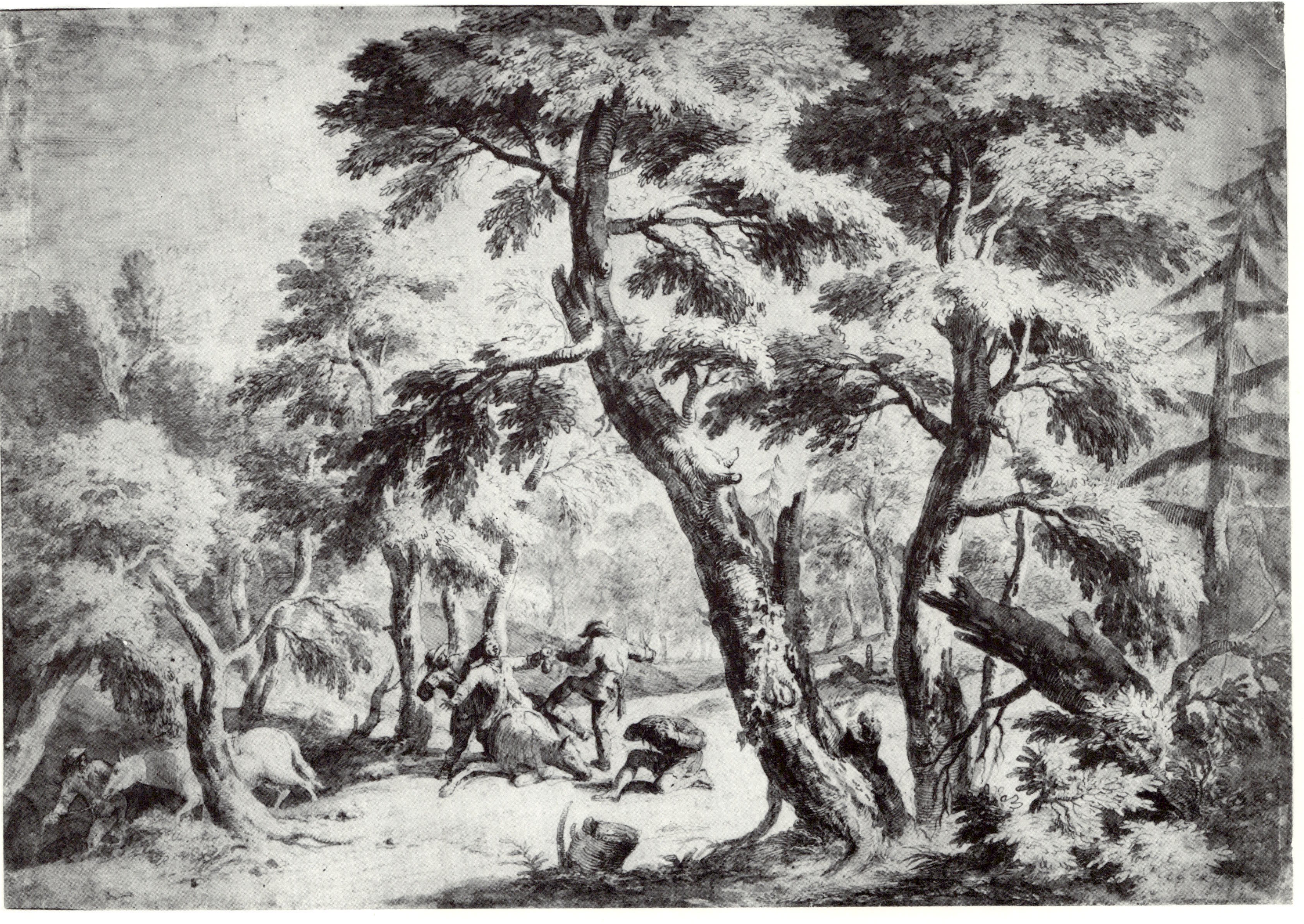

131. *Marco Ricci (Venetian, 1676–1729).* BRIGANDS ATTACKING TRAVELERS.

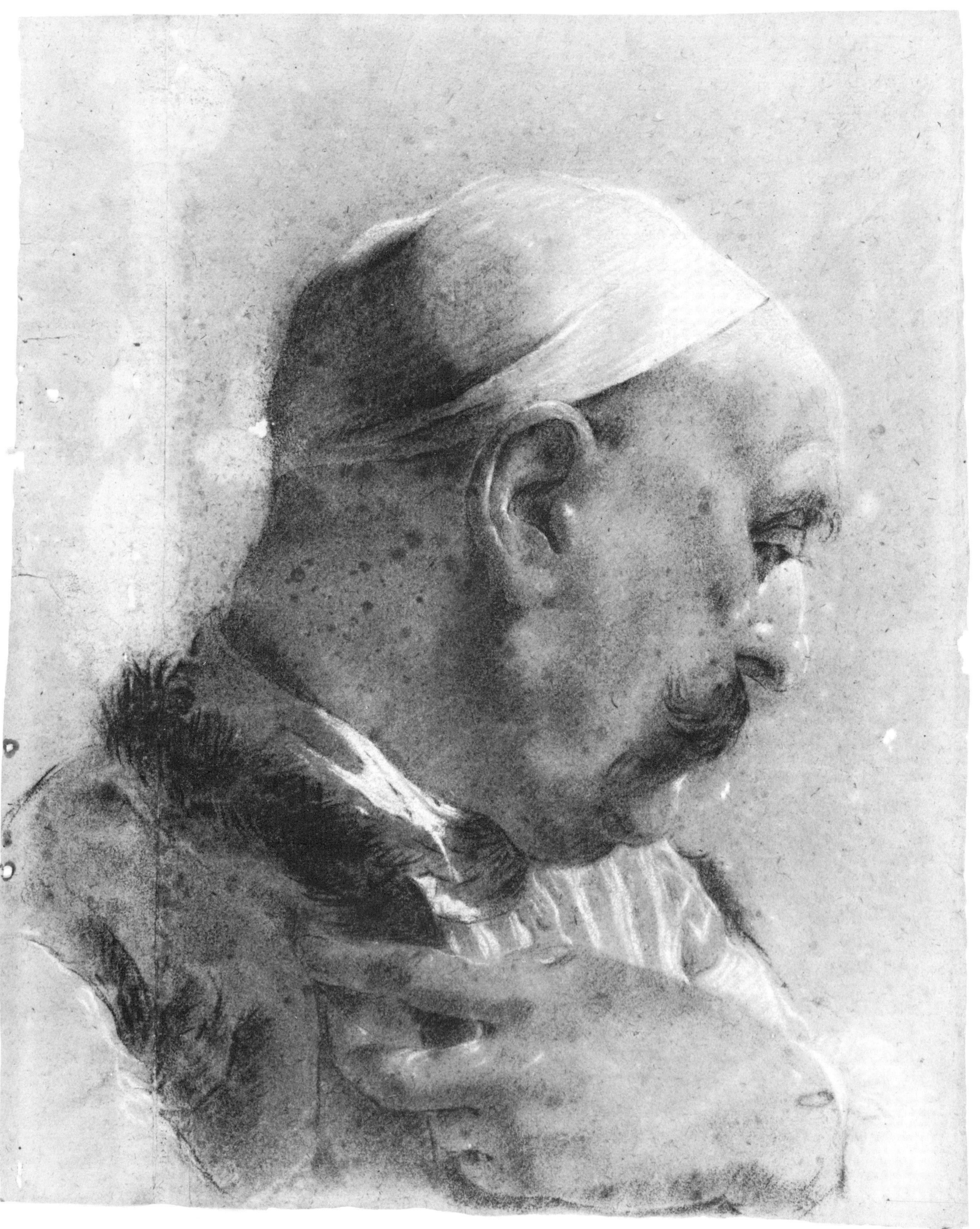

The Pierpont Morgan Library, Janos Scholz Collection

132. *Giovanni Battista Piazzetta (Venice, 1682–1754).* HEAD OF A LEVANTINE.

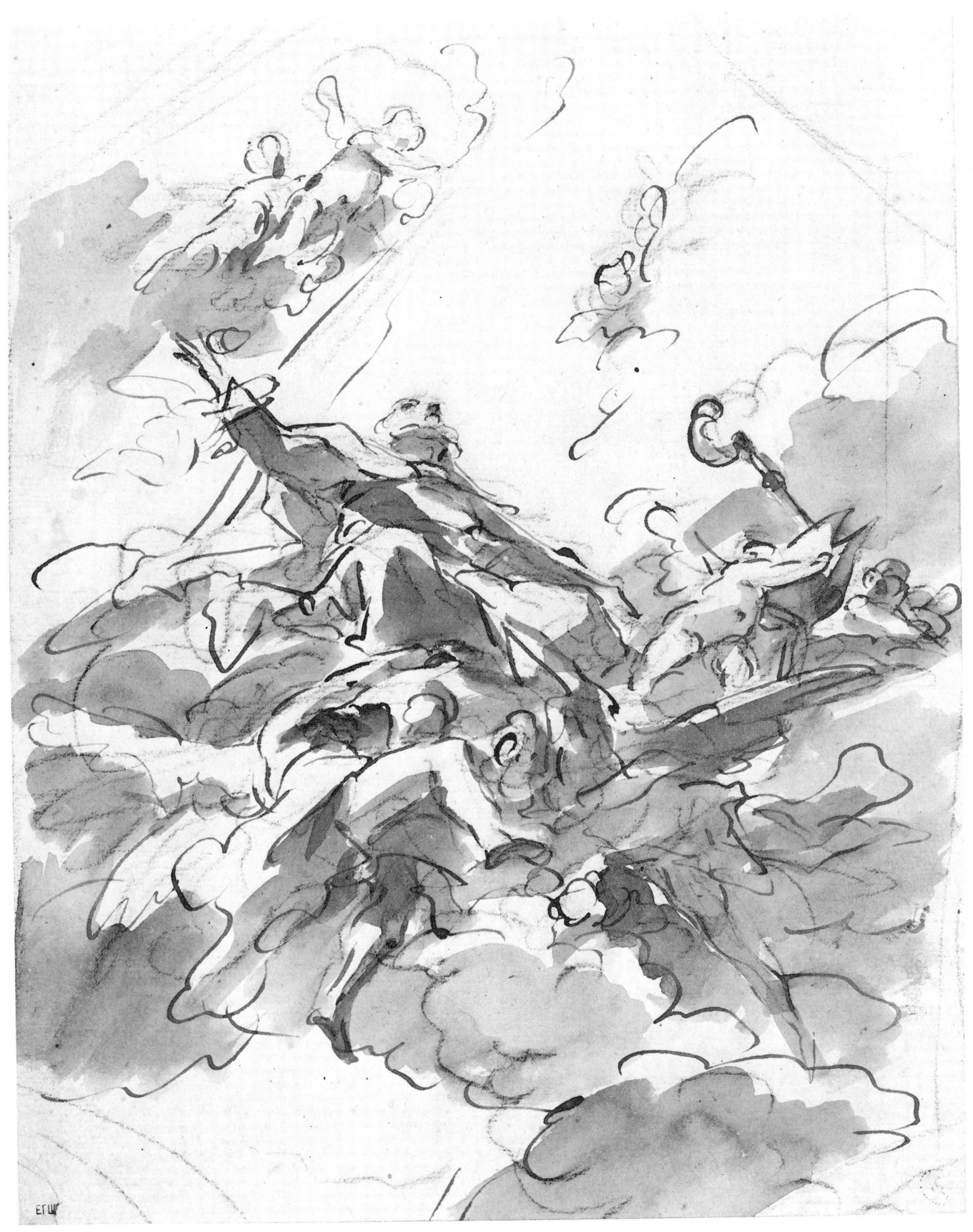

*133. Giovanni Antonio Pellegrini (Venetian, 1675–1741).* HOLY BISHOP IN GLORY.

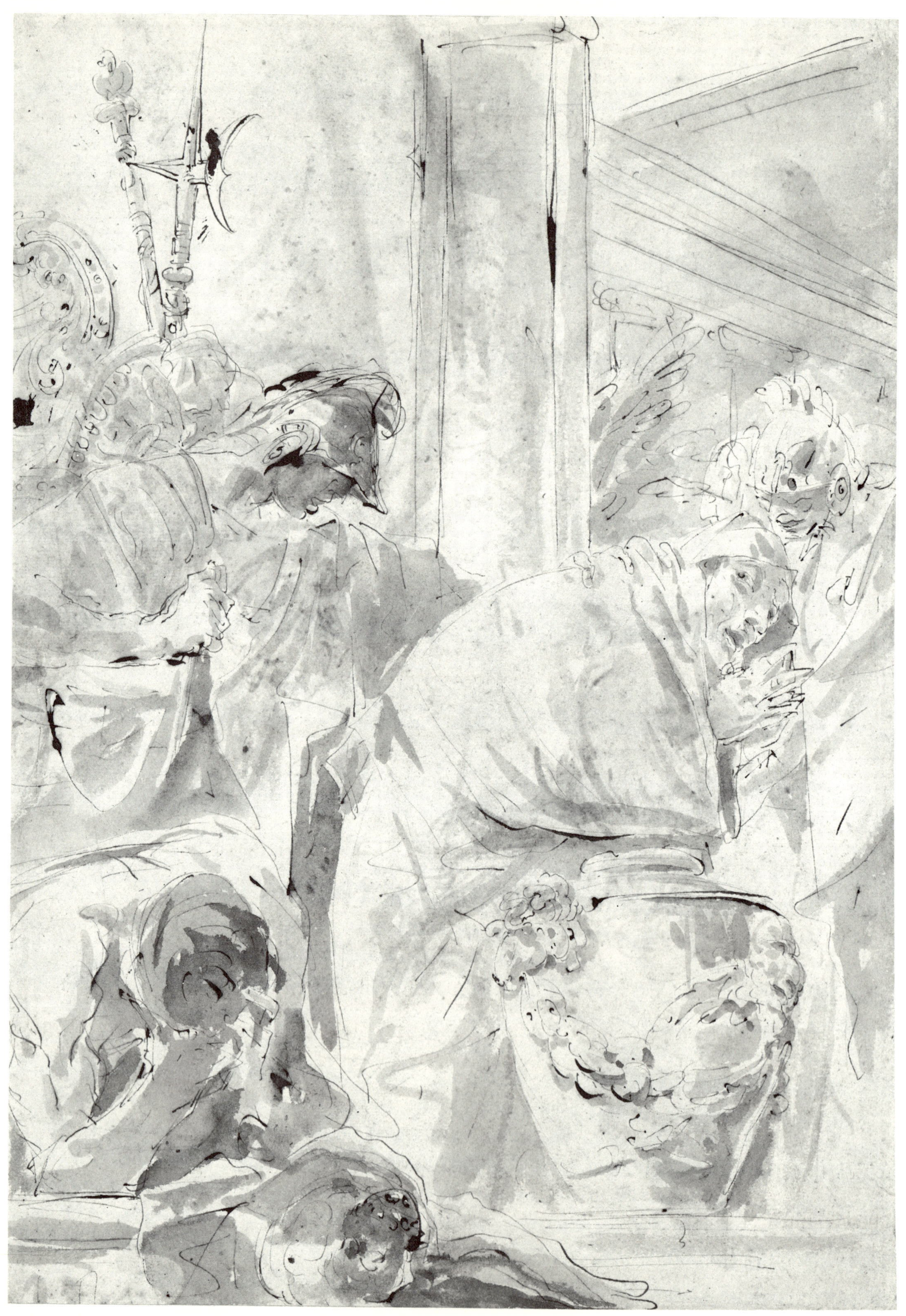

*134. Giovanni Battista Tiepolo (Venice-Madrid, 1696–1770).* MAN LED INTO PRISON.

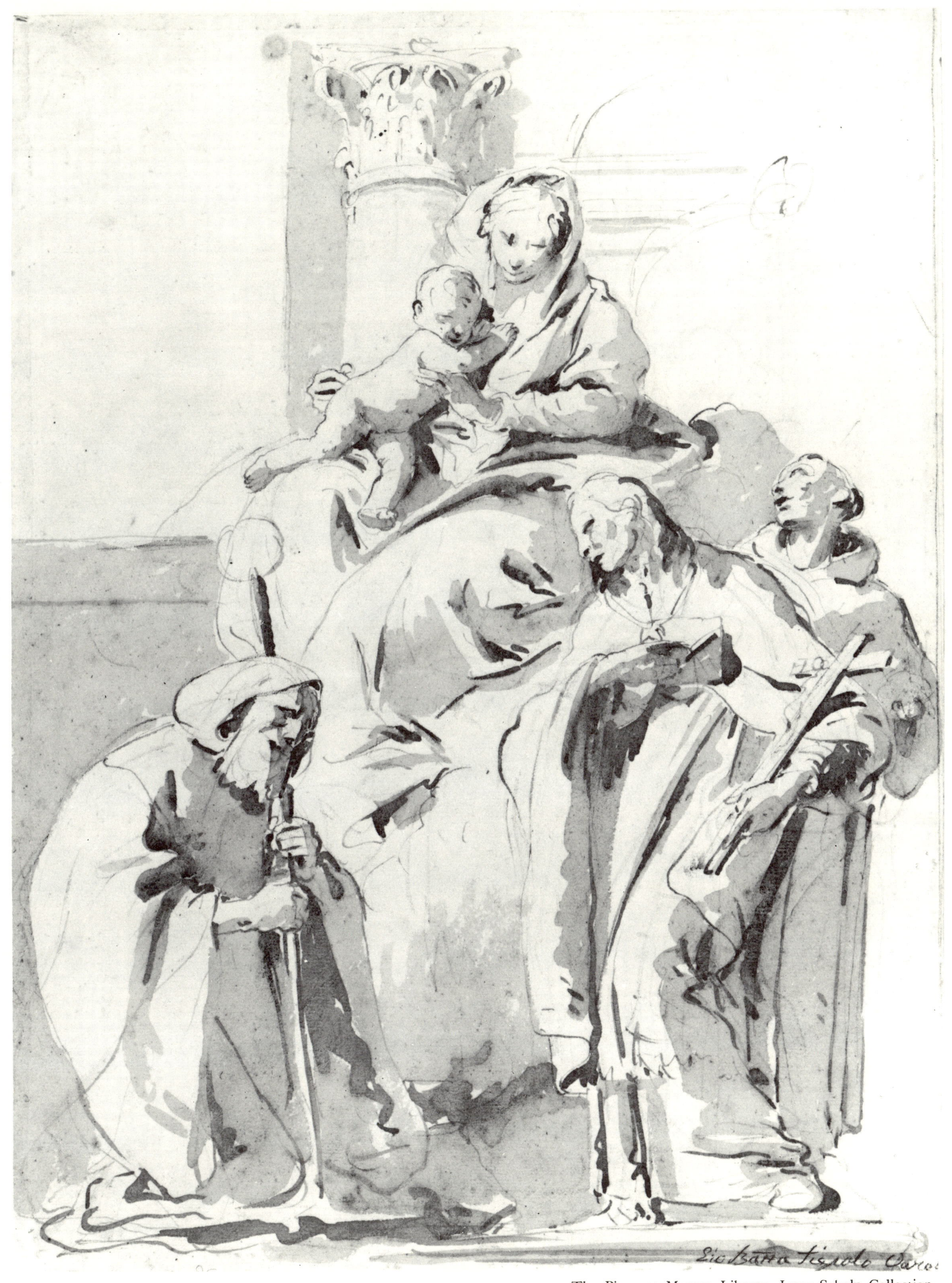

The Pierpont Morgan Library, Janos Scholz Collection

135. *Giovanni Battista Tiepolo.* MADONNA AND CHILD ADORED BY SAINTS.

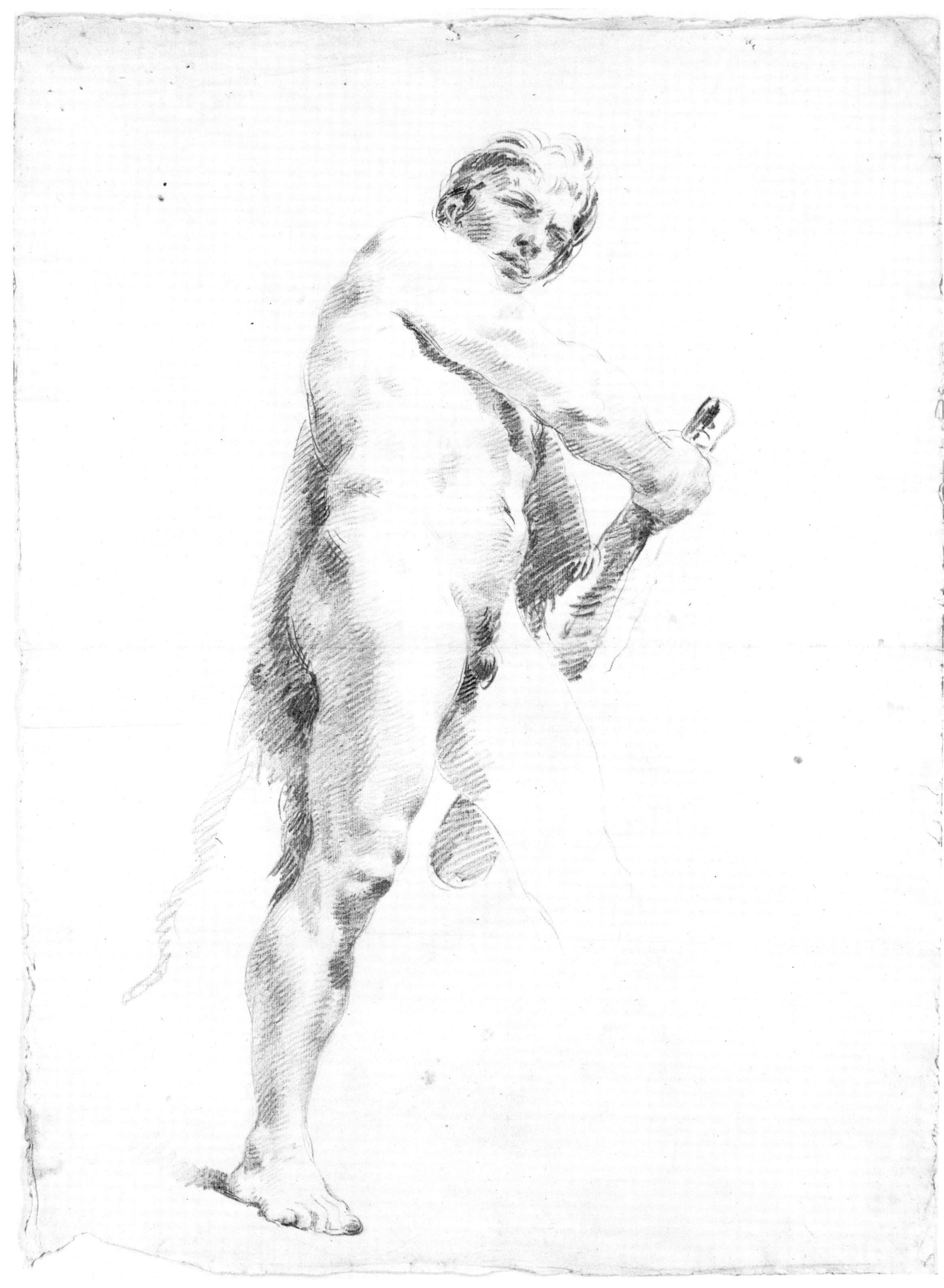

*136. Giovanni Battista Tiepolo.* HERCULES STANDING.

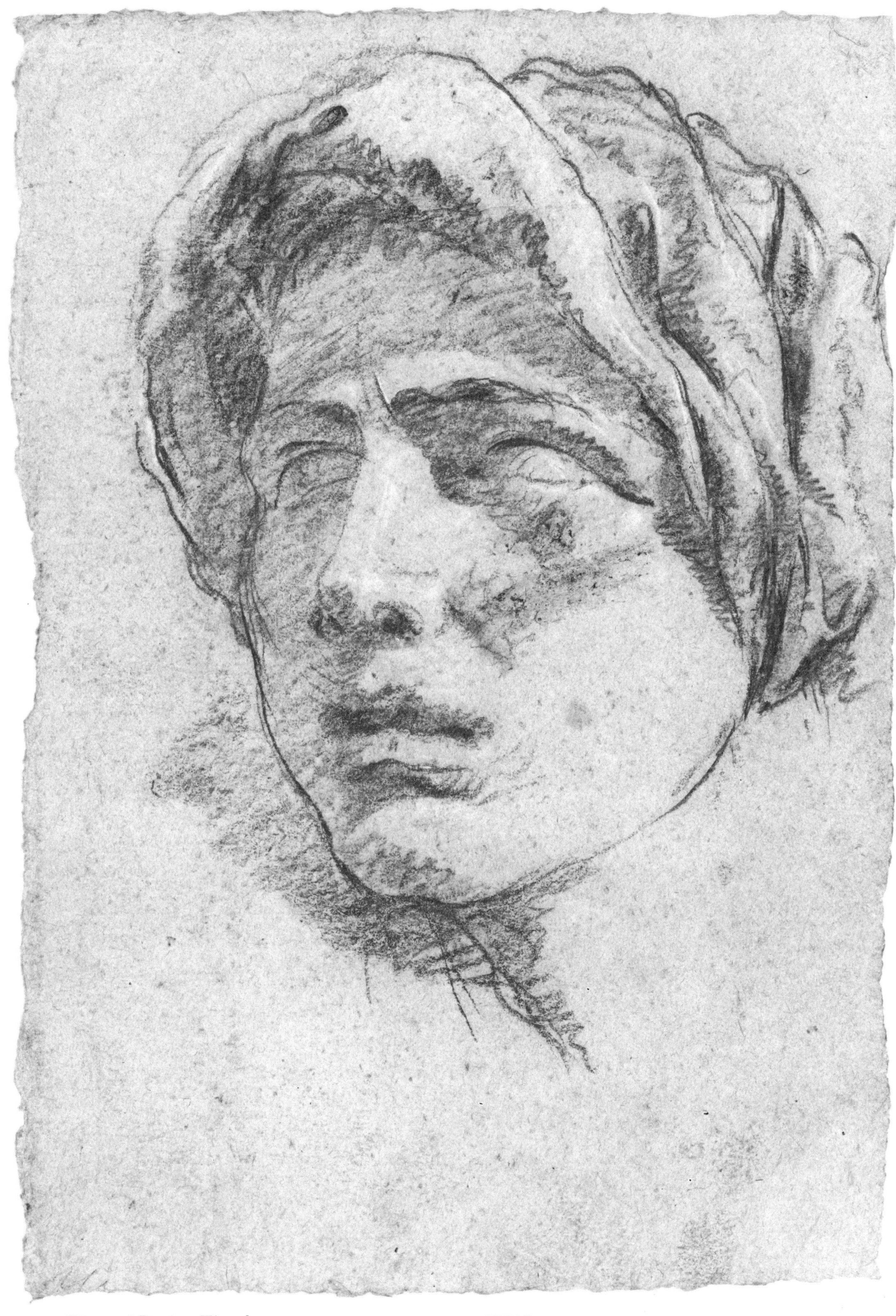

137. *Giovanni Battista Tiepolo.* HEAD OF A MAN WEARING A TURBAN.

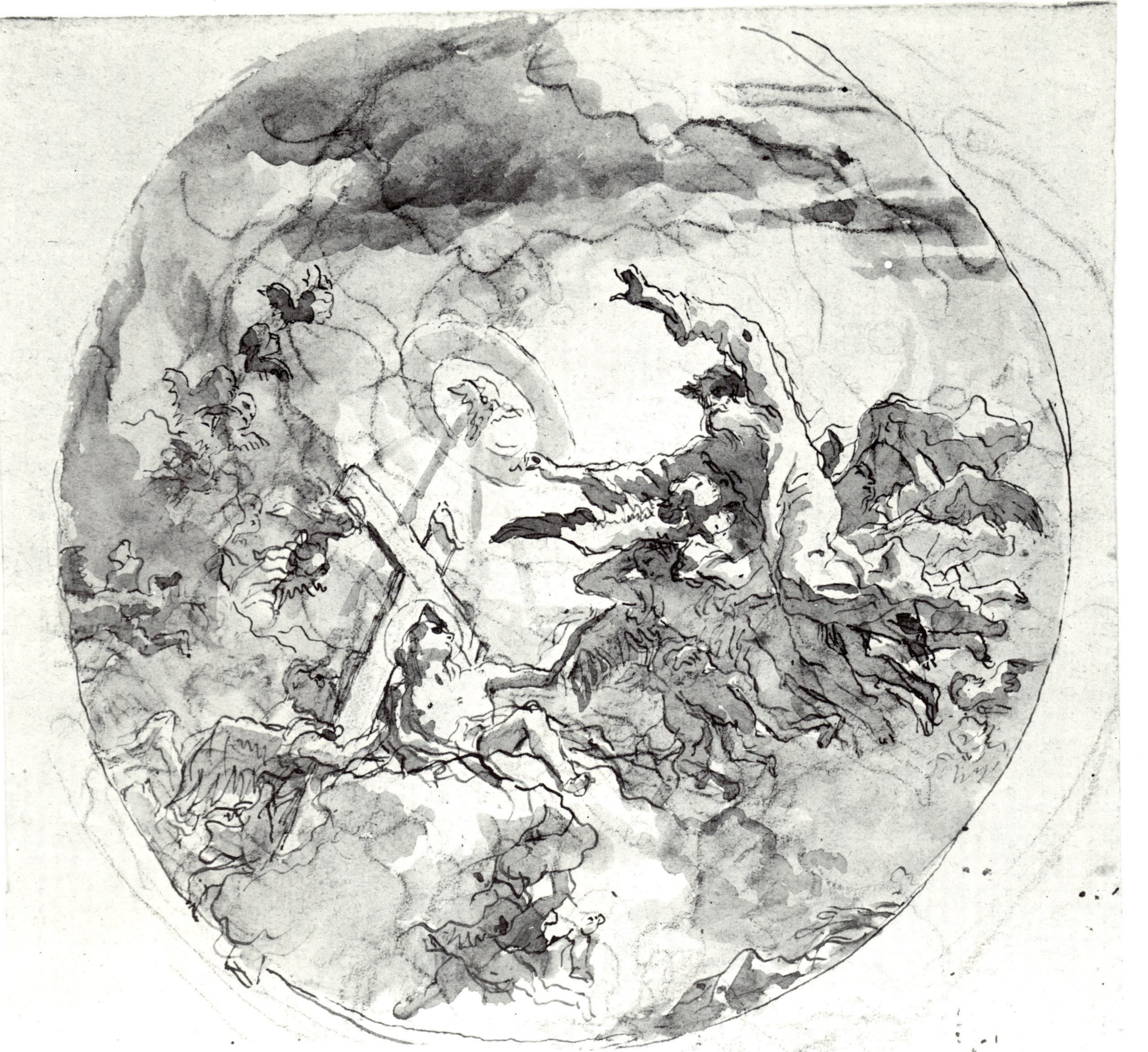

The Pierpont Morgan Library, Janos Scholz Collection

138. *Giovanni Domenico Tiepolo (Venetian, 1727–1804).* THE HOLY TRINITY IN GLORY.

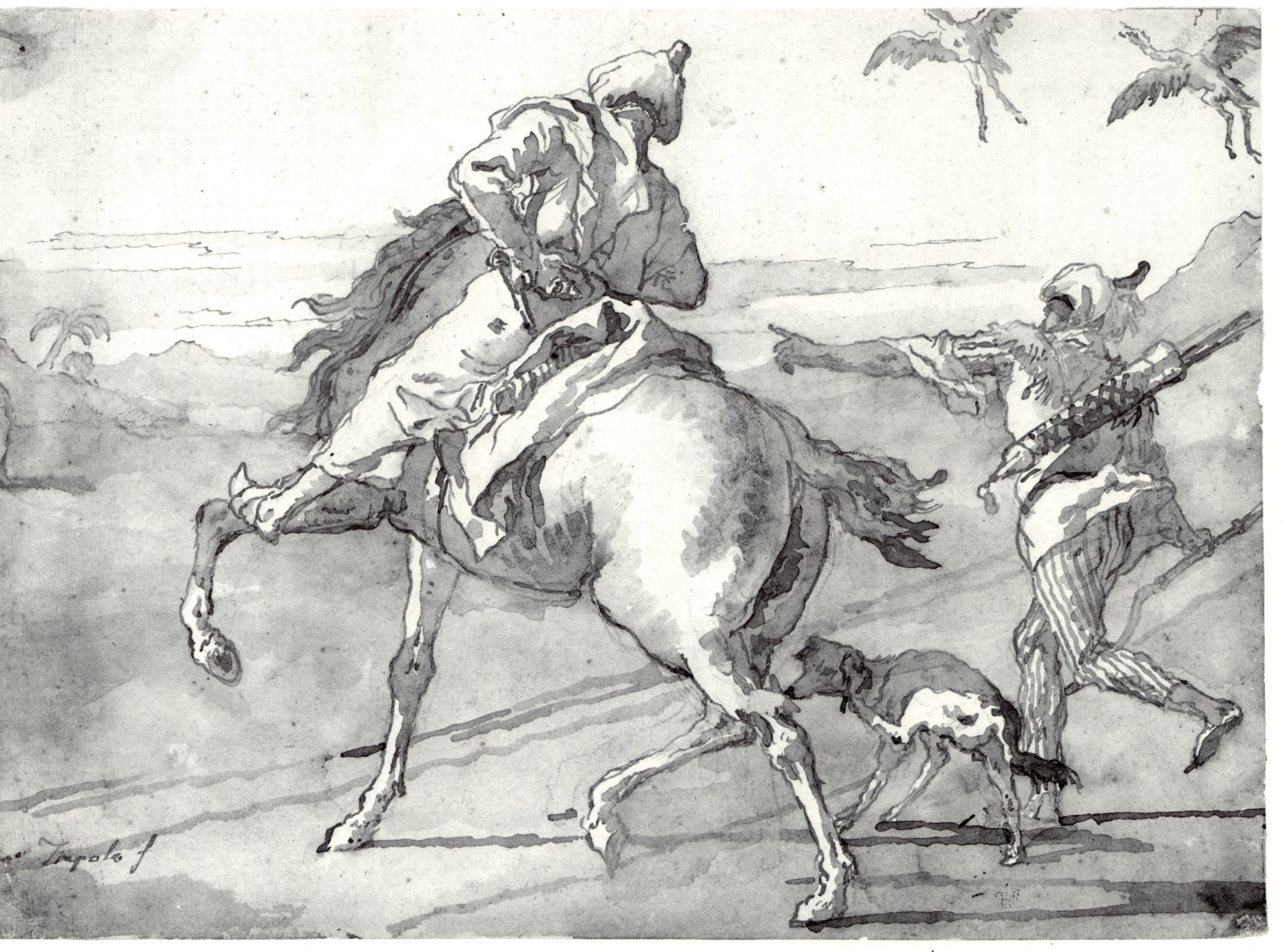


139. *Giovanni Domenico Tiepolo.* ORIENTAL RIDER AND ANOTHER FIGURE.

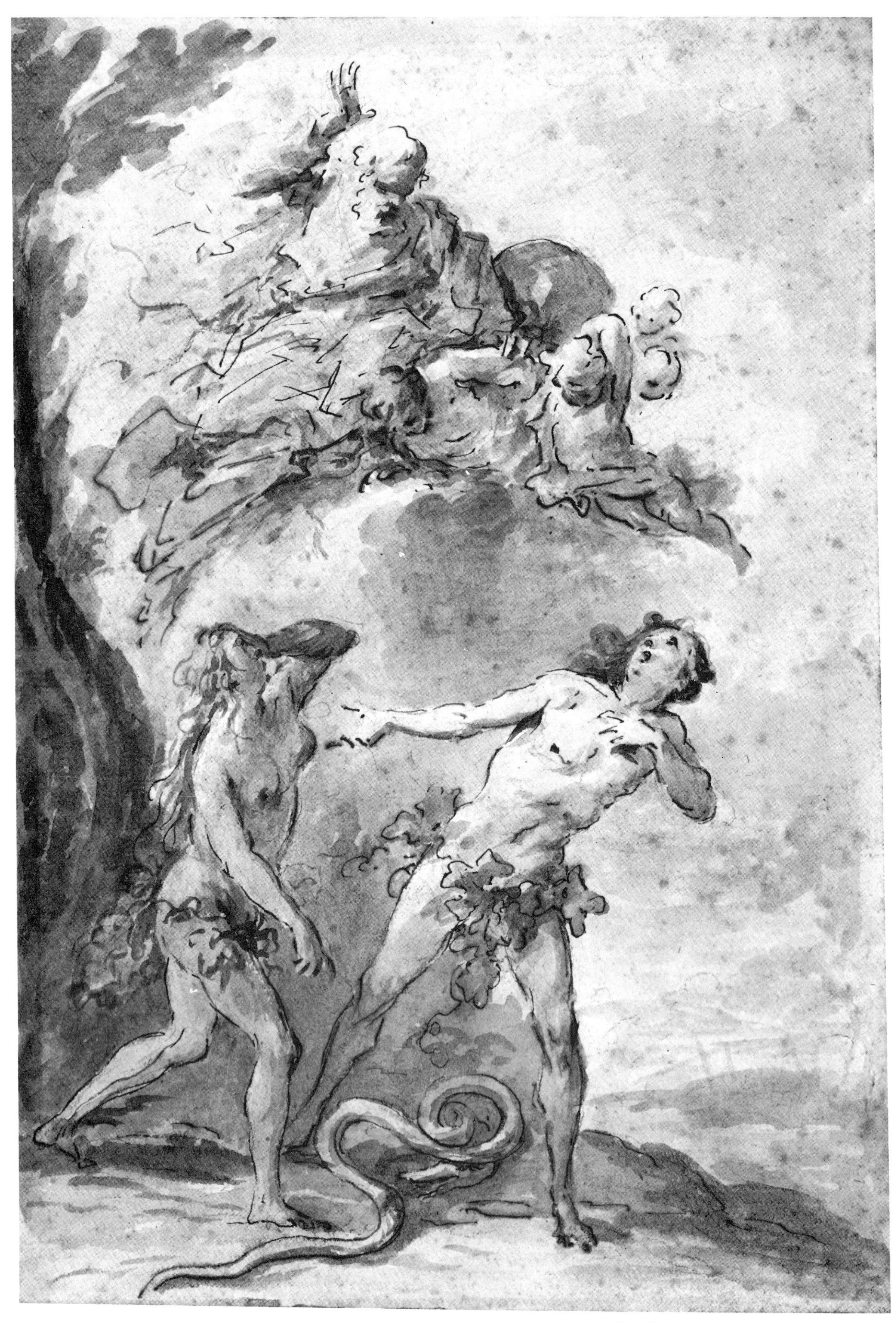

*140. Gaspare Diziani (Bologna-Venice, 1689–1767).*
ADAM AND EVE EXPELLED FROM PARADISE.

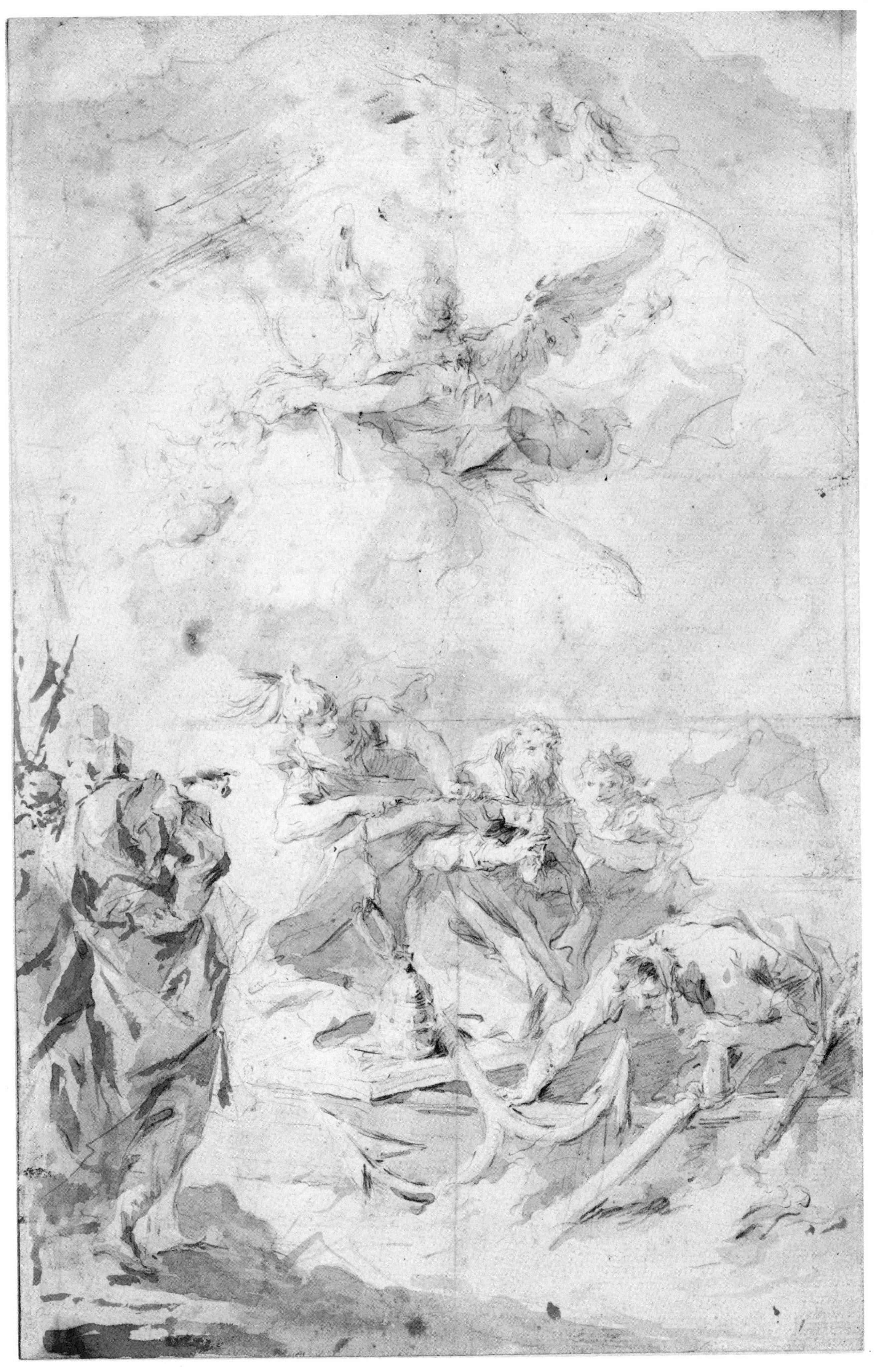

*141. Giovanni Antonio Guardi (Venetian, 1699–1760).*
THE MARTYRDOM OF SAINT CLEMENT.

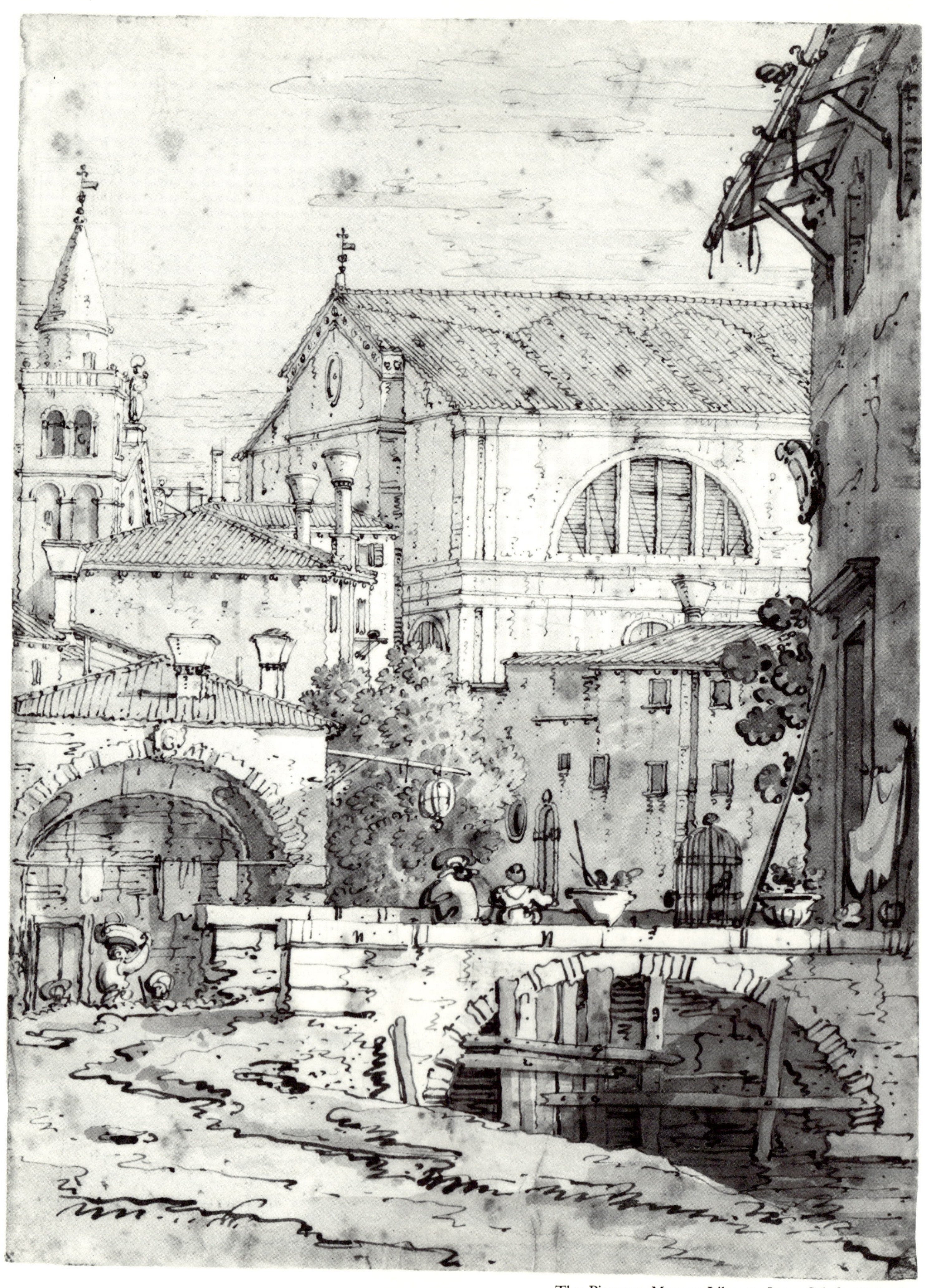

The Pierpont Morgan Library, Janos Scholz Collection

142. *Antonio Canal, called Canaletto (Venetian, 1697–1768).*
IMAGINARY VENETIAN VIEW.

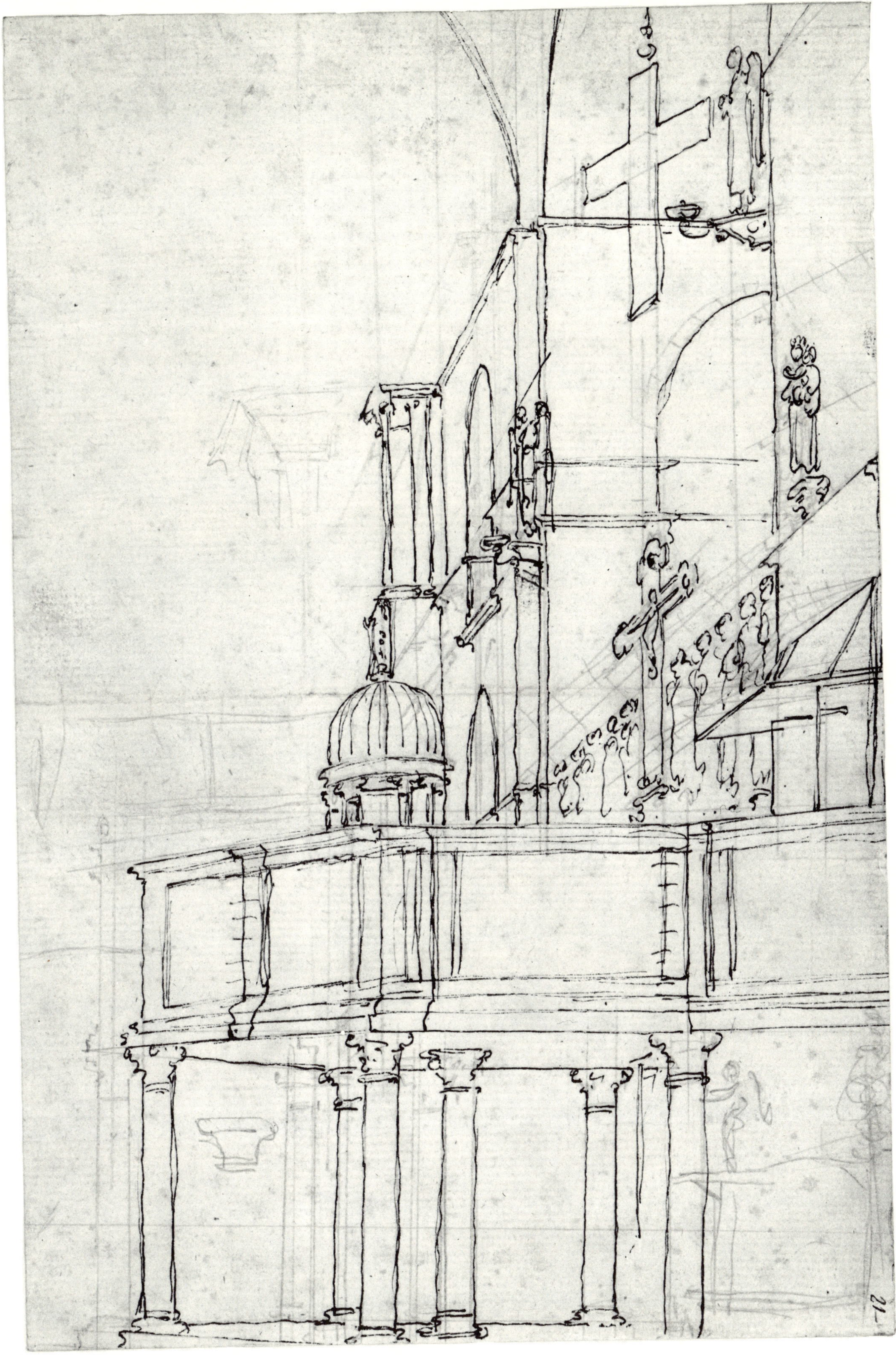

*143. Antonio Canal, called Canaletto.* THE PRESBYTERY OF S. MARCO.

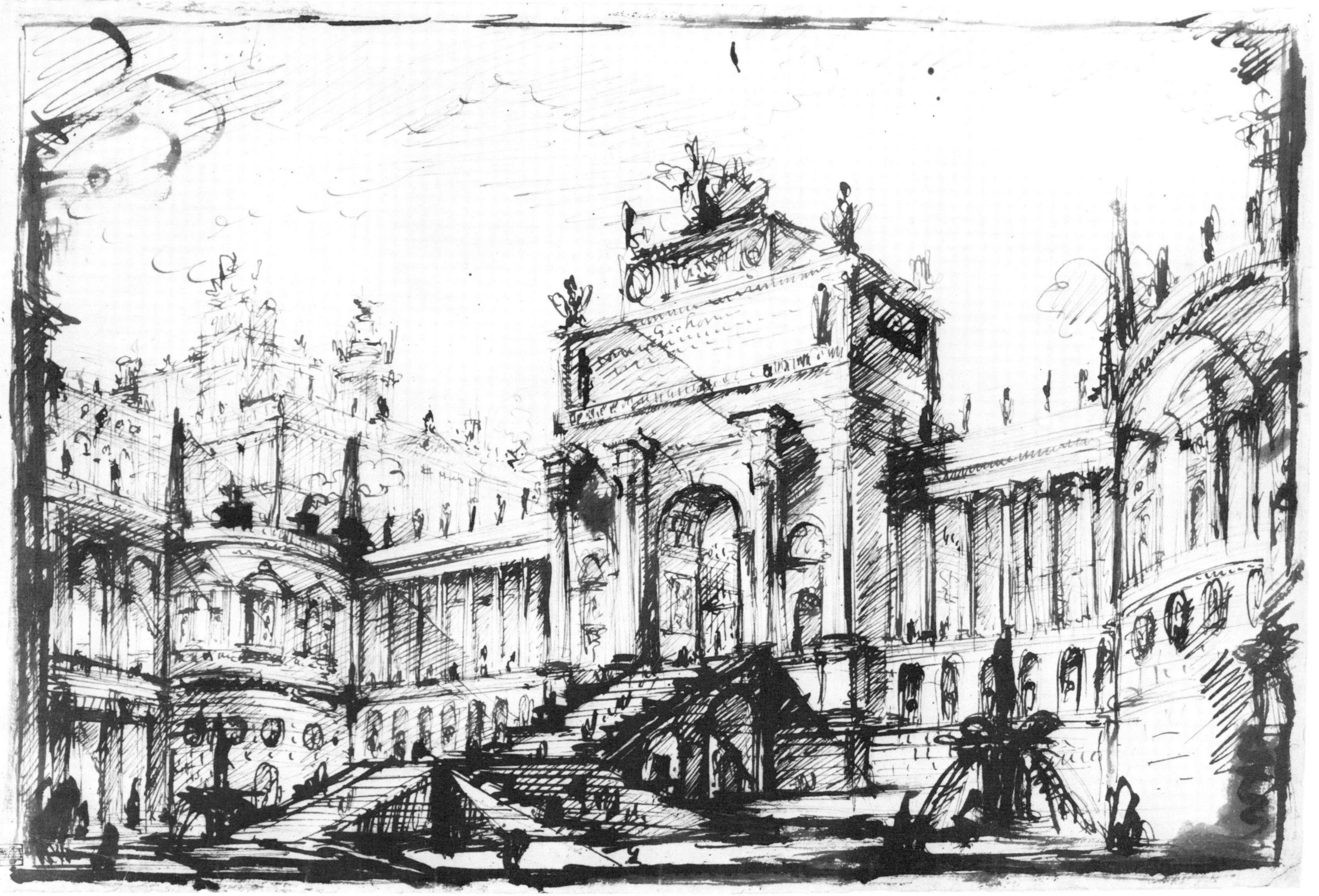

The Pierpont Morgan Library, Janos Scholz Collection

144. *Giovanni Battista Piranesi (Venetian, 1720–1778).* ARCHITECTURAL FANTASY.

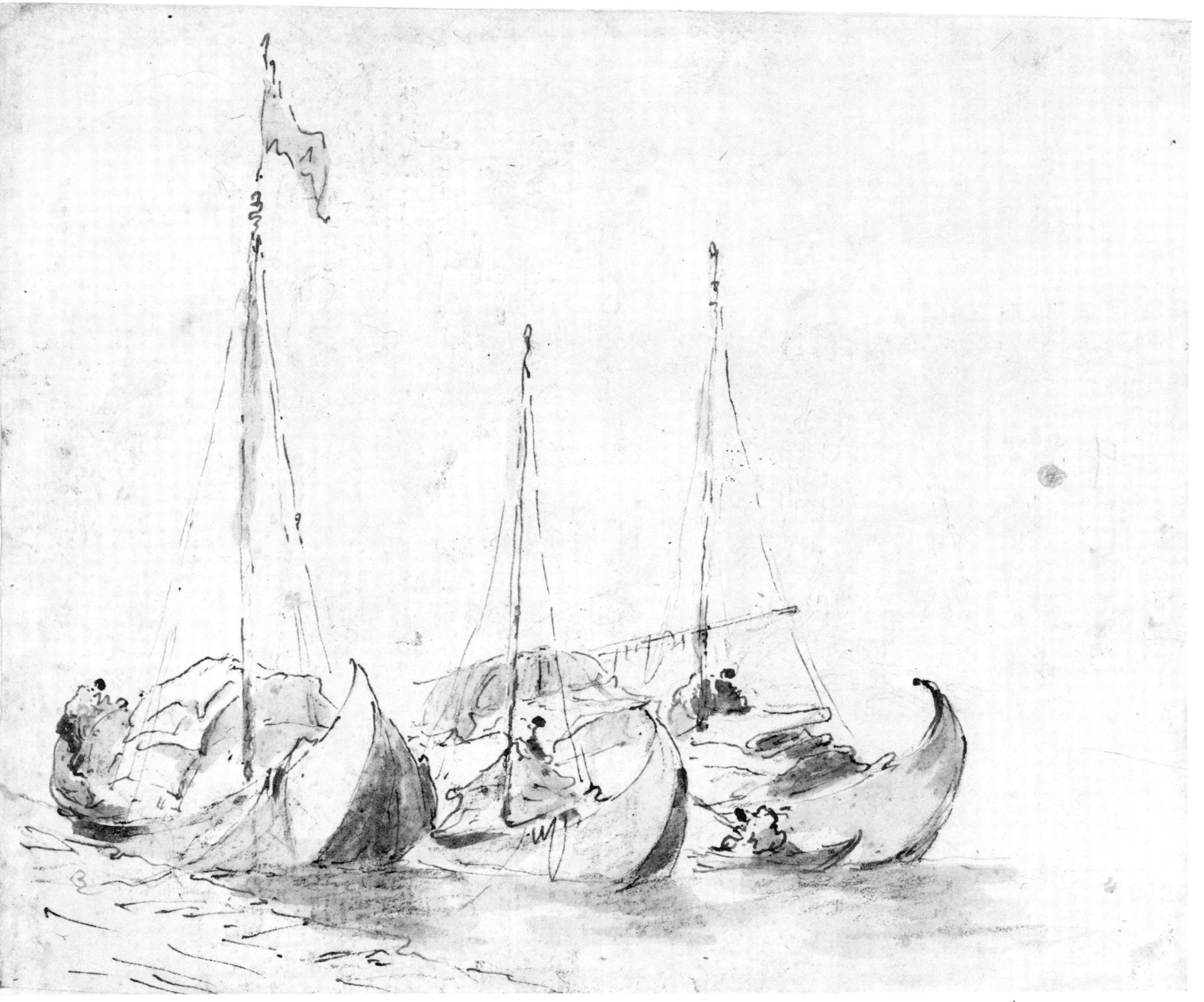

145. *Francesco Guardi (Venetian, 1712–1793).* THREE SAILING BOATS AND A GONDOLA.

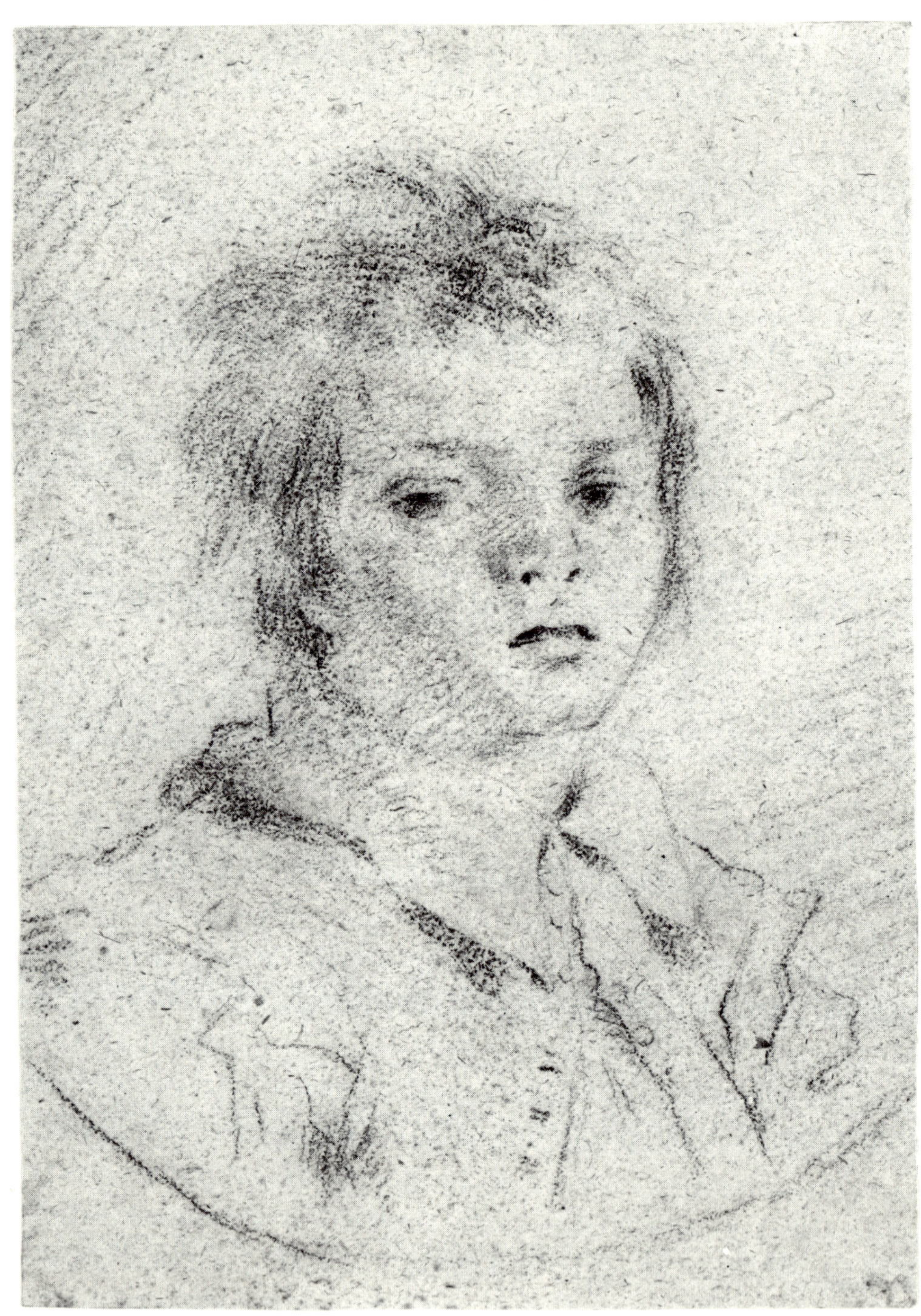

*146. Francesco Guardi.* HEAD OF A BOY.

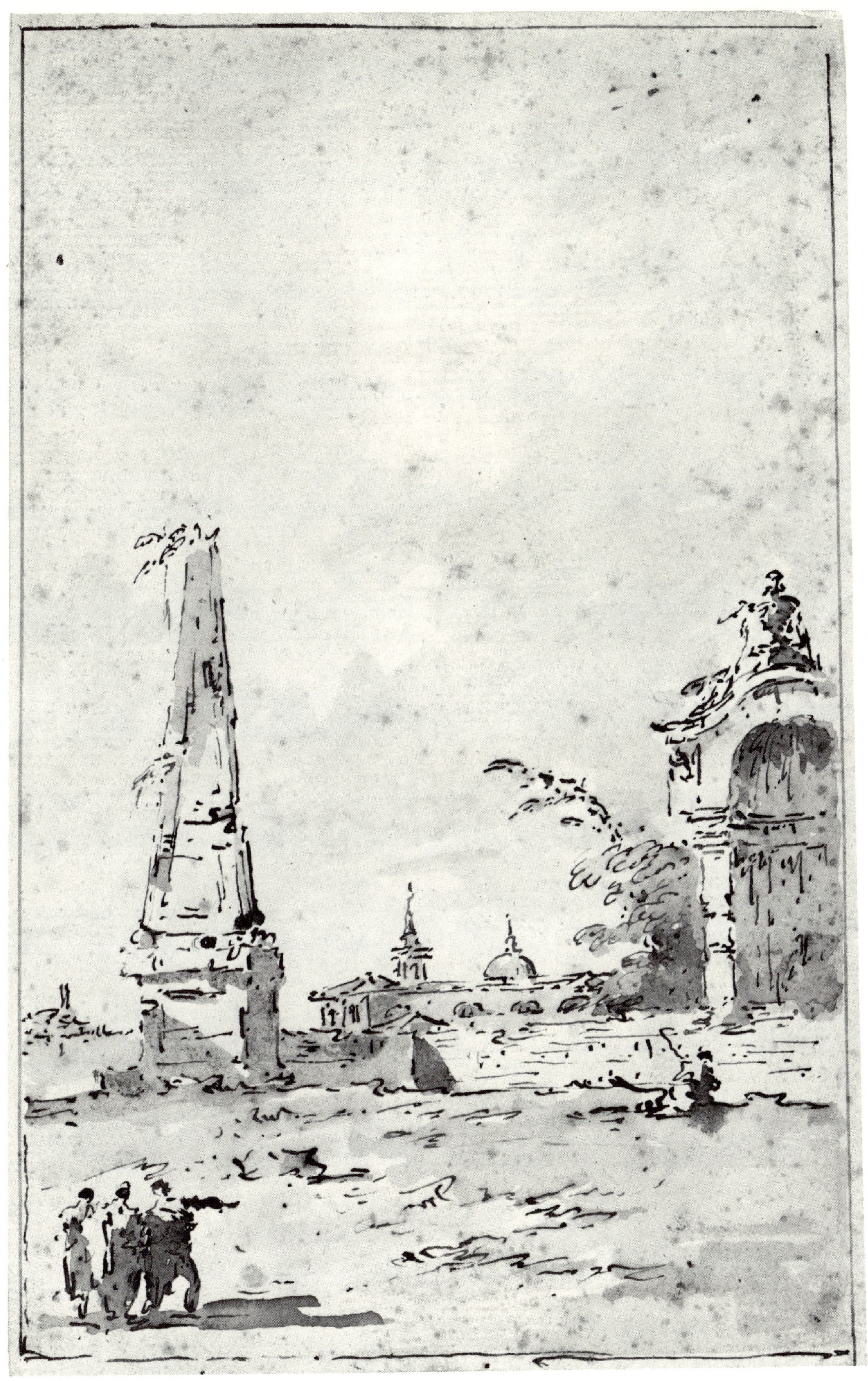

147. *Francesco Guardi.* VIEW WITH AN OBELISK AND FIGURES.

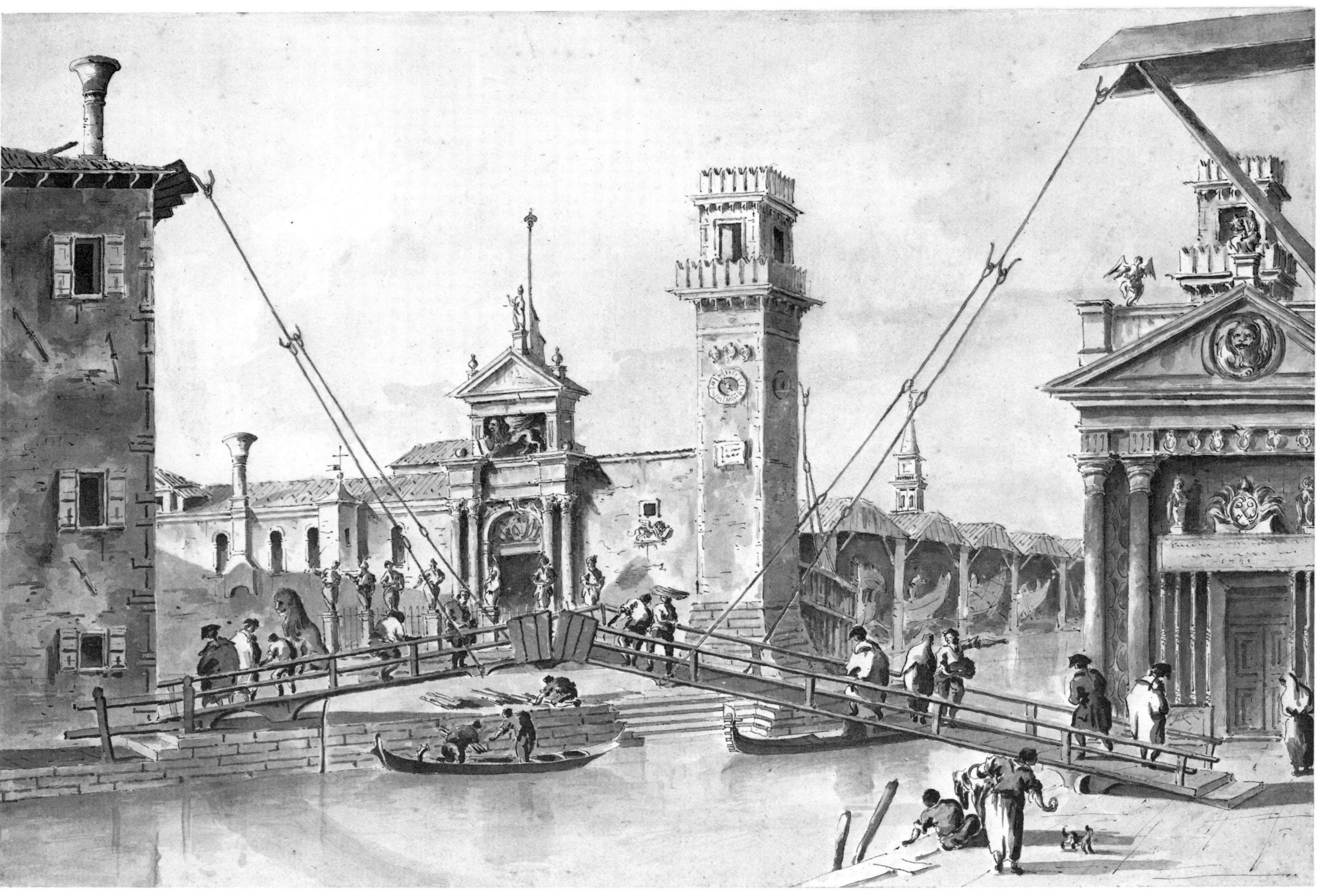

148. *Giacomo Guardi (Venetian, 1764–1835).* ENTRANCE TO THE ARSENAL IN VENICE.

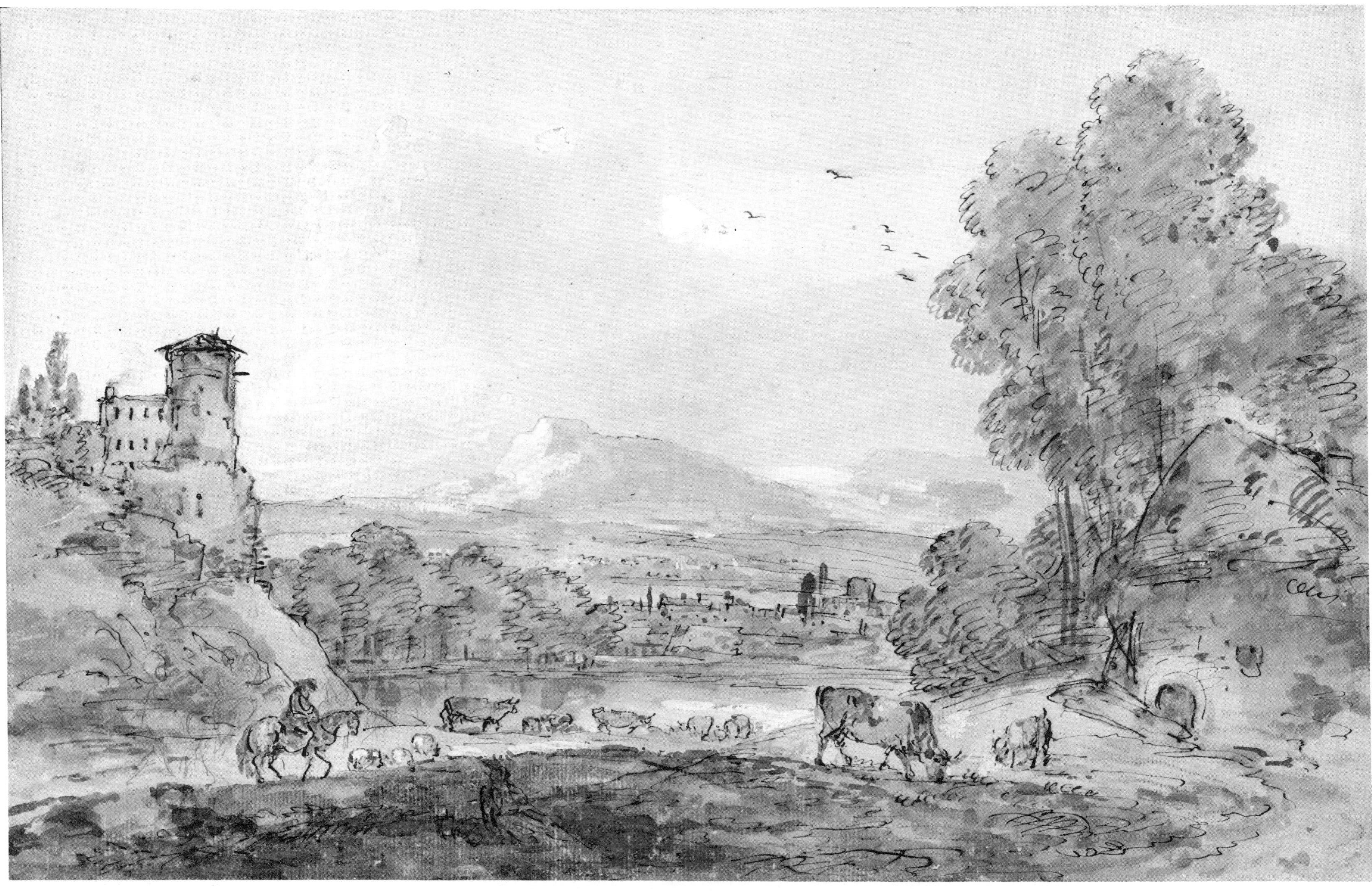

149. *Francesco Zuccarelli (Tuscan, 1702–1788).* LANDSCAPE WITH A LAKE AND A HORSEMAN.

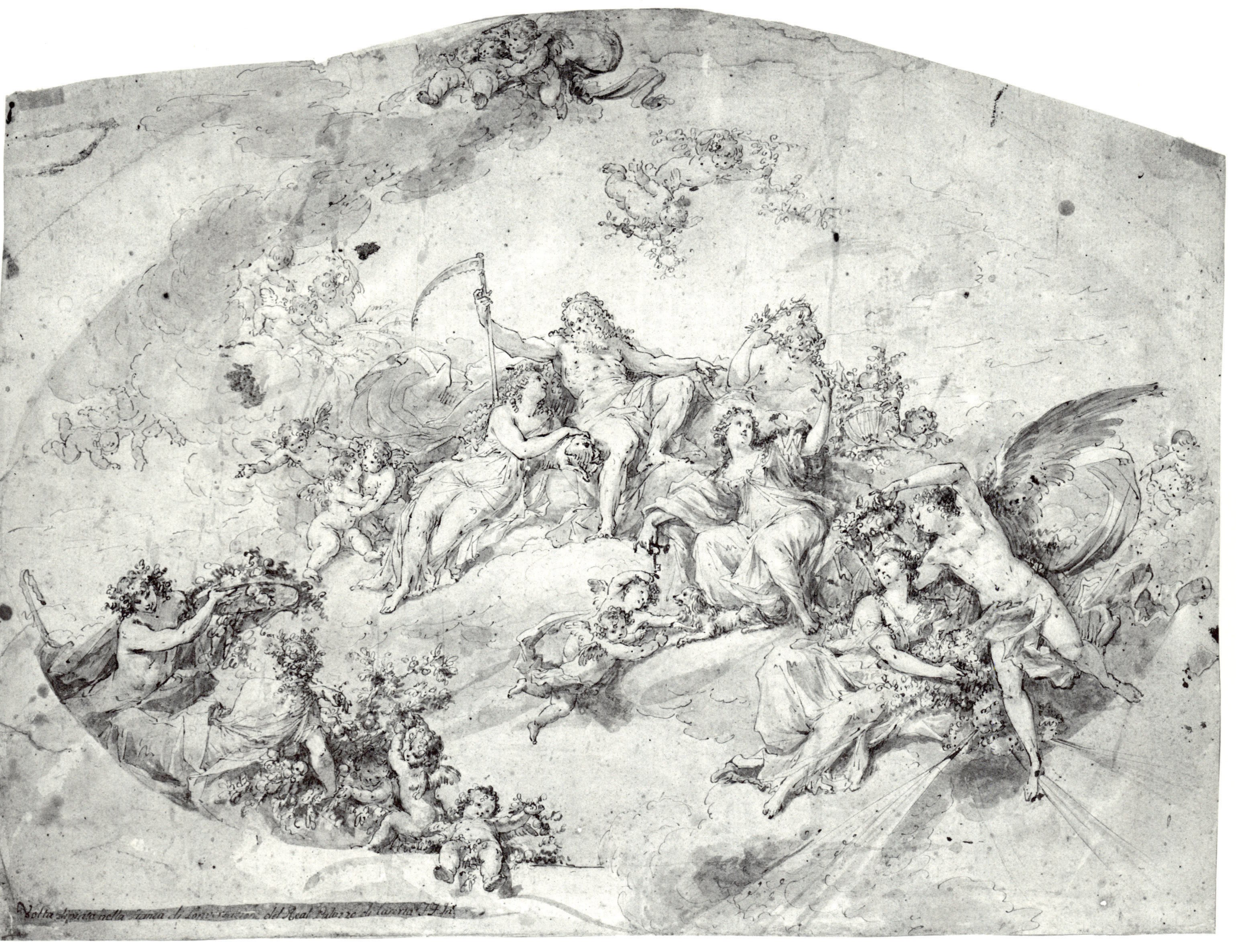

150. *Fedele Fischetti (Neapolitan, 1734–1789).* THE AGE OF GOLD.